Nelson's Annual Preacher's Sourcebook

2008 EDITION

ROBERT J. MORGAN, EDITOR

THOMAS NELSON
Since 1798

NASHVILLE   DALLAS   MEXICO CITY   RIO DE JANEIRO   BEIJING

Published in Nashville, Tennessee, by Thomas Nelson, Inc.

Thomas Nelson, Inc., titles may be purchased in bulk for educational, business, fundraising, or sales promotional use. For information, please email Special Markets@ThomasNelson.com.

Unless otherwise indicated, Scripture quotations are from the New King James Version of the Bible, copyright © 1979, 1980, 1982, 1990, Thomas Nelson, Inc., Publishers.

Scripture quotations noted KJV are taken from the Holy Bible, King James Version.

Verses marked NIV are taken from the Holy Bible: New International Version, copyright © 1973, 1978, 1984 by the International Bible Society. Used by permission of Zondervan Publishing House. All rights reserved.

Scripture quotations noted NASB are from the NEW AMERICAN STANDARD BIBLE®, copyright © 1960, 1962, 1963, 1968, 1971, 1972, 1973, 1975, 1977, 1995 by The Lockman Foundation. Used by permission.

Scripture quotations noted NRSV are from the NEW REVISED STANDARD VERSION BIBLE, copyright © 1989 National Council of the Churches of Christ in the United States of America. Used by permission. All rights reserved.

Scripture quotations marked NLT are taken from the Holy Bible, New Living Translation, copyright © 1996. Used by permission of Tyndale House Publishers, Inc., Wheaton, Illinois 60189. All rights reserved.

Typesetting by ProtoType Graphics, Inc., Nashville, Tennessee.

Morgan, Robert J. (ed.)
  Nelson's annual preacher's sourcebook, 2008 edition.

ISBN 10: 1-4185-2538-3
ISBN 13: 978-1-4185-2538-5

Printed in the United States of America

07 08 09 10 11 — 7 6 5 4 3 2 1

Contents

SPECIAL FEATURES:

Introduction and Acknowledgments

When I first began pastoring thirty years ago, I knew very well how to do it. Now I sometimes wonder if I have a clue. Things have gotten tougher, church life has become more complex, and the times are more complicated. Our nation is consumer-based rather than loyalty-based, and thousands of smaller congregations are finding it hard to compete with scores of mega-churches.

Knowing firsthand the pangs of discouragement, I have wanted *Nelson's Annual Preacher's Sourcebook* to be an endless resource of uplifting articles, timely truths, and spiritual encouragements. Here you'll find a rich collection of old prayers, new insights, heroic mentors, contemporary illustrations, practical helps, and timeless sermon outlines.

I want to thank four people for making this book possible. My literary agent and friend, Chris Ferebee, is selfless, reassuring, and so very helpful. My editor, Michael Stephens, is a skillful teacher, editor, friend, and conversationalist. My co-author is my son-in-law, Joshua Rowe, a gifted student at Southern Seminary in Louisville. And the fifty-two collections of hymns and songs for 2008 were compiled by my associate, Corey Hawkins, Minister of Music at The Donelson Fellowship in Nashville.

To him this volume is gratefully dedicated.

Editor's Preface

The Self-Replenishing Pastor

There *are* some lazy pastors out there; but most of us are hard-working, devoted, and passionate. We've never lost our vision of changing the world, and we long to make an impact for the kingdom that outgrows our life and outlasts our tenure. But it's a draining profession. When the bleeding woman touched Jesus, the Bible says virtue went out of Him; every time our ministry touches another person, virtue goes out of us—and we don't have much virtue to spare.

The greatest saints of all the ages have discovered the fine art of ministerial replenishment. Sad old Jeremiah fell asleep one night weary and worried, but as he tossed on his bed, he dreamed God was speaking to him, and the message was this: "I will satisfy the weary, and all who are faint I will replenish."

"Thereupon I awoke and looked," recalled Jeremiah, "and my sleep was pleasant to me" (Jer. 31:25–26 NRSV).

An ante-Nicene prayer for the ordination of presbyters included this timely petition: "Look down upon this Thy servant . . . and do Thou replenish him with the Spirit of grace and counsel, to assist and govern Thy people with a pure heart."[1]

John Calvin, in the *Institutes,* wrote: "We cannot gain the victory unless we are filled with Him . . . . Therefore, when we pray to be delivered from sin and Satan, we at the same time desire to be enriched with new supplies of divine grace, until completely replenished with them, we triumph over every evil."[2]

---

[1] Roberts, A., Donaldson, J., & Coxe, A. C. (1997). *The Ante-Nicene Fathers Vol. VII: Translations of the writings of the Fathers down to A.D. 325.* Fathers of the Third and Fourth Centuries: Lactantius, Venantius, Asterius, Victorinus, Dionysius, Apostolic Teaching and Constitutions, Homily and Liturgies. (492). Oak Harbor: Logos Research Systems.

[2] Calvin, J., & Beveridge, H. (1997). *Institutes of the Christian religion.* Translation of: Institutio Christianae religionis.; Reprint, with new introduction. Originally published: Edinburgh : Calvin Translation Society, 1845–1846. (III, xx, 46). Oak Harbor, WA: Logos Research Systems, Inc.

Charles Spurgeon once said, "The lamp which was burning in the temple was never allowed to go out, but it had to be daily replenished with fresh oil; in like manner, our faith can only live by being sustained with the oil of grace, and we can only obtain this from God himself."[3]

How, then, do we learn to replenish the soul? Here are ten ideas that have helped me over three decades of pastoral work.

1. Keep a Journal

Your journal is a confessional booth, confidential friend, memory archive, prayer list, accountability device, pressure valve, a running commentary on your life, a record of lessons learned, and a problem-solving technique—all within the covers of a small notebook. I use my journal to record my thoughts during my morning devotions, but in times of unusual stress, I may write page after page, much of it in the form of prayer. Some of the psalmist's prayers were, in my opinion, pages from his journal, as it were. For me, my journal is a spiritual tool that helps open the prayer-doors and Scripture-windows of my heart each day, keeping the air fresh and the sunshine streaming in.

2. Take Breaks

When Jesus told the disciples to come apart and rest awhile, He knew they were depleted, needing a physical separation from the demands of their work. Many ministers are workaholics, but even the mechanical engine of a car has to check into the garage occasionally for maintenance. We need a Sabbath-rest each week, but we also need sufficient time away throughout the year. Whether it's a week at the beach, a tent in the mountains, or a conference in another city, get away and rest. Just go. Delegate things as well as you can, find the best replacement available for the pulpit, and don't give too many people your contact information. If you're exhausted right now and can't get away for a week, check into a state park for a night just to sleep, walk, pray, and exercise.

3. Have a Hobby

One way of diverting our mind from the stresses of ministry is having a good hobby. Golf, maybe, or tinkering with cars. Franklin Roosevelt's

---

[3]Spurgeon, C. H. *Morning and Evening*, entry for November 15th P.M.

stamp collection and Winston Churchill's oil paintings kept them sane during the rigors of the Second World War. I'd love to be able to paint, too; but as it is, my hobby is cooking, owing primarily to my wife's multiple sclerosis. I don't tend to brood over all the problems of family or church life when I'm in the kitchen with my music going like a symphony and ingredients flying through the air like missiles.

There's a legend that the aged John the Apostle was criticized once for tending to his hobby, which was keeping pigeons. He replied that his mind was like the critic's bow and arrow. If the string was always taut, the bow would soon warp.

4. Work on Your Attitude

Elsewhere in this *Sourcebook* I've included an interview with 91-year-old Michael Guido, one of America's pioneer radio evangelists. His exuberance is unstoppable, and when I asked him how he managed to have such a positive attitude at his age, he simply replied, "I work on it."

We've all got to work on our attitudes. Dr. Russell Mixter, beloved Wheaton College professor still going strong at age 100, summed it up this way in his personal maxim: "Life worth living depends on the liver."

Most burnout in ministry comes not from overwork or exhaustion but from conflicts and interpersonal clashes. Acrimony is hard to shrug off, but we can learn to gradually cast off bitterness, anger, and frustration like a schoolboy casting off his clothes while running to the swimming hole. Life is too short to ruin by rancor.

5. Exercise

Exercise keeps the preacher's lungs clear and stamina strong. It lowers our blood pressure, drains away stress, releases our endorphins, and builds a congregation-impressing physique. Well, that may be stretching it a bit, but every church wants a healthy pastor; and nothing can take the place of exercise.

6. Read Old Books

Since I write contemporary books, I hope you read a few of them. But a wise mentor once advised me to read an old book for every one or two modern ones. I took the advice, and now I'm addicted. Spurgeon's sermons. Lewis' apologetics. Luther's Tabletalk. Bunyan's allegories. Herbert's poetry. Gerhardt's hymns. Havergal's devotions. Eusebuis' history. And those Puritans! All of Christian thought and history, stretching back two millennia, is sitting on our doorstep waiting to come into our minds through the gateway of our books. Two thousand years of theologians and mystics are too rich to ignore.

7. Read Biography

Similarly, read biography. I started reading biographies and autobiographies to find sermon illustrations, but I soon realized that its greater value is personal inspiration. I just finished a biography of two Vietnam War POW's whose seven years of torment in the Hanoi Hilton made my most difficult problems look like a walk down Fifth Avenue.

I'm especially fond of missionary biography, and it's too bad that little of it is being published nowadays. Most missionaries must self-publish their autobiographical accounts, hoping to sell enough copies to friends and supports to recoup the cost. When you run across one of these, you're likely to find a hidden treasure, and a great source of original stories for your sermons.

Still, the personal benefit of biography outweighs its professional use. Imagine being personally mentored by Rev. Whitefield, Brother Lawrence, Dr. Luther, President Edwards, or Missionary Carmichael. Reading their stories is a personal mentoring program for me, and I've learned much from their examples.

8. Get Enough Sleep

About a year ago, I nearly collapsed from exhaustion, so I took some time away to process what was wrong. Sitting at a little coffee shop in the sunshine, I made notes in my journal, pondered and prayed deeply, and came to a revolutionary realization. I needed more sleep. I started going to bed a half-hour earlier and getting up a half-hour later.

Amazing what a difference that makes! The Lord doesn't want us to serve Him in a permanent state of exhaustion.

9. Process Mistakes

Our churches may expect perfection from us, but they aren't likely to get it. They've got to realize we're imperfect humans serving other imperfect humans in an imperfect environment. Along the way, we'll make some blunders. While we shouldn't be too cavalier about it, there's no need to anguish unduly over spilled milk. When you make a mistake, apologize, confess it, try to rectify it, and commit it to the Lord. He turned the cook's mistaken pot of poison into the best soup ever served at the School of the Prophets. God's secret ingredient was a hefty dose of Romans 8:28, and that same spice can cover our mistakes, too.

But learn to learn from mistakes. Take a long walk, mull over your goof, ponder it, and ask yourself, "How could I have handled that better?" By visualizing how you should have dealt with a situation, you'll be preparing your mind to react more wisely next time. A day is never lost if a lesson is learned.

10. Spend Time with Your Life-Partner

Finally, hug someone you love. Good friends are important, but none more than the one to whom you're married. Have frequent dates. Pray together. Play together. Share your burdens. Take mini-vacations. Relax in each other's embrace.

Practice these ten suggestions, or come up with your own; but whatever you do, remember Paul's advice to the Ephesian elders: "Take heed to yourself."

If you don't take heed to yourself, you can't take heed to the flock under your care.

Over a hundred years ago, Rev. Martyn L. Williston wrote: "Preachers who grow duller as they count their years . . . do so from simple mental shiftlessness, very much as the Virginia planters have let their lands run waste from mere depletion. We must perpetually replenish heart and brain, or the fields of thought will turn meager and barren."

Learning the secrets of self-replenishment adds years to your ministry and miles to your smiles; and that pleases the Lord.

Create a Sermon Series!

If you would like to publicize and preach a series of messages, you can assemble your own by mixing and matching various sermons and sermon outlines in this *Sourcebook*. Here are some suggestions:

Body Building: Practical Lessons About the Church
- Church Building (April 27)
- How Does It Look to You? (April 27)
- The Church Is Your Family (July 27)
- Not "What's Wrong" But "What's Right" with the Church (October 12)
- My Attitude Toward the Church (November 16)

Help for Life's Trials
- You Cannot Lose (January 6)
- Words of Comfort (January 13)
- Understanding Our Spiritual Battle: Part 1 (February 10)
- He Gives Me Comfort (March 9)
- Thank God for Pressure (April 6)
- Understanding Our Spiritual Battle: Part 2 (June 15)
- Tearing Down or Building Up? (August 24)
- Pulling Yourself Together (November 2)
- State of Readiness (November 9)
- The Brutal Facts of Life (December 7)

Bringing in the Sheaves
- Principles of Witnessing (February 3)
- Fishers of Men (August 17)
- The Gospel Will Be Heard (September 21)
- A Game Plan for Witnessing (September 28)

Family Focus
- When Momma Ain't Happy (May 11)
- Keeping Your Marriage Vows: Part 1 (May 11)
- Keeping Your Marriage Vows: Part 2 (May 11)
- Pleasing Father (June 15)
- Men Behaving Dadly (June 15)

- Marriage Sizzle (August 24)
- Does a Godly Home Guarantee Godly Kids? (October 5)

Things to Remember When the Plate Is Passed

- We Give Thee But Thine Own (February 3)
- Everything I Needed to Know About Giving I Learned in First Grade (February 10)
- The God-Prompted Heart (March 2)
- The Almost Forgotten Beatitude (July 6)
- Financial Integrity (September 7)
- Tithing Is Not a Four-Letter Word (October 19)

Practical Theology

- It's SO Not About Us! (June 8)
- A Guiding Star for the Journey of Faith (June 8)
- We Will Tell of God's Greatness (June 22)
- Deity Described (October 12)
- The Persistence of Grace (October 26)
- Living for the Glory of God (November 9)

Prayer and Praise

- Let's Praise the Lord (March 2)
- The Hannah Pathway (March 16)
- Listening to God (April 13)
- When Worship Turns to War (May 25)
- Praise the Lord! (June 8)
- Prayer: What, Why, Where, When (July 20)
- Morning and Evening Songs (August 24)
- Rejoice in All of Life's Circumstances (October 19)
- Prayer: Three Mistakes We Don't Want to Make (October 26)
- Be Thankful Anyway (November 9)
- Rejoice! God Is in Control (November 16)

Why All the Fuss About a Jewish Carpenter?

- You Must Be Born Again (March 16)
- "He's Alive (But Don't Tell Anyone)" (March 23)
- A Different King (April 13)
- The Servant Solution (April 20)

- Confidence in God (April 27)
- Who Is Jesus to You? (May 18)
- Jesus the Shepherd (July 6)
- The Source of Salvation (October 26)
- The Glorious King (December 7)
- The Eternal Son (December 14)
- The Consolation of Israel (December 14)
- A Stocking Full of Love (December 21)
- The Life Appeared! (December 21)
- One Starry Night (December 21)
- Safe on the Rock (December 28)

Contributors

Dr. Timothy K. Beougher
Billy Graham Professor of Evangelism and Associate Dean of the Billy Graham School of Missions, Evangelism and Church Growth, The Southern Baptist Theological Seminary, Louisville, Kentucky

> **What Really Matters (January 6)**
> Principles of Witnessing (February 3)
> **The Ring of Authority (March 30)**
> Who Is Jesus to You (May 18)
> **It's SO Not About Us! (June 8)**
> **A Fresh Vision for Revival (August 17)**
> **Religion or Relationship (November 30)**
> Making Resolutions Realities (December 28)

Pastor Al Detter
Senior Pastor, Grace Baptist Church, Erie, Pennsylvania

> The Hannah Pathway (March 16)
> Listening to God (April 13)
> **When Momma Ain't Happy (May 11)**
> **Pleasing Father (June 15)**
> We Will Tell of God's Greatness (June 22)
> Stay Away from Trouble (July 13)
> Heroes of Violence (August 31)
> How to Tell God You Love Him (December 7)
> **Funeral Sermon (Suitable for a Suicide Victim)**

Dr. Ed Dobson
Pastor, Calvary Church in Grand Rapids, Michigan, and Moody Bible Institute's 1993 Pastor of the Year

> **You Must Be Born Again (March 16)**
> **Cultivating Our New Life in Jesus (August 31)**
> **Youth Sermon—How to Avoid Losing Your Faith**

Dr. Michael Easley
President, Moody Bible Institute, Chicago IL. Former Pastor and Teacher, Immanuel Bible Church, Springfield, Virginia and Grand Prarie Bible Church in Texas.

> **The Character of a Leader (February 3)**

Rev. Billie Friel
Pastor, First Baptist Church, Mt. Juliet, Tennessee

> Honoring God's Order (March 9)
> The Great Problem of Loneliness (April 6)
> The Mercy of God (November 16)

Rev. Peter Grainger
Pastor, Charlotte Baptist Chapel, Edinburgh, Scotland

> **Servants of Christ (February 10)**
> **Church Building (April 27)**
> **Courting Disaster (June 22)**
> **Settled Out of Court (July 27)**

Dr. Michael A. Guido
Founder of the Guido Evangelistic Association (1957), Devotional Column Writer, Radio and Telecast Host, and Writer of "Seeds from the Sower" Publication

> Let's Praise the Lord (March 2)
> The Extraordinary Christian (March 30)
> Taming the Temper (April 13)
> Prayer: What, Why, Where, When (July 20)
> Fishers of Men (August 17)
> Taming the Tongue (November 23)

Rev. Mark Hollis
Former Minister of 15 Years and Current Freelance Writer in Nashville, Tennessee. Master of Arts in Pastoral Counseling.

> You Cannot Lose (January 6)
> Everything I Needed to Know about Giving . . . (February 10)
> The Gospel Will Be Heard (September 21)
> Rejoice in All Life's Circumstances (October 19)
> Rejoice! God Is in Control (November 16)

Rev. David Jackman
President, Proclamation Trust; Director, Cornhill Training Course, London, England

> **A Different King (April 13)**
> **The Path of Wisdom (June 1)**

Dr. David Jeremiah
Senior Pastor of Shadow Mountain Community Church, El Cajon, California, and Chancellor of Christian Heritage College

> **The Godly Life (February 17)**
> Loving Your Enemies (February 17)
> **When Worship Turns to War (May 25)**
> Three-Dimensional Giving (May 25)
> **Tearing Down or Building Up? (August 24)**
> **Living for the Glory of God (November 9)**

Rev. Todd M. Kinde
Pastor of Grace Bible Church, Grandville, Michigan. Former Pastor of North View Alliance Church, Grand Rapids, Michigan.

> **Words of Comfort (January 13)**
> **He Gives Me Comfort (March 9)**
> **Prepare the Way with Readiness (September 28)**
> **Unity and Humility (November 23)**
> The Mind of Christ (November 23)
> **Funeral Sermon (Suitable for Death of a Believer)**
> **Communion Sermon—The Source of Joy**

Rev. Larry Kirk
Christ Community Church, Daytona Beach, Florida

> Beloved Children Walking in the Light (May 18)
> A Guiding Star for the Journey of Faith (June 8)
> **The Persistence of Grace (October 26)**

Dr. Woodrow Kroll
President and Senior Bible Teacher of Back to the Bible Broadcast

> **Seven Steps for Trusting God as We Get Older (June 29)**
> The Landmark of Christ's Atonement (June 29)

Dr. Martin Luther (1483–1546)
Writer, Preacher, Reformer

> The Manifestation and Sermon of Christ After His Resurrection (March 23)

Dr. Robert M. Norris

Senior Pastor of Fourth Presbyterian Church in the Washington Suburb of Bethesda, Maryland

Dr. Stephen Olford

Evangelist, Founder of the Stephen Olford Center for Biblical Preaching, Memphis, Tennessee

Dr. Larry Osborne

Senior Pastor, North Coast Church, Vista, California

The Power of Significant Relationships (November 30)
You Tell Them! (December 28)

Dr. A. T. Pierson (1837–1911)
Preacher, Writer, Speaker at Keswick Convention

The Fourfold Force of Scripture (January 13)

Dr. Kevin Riggs
Senior Pastor, First Free Will Baptist Church, Russellville, Arkansas

The Tough News of the Gospel (January 20)
It's Not About You (January 27)
It's a Matter of the Heart (February 24)
Wild at Heart (September 21)
Tithing Is Not a Four-Letter Word (October 19)
The Brutal Facts of Life (December 7)

Joshua D. Rowe
Assistant Editor to Robert J. Morgan, Summa Cum Laude Graduate of Columbia International University, Master of Divinity Student at The Southern Baptist Theological Seminary

Praise the Lord! (June 8)
Stop Passing the Blame (July 13)
The Church Is Your Family (July 27)
The Difficulties of Discipleship (August 10)
Forget Not His Benefits (August 17)
Patience in Hardship (September 21)
The Consolation of Israel (December 14)

Rev. Richard S. Sharpe, Jr.
Director of Small Church Ministries and President of Christian Home Crusade

Prayer for Revival (May 4)
Partial Obedience (August 3)

Rev. Charles Haddon Spurgeon (1834–1892)
Pastor, Metropolitan Tabernacle, London

Morning and Evening Songs (August 24)
The Pearl of Patience (September 14)

Rev. Melvin Tinker

Vicar of The Church of St John Newland since 1994. Editor of "Restoring the Vision—Anglican Evangelists Speak Out," and The Anglican Evangelical Crisis.

A Call to Submission (February 24)
Who Rules? (March 16)
A Constant Temptation (April 6)
The Servant Solution (April 20)
The Creator (June 1)
Jesus the Shepherd (July 6)
Sez Who? (August 3)
The Trap of Cynicism (September 28)
Good Timing/God's Timing (November 2)
The Glorious King (December 7)

Dr. Melvin Worthington

Executive Secretary, National Association of Free Will Baptists

The Pastoral Pattern (January 13)
The Biblical Bishop (July 20)
The Christian's Compass (September 14)
Moses' Miracles (October 5)
Deity Described (October 12)
Jacob's Journey (November 30)
The Disciple's Diet (December 14)
Pastoral Preaching (Ordination Sermon)

(Note: Bold Print indicates main outlines)

All other outlines are from the pulpit ministry of the general editor, Pastor Robert J. Morgan, of The Donelson Fellowship in Nashville, Tennessee. Special appreciation goes to Corey Hawkins, music minister of the Donelson Fellowship, for his invaluable assistance.

2008 Calendar

January 1	New Year's Day
January 6	**Epiphany**
January 13	
January 20	**Sanctity of Human Life Sunday**
January 21	Martin Luther King, Jr. Day
January 26	Australia Day
January 27	
February 1–29	Black History Month
February 3	**Transfiguration Sunday; Super Bowl Sunday**
February 6	Ash Wednesday
February 10	**First Sunday of Lent**
February 12	Lincoln's Birthday
February 14	Valentine's Day
February 17	**Second Sunday of Lent**
February 18	Presidents' Day
February 22	Washington's Birthday
February 24	**Third Sunday of Lent**
February 29	Leap Day
March 2	**Fourth Sunday of Lent**
March 9	**Fifth Sunday of Lent; Daylight Saving Time Begins**
March 16	**Palm Sunday**
March 17	St. Patrick's Day
March 20	Maundy Thursday; First Day of Spring
March 21	Good Friday; Purim
March 23	**Easter Sunday**
March 30	

April 6

April 13   **Jefferson's Birthday**

April 20   **Passover**

April 22   Earth Day

April 23   Administrative Professionals Day

April 27

May 1   Ascension Day; National Day of Prayer

May 4

May 11   **Mother's Day; Pentecost**

May 17   Armed Forces Day

May 18   **Trinity Sunday**

May 25

May 26   Memorial Day

June 1

June 8

June 14   Flag Day

June 15   **Father's Day**

June 20   First Day of Summer

June 22

June 29

July 4   Independence Day

July 6

July 13

July 20

July 27   **Parent's Day**

August 3   **Friendship Day**

August 6   Transfiguration Day

August 10

August 17

August 24

August 31

September 1   Labor Day

September 7   **Grandparent's Day**

September 14

September 21

September 22   First Day of Autumn

September 26   Native American Day

September 28

September 30   Rosh Hashanah

October 1–31   Pastor Appreciation Month

October 5

October 9   Yom Kippur

October 12

October 13   Columbus Day

October 19

October 26   **Reformation Day; Mother-in-Law Day**

October 31   Halloween

November 1   All Saints' Day

November 2   **Daylight Saving Time Ends**

November 9   **International Day of Prayer for the Persecuted Church**

November 11   Veterans Day

November 16

November 23

November 27   Thanksgiving Day

November 30   **First Sunday of Advent**

December 7   Second Sunday of Advent; National Pearl Harbor Remembrance Day

December 14   Third Sunday of Advent

December 21   Fourth Sunday of Advent; First Day of Winter

December 22   Hanukkah Begins

December 24   Christmas Eve

December 25   Christmas Day

December 26   Kwanzaa Begins

December 28

December 31   New Year's Eve

Boldface dates are Sundays

SERMONS AND
WORSHIP SUGGESTIONS
FOR 52 WEEKS

JANUARY 6, 2008

SUGGESTED SERMON

What Really Matters

Date preached:

By Dr. Timothy K. Beougher

Scripture: Mark 1:9–20, especially verse 15
The time is fulfilled, and the kingdom of God is at hand. Repent, and believe in the gospel.

Introduction: When a year closes out and the hustle and bustle of the holidays have passed, we often have just enough time to think about the New Year as a new beginning. It's wonderful to reevaluate what's most important in our lives and to determine what deserves more of our attention. In our passage today, Jesus gives us some great guidance as we gear up for 2008. According to Scripture, what really matters?

1. **Pleasing God in the Ordinary Events of Life (vv. 9–11).** We could spend all day on this passage, but understanding the context gives us great insight. Jesus hadn't preached a sermon (unless you count His excursion in the temple at age 12 in Luke 2); He hadn't performed any miracles; He had done nothing in the category of "full-time" Christian work! What had He done? He worked in a carpenter's shop. It doesn't matter what our occupation is, but what matters is our obedience in whatever we do.

2. **Following God Even When Tempted to Turn Away (vv. 12–13).** What really matters? Following God even when tempted to turn away, saying no to the enticements of sin. We need to understand that temptation is not sin (Heb. 2:14). Jesus Himself was tempted, but He followed God even when tempted to turn away. We can apply the ideas here by asking ourselves some difficult questions:

   A. What are my most difficult temptations?
   B. When do they most commonly strike?
   C. Why do they come at that time and place?
   D. How can I avoid them?

   We must be "pro-active" in dealing with temptation, and not simply "re-active."

3. **Telling Others about God's Wonderful Salvation (vv. 14–15).** Jesus preached repentance and shared the gospel, the Good News. Repentance is turning away from our sins. The gospel would be incomplete, however, if we had nowhere to turn to: That's why Jesus preached the Good News, too! He once told the story of a woman who lost a silver coin and the frantic search which ensued. What did she do when she found it? She rejoiced and called together her friends to celebrate! You see, good news is for sharing; there's no better news than the gospel of Jesus Christ!

4. **Living as a Disciple (vv. 16–20).** These verses show us how Jesus called His disciples, unique in some ways, but very much the same as He calls us to discipleship today.

   A. **The Call to Discipleship.** Jesus was walking along the Sea of Galilee. But this was more than a casual afternoon stroll. Jesus was looking for people. He found Peter and Andrew, James and John. They were fisherman. They were not from the religious elite. They were not scribes, or Levites, or priests, or rabbis. They were not Pharisees or Sadducees. They were common people, ordinary individuals like you and me. In choosing these individuals, Jesus is making a statement to us. He can use ordinary people if we are willing to follow Him.

   B. **The Meaning of Discipleship.** The word *discipleship* has been used in a variety of different ways in our culture. What does it mean to be a disciple of Jesus Christ? Jesus asks us to *leave other things behind and follow Him.* Christ's call demands that we give Him our supreme allegiance (Luke 14:26). Scripture teaches us that *who He is demands that we follow.* Jesus is no ordinary man: He is God come in the flesh. How could we do anything but follow Him?

   C. **The Rewards of Discipleship.** First, *we are transformed by His power!* Our job is to follow; His job is to transform. As we follow Jesus, He gives us the power to become what He wants us to be. Secondly, *we are fulfilled beyond measure* (John 12:24). One of the paradoxes in Scripture is that if a person seeks to save his or her life, they will lose it.

   It is only in losing our lives that we find them. Only as we turn our lives over to Jesus wholeheartedly can we find true fulfillment in life.

Conclusion: Jesus began His ministry exemplifying these four things that really matter. During His ministry, He taught them to be His followers in what we know as the Great Commandment and the Great Commission. The Great Commandment is to love the Lord with all our heart, soul, mind, and strength and our neighbor as ourselves (Matt. 22:37–38). This leads to the Great Commission, to tell the world about Christ (Matt. 28:18–20)!

STATS, STORIES, AND MORE

More from Dr. Beougher
My background is engineering. As a senior in college, I won a national design competition and eventually received a U.S. Patent for the design. But God had called me into ministry and so I headed off that next year for Southwestern Seminary in Fort Worth. When I left for seminary, I wish I had $1 for every person who said to me, "You're really committed." I'll be honest, at first those compliments stroked my ego. But it didn't take long before they really bothered me. Why? Because the implication was that I wasn't committed to Christ as an engineer, and that just wasn't true. When I was working as an engineer my highest goal in life was to please God. That didn't change when I left for seminary. I believe God was just as pleased with my work as an engineer, trying to bring glory to Him, as He is with my work as a pastor or professor. The key is not so much what is being done but that it is being done in obedience to the Father.

APPROPRIATE HYMNS AND SONGS

"Another Year Is Dawning," Frances R. Havergal, Public Domain.

"All That Thrills My Soul Is Jesus," Thoro Harris, 1931 Mrs. Thoro Harris. Renewed 1959 (Nazarene Publishing House).

"Wonderful, Merciful Savior," Dawn Rodgers & Eric Wyse, 1989 (Word Music, LLC; Dayspring Music, LLC).

"Famous One," Chris Tomlin & Jesse Reeves, 2002 worshiptogether.com songs (Admin. by EMI Christian Music Pub.), Sixsteps Music (Admin. by EMI Christian Music Pub.).

FOR THE BULLETIN

On January 6, 1519, Martin Luther met with Karl von Miltitz, representing Pope Leo X, in an effort to prevent a church schism. Miltitz left the meeting thinking he had accomplished his purpose, but Luther would not be silenced. ● January 6, 1739, marks the birth of John Fawcett, author of "Blest Be the Tie that Binds." He was converted at age 16 by George Whitefield and became a Baptist pastor. He wrote his famous hymn after he and his wife could not bear leaving their beloved rural congregation for a famous pastorate in London. ● On Sunday, January 6, 1850, the "Prince of Preachers," Charles Haddon Spurgeon, was converted. A snowstorm forced 15-year-old Charles to duck into a Primitive Methodist Church. Only a few people were there, and not even the preacher showed up. A thin-looking man finally stood and read Isaiah 45:22. Spying Charles in the back, he pointed his finger, crying, "Look, young man! Look! Look to Christ!" Charles did look and was saved. ● On this day in 1884, Gregor Mendel, Austrian Augustinian monk, biologist and botanist, died. He pioneered the study of biological heredity and laid the mathematical foundation of the science of genetics. ● Alexander Whyte, one of Scotland's greatest preachers, died on January 6, 1921. ● On this day in 1947 another Scottish preacher, Peter Marshall, became Chaplain of the United States Senate. Two years later, he suffered a heart attack and died. His widow, Catherine Marshall, assuaged her grief by writing his biography, *A Man Called Peter.* She went on to become one of the twentieth century's most gifted authors.

WORSHIP HELPS

Call to Worship

> O Trinity! O Unity!
> Be present as we worship Thee;
> And with the songs that angels sing
> Unite the hymns of praise we bring.
> —From an eleventh-century Latin
> hymn titled "All Hail Adored
> Trinity"

Offertory Scripture Reading

Command those who are rich in this present age not to be haughty, nor to trust in uncertain riches but in the living God, who gives us richly all things to enjoy. Let them do good, that

Continued on the next page

WORSHIP HELPS—*Continued*

they be rich in good works, ready to give, willing to share, storing up for themselves a good foundation for the time to come, that they may lay hold on eternal life (1 Tim. 6:17–19).

Invitation

What new beginnings have you committed to this New Year? For any of you here today who have never committed your life to Christ, listen to Jesus' words about the most important new beginning: "Jesus answered and said . . . 'unless one is born again, he cannot see the kingdom of God'" (John 3:5). In our passage we looked at today, Jesus gave us two key steps to being born again. He said, first, "repent." Repentance is admitting that you have sinned against God, acknowledging He's right and you are wrong, and turning away from your sinful lifestyle. The second step Jesus gave us was "believe in the gospel!" Faith is the other key to being born again. We must trust Jesus to forgive us of sin, and we must follow Him as the Son of God and the Lord of our lives. Please come and talk with me or our staff if you would like to make this decision today, to have the ultimate new beginning, to be born again into a new life with Christ!

PRAYER FOR THE PASTOR'S CLOSET

Revive us, Lord! Is zeal abating
While harvest fields are vast and white?
Revive, us Lord, the world is waiting,
Equip Thy church to spread the light.
—BESSIE HEAD, 1914

Additional Sermons and Lesson Ideas

You Cannot Lose
By Rev. Mark Hollis

Date preached:

SCRIPTURE: Philippians 1:18–26

INTRODUCTION: We focus our camera; we focus our attention, but how often do we focus on Christ despite our circumstances? Paul's focus allowed him to stare death in the face knowing that whether he lived or died he could not lose.

1. Deliverance Is Coming (vv. 18–19). In the face of adversity God has given us the resources of prayer and the Holy Spirit.
2. Losing Is Not an Option (vv. 20–21). Paul had come to know Christ so intimately that he recognized death as the only barrier between him and the One he loved.
3. God Has a Plan and Purpose (vv. 22–26). Paul trusted that he would be delivered for at least these three purposes:
   A. Fruitful Labor in the Gospel (v. 22).
   B. Helping Believers to Progress in Joy and Faith (v. 25).
   C. Joyful Reunion with those He Loved (v. 26).

CONCLUSION: When we place our circumstances in God's hands, we realize His will is good and acceptable (Rom. 12:2).

Stay Focused!
By Dr. Larry Osborne

Date preached:

SCRIPTURE: Various, especially Matthew 28:19–20

INTRODUCTION: Today we will look at how we can restore our focus, get back on track, and stay there. To be spiritually contagious, we must stay focused on:

1. Disciples, Not Just Decisions (Matt. 13:1–23; 28:19–20; Luke 10:25–28; Mark 10:17–22; Col. 1:28–29).
2. Obedience, Not Just Doctrine (Matt. 28:20; John 8:31–32; 14:21, 23–24; 1 John 2:3–5; 1 Cor. 13:2).
3. Persuasion Not Debate (2 Tim. 2:24–26; 1 Cor. 9:19–22; Matt. 5:43–48; John 13:34–35).
4. Relationships, Not Attendance (Heb. 10:24–25; Prov. 13:20; 27:17).

CONCLUSION: God wants us to be spiritually contagious: influencing and impacting our world for the Lord.

JANUARY 13, 2008

Words of Comfort

Date preached:

By Rev. Todd M. Kinde

Scripture: Isaiah 40:1–11, especially verses 1, 10–11
"Comfort, yes, comfort My people!" says your God. Behold, the Lord GOD shall come with a strong hand, and His arm shall rule for Him; behold, His reward is with Him, and His work before Him. He will feed His flock like a shepherd; He will gather the lambs with His arm, and carry them in His bosom, and gently lead those who are with young.

Introduction: Have you ever received a bit of bad news that made your heart sink? Imagine receiving news like this only to discover that the consequences of that bad news will come around while you're on vacation! Israel received some bad news in Isaiah 39. Israel was to be invaded by Babylonian forces and taken into captivity. Hezekiah, king of Israel, was told, however, that this would not happen during his reign but during the time of his sons. Hezekiah took consolation in this fact. In reaction to Hezekiah's cavalier attitude about the condition of God's people, God Himself brought a word in 40:1, "Comfort, yes, comfort My people." God comes with His comforting words of salvation through Jesus. The Lord is coming and we ought to find comfort in Him.

1. **Comfort in God's Tender Forgiveness (40:1–2).** Comfort comes to us through words. The company of prophets was told to speak and cry to God's people, indicating the prophetic work of preaching. Israel had been disciplined for ignoring God and His Word. God was now bringing forgiveness and ending this exile. Even in the exile, God called His people by name. Today we, as the church, the people of God, enjoy the perfect fulfillment of His tender forgiveness in Jesus Christ (Eph. 1:7). Yet, we, too, live in a type of exile awaiting the coming of Christ in glory. Our exile is not one of punishment, but one of patient endurance and purification. Peter identifies us as sojourners, those in exile. Yet, we find comfort in the tender forgiveness of God having received mercy (1 Pet. 1:1; 2:10).

2. **Comfort in God's Revealed Glory (40:3–5).** When a king was to visit a region or a city it would be announced well in advance so that the

people could prepare the way for him, making the roads worthy of His presence. The coming of the king was not a one-day event. It was an extended season of time of unfolding revelation. Here, the way is made smooth, clear, level, and straight as is characteristic of God's holiness, purity, and righteousness. When He comes, He will come in the fullness of His glory and nothing will get in His way. This passage is applied to John the Baptizer in the Gospel accounts. He prepares the way for the Lord Jesus who is the very essence of God's glory (John 1:14; Heb. 1:1–3).

3. **Comfort in God's Enduring Word (40:6–8).** Isaiah, being among the school of the prophets responded, "What do I say?" God gave him the very message he was to preach. The message details the mortality of man and the eternality of God's Word, the fading nature of humanity, and the enduring nature of God's Word. We are temporary; He is permanent. We are morally and spiritually unreliable. This message we resist. We do not like to be reminded of nor told of our inability and frailty. Christianity is not about human power, but about Divine power. Christianity is not about commitment, but about confidence in God who is enduring and in His unchanging Word (Num. 23:19; Ps. 119:89). Jesus says that the whole earth will pass away but His words will remain (Mark 13:31).

4. **Comfort in God's Strong Arms (40:9–11):** Lastly, as we await the coming of Jesus, we find comfort in God's strong arms. The strong arms of God are illustrated for us in two images—the Warrior and the Shepherd. God comes as the Warrior 1) to rule, 2) with reward, and 3) with recompense (v. 10). God comes as the Shepherd 1) to gather, 2) to carry, 3) to lead (v. 11). Jesus came as the Good Shepherd to gather us together and to provide for our salvation (John 11:51–52). Jesus will come again as the mighty Warrior to judge the living and the dead. God leads us—He leads us to repentance (Rom. 2:4). When we come to the Lord in repentance and faith, then we will find comfort in Him.

Conclusion: Are you resting in the comfort of the Lord? Are you numbered among His people?

STATS, STORIES, AND MORE

In "real life," actress Lisa Whelchel is a busy mother, a pastor's wife, and a popular Christian writer and speaker. One of her specialties is teaching busy mothers how to take time for spiritual nourishment in the Word of God every day. On her bookshelf is a copy of *Wuest's Word Studies from the Greek New Testament,* and one day she noticed something. In the Bible, the term "word" is sometimes translated from the Greek word *rhema.* For example, in Matthew 4:4, Jesus said that we cannot exist on bread alone, but by every *rhema* that proceeds from the mouth of God. The term "word" in this verse is the Greek word *rhema,* which means something that has been definitely stated, a pronouncement, a specific word uttered by a living voice. This term struck Lisa and she began thinking of specific Bible verses as "Rhema Rays." She wrote, "When I sit down in my recliner, snuggle up with a cozy blanket, a hot cup of coffee, and my favorite comfy Bible every morning, there are some days, as I am reading the Word to know God personally, that He reveals Himself in an especially intimate way. It is as if the Lord shines a ray of light on a verse, even if I have read it a hundred times before but, suddenly I understand how it specifically applies to me and my life. I call these moments 'Rhema Rays.'" This is God's primary way of dispensing comfort to our hearts—through the truths and promises of His enduring and infallible Word.

APPROPRIATE HYMNS AND SONGS

"Straight to the Heart," Brent Bourgeois & Michael W. Smith, 1995 (Sony/ATV Milene Music; ADC Music; W. B. M. Music; Deer Valley Music).

"He's Been So Good to Me," R. Doug Little, 1978 (Heart Warming Music Co./BMI).

"Abide with Me," Henry Francis Lyte & William Henry Monk, Public Domain.

"Hungry," Kathryn Scott, 1999 Vineyard Songs (Admin. by Vineyard Music UK)."Blessed Be Your Name," Beth Redman & Matt Redman, 2002 ThankYou Music (Admin. by EMI Christian Music Pub.).

FOR THE BULLETIN

On January 13, 1522, Martin Luther, exhausted in his efforts of translating the New Testament into German, wrote a friend that he had undertaken a task beyond his power, and that he now understood why no one had attempted it before. His translation was published later that year. ● January 13 marks the death of George Fox, founder of the Society of Friends, or Quakers, in 1691. ● Torrential rain on January 13, 1856, kept missionary J. Hudson Taylor confined to a little boat during a preaching tour of China. His diary on that day reads, "The rain was so heavy all day that no one could leave the boats. Thus we enjoyed a delightful day of rest, such as we had not had for some time; and the weather prevented much inquiry being made for us. Had the day been fine we should most likely have been discovered, even if we had not left the boats. As it was, we were allowed to think in peace, and with wonder and gratitude, of the gracious dealings of our God, who had thus led us apart into "a desert place" to rest awhile. ● On this day in 1892, Amy Carmichael responded to God's call to be a foreign missionary. ● On January 13, 1915, Mary Slessor passed away at age 66, following nearly 39 years of remarkable missionary service in Nigeria. Her last words were, "Do not weep, do not weep; the Lord is taking me home."

WORSHIP HELPS

Call to Worship

All heaven will praise your great wonders, LORD; myriads of angels will praise you for your faithfulness. For who in all of heaven can compare with the LORD? What mightiest angel is anything like the LORD? The highest angelic powers stand in awe of God. He is far more awesome than all who surround his throne. O LORD God of Heaven's Armies! Where is there anyone as mighty as you, O LORD? You are entirely faithful (Ps. 89:5–8 NLT).

Scripture Reading Medley

LORD, you know the hopes of the helpless. Surely you will hear their cries and comfort them. / Even when I walk through the darkest valley, I will not be afraid, for you are close beside me. Your rod and your staff protect and comfort me. / When doubts filled my mind, your comfort gave me renewed hope and

Continued on the next page

WORSHIP HELPS—*Continued*

cheer. / Your promise revives me; it comforts me in all my troubles . . . I meditate on your age-old regulations; O LORD, they comfort me . . . now let your unfailing love comfort me, just as you promised me, your servant. / All praise to God, the Father of our Lord Jesus Christ. God is our merciful Father and the source of all comfort. He comforts us in all our troubles so that we can comfort others. When they are troubled, we will be able to give them the same comfort God has given us (Ps. 10:17; 23:4; 94:19; 119:50, 52, 76; 2 Cor. 1:3–4 NLT).

Benediction
Now may our Lord Jesus Christ himself and God our Father, who loved us and by his grace gave us eternal comfort and a wonderful hope, comfort you and strengthen you in every good thing you do and say (2 Thess. 2:15–17 NLT).

Quote for the Pastor's Wall

Success is going from failure to failure without losing your enthusiasm.

—WINSTON CHURCHILL

Additional Sermons and Lesson Ideas

The Fourfold Force of Scripture
Adapted from a message by Dr. A. T. Pierson

Date preached:

SCRIPTURE: Psalm 119:89

INTRODUCTION: There are four grand utterances in the Bible that constitute a basis for biblical authority.

1. His Word Is Settled. "Forever, O LORD, Your word is settled in heaven" (Ps. 119:89). This was Luther's maxim, inscribed on the walls of his chamber and embroidered on his robe. It means that the Word of God is established in heaven, beyond the reach of all disturbing causes.
2. His Word Is Magnified. "You have magnified Your word above all Your name" (Ps. 138:2). This suggests that beyond all other previous manifestations of the Divine character, His written Word reveals Him.
3. His Word Is Priceless. "Buy the truth, and do not sell it" (Prov. 23:23). This advises us to give any price for the truth, but to take no price to part with it.
4. His Word Is Authoritative. "These are the true sayings of God" (Rev. 19:9). What God has said in His sixty-six books is faithful, true, established, authoritative, and represents the standards by which the universe is governed.

CONCLUSION: "Holy Bible, book divine, precious treasure, thou art mine."

The Pastoral Pattern
By Dr. Melvin Worthington

Date preached:

SCRIPTURE: 1 Timothy 1—3; 2 Timothy 4; 1 Corinthians 11

INTRODUCTION: Today's ministers face a complex and corrupt society. They are expected to be role models for their congregations. Ministers who effectively provide a role model must progressively develop as a person, preacher, and pastor.

1. The Pastor as a Person. In our personal lives, ministers must develop the *proper disposition* which manifests itself under all circumstances. They must manifest the *proper development* of the qualities that make a good minister, maintaining *proper discipline* and developing *proper doctrine*.
2. The Pastor as a Preacher. As preachers develop in the pulpit, they will preach the Word of God *comprehensively, conscientiously, continually, clearly, compassionately, correctly*, and *contextually*.
3. The Pastor as a Pastor. Pastoral work is rugged but rewarding. Pastors must polish their ability to *educate the congregation, encourage the congregation, exhort the congregation*, and *establish the congregation*.

CONCLUSION: Will you allow God to make you a pastoral pattern as a person, preacher, or pastor?

Thomas Watson's Rules of Contentment

Thomas Watson, the most quotable of the Puritans, wrote a wonderful book entitled *The Art of Divine Contentment: An Exposition of Philippians 4:11*. In Chapter 14, condensed and adapted below, Watson gave his "Christian directory," listing his rules of contentment.

Rule 1: Advance faith. All our disquiets issue from unbelief. O set faith a-work! It is the property of faith to silence our doubtings, to scatter our fears, to still the heart when the passions are up. Faith works the heart to a sweet serene composure. It is not having food and raiment, but having faith, which will make us content. Faith sucks the honey of contentment out of the hive of the promise.

Rule 2: Labor for Assurance. He who can say, "I know whom I have believed"—that man has enough to give his heart contentment. If any thing in the world is worth laboring for, it is to get sound evidences that God is ours. If this be once cleared, what can come amiss? No matter what storms I meet, so that I know where to put in for harbor. He that has God to be his God is so well contented with his condition that he does not much care whether he has anything else.

Rule 3: Get a Humble Spirit. The humble man is the contented man. He does not say his comforts are small, but his sins are great. He thinks it is mercy he is out of hell, therefore he is contented. A proud man is never contented; he is one that has a high opinion of himself, therefore under small blessings is disdainful, under small crosses impatient. The humble spirit is the contented spirit; if his cross be light, he reckons it the inventory of his mercies; if it be heavy, yet he takes it upon his knees, knowing that when his estate is worse, it is to make him better.

Rule 4: Keep a Clear Conscience. Contentment is the manna that is laid up in the ark of a good conscience. Oh, take heed of indulging any sin! It is as natural for guilt to breed disquiet as for putrid matter to breed vermin. Would you have a quiet heart? Get a smiling conscience.

Rule 5: Learn to Deny Yourselves. Look well to your affections, bridle them in. Do two things: Mortify your desires; moderate your delights.

Rule 6: Get Much of Heaven into Your Heart. Spiritual things satisfy; the more of heaven is in us, the less earth will content us. He that has once tasted the love of God, his thirst is much quenched towards sublunary things; the joys of God's Spirit are heart-filling and heart-cheering joys; he that has these, has heaven begun in him. Seek those things which are above. Fly aloft in your affections, thirst after the graces and comforts of the Spirit; the eagle that flies above in the air, fears not the stinging of the serpent.

Rule 7: Look Not So Much on the Dark Side of Your Condition, as on the Light. The pillar of cloud had its light side and dark; look on the light side of the estate. Suppose you are in a lawsuit, there is the dark side; yet you have some land left, there is the light side. You have sickness in your body, there is the dark side; but grace in your soul, there is the light side. You have a child taken away, there is the dark side; your husband lives, there is the light side. Look on the light side of your condition, and then all your discontents will easily disband; do not pore upon your losses, but ponder upon your mercies.

Rule 8: Consider in What a Posture We Stand in the World. We are *soldiers;* a soldier is content with anything though he has not his stately house, his rich furniture, his soft bed, his full table, yet he does not complain. We are *pilgrims,* in the world but not of the world. We are *beggars* at heaven's gate, begging this day for our daily bread. *Continued on the next page*

THOUGHTS FOR THE PASTOR'S SOUL—*Continued*

Rule 9: Let Us Often Compare Our Condition. Let us compare our condition with others; and this will make us content. Am I in prison? Was not Daniel in a worse place in the lion's den? Do I live in a mean cottage? Read of the primitive saints, that they wandered in sheep and goat skins, of whom the world was not worthy. Let us compare our condition with Christ's upon earth. What a poor condition was He pleased to be in for us; for you know the grace of our Lord Jesus Christ, that though He was rich, yet for our sakes He became poor. Let us compare our condition with what it shall be shortly. God may presently seal a warrant for death to apprehend us: and when we die, we cannot carry estate with us: honor and riches descend not into the grave, why then are we troubled at our outward condition?

Rule 10: Do Not Bring Your Condition to Your Mind, but Bring Your Mind to Your Condition. The way for a Christian to be contented, is not by raising his estate higher, but by bringing his spirit lower; not by making his barns wider, but his heart narrower.

Rule 11: Study the Vanity of the Creature. The world is like a shadow that declines; it is delightful, but deceitful, promising more than we find. The world may be compared to ice, which is smooth but slippery.

Rule 12: Get Fancy Regulated. The water that springs out of the rock drinks as sweet as if it came out of a golden chalice. Things are as we fancy them. Ever since the Fall, the fancy is distempered; God saw that the imagination of the thoughts of his heart were evil. Fancy looks through wrong spectacles. Pray that God will sanctify your fancy. Could we cure a distempered fancy, we might soon conquer a discontented heart.

Rule 13: Consider How Little Will Suffice Nature. Christ taught us to pray for our daily bread. Nature is content with a little. Not to thirst or to starve is enough. Having food and raiment let us be content.

Rule 14: Believe the Present Condition Is Best for Us. A wise Christian has his will melted into God's will. God is wise. God knows which is the fittest pasture to put His sheep in; sometimes a more barren ground does well, whereas rank pasture may rot. Did we believe that condition best which God doth parcel out to us, we should cheerfully say, "The lines are fallen in pleasant places."

Rule 15: Do Not Too Much Indulge the Flesh. The flesh is a worse enemy than the devil, it is a bosom-traitor; an enemy within. O let it not have the reins! Martyr the flesh! Keep it under! Put its neck under Christ's yoke, stretch and nail it to His cross.

Rule 16: Meditate Much on the Glory Which Shall Be Revealed. There are great things laid up in heaven. It is but awhile and we shall be with Christ, bathing ourselves in the fountain of love; we shall never complain of wants and injuries anymore. The hope of this is enough to drive distempers from the heart. Blessed be God, it will be better.

Rule 17: Be Much in Prayer. Is any man afflicted? Let him pray. Is any man discontented? Let him pray. When the heart is filled with sorrow and disquiet, prayer lets out the bad blood. Prayer is a holy spell to drive away trouble; prayer is the unbosoming of the soul, the unloading of all our cares in God's breast; and this ushers in sweet contentment. Paul could be in every state content, yet it was through Christ strengthening him.

JANUARY 20, 2008

Be of Good Cheer! Your Sins Are Forgiven!

Date preached:

Scripture: Matthew 9:1–8, especially verse 2
Son, be of good cheer; your sins are forgiven you.

Introduction: Jesus used a wonderful phrase on five occasions. Though only one word in the Greek, our English versions use four words to describe it. These words are part promise, part command: *Be of Good Cheer.* No message is more needed. Our society is awash in depression, but Jesus wants to give us joy and cheer.

1. **Sin Can Paralyze Us.** This man had two heartrending problems, an exterior dilemma and an interior one. The inner, invisible problem was the worse of the two. On a physical level, this man was paralyzed, either a paraplegic or a quadriplegic. But that wasn't the worst of it. He was paralyzed in his heart. He felt guilty, at fault, culpable, to blame, wicked, ashamed, and self-condemning. I have a theory that his two problems were intertwined. I think he was a relatively young man whose goofing off had caused an accident. We read all the time in the newspapers about people who cross the "Stupid Line." This man in Matthew 9, in my speculative opinion, had crossed the Stupid Line and had caused an accident resulting in his own paralysis. He had perhaps injured someone else, too. Guilt can cripple and paralyze. It can alter your personality and relationships. It can erode your self-image and sap your morale. Perhaps you had an affair in the past, or you were promiscuous at some point in your history. Maybe you've had an abortion, which almost no one knows of; but the guilt of it is affecting your life now. I've had people who told me about a same-sex encounter they had in the past, just a momentary incident; but over the years the memory of it has tormented them. Well, this is where Jesus Christ excels. He's an expert in dealing with these matters. In our passage today He deals with the problem headlong, and His words are for us just as much as they were addressed to the man on the cot. What does

Jesus say to us? How does He address our guilt? He speaks eight words: "Be of good cheer! Your sins are forgiven."

2. **Jesus Can Pardon Us.**

   A. **Jesus Pronounces Forgiveness.** You and I have the capacity to forgive sins in a limited and secondary sense. In an ultimate, primary sense, only God can extend true forgiveness because it is His law that has been broken, and it is against Him that all sin occurs. When Jesus said, "Your sins are forgiven," He was claiming to do something only God could do and acting on a prerogative that only God could exercise. Nothing in this passage makes sense if we don't accept the biblical premise that Christ is fully God. Looked at from another perspective, we recognize our Lord's divinity here in three ways. We see His omniscience, for He read the need of the paralytic and the minds of the scribes. We see His omnipotence, for He said, "Rise up and walk," and the man's paralysis fell away. And we see His authority to forgive sins, which is a prerogative of God and God alone.

   B. **Jesus Provides Forgiveness.** The act of forgiving this man was very costly, for it required our Lord Himself to be paralyzed on the cross, bearing that man's sin, and mine and yours. Hebrews 9:12 says, "Not with the blood of goats and calves, but with His own blood He entered the Most Holy Place once for all, having obtained eternal redemption."

3. **Faith Can Prove It to Us.** You say, "Can I really accept the reality of total, complete, and ultimate forgiveness?" Yes, faith can prove it to us. This man could have said, "What a bunch of rubbish. I don't believe a word of it; I'm not going to accept it. This is a waste of time, boys, carry me home." But he didn't. He flexed his muscles, stretched his legs, took a deep breath, rose from his stretcher, and departed to his house. When the multitudes saw it, they marveled and glorified God who had given such power to men. Isn't it time for you to rise up and walk? It's time for you, too, to say: "I've wallowed around in guilt and sin and shame long enough. I'm going to embrace God's forgiveness. I'm going to forgive myself. I'm going to live a life set free." What can wash away our sin? Nothing but the blood of Jesus.

STATS, STORIES, AND MORE

The Epidemic of Depression

Peter D. Kramner, in his book, *Against Depression*, warns that depression is at epidemic levels, and it is an affliction that destroys us in both body and soul. Depression endangers nerve cells, disrupts brain functioning, damages the heart and the blood vessels, alters personal perspective and judgment, and interferes with parenting and family life."[1] Another recent book on the subject of depression defines it as "a state of existence marked by a sense of being pressed down, weighed down, or burdened which affects a person physically, mentally, spiritually, and relationally."[2] According to experts, at this very moment somewhere between 14 and 28 million Americans are suffering from depression, but multitudes of others of us are battling other related mood disorders that stem from many causes and require many courses of treatment.

Written in Blood

In 2005, a commuter train in Los Angeles struck an SUV on the tracks. The train derailed and struck another train, causing eleven deaths and over 200 injuries. There was one story coming out of that accident that gripped California. It involved a man who was on the train. Normally, he later said, he would not have taken the train, but he was called in early to work at an aerospace plant in Burbank. He was sitting upstairs in the double-decker car when the wreck occurred. He recalled waking up to find himself trapped under the debris and covered with blood. He realized he had been badly injured, and using the blood that was oozing from his own body, he used his finger to write a note to his family, telling them that he loved them.[3] That is what Christ did for us. Using His own blood, He wrote a message of love for you and me, and the blood of Jesus Christ, God's Son, cleanses us from all sin. So sin can paralyze us, but Jesus can pardon us. He pronounces forgiveness because He provides it.

---

[1] Peter D. Kramer, *Against Depression* (New York: Viking Press, 2005), from the dust jacket.
[2] David B. Biebel and Harold G. Koenig, *New Light on Depression* (Grand Rapids: Zondervan, 2004), p. 19.
[3] "Train Passenger Recalls Blood Message" by Greg Risling (AP) in NorthWest Cable News, at http://www.nwcn.com/sharedcontent/nationworld/nation/020405ccjccwNat TrainBlood.75ecod82.html, accessed November 7, 2005.

APPROPRIATE HYMNS AND SONGS

"There Is a Fountain Filled with Blood," Lowell Mason & William Cowper, Public Domain.

"Nothing But the Blood," Robert Lowry, Public Domain.

"For Who You Are," Marty Sampson, 2006 Hillsong Publishing (Admin. in U.S. & Canada by Integrity's Hosanna! Music).

"Sing for Joy," Lamont Hiebert, 1996 Integrity's Hosanna! Music.

FOR THE BULLETIN

Decius Trajan, Emperor of Rome, executed Fabian, Bishop of Rome, on January 20, 250. ● January 20, 1669, is the birthday of Susanna Wesley. ● On this date in 1828, early American evangelist, David Marks, preached all day and retired to bed exhausted. Just past midnight, he felt so ill he thought he was going to die. Marks grew joyous at the prospect of heaven. But suddenly, thinking of sinners bound for hell, he seemed to hear a whisper: "Will you still go and warn them?" Weeping, Marks replied, "Yes, Lord, I will go and warn them as long as it shall be Thy will." His recovery began instantly, adding years to his evangelistic labors. ● On January 20, 1858, missionaries Hudson and Maria Taylor were married. ● During the Revival of 1905, a Day of Prayer was proclaimed in Denver, Colorado, on Friday, January 20. So many people flocked to churches and theaters for prayer that most of the city's stores and schools closed. The impact of the revival was felt for months. ● Eliza Davis served many years as the first black woman from Texas to go to Africa as a missionary. At age 65, she was recalled by her denomination, the National Baptist Convention, for retirement. But two years later, Eliza raised her own support and returned to Africa to serve another 25 years. On January 20, 1979, she celebrated her 100th birthday. ● On January 20, 1987, Terry Waite, the Archbishop of Canterbury's envoy in Lebanon, was kidnapped. He was not released until November, 1991.

WORSHIP HELPS

Call to Worship

Sing to God, you kingdoms of the earth; oh, sing praises to the Lord, to Him who rides on the heaven of heavens, which were of old! Indeed, He sends out His voice, a mighty voice. Ascribe strength to God; His excellence is over Israel, and His strength is in the clouds (Ps. 68:32–34).

Kid's Talk

(You can illustrate this story with pictures of Hattie May, Dr. Conwell, and the Baptist Temple of Philadelphia by searching for their images on an Internet search engine.)

Do you ever put some money in your Sunday school offering or in the collection plate in our church service? That money is just as important to God as what anyone puts in. I want to tell you the story of Hattie May Wiatt. This little girl lived in a house near her church, but her church was meeting in a small building and sometimes Hattie had trouble finding a place to sit. One day the pastor walked by on his way to church, and he saw little Hattie standing by the gate of the church, about to turn around and go home. The pastor, Dr. Russell H. Conwell, lifted her onto his shoulders and carried her through the crowd and took her into Sunday school and found a chair for her in the corner.

The next day, he met her again as she was going down the street to school. "Hattie," he said, "we are going to have a larger Sunday school room soon."

She said, "I hope you will. It is so crowded that I am afraid to go there alone."

Later Pastor Conwell heard Hattie was sick, and he visited her and prayed with her. But she didn't get better. She passed away. At the funeral, Hattie's mother handed Pastor Conwell a little bag containing 57 pennies. Hattie had saved that much money to help build a new church building.

Dr. Conwell took those pennies to his pulpit the next Sunday and said that the church now had its first gift toward the new building. The story gets rather long after that; but to make a long story short, as time went by those 57 pennies kept multiplying as people were moved and impressed to give, until finally the church had a new piece of land, a new building, and a new children's Sunday school—all because of one little girl who gave 57 pennies to the Lord. So I want to remind you that your pennies and nickels and dimes and dollars are just as important in God's sight as the largest gift that comes in. And if we all pray and give as the Lord wants us to, great things will happen.

Additional Sermons and Lesson Ideas

The Tough News of the Gospel
By Dr. Kevin Riggs

Date preached:

SCRIPTURE: Mark 8:31—9:1

INTRODUCTION: Confessing that Jesus is the Christ means I must nail some things to the cross. What should I nail?

1. I Must Nail My "Self" to the Cross (v. 34). Following Jesus means I am no longer at the center of my life, He is.
2. I Must Nail My Security to the Cross (v. 35). What a paradox we find in this verse! If I hold on to my life I will lose it, yet if I let go of my life I will save it.
3. I Must Nail My Success to the Cross (vv. 36–37). Is your soul worth the cost of that new car or nice home? Is your soul worth that new title and new prestige at work?
4. I Must Nail My Status to the Cross (v. 38). This verse presents radical claims and hard words. I imagine Mark's first readers, who were undergoing tremendous persecution at the hands of Nero, found strength and encouragement in them.

CONCLUSION: The tough news of the gospel is that you must confess Christ and accept His cross. Anything less is cheap grace.

Facing Detractors
By Dr. Robert Norris

Date preached:

SCRIPTURE: 1 Thessalonians 2:1–12

INTRODUCTION: Jesus made it clear from the outset that we as kingdom people will always face opposition. How should we react when facing such conflict?

1. Meet Conflict with Courage in God (vv. 1–2).
2. Meet Conflict with Confidence in Your Calling (vv. 3–4).
3. Meet Conflict by Honoring the Lord (v. 4b).

CONCLUSION: Kingdom people will always face opposition in this world. However, through these trials, God is glorified and His kingdom advances. We can look forward to the day when the kingdom will be completed and our suffering will be rewarded.

JANUARY 27, 2008

SUGGESTED SERMON

How to Cult-Proof Your Faith

Date preached:

By Dr. Larry Osborne

Scripture: Philippians 3:17—4:1, especially 4:1
Therefore, my beloved and longed-for brethren, my joy and crown, so stand fast in the Lord, beloved.

Introduction: A cult is a group who claim to be Christians, but aren't. The easiest way to spot a cult is by their view of Jesus: who He is and what He did and does. If any group's view of Jesus' ultimate person and work does not line up with Scripture and 2,000 years of historic Christianity, then you're looking at a cult.

1. **Know Your Enemy (Matt. 13:24–30; 7:15–16; John 8:44; 2 Cor. 11:14–15; 1 Cor. 10:20).**

   A. **The Most Dangerous Enemy Is the One that Looks Like a Friend.** Whether it's a business deal or a relationship that turns deceptive, the principle holds true that we're the most vulnerable when we let our guard down. The enemy comes well disguised (2 Cor. 11:13–15).

   B. **Satan's Goal Isn't to Make Us Outwardly Evil; It's to Keep Us from Christ.** The self-righteous are the most likely to reject the idea that they need Jesus (Luke 18:9–13; John 8:12–59).

2. **Enemies or Citizens (Phil. 3:17—4:1).** Paul sets apart two distinct groups that we should be aware of.

   A. **Enemies Claim to Be Followers of Jesus (vv. 17–19).** The enemies of Christ will certainly be destroyed in the end, and there are ways to spot and avoid them now. Paul teaches that their god is their belly. In other words, they may make their dietary laws as if they are the way to heaven. They glory in what should be to their shame, and their ultimate hope is in human systems. By raising the bar with man-made rules, the enemy keeps people from God. By turning religion into a set of rituals and rules, the enemy fills people with pride (Luke 18:9–14).

B. **True Followers of Jesus Are Citizens of Heaven (vv. 20–21).** They trust Jesus to make them right with God. Notice the hope of those who follow Christ! They eagerly wait for the Savior, the Lord Jesus Christ, to make them ultimately right with God. We don't trust our own works, our diet, or anything except the divine, resurrected Jesus Christ! Only through Christ will we be ultimately made perfect.

3. **Watch Out for Those Who:**

A. **Devalue the Cross (Phil. 3:18).** When Jesus said "It is finished" (John 19:30) from the Cross, we know that He atoned for our sins. Cults will often say, "Jesus plus . . ." as if the Cross wasn't enough. The plus may be baptism, temple rights, special sayings, rituals, sacraments, or any number of things that make us feel righteous based on our works. We see these ideas emerge with the Jehovah's Witnesses, with Mormons, and even sometimes in formerly orthodox churches that have fallen from the truth. If good works and added rituals could have saved us, Jesus' death was in vain (Gal. 2:21ff).

B. **Focus More on What We Eat Than Who We Are (Phil. 3:19).** Cults often present righteousness by subtraction. They often rank one's standing with God by what he or she doesn't do. The New Testament speaks directly to dietary laws, making it heretical to preach that righteousness comes through what we physically consume (Mark 7:1–23; 1 Tim. 4:1–5).

C. **Breed an Attitude of Elitism and Pride (Phil. 3:19).** Underneath almost every cult is a separatist idea that only they have the actual truth of the gospel. Mormons, for example, will tell you they (and not anyone else) have the "fullness" of the gospel. Beware of such groups.

D. **Focus on Brand New Insights and Special Teachers (1 Cor. 3:1–4; Acts 17:11; Gal. 1:6–9; Deut. 18:21–22).** Insights must be gleaned through the insights of a special prophet or teacher. Whenever someone's insight or teaching comes between you and the Bible, you very well may be in a cult or headed down a cult-like path. Biblical Christianity is built on the Bible (Acts 17:11).

4. **Never Confuse a Victim of the Enemy with the Enemy Himself (2 Tim. 2:24–26).** Our ultimate goal should be to win over the enemies

of God, not to have angry debates for argument's sake. Paul spoke of his tears over those who were enemies of God in Philippians, and here in 2 Timothy he speaks of humility, patience, and correction for the purpose of repentance and truth, that they may escape the snare of the enemy.

Conclusion: Cult-proofing our faith means devoting ourselves wholly and completely to Jesus Christ, for our only hope of righteousness is through Him.

STATS, STORIES, AND MORE

More from Dr. Osborne

I spoke at a camp some years back and said some things that shook a few people up. Afterwards there was a particular couple that came to me saying they had to talk with me about what I said. I showed them the verse of Scripture where I got the ideas I preached. They weren't satisfied with just seeing that Scripture. First, they had to check with their study Bible that had notes from their special favorite teacher. After every talk, they wanted to be sure, not that my teaching came from Scripture, but that my teaching lined up with their favorite teacher's.

In her book, *Another Gospel,* Dr. Ruth Tucker wrote, "Jesus is the focus of any true Christian belief system, and His life and ministry is open for scrutiny. This is well illustrated by the evangelistic focus of E. Stanley Jones, the great Methodist missionary to India. 'I defined Christianity as Christ,' wrote Jones, in reference to a debate with a Jain scholar. 'If you have any objections to make against Him, I am ready to hear them and will answer them if I can.' On another occasion, he responded, 'My brother, I am the narrowest man you have come across. I am broad on almost everything else, but on the one supreme necessity for human nature I am absolutely narrowed by the facts to one—Jesus.'"[1]

---

[1] Ruth Tucker, *Another Gospel* (Grand Rapids: Zondervan, 1989), pp. 12–13.

APPROPRIATE HYMNS AND SONGS

"Onward Christian Soldiers," Sabine Baring-Gould, Public Domain.

"Stand Up, Stand Up for Jesus," George Duffield, Jr., Public Domain.

"Shout to the Lord," Darlene Zschech, 1993 Hillsong Publishing (Admin. in U.S. & Canada by Integrity's Hosanna! Music).

"One Way," Joel Houston & Jonathon Douglass, 2003 Hillsong Publishing (Admin. in U.S. & Canada by Integrity's Hosanna! Music).

"Because We Believe," Jamie Harvill & Nancy Gordon, 1996 Mother's Heart Music (Admin. by ROM Administration).

FOR THE BULLETIN

Robert Murray McCheyne, born in 1813, was a Scottish minister and disciple of the godly Andrew Bonar. He was a sickly man and died very young, but the spiritual quality of his life and ministry live to this day. On January 27, 1842, he sat down with pen and paper to reply to a young boy named Johnnie who was anxious about his soul. McCheyne began: "I was very glad to receive your kind note, and am glad to send you a short line in return, although my time is much taken up. You are very dear to me, because your soul is precious; and if you are ever brought to Jesus, washed and justified, you will praise Him more sweetly than an angel of light. I was riding in the snow today where no foot had trodden, and it was pure, pure white; and I thought again and again of that verse: 'Wash me, and I shall be whiter than snow.'" ● On January 27, 1880, U.S. Patent No. 223,898 was granted to Thomas Alva Edison for his electric lamp. ● January 27, 1908, Charles M. Alexander, evangelistic gospel song leader and associate of D. L. Moody and R. A. Torrey, made up his mind to join Wilber Chapman in evangelistic campaigns around the world. The two worked together until Alexander's death in 1920 and are considered one of the most effective evangelistic partnerships of the twentieth century. ● The Russians liberated Auschwitz concentration camp on January 27, 1945, where the Nazis had murdered 1.5 million men, women and children, including more than one million Jews. ● On January 27, 1980, Christian Adventist leader Vladimir Shelkov, 84, died in the Soviet labor camp of Tabaga where temperatures often dropped to eighty degrees below zero. He had spent 23 years in such labor camps because of his faith in Christ.

WORSHIP HELPS

Call to Worship

Make a joyful shout to the LORD, all you lands! Serve the LORD with gladness; come before His presence with singing. Know that the LORD, He is God; it is He who has made us, and not we ourselves; we are His people and the sheep of His pasture. Enter into His gates with thanksgiving, and into His courts with praise. Be thankful to Him, and bless His name. For the LORD is good; His mercy is everlasting, and His truth endures to all generations (Ps. 100).

Offertory Comments

> Lord, Thou lov'st the cheerful giver,
> Who with open heart and hand
> Blesses freely, as a river
> That refreshes all the land.
> Grant us then the grace of giving
> With a spirit large and free,
> That our life and all our living
> We may consecrate to Thee.
> —ROBERT MURRAY, 1898

Invitation

Perhaps some in this very room are part of a cult, or maybe hearing this message awakened you to some fundamental truths of the Christian faith that you have never truly believed by faith. Many of the greatest heroes of Christianity were once in the same place you are now. Jesus Christ has offered us His forgiveness, even to us who once believed the lies of the enemy concerning Him. I invite you to come today and speak to me or one of the church leaders. If you are willing to repent, the blood of Jesus Christ will atone for your every sin.

Additional Sermons and Lesson Ideas

It's Not About You

By Dr. Kevin Riggs

Date preached:

SCRIPTURE: Mark 1:1–13

INTRODUCTION: Sidekicks have one thing in common—*they are not the hero, they never receive the glory the hero receives, and they seem to like it that way.* Did Jesus have a sidekick? If He did, it would have been John the Baptist. Consider four characteristics in John's life that pointed others to Jesus:

1. Simplicity. John had a simple message and an even simpler lifestyle. We need to reevaluate our priorities, and recognize that life is pretty simple. Jesus said, "But seek first the kingdom of God and His righteousness . . ." (Matt. 6:33).
2. Integrity. John's message was plain, his lifestyle was simple, and he backed up what he preached. He refused to compromise his values. John was a person of integrity, and that pointed others to Jesus.
3. Distinctiveness. John's lifestyle was proof that his message would result in true change. Likewise, the life of a disciple of Jesus should be distinctively different from the rest of society.
4. Humility. Matthew tells us that when Jesus came to John to be baptized, John felt he did not deserve such an honor (Mark 3:14). Humility is seeing yourself for who you are in Christ.

CONCLUSION: When Jesus appeared on the scene, John the Baptist slid into the background, but he did not keep quiet. We should follow his example by preaching the same message, pointing people to Jesus.

The Two Things that Make Us Special

Date preached:

SCRIPTURE: Deuteronomy 4:5–8 (NIV)

INTRODUCTION: If we face self-esteem issues, this is a great passage to learn, for here the Lord gives us two traits that make us wonderfully different from everyone else on earth. In context, Moses, addressing the Israelites before they entered the Promised Land, told them two ways in which they were unique.

1. We Have God's Nearness (v. 7). "What other nation is so great as to have their gods near them the way the LORD our God is near us whenever we pray to him." The Bible repeatedly tells us of God's presence, His nearness, His "with us." Through prayer, we draw near, and experience His presence personally.
2. We Have God's Laws (v. 8). "What other nation is so great as to have such righteous decrees and laws . . . ?" The Word of God is great treasure, giving us wisdom from above and a perspective on life that nonbelievers don't enjoy.

CONCLUSION: This passage reminds us of the importance of our daily quiet time and of the wonderful privilege of walking with the Lord 24 hours a day.

FEBRUARY 3, 2008

SUGGESTED SERMON

The Character of a Leader

Date preached:

By Dr. Michael Easley

Scripture: Nehemiah 5:1–19, especially verse 19
Remember me, my God, for good, according to all that I have done for this people.

Introduction: Conversations around the coffee pot or copy machine reveal a lot about an organization. Office politics consume a great deal of time, energy, and resources. Unhealthy gossip distracts from the work and demoralizes the troops. This shows that even if an outside enemy fades from view, an enemy from within is exposed. We see this situation played out in the rebuilding of Jerusalem's city wall under Nehemiah's leadership. Hunger and exploitation are the presenting problems in Nehemiah 5, but the threat is to the community and the effort to build the wall. The solution to this enemy from within is godly leadership.

1. **Threats from Within (vv. 1–5).** Those who returned with Nehemiah to rebuild the city wall faced their fair share of difficulty. In previous chapters, external enemies taunted and threatened them. However, at this point in the text, the enemy was internal:

   A. **Hunger (vv. 2–3).** Evidently because of their work on the wall, they neglected their crops, resulting in famine.

   B. **Mortgage (v. 3).** To get grain, many mortgaged their fields, vineyards, and houses. The situation was desperate and cost many their shelter.

   C. **Debt/Usury (v. 4).** To avoid selling their possessions, many borrowed money from their Jewish brothers to pay taxes to Artaxerxes. This put them in debt. The problem was compounded by high interest rates from their Jewish brothers (cf. Ex. 22:25; Lev. 25:38; Deut. 15:1–11).

   D. **Exploitation (v. 5).** Whereas Nehemiah and some others had purchased indentured Jews who had been sold as slaves to foreigners (cf. Lev. 25:47–55), others had done the opposite, selling sons and daughters into slavery for survival.

2. **Leadership's Reply (vv. 6–11).** Nehemiah's initial response was anger (v. 6) at the selfishness and greed of those exploiting each other. Nehemiah, exhibiting the character of a good leader, had the courage to face opposition. He rebuked them, pointed out their offenses, and displayed himself as an example. Nehemiah had redeemed Jewish brothers who had been sold into slavery (v. 8). He helped the needy by lending money and grain without usury (vv. 10–11).

3. **The People's Response (vv. 12–13).** The people's immediate response was: "We will restore it . . . we will do as you say" (v. 12). Nehemiah knew that words are cheap, so he called the priests together and required an oath from the people. He then proclaimed God's judgment should any of them falter in their fulfillment of their oath (v. 13).

4. **A Pattern of Leadership (vv. 14–19).** When Nehemiah was appointed governor of Judah, a term of twelve years, he was at the highest position of leadership in the nation at that time. Despite his high position, he demonstrated principles of good leadership:

   A. **Godly Leadership Does Not Take Advantage of Position (vv. 14–15).** Nehemiah's position afforded him the right to feed and entertain the officials of his leadership. While he had this fringe benefit, he didn't exploit it. He could have imposed heavy taxes, but refrained from this as well.

   B. **Godly Leadership Shares the Work (v. 16a).** Many leaders delegate from a distance, but Nehemiah applied himself to the work.

   C. **Godly Leadership Does Not Take Unfair Advantage of a Situation (v. 16b).** Similar to what we know as "insider trading," Nehemiah was a man of wealth and could have easily bought up a lot of land for himself, but he did not.

   D. **Godly Leadership Commits One's Own Resources (vv. 16c–18).** Nehemiah committed his own servants (v. 16), his table (v. 17), and wealth (vv. 17–18).

   E. **Godly Leadership Evidences Compassion for Those Being Led (vv. 15, 18).** Nehemiah knew the heavy burden of the people and would not impose heavy taxes as previous governors had.

F. Godly Leadership Prays and Trusts God with Confidence and a Clear Conscience (v. 19). "Remember me, my God, for good, according to all that I have done for this people."

Conclusion: Perhaps today you can identify with the Jews who were oppressed by enemies of hunger, mortgage, or high interest rates. Maybe you are guilty of collecting high interest or burdening the poor. Follow the example of Godly leaders such as Nehemiah, the apostles (cf. 2 Thess. 3:7–15), heroes of Scripture (Heb. 11), or godly leaders in this very church. We must depend on God in our most desperate times, and we must reflect the grace we have been given when others are in need (Phil. 4:12–13).

STATS, STORIES, AND MORE

One of the most basic principles of business and leadership success is the maxim: "Find a need and fill it." In the 1800s there was a Vermont blacksmith who became known for his solid, sturdy workmanship. When word came from the West of vast fields capable of growing produce far in excess of what Vermont could grow, hundreds of people migrated. This blacksmith went with them, and soon detected a serious problem. The cast iron plows the pioneers had brought with them from the East didn't work well in the Midwest. The rich, Midwestern soil clung to them, and it was necessary every few steps to stop and scrape the soil from the plow. In 1837, through trial and error, the blacksmith designed a plow from a discarded saw mill blade. It was a polished steel plow that cleaned itself as it plowed. He built and sold ten of them, and then orders came for more and more. As he manufactured these plows, he kept changing them, causing some to criticize him. But he replied, "If we don't improve our product, somebody else will." By 1868, he was producing 13,000 plows a year in the largest plow factory in the United States. The blacksmith's name was John Deere. He was a man who just saw a need and filled it. The same principle is true spiritually. Sometimes we feel like shaking our heads and wringing our hands over the immoral conditions of our day. But instead, remember this first principle of leadership: Good leadership meets the needs of the hour.

APPROPRIATE HYMNS AND SONGS

"My Hope Is You," Brad Avery, David Carr, Johnny Mac Powell, Mark D. Lee, & Sam Anderson, 1997 New Song (Vandura 2500 songs & Gray Dot Songs).

"He Leadeth Me," Emma L. Ashford, Public Domain.

"Lead Me Lord," Elizabeth & Wayne Goodine, 1994 New Spring.

"Take My Life," Scott Underwood, 1995 Mercy/Vineyard Publishing (Admin. by Music Services).

FOR THE BULLETIN

February 3, 865, marks the death of Anskar, the "Apostle to the North." Anskar (or Ansgar) was a French Benedictine monk who gave himself to missionary service, planting the gospel in Scandinavia. ● Rev. John Rogers spent his last Sunday, February 3, 1555, quietly in Newmarket Jail where he had been interred for preaching the gospel. Rogers was a convert of William Tyndale and Miles Coverdale, whom he had met in Antwerp. Returning to England, Rogers had become a proponent of the Reformation, hence his imprisonment during the reign of Queen Mary. On Monday morning, February 4, 1555, the jailer's wife woke him with a rumor that his death was imminent. Later that morning, he was led to the stake and burned to ashes, leaving behind a wife and eleven children. ● On this day in 1675, King Charles II of England revoked the Declaration of Indulgence. John Bunyan was among those arrested. His writings from prison (including *Pilgrim's Progress*) immortalized him and spread the message of Christ around the world. ● February 3, 1816, is the birthday of the English preacher, F. W. Robertson, whose sermons, published posthumously, made him better known after his death than while he was living. ● On Thursday, February 3, 1898, George Truett, the new, young pastor of the First Baptist Church of Dallas, Texas, went quail hunting with the city's police chief, J. C. Arnold. Somehow Truett's gun discharged, killing Arnold. In the days to follow, Truett nearly lost his mind from anguish. But at length, he had a dream in which he saw Jesus saying to him, "You are My man from now on." Truett eventually returned to the pulpit to become one of the most powerful preachers of the twentieth century. ● On February 3, 1913, the sixteenth amendment to the constitution was ratified, giving the U.S. Government the power to impose and collect income taxes.

WORSHIP HELPS

Call to Worship
Blessed be the LORD God of Israel, from everlasting to everlasting! And let all the people say, "Amen" (Ps. 106:48)!

Welcome
Good morning and welcome to Sunday morning at our church! Someone recently said that according to the Bible, worship is something we do, not something we attend. As we sing and pray and express our thanksgiving to God, and as we present our tithes and offerings and listen to His Word, we invite you to be fully engaged with us. We're here in the presence of the living God, and He is in this very room, deserving of our worship.

Offertory Comments
Today we will learn about the great prophet and leader, Nehemiah, who was exemplary in his generosity as opposed to the wickedness of many Israelites under his rule. You know, often our willingness to sacrifice for God's work and for others is an indicator of our spiritual condition. If you are a church member, and you haven't been involved in regular and joyful giving to this church and others in need, I'm not going to ask you to submit a tithe this morning. I want you to do something more important. I ask you to examine your heart and see what might be hindering this spiritual discipline in your life. Spend some time this week in repentance and consideration of what the Lord might have you give on a regular basis from this point on. The Lord doesn't need your money; He wants your heart in submission to Him.

Benediction
Grace to you and peace from God our Father and the Lord Jesus Christ (Phil. 1:2).

Additional Sermons and Lesson Ideas

Principles of Witnessing
Date preached:

By Dr. Timothy K. Beougher

SCRIPTURE: Acts 8:25–40

INTRODUCTION: In this portion of Scripture, we find five key principles for witnessing based on Philip's example:

1. The Principle of Sensitivity: Respond to God's Leading (vv. 25–26).
   A. The Strategic Response (v. 25). The Spirit strategically called the apostles and us to preach beginning where we are, and as we go to spread the gospel outward.
   B. The Spontaneous Response (v. 26). Like Philip, we should not be restricted by programs or goals, but sensitive to the Spirit's leading.
2. The Principle of Observation: Keep Your Eyes Open (vv. 27–30). Often we miss opportunities to witness simply due to spiritual dullness, but like Philip we must be aware of the Spirit's leading.
3. The Principle of Scripture: Share the Bible (vv. 31–34). Scripture must be central, since it's the primary source concerning all spiritual reality.
4. The Principle of Christ: Point People to Christ (v. 35). Like Philip, we must always point to Christ or we have missed the point!
5. The Principle of Response: Encourage a Response to Christ (vv. 37–39). We should encourage a response from those with whom we share, especially as displayed in these verses; we must encourage repentance and faith followed by baptism.

CONCLUSION: Are you ready to make a fresh commitment to witnessing?

We Give Thee But Thine Own
Date preached:

SCRIPTURE: 1 Chronicles 29:1–20

INTRODUCTION: God's work depends on the willingness of leadership and membership to provide the financial support. We have a great example of this in today's text, as King David raises funds for the temple.

1. We Have a Great Task (v. 1). David said this was a great task, done not for himself but for the Lord, and that his son, Solomon, was inadequate for the job. We are inadequate in ourselves, our task is great, and our work is for the Lord.

2. We Have a Great Team (vv. 2–9). David gave, the leaders gave, and the people gave. It required everyone "consecrating themselves."
3. We Have a Great Truth (vv. 10–19). All that we have is from His hand, and we give back to Him only what He has already given to us (v. 14).
4. We Have Great Thanksgiving (v. 20). Everyone, youngest to greatest, praised God as the needs were met for the accomplishing of God's work.

CONCLUSION: Hymnist William How wrote: "We give Thee but Thine own, / Whate'er the gift may be; / All that we have is Thine alone, / A trust, O Lord, from Thee."

PRAYER FOR THE PASTOR'S CLOSET

Amid all the wonders of heaven and earth, there is no one like You. Your works are exceedingly good. Your judgments are true, and by Your providence You rule the universe. Therefore, praise and glory to You, who are the Wisdom of the Father; my lips, my soul, and everything created join in praising and blessing You.

—THOMAS À KEMPIS

A Pastor's Sketches
By Ichabod Spencer

In an inquiry meeting of about seventy people, Rev. Ichabod Spencer came across a man struggling with deep conviction of sin. When Spencer asked the man about the state of his soul, the man replied, "I feel that I have a very wicked heart."

"It is a great deal more wicked than you think it," replied Spencer before turning and walking away.

The man was understandably angry at the preacher's curt response, but upon further reflection he admitted to himself that it was true and that Christ was the only remedy. Later he met Spencer again and shared his testimony. The man then said, "I want to ask you a question. I have been thinking of it a great deal, and I cannot conceive how you know what to say to each one, where there are so many. We have been talking about it, some of us, and we cannot understand how it is that you can know our thoughts and feelings, when nobody has told you."

"I have only one rule on that subject," replied Spencer. "I am to conspire with the Holy Spirit. If I perceive that any one truth has impressed the mind, I am to make its impression deeper, and I would not diminish it by leading the mind off to something else . . . . I just aim to conspire with the Holy Spirit."[1]

Ichabod Spencer was born in 1789 in Vermont and converted to Christ at age eighteen, following the death of his father. He became a school teacher in New York State, and it appeared he had a bright future in academia. But the burden of preaching pressed on his soul, and he felt God's call to be a pastor. Most of his ministry was spent at Brooklyn's Second Presbyterian Church, taking the church from a handful of weary souls to one of the largest congregations in New York City. His ministry was noted for his commitment to visit every home represented by his church

Continued on the next page

---

[1]Ichabod Spencer, *A Pastor's Sketches* (Vestavia Hills, AL: Solid Ground Christian Books, 2001), p. 153.

on an annual basis. For over twenty years, he averaged over 800 visits a year.

Even more remarkable is this: After each visit, Spencer would go home and record the conversation that had occurred and make extensive notes of his observations. From those notes have come the two volumes of *Sketches*. The books could be called *Applied Pastoral Theology*, for Spencer was a master of intersecting the truths of Scripture with the needs of the human heart. His approach was different with every person, and reading his *Sketches* is like sitting in the parlor, watching him interact with an interesting assortment of saints and sinners.

When the first volume was published in 1850, the sales were phenomenal, and *A Pastor's Sketches* became a blockbuster in Christian publishing for its day. The introduction to my edition says, "No one living in the northeastern part of the United States in the middle 1800s would have believed that Spencer or his *Sketches* would ever be forgotten."

Sadly, however, Spencer's *Sketches* are largely neglected today; but I have a conviction that we read too many trendy, contemporary books at the expense of the ageless classics that really have something of substance to say to us. Spencer, a staunch Reformed theologian, wasn't afraid to be confrontational; but he displayed a gift of discernment that I, for one, need now more than ever. I'm eager to "conspire with the Holy Spirit" in the saving and settling of souls.

FEBRUARY 10, 2008

SUGGESTED SERMON

Servants of Christ

Date preached:

By Rev. Peter Grainger

Scripture: 1 Corinthians 4:1–21, especially verse 1
Let a man so consider us, as servants of Christ and stewards of the mysteries of God.

Introduction: There was somewhat of a media frenzy when the First Lady Laura Bush revealed that President George W. Bush began each day by reading an excerpt from a devotional book, *My Utmost for His Highest,* by Oswald Chambers. The media referred to Chambers as obscure, citing him as the spiritual inspiration for Bush. Chambers would probably be honored to be considered obscure by this age, since his God-centered writings are foreign to them. However, it's not only the media that misunderstand Christian leaders and leadership. Paul addressed this problem in the Corinthian church, explaining what it truly means to be a servant of Christ. He used three descriptions to explain his own role as a Christian pastor/teacher, each contrasting sharply with the wrong ideas of Christian leadership that the Corinthians held and which were being modeled by teachers who had come into the church.

1. **A Steward and His Master (vv. 1–7).** The word Paul used for "servant" here was originally used to describe a rower in the lower part of a *trireme*—a Greek galley with three banks of oars on each side. It then came to mean anyone involved in service of a lowly kind, but who was subject to direction by and held accountable to his master. Thus Paul explained that he was the Corinthians' servant, but they were not his master. The word "steward" was used to show that Paul had been entrusted with the "mysteries" of God, namely the gospel, which he must preach. Therefore:

    A. **Do Not Judge, for Judgment Is the Lord's (vv. 2–5).** The Corinthians judged Paul's performance, but he explained that God's judgment is based on faithfulness. All are ultimately accountable to God.

    B. **Do Not Boast, for Your Gifts Are from the Lord (vv. 6–7).** The church at Corinth seemed to have been a first-century preacher's talent show. The Corinthians charged that some teachers such as Apollos were better speakers or more sophisticated thinkers than Paul. He explained that whatever Christians have is given to them, so there is no room for boasting.

2. **An Apostle and His Sufferings (vv. 8–13).** With biting irony, Paul challenged the self-sufficiency and complacency of his critics, and contrasted their circumstances and claims with his own contrasting circumstances. The Corinthians had taken the future blessings promised in Christ and applied them to the present (v. 8). However, Paul described himself and his fellow apostles as public spectacles (v. 9). He went on to contrast every aspect of the Corinthians' lives to his own experience (vv. 10–13): His was a life of suffering for the gospel's sake, while theirs was a comfortable experience of blessings. The way of Christ is the way of the Cross—the way of suffering. We will reign with Christ only if we suffer with Him (Matt. 5:1–12).

3. **A Father and His Children (vv. 14–21).** Paul's aim in this exhortation is not destructive but constructive. He wrote to warn them ". . . as my beloved children . . . I have begotten you through the gospel" (vv. 14–15). The role model for children is their father. We're often hesitant to tell new Christians to imitate us: "Don't imitate me, imitate Christ," we say. However, Paul would say, "Imitate me, as I imitate Christ." The only way Jesus' life can be seen lived out in human flesh today is through His followers. Paul intended to come to Corinth either with a rod or with a gentle spirit, depending upon how they responded to his exhortations.

Conclusion: Paul's message to the Corinthians is just as applicable to us today! Many of us treat the church like a theater for the best speakers or entertaining singers. While ministry should certainly be carried out with due reverence and skill, we mustn't judge ministers according to the level of their gifts. Those we see as Christian celebrities very well may be humbled before the judgment seat of Christ, while the true servants who take the way of the Cross, who become spectacles before men and angels, who act as fools for Christ, being mocked, even slaughtered by ruthless leaders of this age: those will one day be exalted and praised in the day of judgment. Let us humble ourselves and be thankful for the gifts God has granted for the building up of His church.

STATS, STORIES, AND MORE

More from Rev. Grainger
In Old Cairo Cemetery is a simple stone over a grave. Inscribed with the name Oswald Chambers it simply states: A BELIEVER IN JESUS CHRIST. Underneath these words is the image of a Bible opened to Luke 11:13, the promise Chambers courageously appropriated and through which he faithfully served: "If you then, being evil, know how to give good gifts to your children, how much more will your heavenly Father give the Holy Spirit to those who ask Him!" (Luke 11:13). Only the indwelling Holy Spirit can make us faithful stewards of Christ, suffering servants for Christ, and spiritual parents to others—not skills or attributes the world may count very highly. But it is God's estimation and judgment that will finally count. And who knows how He may judge an obscure Baptist preacher and the President of the United States.

Fame or Faithfulness?
Over his 19-year career, Gary Carter hit 324 home runs and drove in more than 1,200 runs. When he was inducted into Baseball's Hall of Fame, he said this: "Above all I want to thank my Lord and Savior Jesus Christ. A great verse that spoke to me while writing my speech that kind of explains what it's all about comes in Psalm 18. 'I love you, Lord, You are my strength. The Lord is my rock, my fortress, my Savior; my God is my rock, in whom I find protection. He is my shield, the strength of my salvation, my stronghold. I will call on the Lord, who is worthy of praise.'"

APPROPRIATE HYMNS AND SONGS

"There Is None Like You," Lenny LeBlance, 1991 Integrity's Hosanna! Music.

"If We Are the Body," Mark Hall, SWECS Music (Admin. by EMI Christian Music Pub.).

"I Will Follow Christ," Clay Crosse & Steve Siler, 1999 Word Music, LLC.

"Praise You," Elizabeth Goodine, 1992 New Spring.

"I Will Serve Thee," Gloria and William Gaither, 1969 William J. Gaither, Inc. (AAR UBP of Gaither Copyright Management).

FOR THE BULLETIN

On February 10, 754, Emperor Constantine V called an iconoclastic council in Constantinople. The 330 bishops denounced artists who made pictures of the Savior, saying that the Eucharist alone presents the proper image of Christ. ● John Wesley fell on ice-covered London Bridge, on February 10, 1751, and was carried to the home of nurse Mary Vazeille. During his recuperation, he proposed to her. "I groaned all day, and several following ones," his brother Charles wrote. "I could eat no pleasant food, nor preach, nor rest, either by night or by day." John and Mary's marriage, unfortunately, was not a happy one. ● A. B. Earle, author of "Bringing in the Sheaves," was a well-known evangelist who began preaching in 1830 at age 18. During the next 50 years he preached 19,780 times, with 150,000 people professing Christ. On February 10, 1859, Earle, dedicating himself anew to Christ, wrote: "This day I make a new consecration of my all to Christ. Jesus, I now forever give myself to Thee; my soul to be washed in Thy blood and saved in heaven at last; my whole body to be used for Thy glory; my mouth to speak for Thee at all times; my eyes to weep over lost sinners." ● February 10, 1859, is the birthday of the famous missionary to China, Jonathan Goforth.

WORSHIP HELPS

Call to Worship
Let, I pray, Your merciful kindness be for my comfort, according to Your word to Your servant. Let Your tender mercies come to me, that I may live; for Your law is my delight (Ps. 119:76–77).

Scripture Reading
Then the mother of Zebedee's sons came to Him with her sons, kneeling down and asking something from Him. And He said to her, "What do you wish?" She said to Him, "Grant that these two sons of mine may sit, one on Your right hand and the other on the left, in Your kingdom." But Jesus answered and said, "You do not know what you ask. Are you able to drink the cup that I am about to drink, and be baptized with the baptism that I am baptized with?" They said to Him, "We are able." So He said to them, "You will indeed drink My cup, and be baptized with the baptism that I am baptized with; but to sit on My right

hand and on My left is not Mine to give, but it is for those for whom it is prepared by My Father." And when the ten heard it, they were greatly displeased with the two brothers. But Jesus called them to Himself and said, "You know that the rulers of the Gentiles lord it over them, and those who are great exercise authority over them. Yet it shall not be so among you; but whoever desires to become great among you, let him be your servant. And whoever desires to be first among you, let him be your slave—just as the Son of Man did not come to be served, but to serve, and to give His life a ransom for many (Matt. 20:20–28).

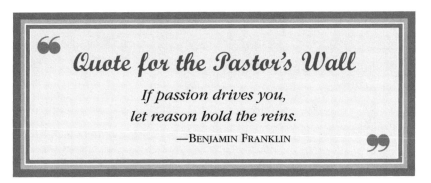

Quote for the Pastor's Wall

If passion drives you,
let reason hold the reins.

—BENJAMIN FRANKLIN

Additional Sermons and Lesson Ideas

Everything I Needed to Know About Giving I Learned in First Grade

Date preached:

By Rev. Mark Hollis

SCRIPTURE: Various from Malachi and 2 Corinthians

INTRODUCTION: Most of what we need to know about life can be gained from a first grade classroom. Here are some things I learned about giving . . .

1. Respect the One Who Is in Charge (Mal. 1:6,7).
2. Always Give Your Best (Mal. 1:8).
3. Don't Take Things That Don't Belong to You (Mal. 3:6–9).
4. Give According to What You Have (2 Cor. 8:12).
5. Giving Is Part of a Transformed Life (2 Cor. 9:7).
6. Giving to God First Is an Opportunity to Trust Him for All You Need (Mal. 3:10–12).

CONCLUSION: When we give to God first we demonstrate that we trust Him to meet all of our needs. He owns it all anyway, so certainly He is able to meet any needs you and I may have. Will you trust Him?

Understanding Our Spiritual Battle (Part 1)

Date preached:

By Dr. Larry Osborne

SCRIPTURE: Ephesians 6:10–18

INTRODUCTION: Notice the imagery of these verses describing our spiritual battle: a soldier under fierce attack, an enemy we can't see, an enemy we can't beat on our own. How can we prepare to face such an enemy?

1. Know Your Enemy (vv. 11–12). We must realize that our enemy is not Christians with whom we disagree or worldly people, but Satan and his demonic worldview (cf. Eph. 2:1–3; 1 John 5:19).
2. Understand His Strategy (v. 13). Satan primarily uses trials and hardships to get us to question either God's goodness or His dependability (cf. 1 Pet. 5:8–10; John 8:44; Rev. 12:9–11; Gen. 3:1–6).
3. Recognize Your Vulnerability. Humanly speaking, we are susceptible to the attacks of our enemy (1 Cor. 10:12–13; Jude 9–10; 2 Chr. 26:1–23).
4. Follow Your Assignment (vv. 11–13). We are to put on the full armor of God. We must hang tough and do the right thing no matter what happens!

CONCLUSION: Which of these ideas most applies to you? What can you do as a result to prepare yourself for the spiritual battle that wars around you?

FEBRUARY 17, 2008

SUGGESTED SERMON

The Godly Life

Date preached:

By Dr. David Jeremiah

Scripture: 2 Timothy 3:10–13
But you have carefully followed my doctrine, manner of life, purpose, faith, longsuffering, love, perseverance, persecutions, afflictions, which happened to me at Antioch, at Iconium, at Lystra—what persecutions I endured. And out of *them* all the Lord delivered me. Yes, and all who desire to live godly in Christ Jesus will suffer persecution. But evil men and impostors will grow worse and worse, deceiving and being deceived.

Introduction: Somebody once told me: "Pastor Jeremiah, you will learn in your ministry that if you communicate from your head you may change somebody's mind. If you communicate from your heart you might change their attitudes. But if you communicate from your life you have the potential of changing their lives." That dynamic truth is illustrated in three verses we're studying today. Here Paul cited nine qualities of life that he had transmitted to Timothy.

1. **We Communicate Through Our Preaching (v. 10).** *You have carefully followed my doctrine.* When Paul first visited Timothy's home city, he preached with such power the people thought he was a god. Timothy had had the privilege of being under his ministry and hearing his sermons. All of us are pastors and preachers whenever we share with others the truth of Scripture.

2. **We Communicate Through Our Practice (v. 10).** *My manner of life.* The only Christ I've ever seen is the Christ I see in the Word of God and the Christ I see reflected in the lives of other people. Paul said: "Follow me as I follow Christ." Is that what your life is saying?

3. **We Communicate Through Our Purpose (v. 10).** . . . *purpose.* Our life's purpose is whatever we would die for right now. What is your purpose? When people see us living with a sense of Christian purpose, it inspires them toward Christ.

4. **We Communicate Through Our Perseverance (v. 10).** . . . *faith.* The word "faith" here means being faithful under pressure, or fidelity. It influences people when they see our doctrine sustain us during

difficult days. We don't abandon it, nor do we abandon ourselves to despair. We persevere because of the promises of God.

5. **We Communicate Through Our Patience (v. 10).** . . . *longsuffering.* This word means to have patience with people. It's hard to communicate Christ when you're easily frustrated by others, or when you grow irritable and lose your patience. People can bring out the worst in us, but the fruit of the Spirit is patience. Our gospel is communicated best when we learn from it how to remain calm with difficult people.

6. **We Communicate Through Our Philanthropy (v. 10).** . . . *love.* The older translations say "charity." Paul was a God-lover and a good-lover. He seized opportunities to do good to those around him, reaching them with the good things of God.

7. **We Communicate Through Our Patience with Circumstances (v. 10).** . . . *perseverance.* The prior word for patience had to do primarily with putting up with people. This word has to do with putting up with circumstances. When people see us forging ahead by faith, despite discouragements and setbacks, it shows them the fiber of the Christian.

8. **We Communicate Through Our Persecutions (v. 11).** *Persecutions.* . . . The record of Paul's persecutions is given in the books of Acts and 2 Corinthians. We may not be stoned and whipped as Paul was, but we'll suffer rejection or abuse because of our commitment to Christ. This world is gospel-hostile. When we keep sharing the gospel anyway, the message begins cutting through the fog like a spotlight.

9. **We Communicate Through Our Pain (v. 11).** . . . . *afflictions.* In 2 Corinthians 4:7, Paul explained that he possessed the treasure of the ministry in a jar of clay that the excellence might be of God. During times of pain, pressure, and stress, we have the greatest opportunities to let people know that Christianity works.

Conclusion: Our greatest communication isn't with our lips but with our lives. That's especially true when the teacher or communicator is experiencing trouble. I communicate more about Jesus in the midst of difficulty than any other time because I have the opportunity to demonstrate its reality to others. Sooner or later, what we really believe will be seen in what we are. There's coming a day when a crisis will reveal your character. The foundation of your life will be tested by the trials that come your way. You may fool people for awhile. But when the rains come and the floods rise, it becomes evident whether our lives are built on the solid rock or upon the shifting sands. When our lives are Christ-based, we communicate Him through our preaching, our practice, our purpose, our perseverance, our patience, our philanthropy, our patience with circumstances, our persecutions, and our pain. What is your foundation? Is your life built upon Christ and His Word? You have the most wonderful opportunity this morning to accept Christ as your Savior and to build your life on Him and to start communicating Him to others.

STATS, STORIES, AND MORE

"I'd Rather See a Sermon"
Edger (Eddie) Guest was born in Great Britain but moved to America with his family and began his illustrious career as a journalist at age 13, when he signed on with the Detroit Free Press as an office boy. He stayed with the newspaper for sixty years. His column was eventually syndicated in 300 newspapers. He was working as an assistant exchange editor in 1898 when he began writing poems to use as "fillers" in the newspaper. He went on to become "The Poet of the People" and the "Poet Laureate of Michigan." One of his most famous verses says:

> I'd rather see a sermon than to hear one any day;
> I'd rather one would walk with me than merely tell the way.
> The eye's a better pupil and more willing than the ear,
> Fine counsel is confusing, but example's always clear;
> And the best of all the preachers are the men who live their creeds,
> For to see good put in action is what everybody needs.

(This poem, in its entirety, is easily found on the Internet. The whole poem is well worth quoting.)

APPROPRIATE HYMNS AND SONGS

"Forever," Chris Tomlin, 2001 worshiptogether.com songs (Admin. by EMI Christian Music Pub.).

"Open the Eyes of My Heart," Paul Baloche, 1997 Integrity's Hosanna! Music.

"Take My Life and Let It Be," Frances R. Havergal, Public Domain.

"This Is Your Life," Jonathon Foreman, 2002 MeadowGreen Music Co. (Admin. by EMI Christian Music Pub.).

"My Life Is in Your Hands," Kirk Franklin, Lilly Mack Music (Admin. by Lilly Mack Music).

FOR THE BULLETIN

On this day, February 17, 1600, Italian philosopher and mathematician, Giorgano Bruno, whose theories anticipated modern science, was betrayed to the Inquisition and burned as a heretic in Rome. ● Eighty-eight years later, on February 17, 1688, James Renwick, 28, was martyred at the Grassmarket in Edinburgh. Renwick, a Scottish Covenanter, had devoted his young life to preaching through the "mosses, muirs, and mountains" of Scotland, until his arrest. On the morning of his death, as Renwick said grace over breakfast, he prayed, *O Lord, Thou hast brought me within two hours of eternity, and this is no matter of terror to me, more than if I were to lie down in a bed of roses.* ● On February 17, 1739, George Whitefield, being denied a pulpit, preached for the first time in the open air. His sermon near Bristol, England, to coal miners, launched one of the most extraordinary evangelistic ministries in history. ● On February 17, 1795, the London Missionary Society (as it came to be known) was organized by thirty-four men at the Castle and Falcon public house in London. ● February 17, 1850, schoolteacher James Garfield traveled by sleigh to a church meeting where he was so impressed with the gospel that he shortly made a profession of faith. He became a preacher with the Disciples of Christ before entering politics, and later became the only minister to serve as President of the United States (though not ordained, in keeping with the practice of the Disciples of Christ). ● On February 17, 1977, Uganda Radio announced the death of Anglican Archbishop Janani Luwum. He had been arrested by Idi Amin's soldiers, tortured mercilessly, then shot through the heart by the dictator himself.

WORSHIP HELPS

Call to Worship

This is the Sunday God has made. This is the first day of the week, the day when our Lord rose from the dead. This is His day, and ours! Shall we stand and shall we praise Him in song.

Responsive Reading from 2 Timothy 3

Worship Leader: But know this, that in the last days perilous times will come: For men will be lovers of themselves, lovers of money, boasters, proud, blasphemers, disobedient to parents, unthankful, unholy, unloving, unforgiving, slanderers, without self-control, brutal, despisers of good, traitors, headstrong, haughty . . .

Congregation: . . . lovers of pleasure rather than lovers of God, having a form of godliness, but denying its power.

Worship Leader: And from such people turn away!

Congregation: But you have carefully followed my doctrine, manner of life, purpose, faith, longsuffering, love, perseverance, persecutions, afflictions . . .

Worship Leader: Yes, and all who desire to live godly in Christ Jesus will suffer persecution.

Pastoral Prayer

Our Father and God, forgive us if our lives don't produce some measure of persecution. In a world that hates the gospel, may we be identified with it. In a world that dismisses Christ, may we be known as His followers. In a world that eschews preaching, may we hold our doctrine in integrity. In a world that relishes the church's every fault, may we be faultless and pure. And then use us, Lord, through our lives and through our lips to communicate Christ so clearly that all the world will know. We pray in Jesus' name. Amen.

Additional Sermons and Lesson Ideas

Loving Your Enemies
By Dr. David Jeremiah

Date preached:

SCRIPTURE: Matthew 5:43–48

INTRODUCTION: For many of us, the title of this message could be "Mission Impossible." How can we love our enemies? In this paragraph, Jesus tells us how.

1. The Reminder (v. 43). Jesus began by referring His listeners back to Old Testament law and to what the rabbis taught.
2. The Requirement (v. 44a). "But I say to you, love your enemies . . ." This is another one of those very hard sayings, but we see this practiced in the lives of Steven, Paul, and especially Jesus.
3. The Responsibilities (v. 44b).
    A. Bless those who curse you.
    B. Do good to those who hate you.
    C. Pray for those who spitefully use you.
4. The Reason (v. 45). That you might be like your Father in heaven.

CONCLUSION: The Holy Spirit can empower us to live this truth. It's not natural life. It's supernatural life. But it's the life Christ has put in front of us. Through His strength and by His grace we can learn to obey.

What It Takes to Change Things

Date preached:

SCRIPTURE: Ezra 7:1–10

INTRODUCTION: If you want to see someone who could walk into any environment and change things, look at Ezra. When he showed up, things began to change. He makes a rather dramatic biblical entrance in Ezra 7, like the main character of a movie who doesn't make his appearance until halfway through the film. From him we learn the importance of:

1. Our Heritage (vv. 1–5). The first five verses present Ezra's lineage. An appreciation of our history and heritage can help our self-image and give us confidence in leadership.
2. Our Skill (v. 6a). Ezra was competent in his field. He was "well-versed" (NIV).
3. Our Anointing (v. 6b). God's hand was on him. We can't do anything of consequence without the hand of God on our lives.
4. Our Helpers (v. 7). Ezra had a good team with him.
5. Our Devotion to Scripture (vv. 8–10). Ezra's deepest strength was that he had devoted himself to study God's Word, to obey it, and to teach its statutes in Israel.

CONCLUSION: God wants to equip you to lead, to influence, and to change the world. Here are your five greatest tools.

FEBRUARY 24, 2008

Knowing What to Say and When to Say It

Date preached:

Scripture: Proverbs 10:19–21, especially verse 21
The lips of the righteous feed many, but fools die for lack of wisdom.

Introduction: Recently Ted Pollock's interesting column, "Give Instructions in Small Doses," ran in a leadership newsletter for the automotive industry. Pollock said, "When you have complex instructions to give, particularly to inexperienced workers, don't overwhelm them by explaining everything at once. Explain one portion at a time, making sure the employee understands it before you go on to the next instruction."[1] That's excellent advice for all of life, and that's exactly what we see in the book of Proverbs—God's wisdom in small doses. A great number of these deal with our words. Many of our problems in life occur because we say the wrong thing, or we say it at the wrong time, or we say it in the wrong way. A thirty-second tirade can damage a thirty-year career, a thirty-year marriage, or thirty years of reputation. As he wrote Proverbs, Solomon was cognizant of the power of the tongue, and when you read his thoughts on this subject in Proverbs, you find God's wisdom in small doses telling us to. . . .

1. **Shut Up.** Some verses tell us in plain English to be cautious about what we say, to never miss an opportunity to keep our mouths shut (see Prov. 17:9, 14, and 27; also see Prov. 11:12; 12:16; 19:11; 20:3; 26:20–22). Certain things are necessary for life—food, water, and protection; but some things are not life-necessities—it isn't necessary to state our opinion on every subject, to have the last word in every argument, to demand our way in every discussion, to defend ourselves from every criticism, or to draw a line on every issue. Sometimes we just need to keep our thoughts and words to ourselves.

---

[1] Ted Pollock, "Don't Let Fears Cramp Your Creativity," in *Automotive Design and Production*, at http://www.autofieldguide.com/columns/0701mgmt.html, accessed on September 14, 2005.

2. **Build Up.** But it isn't enough just to shut up. God hasn't called us to take vows of silence like medieval monks. He gave us the remarkable capacity for human language, for He wants us to build others up (see Prov. 10:11 and 19; also see 12:18; 15:4 and 23; 16:23–24). When Lou Gehrig was starting his baseball career, he went into a slump and grew so discouraged he thought of quitting. A friend named Paul Krichell heard Lou was slumping, and he took a train to Hartford and invited Lou to join him for a steak dinner at the Bond Hotel. Lou poured out his frustrations, and Paul could see the player's confidence was shot. He spent the evening telling Lou that all hitters go through slumps, that the best ones—even Ty Cobb—don't get hits six or seven out of every ten tries. But eventually good hitters start hitting again; and, said Paul, you're a good hitter. After dinner, Gehrig walked with Paul to the train station and thanked him for coming. The next day, Lou started blasting the ball again, and over the next eleven games he came through with twenty-two hits, including six home runs—and his career took off. "I decided not to quit after all," he said.[2] Sometimes we need to take a train, track down someone, buy them a steak, and encourage them with wise counsel.

3. **Speak Up.** Other times we need to speak up (see Prov. 31:8–9). In 1955, when Rosa Parks was a seamstress in Montgomery, Alabama, the city buses were segregated. One day, Rosa got on the bus, went back to the black section, and took the first available seat. A few stops later, the bus filled up and a white man got on. The bus driver demanded she give him her seat, and she spoke four words that changed history: "No, I will not." With those words, she almost single-handedly launched the Civil Rights movement in America.

Conclusion: If a lightning bolt struck a transformer near your house, it could send a powerful surge of electricity through the lines and into your house, frying your computer. So we have circuit breakers and surge protectors that interrupt the flow of electricity before any damage is done. These verses in Proverbs are the circuit breakers and surge protectors for the soul. The air around us is often static with anger, and our social atmospheres change as often as the weather. We need to install some of today's verses as spiritual circuit breakers committing

---

[2]Jonathan Eig, *Luckiest Man: The Life and Death of Lou Gehrig* (New York: Simon & Schuster, 2005), pp. 48–49.

them to memory and to conscious thought. We must become more and more like Jesus, for no one ever spoke as He did. The great secret of the book of Proverbs is that in describing the wise person it offers us a pen-portrait that was perfectly fulfilled in our Lord Jesus. Receive Him as your Lord and Savior, and grow up into Him in all things. And let the words of your mouth and the meditations of your heart be pleasing in His sight.

STATS, STORIES, AND MORE

In 1960, Nixon was running against Kennedy, and the two men debated on national television, during which Nixon made a comment about the salty language of Harry Truman. Nixon said: "I'm very proud that President Eisenhower restored dignity and decency and, frankly, good language to the conduct of the presidency of the United States. And I only hope that should I win this election, that I could [see] to it that whenever any mother or father talks to his child, he can look at the man in the White House and say: 'Well, there is a man who maintains the kind of standards personally that I would want my child to follow.'"

Nixon lost that election, but eight years later he won the White House; but when the transcription of the Nixon tapes were released during the Watergate scandal, Americans were shocked at the obscene, crude, filthy, profane language captured on tape.

But here's the thing. As shameful as it was, it wasn't Nixon's profanity that cost him the White House; it was another set of words—a few sentences uttered on June 23, 1972, in which he authorized his staff to have the CIA pressure the FBI to stop the investigation into the Watergate Complex. That entire conversation took place in less than ninety minutes just before lunch, but the words on the tape doomed his presidency, ruined his life, and changed the history of our country.

Many a person has ruined a marriage or a reputation or a career or a child's self-image by the unwise use of words. We can spend our entire lifetimes trying to develop something, and with just a few unwise words, we can ruin it all.

APPROPRIATE HYMNS AND SONGS

"Here I Am to Worship," Tim Hughes, 2000 ThankYou Music (Admin. by EMI Christian Music Publishing Co.).

"Rejoice the Lord Is King," Charles Wesley & George Handell, Public Domain.

"We Fall Down," Chris Tomlin, 1998 worshiptogether.com songs (Admin. by EMI Christian Music Publishing).

"Holy, Holy, Holy," John Bacchus Dykes & Reginald Heber, Public Domain.

FOR THE BULLETIN

On this day in A.D. 303, a general persecution of Christians was unleashed in the Roman Empire by edict of Diocletian. The historian Eusebius saw churches razed, Scriptures burned, and pastors torn to pieces in the amphitheater. ● On February 24, 1208, Francis of Assisi attended Mass in the church of Saint Mary of the Angels. As Matthew 10:9 was read, Francis was deeply moved. Shortly thereafter, inspired by that verse, he began his itinerant ministry. ● James Mitchell, Scottish preacher, was tortured for his faith on February 24, 1676. Mitchell's right leg was inserted into a device designed to crush the leg by using an iron wedge and mallet. Mitchell fainted following the ninth blow. ● February 24, 1811, is the birthday of Daniel Payne, first African-American university president in the United States. Payne, sixth bishop of the African Methodist Episcopal Church, helped establish Union Seminary and Wilberforce University in Ohio. ● On February 24, 1812, missionary Henry Martyn finished the Persian translation of the New Testament. ● Amanda Smith (1837–1915) was a black scrub woman and ex-slave who began accepting invitations to preach as a Methodist holiness evangelist throughout the South, traveling alone by train, her belongings rolled in a carpetbag. Her fame leaped the Atlantic, and she was called to England for meetings, then to India, then to Africa. She organized women's bands, young people's groups, temperance societies, and children's meetings. She adopted homeless youngsters and started an orphanage near Chicago. Amanda Smith died on February 24, 1915. ● On February 24, 1945, Olympic hero and missionary Eric Liddell was buried at Weihsien internment camp.

WORSHIP HELPS

Call to Worship

I will sing of the mercies of the LORD forever; with my mouth will I make known Your faithfulness to all generations. For I have said, "Mercy shall be built up forever; Your faithfulness You shall establish in the very heavens" (Ps. 89:1–2).

Suggested Scriptures

- Proverbs 10:11, 19; 11:12; 12:16, 18; 15:4, 23; 16:23–24; 17:9, 14, 27; 19:11; 20:3; 26:20–22; 31:8–9
- Psalm 34:13
- Luke 6:45
- James 3:1–11
- Ephesians 4:29
- Colossians 3:8
- 1 Peter 3:10

Benediction

May the words of my mouth and the meditation of my heart be pleasing in your sight, O LORD my Rock and my Redeemer (Ps. 19:14 NIV).

Kid's Talk

Read Psalm 34:13, "keep your tongue from evil and your lips from speaking lies" (NIV). Tell the children an appropriate story about your own childhood when a lie got you in trouble and the consequences. Explain that God wants us to use every part of us to honor Him, including our mouths. Ask them what they can think of to do this week that would honor God with their mouths and let a few answer out loud. Lead them in a short prayer of praise as an example of honoring God with your mouth.

Additional Sermons and Lesson Ideas

A Call to Submission
Date preached:
By Rev. Melvin Tinker

SCRIPTURE: Hebrews 12:1–13

INTRODUCTION: It is easy to panic and jump ship when things get tough, only to find ourselves in deeper trouble than had we stayed and seen the journey through. Let's look at a passage that encourages us to stay the course in submission to Christ.

1. Go the Distance (vv. 1–3). The most important principle in running a race is to keep our eyes on Christ. Going the distance requires a proper focus.
2. Go with Discipline (vv. 4–13). Staying the course requires the discipline of God in our lives. We must not reject but embrace and endure discipline, for it is proof that we are sons of God.

CONCLUSION: Are you focusing on the Lord Jesus? Have you experienced His discipline? God requires no less of us than complete submission to Him and focus upon Jesus, the Author and Finisher of our faith!

It's a Matter of the Heart
Date preached:
By Dr. Kevin Riggs

SCRIPTURE: Mark 4:1–20

INTRODUCTION: There is an old saying, "Crime doesn't pay . . . and neither does farming." Jesus' parable about sowing, growing, and harvesting, made perfect sense to His audience. In this story about a farmer sowing seed, Jesus mentions four types of dirt. He then turns to explain what each means:

1. Hard Dirt (v. 2): The Hard Heart (vv. 14–15).
2. Rocky Dirt (vv. 5–6): The Shallow Heart (vv. 16–17).
3. Thorny Dirt (v. 7): The Overcrowded Heart (vv. 18–19).
4. Good Dirt (v. 8): The Good Heart (v. 20).

CONCLUSION: In what condition is your heart? How can you know? You can know by taking a spiritual EKG.

E—Examine your own heart.
K—Know for sure your heart belongs to Jesus.
G—Grow.

COMMUNION SERMON

The Source of Joy

Date preached:

By Rev. Todd M. Kinde

Scripture: Ecclesiastes 8:15 (NASB)
So I commended pleasure, for there is nothing good for a man under the sun except to eat and to drink and to be merry, and this will stand by him in his toils throughout the days of his life which God has given him under the sun.

Introduction: What will bring you joy? Where will you find the greatest pleasure? What will make you happy? Ponder this. Solomon commends to us the virtue of joy (v. 15). It would seem to us in this day and age that joy is impossible if there is injustice and suffering. If life under the sun is filled with vanity, how can the preacher commend joy? What is your first response to the question of joy? Perhaps the problem in our thinking, and as a result with our life as a whole, is not that we have the wrong desire for joy or the wrong definition of joy but that we seek the wrong source for joy. I wonder, how many of us at first thought believed that the revelation of God's grace in Christ was the place we would find the greatest joy. If our gaze does not transcend this realm and falls short of the heavenly vision then we will not know joy in this life. When we worship God as the source of wisdom and joy we will have lives marked by labor, simplicity, and contentment.

1. **Labor.** Again, we might be uncomfortable to place work as a mark of the joyful Christian life. Our society has developed a perspective that work is something to be avoided or done with as soon as possible and we have an acronym to go along with it as a motto, TGIF or Thank God It's Friday. Many are caught up in living for the weekend as if fun is the highest good one could pursue. This reveals an idolatrous heart that seeks the source of joy in earthly fun rather than in the heavenly Father. To avoid work is actually to deny God. God created man in the garden for the purpose of working the garden. The first task was to identify, categorize, and name the animal kingdom. Adam was so exhausted from that work that he took a nap in the heat of the day. It was after the work that God came and took from Adam's side a body part and fashioned the

woman who would be his wife. But when his focus shifted from God to Eve then came the fall into sin. When Adam became more concerned to please Eve by compliance than to please God by obedience, he sinned. He sought the source of joy in the gift rather than in the Giver.

2. **Simplicity.** Life is not really all that complicated. Solomon highlights food and drink and the ability to enjoy them as the gifts of God. Now this summary statement must be kept in context with the other summaries that have been made earlier (Eccl. 2:24–26; 5:18–20). God gives these gifts to humanity. These gifts seem to define culture. See the sort of society that Solomon developed (1 Kin. 4:20–21). The teaching of Jesus resonates with this simplicity of life (Matt. 6:25; 8:20). As followers of Christ we will find joy in the Lord and our lives will be uncomplicated, without worry, and in need not much beyond food, drink, and clothing.

3. **Contentment.** Contentment is finding pleasure and fulfillment in what God has chosen to give. God gave the blessing, the suffering, the toil, the days, the food, the drink. God also gives the gift of joy the ability to enjoy the simple life. It is one thing to have a simple life; it as another thing to be content with it. True contentment is a gift that comes from godliness (1 Tim. 6:6–8). The source of contentment is the fear of the Lord (Prov. 19.23). Now we have come full circle. The source of joy is found in the worship of God. Are you satisfied with Christ? Are you satisfied with the culture He has built in this community of faith that is defined and gathers around the actions of eating and drinking at the Lord's Table?

Conclusion: Friends, fear God. Worship God. Be satisfied with God revealed in Christ, crucified for our sin, and glorified for our life. Come to Him and to His Table of food and drink, and be satisfied.

Interview with Dallas Willard

Christian Philosophy Professor and Author

In your books and lectures, you're a keen advocate of Scripture memory as a powerful tool in spiritual formation. Why do you feel so strongly about that?

There are two main explanations of that. The first is the way I was brought up, and that is not an insignificant thing for me. Ever since I can remember in Sunday school, Bible school, and other avenues of church activity there's been an emphasis on memorization of Scripture. I'm very thankful for that. Second, I've found that through Scripture memory the incredible treasures of Scripture are not only just available to my mind, but they inform my whole being in a way that is a testimony to the substantial power of the Word of God.

You're not just talking about memorizing a verse here or there, are you?

Memorizing miscellaneous verses is a good thing, but when I talk about memorizing Scripture, I'm really talking about memorizing passages, whole psalms, or long parts of the letters or the Gospels. That does something not only to your mind but to your outlook. For me, anything that is going to be effective in spiritual formation or growth in grace has got to be holistic. It can't be a little side thing that you have a few Scriptures memorized. A simple illustration is the Twenty-Third Psalm. Many, many people have that memorized, but they don't allow it to inform their thinking and their acting by meditating on it as they should. Having it stored in your mind is a powerful resource for inner development. It's also important for preaching, because it's strange how having long passages of the Word of God inscribed in your mind just brings outlines, insights, and ways of putting things that will inform your speaking, your conversation, and your preaching. That's the main thing I have found out by use, that there's power in long passages of the Word being committed to memory.

Continued on the next page

CONVERSATIONS IN THE PASTOR'S STUDY—*Continued*

What is your own personal daily habit as it relates to Scripture memory?

Well, it is above all to use what I have memorized. For example, one of my favorite passages and one that I encourage others to learn is Colossians 3:1–17. Now, suppose I am driving to my office on the freeway. I will take that up. When you use what you have memorized, you don't just rattle it off; you just soak yourself in it. You bring it carefully to mind and receive from it always more than you had realized was in it. It seems like you never reach the bottom. I do not daily memorize new passages, but during one week there will be periods when I will take up some new passages and begin to work on them. The way I do it is that I don't try to just sit down and memorize them right now. I select a passage and I will work on it by reading it, thinking about it, and studying it. Then I begin to take a three-, four-, or five-verse section, and I will repeat that until I have it down. The words won't stay there fully in my mind on the first or second time through them. I relax about that and just keep going back over it for a period of days or weeks until it is pretty solidly set in my mind. Then I'll use it for a period, and then I'll memorize another.

Do you find that your sermon outlines very often flow from your Scripture memory?

That's absolutely right. The issue of hermeneutics is an interesting one. The texture of a passage from the Scripture will have many different ways of breaking up into segments. You won't see those all at once; in fact, you'll never see all of them because there's such depth to the way Scripture is composed. But very often as in Colossians 3:17, it outlines itself in various ways. You start out with the resurrection life you've been given and the next step is mortification, letting the old life die off; and then comes the responsibility of an individual to grow by putting off the old person and putting on the new. Each of those sections breaks down into parts that outline like the first four verses, which are about, "If you, then, be raised with Christ," and so on. It has four or five points that you can preach on at the drop of a hat. So it's just amazing how the little particles come out when you know the passages by heart.

How would you advise a minister not in this habit to go about it?

I'd begin with some of the most well-known and familiar passages. For example, if one has not yet memorized 1 Corinthians 13, that's a great passage to start. It's the kind of passage that people have a rough familiarity with because they've just heard it so much. In a group setting, this passage is a good one for the members of the group to memorize in the next three days or whatever. I don't know how frequently I've had people write me and talk about how that's changed their whole re-entry into their church setting, work setting, and home setting, just having that in their minds.

This is a major discipline for the spiritual life, and as you practice it you find you come to hunger inwardly for the practice. That's where it really gets good. Don't make it a kind of job, but a joy.

MARCH 2, 2008

Do Dead People Go to a Better Place?

By Dr. Larry Osborne

Date preached:

Scripture: Various, especially John 14:6
Jesus said . . . "I am the way, the truth, and the life. No one comes to the Father except through Me."

Introduction: How many times have you found yourself at a funeral where family is assured their loved one is "in a better place?" It seems more often than not this phrase is used of the deceased despite the kind of lives they lived or what they believed. I call these "funeral assurances," a false hope given when the salvation of the deceased is actually unknown. Today we want to look at Scripture and see what actually qualifies a person for heaven.

1. **What Our Culture Believes: Dead People Go to a Better Place Because . . .**

   A. **God Grades on a Curve.**

   B. **As Long as We Are Sincere, Any Spiritual Path Works.**

   C. **A God of Love Would Not Send Anyone to Hell.**

   D. **Only an Ignorant Bigot Thinks Jesus Is the Only Way.**

2. **What the Bible Actually Says:**

   A. **There Is a Real Place Called Hell.** If hell was a myth, Jesus certainly would never have given such a strong warning and frightening description of it: ". . . It is better for you to enter into life maimed, rather than having two hands, to go to hell, into the fire that shall never be quenched—where *'Their worm does not die and the fire is not quenched'*" (Mark 9:42–45).

   B. **It Was Made for Satan and His Angels.** Scripture is clear that hell was not originally intended for us. In fact, Jesus prophesied about the Day of Judgment: "Then He will also say to those on the left hand, 'Depart from Me, you cursed, into the everlasting fire prepared for the devil and his angels'" (Matt. 25:41; see Rev. 20:10).

C. **God Doesn't Grade on a Curve.** We often compare ourselves to others who are "less righteous" than we presume ourselves to be. Scripture, however, teaches us that God is the standard against which we are judged: ". . . for all have sinned and fall short of the glory of God" (Rom. 3:23).

D. **Jesus Is the Only Ticket to Heaven.** It doesn't get much clearer than this: "Jesus said . . . 'I am the way, the truth, and the life. No one comes to the Father except through Me'" (John 14:6). We need to keep in mind that not every slight acknowledgment of God makes us true disciples of Christ who will share eternity with Him. Jesus never says "accept Me" in the Bible; He says "follow Me!"

3. **How Should We Then Live?**

A. **Trust God with Your Questions.** If you're a thinking person, you will have questions about God's ways. Faith does not mean complete absence of doubt. In fact, faith is at its best when we struggle with doubt and obey anyway (Heb. 11:6). We can trust God not just because "He says so," but because He has proven Himself faithful.

B. **Tell People the Good News About Jesus.** Before He ascended into heaven, Jesus gave the command, "Go therefore and make disciples of all the nations, baptizing them in the name of the Father and of the Son and of the Holy Spirit, teaching them to observe all things that I have commanded you; and lo, I am with you always, even to the end of the age. Amen" (Matt. 28:19–20). Far from being a simple recruiting speech, this was Jesus' command to carry out the whole reason He came, that sinners might be reconciled to God (2 Cor. 5:18)!

C. **Be Winsome, Not Combative (2 Tim. 2:24–26).** Even those who do the will of the enemy deserve respect. Our goal is not to win an argument! If there's a real place called hell, I want to do everything I can to keep others from going there. Our job is to be part of the "rescue squad."

D. **Remove Every Obstacle You Can (1 Cor. 9:19–23).** When it comes to those who don't know Jesus, you should be on the front line helping others come to Christ no matter what it takes: whether it takes putting up with a different style of music, leaving visitors the best parking spaces at church, or any other "inconveniences" to us. We must realize that our preferences do not matter.

Conclusion: Do dead people go to a better place? Only when they follow Jesus.

STATS, STORIES, AND MORE

More from Dr. Osborne

Years ago I was pastor of a Baptist church located in a suburb right outside of Los Angeles. I was a twenty-five-year-old youth pastor in a large church, ready to take any opportunity to learn and gain experience. I love to teach and preach, but one thing no one really asked of a youth pastor was to do a funeral. At one point in my ministry, however, a young girl died in a motorcycle accident nearby. Evidently she had a Baptist background, so the funeral home called asking for a young Baptist preacher. I had it all worked out in my mind, how to address the audience with the truth of the gospel and a challenge to respond to the Lord. As I drove to the funeral home, I felt very uneasy and nervous.

When I approached the funeral home, there were about 150 motorcycles parked there. I realized this wasn't just a girl who died in a motorcycle accident; she was in a motorcycle gang! This was a group known as "The Sundowners," a drug-running, hard-core, criminal-type motorcycle gang. I began to think, *Maybe I shouldn't say what I wanted to say.* I decided to keep driving past! The Holy Spirit convicted me, and I turned around. I ended up delivering the message as I planned. After the funeral, we went to the graveside. After I read the twenty-third Psalm, each of the gang members grabbed a beer from their motorcycle, drank it, and threw it into the hole with the casket! As I drove back, for the first time, I understood the cultural pressure of assuring friends and family of a dead person that their loved one is in heaven.

APPROPRIATE HYMNS AND SONGS

"Come, Now Is the Time to Worship," Brian Doerksen, 1998 Vineyard Songs.

"O For a Thousand Tongues to Sing," Charles Wesley, Public Domain.

"Come Thou Fount," John Wyeth & Robert Robinson, Public Domain.

"Agnus Dei," Michael W. Smith, 1990 Sony/ATV Milene Music.

FOR THE BULLETIN

The Lollards, John Wycliffe's traveling preachers, were early pre-Reformation evangelists who were bitterly persecuted. The first Lollard martyr was William Sawtré, who was burned to death on March 2, 1401. ● Henry Venn was born on March 2, 1724. He was an Anglican clergyman and close friend of George Whitefield, born near London and ordained in 1749, whose sermons fascinated the industrial and manufacturing classes of eighteenth-century England. ● On March 2, 1783, New England evangelist Benjamin Randall was struck with a violent fever, which nearly killed him. He later wrote in his journal, "Through the whole illness, I enjoyed a heavenly calm. I found my faith strong in the Lord Jesus Christ. . . . I laid basking and solacing in divine consolation and felt the streams of heavenly love flow sweetly into my soul." ● John Wesley died on March 2, 1791. ● March 2, 1848, marks the birthday of Christian entrepreneur, A. A. Hyde, creator of Mentholatum. ● American missionary Gustav Schmidt, 39, opened the Danzig Instytut Biblijny in the Free City of Danzig (Gdansk), Poland, on March 2, 1930. It was the first Pentecostal Bible Institute established in Eastern Europe. ● On March 2, 1979, over 1,100 Christian organizations joined together to form the Evangelical Council for Financial Accountability (ECFA), an oversight agency that helps insure financial integrity among evangelical ministries.

WORSHIP HELPS

Call to Worship
"Great and marvelous are Your works, Lord God Almighty! Just and true are Your ways, O King of the saints! Who shall not fear You, O Lord, and glorify Your name? For You alone are holy. For all nations shall come and worship before You, for Your judgments have been manifested" (Rev. 15:3–4).

Closing Prayer/Invitation
Father, would You take these things, and would You help us to study these Scriptures, and to hold on to that which matches Your Word and Your truth?

With your heads bowed, I want to speak to those who have been checking out Christianity or those who have come to church but never taken the step to follow Jesus with your life. Jesus' death on the Cross made possible three things: the

Continued on the next page

WORSHIP HELPS—*Continued*

forgiveness of your sins, your adoption as a son of God, and the release of the Holy Spirit to change you from the inside out. There is one condition to receiving these things: You have to give Him the steering wheel of your life. If you have never given Him the steering wheel, if today is the day you want to make that choice, would you pray this prayer with me right now:

> "Dear Jesus, would You forgive my sins? Would You adopt me into Your family? Would You come and change me from the inside out. Here is the steering wheel of my life. From this point forward, You take control."

Suggested Scriptures

- Deuteronomy 29:29
- Isaiah 55:8–9; 64:6
- Matthew 10:28
- John 1:12–13
- Galatians 2:21
- 2 Thessalonians 1:6–10
- Hebrews 10:26–27
- 1 Peter 3:15
- 1 John 2:3–5
- Revelation 20:11–15

Additional Sermons and Lesson Ideas

Let's Praise the Lord
Date preached:

By Dr. Michael A. Guido

SCRIPTURE: Psalm 138

INTRODUCTION: Paganism has its prayers, but not any praise. It has teaching, but not any thanksgiving. Sometimes unthinking Christians express no thanksgiving. But praising, like praying, should be a habit. It should be done continually, not casually. David, who had this habit, listed four reasons for praise in Psalm 138.

1. Praise the Lord for His Revelation (v. 2).
2. Praise the Lord for His Response (v. 3).
3. Praise the Lord for His Reviving (v. 7).
4. Praise the Lord for His Redemption (v. 8).

CONCLUSION: Has your life become shattered by sin? Have you made a mess of things and are you wondering what's the use? Oh the Lord loves you. Bring Him into your broken heart and you will soon know what it is to praise Him for His redemption!

The God-Prompted Heart
Date preached:

SCRIPTURE: Exodus 25:1–9

INTRODUCTION: The tabernacle represented a "building program" for ancient Israel, and by its example we can learn how God wants to fund His work today.

1. God Puts the Opportunities in Our Pathway. The Israelites had an opportunity to build a dwelling for God's presence among them. The tabernacle was a scale model of the real temple in heaven and an object lesson of Christ and His salvation. It was an expensive task. Where did the funding come from?
2. God Puts the Money in Our Pockets. God anticipated the need in advance (see Ex. 3:21–22; 12:31–36). In plundering the Egyptians, the Lord provided the Israelites with wherewithal, not for their own affluence, but as a means of pre-funding His work.
3. God Puts the Willingness in Our Hearts. Exodus 25:2 says the offering would come from those who gave with willing hearts, and the NIV says from those whose hearts were prompted to give. The outcome is seen in Exodus 36:3–7.

CONCLUSION: It's not anyone's job to prod or pressure others regarding giving. Our job is praying, and the Lord's job is prompting. We have great opportunities in our pathway, money in our pockets, and the prompting of God in our hearts.

Interview with Dr. Michael Guido
Pioneer Radio and Television Evangelist

Have you ever had bouts of discouragement in the Lord's work?

Oh, yes, sir! Whenever I have gone through those times of discouragement, I have always gone to the Bible and have selected Bible verses that fit into my problem and my pain. Through my tears I have memorized those verses, meditated upon them, and asked the Lord to make them real in my life, to deliver me from that sorrow, from that loss, from that heavy burden. And He did it every time. May I tell you about the thing that led us into this ministry? Audrey and I were in evangelistic work. Audrey used magic to illustrate the Bible. She was considered one of the nation's greatest professional magicians, and God greatly used her ministry. When we were on our way to Atlanta, a truck hit us. We had new one-day-old car, and it was completely demolished. When I came to, I couldn't find Audrey. I saw a thin line of blood and I followed it and found her in a pool of blood. Her face was cut from her hair, down through her nose, lips, and chin. The doctors said, "Your wife won't see. We don't think she will ever appear lovely enough to stand before an audience again." The plastic surgeons just shook their heads. But the next day, a stranger came in and said, "I'm one of the leading plastic surgeons from Paris. I wondered why God wanted me in Atlanta. It's to make you beautiful again." And he operated on Audrey and you could hardly tell she was ever cut so hideously. Coming home in the ambulance I said to her, "God spared our lives. Let's promise that we will do the work of four people instead of two." She started to cry and said, "I like that. Let's ask Him what to do silently." We did. I said, "Did He tell you?" She said, "You're going to laugh." I said, "Try me!" She said, "A radio and television ministry." I said, "That's what He put on my heart." Audrey said, "Let's ask God to give us a name," and all I could think of was Monet's painting of *The Sower*. I said, "We'll call it 'The Sower.'" Audrey said, "Let's promise God we will never ask anybody for money." I said, "I like that." And in the ambulance we chose the verse, "Seek first the kingdom of God and His righteousness, and all these things shall be added unto you." And from that day to this, we have never asked for money, never hinted for money, never suggested for money. We have run everything by prayer. There have been days when we would be so discouraged that we wouldn't have enough money for the work, but the Lord always came through.

Someone said that all discouragement is from the devil. Do you agree?

Oh, I think the Lord uses it to make us become people of faith. We must turn our obstacles into opportunities and our scars into stars.

You counsel a lot of ministers who are facing discouragement. What seems to be some of the main causes for discouragement in the ministry today?

Prayerlessness. Biblelessness. Sometimes being married to the wrong person. A lack of passion for souls. It hurts me whenever I see a minister who has no passion for souls. I pray, "Lord, if the time ever comes in my life when I fail to save souls in a personal way, kill me and take me home to heaven."

What would you say to someone who is laboring, but without a lot of observable fruit?

Whenever I'm in a meeting and no souls are being saved, I pray, "Oh God, what's wrong with me?" He usually shows me, then I right the wrong, then I submit myself to the Lord and say, "Lord, send me out. Let me lead somebody to Thee." And every time I see a person, I see written across their forehead the Bible verse, "For whom Christ died." I find it easy when I think of that to give them a tract, to ask them a question, to lead them to the Lord. *Continued on the next page*

CONVERSATIONS IN THE PASTOR'S STUDY—*Continued*

May I ask how old you are?

Yes, sir. I'm 91.

Do you ever fret about growing older?

No, sir. I just thank the Lord that He lets me live another day.

Your energy seems to be as strong now as ever.

Well, it takes me a little longer to do things, but I do as much today as I did yesterday, or last week or last month. I get up every morning at 5:30 and go to bed at night at about 10:30. I get calls almost every night from all over the world from people who hear our broadcast. The other morning at 2:30, a girl called and said, "I'm a Muslim and I live in Damascus, Syria. I just saw your telecast. Can I, a Muslim, become a Christian?" I led her to the Lord and she called me every morning for seven mornings at 2:30 to thank me for leading her to Jesus.

Have you always been so enthusiastic?

I think it's been cultivated. I work hard on it. I try never to let anything make me bitter. "All things work together for good to them that love God." Every morning I say, "Lord, give us more radio and television stations." And no station charges us for time. We're on over 400 radio stations and they all air our program free of charge.

MARCH 9, 2008

SUGGESTED SERMON

He Gives Me Comfort

Date preached:

By Rev. Todd M. Kinde

Scripture: Psalm 23:4b
Your rod and Your staff, they comfort me.

Introduction: Psalm 23 teaches us that Yahweh is the Shepherd. The tools of the shepherd are a rod and a staff. These tools become the symbol of his trade and the status of his role in the community. Shepherds were not necessarily the highest esteemed in any given society. Yet from the beginning of creation it would seem God has chosen to reveal His relationship to humanity in terms of the shepherd. In the Old Testament, the word "shepherd" refers to kings, judges, and other leaders of the people (Num. 27:17; 2 Sam. 5:2; 7:7; Ps. 78:70–72). As the Good Shepherd, Jesus fulfills the type of the shepherd we see in Psalm 23:4 in at least four ways:

1. **Christ Defends and Protects Us.** Not all will submit to the sovereign rule of the Lord. Some resist the Shepherd. To these the Lord applies the rod. The shepherd's rod was about two feet in length with a knot at one end and a handle carved in the other. The knotted end might be weighted and impressed with sharp metal or stones. A skilled shepherd could wield it like a cudgel or mace to crush a predator's head or he could throw it with precision at a charging attacker. To the sheep this rod is a comfort giving strength in the face of dangers. The rod defends and protects the sheep within the flock. But to the enemy the rod is a fearful thing, a sign of power that threatens to undo the devious plan. The fulfillment of the Shepherd is Christ. He is the Sovereign who reigns (Rev. 19:15–16). To the enemies this is a terror. To the sheep this is a comfort.

2. **Christ Disciplines and Watches Us.** Those who work with animals know that there are times when the master must use a firm hand. Christ uses a firm hand to enforce His covenant with us at times when we act against it. This is not His *punishing* act as with those outside the fold. This is His *purifying* act to make us more obedient

and loyal members of the kingdom (Deut. 8:5–7; Heb. 12:5–6, 10–11; cf. Prov. 3:11–12). To the sheep this is comfort though we are slow to understand it. The Good Shepherd will not let us get away with disobedience. Christ will not let us go too far. He will stop us with His firm hand and His tough love.

3. **Christ Directs and Guides Us.** We know from the verbs of verses 2–3, "He leads me . . . He guides me . . ." The shepherd uses the staff to direct the sheep. The shepherd's staff is more recognizable to us. That long piece of slender wood with a crook formed at one end. With the length of the staff the shepherd can reach ahead or behind or to the side to tap the lamb into movement away from or toward a certain direction. Christ is the Good Shepherd who directs us maintaining our covenant relationship with Him. He leads us in paths of righteousness for His name's sake. This certainly applies to obedience as we saw earlier. It also applies to wise living. His Word, the Scriptures, are like a rod and a staff that direct us in godly decision making.

4. **Christ Delivers and Frees Us.** Sometimes the sheep will stumble into a hole. Sometimes they will get so enraptured with that lush green grass that they nose themselves into a thorn bush trying to reach for more and the fleecy wool gets tangled in the thorns. The shepherd's staff has that crook in the end which is used to pull sheep out of a hole or to reach around the neck of an entangled lamb and, with a firm but gentle tug, free the lamb from the snare. So Christ delivers and frees us from pitfalls and snares.

Conclusion: Our greatest deliverance and freedom is from sin. Having received this deliverance we are free to enjoy the Shepherd's presence and to find comfort in His rod and staff. Christ is the Shepherd of the sheep who has given His life on the Cross for the sheep (John 10:11). God the Father raised Him to life and He has freed us to serve Him. Yield to Him. Submit to His reign. Surrender all care and trust to Him (Rev. 1:5–6).

STATS, STORIES, AND MORE

Psalm 23 occupies a curious place in the book of Psalms, preceded by Psalm 22 and followed by Psalm 24. Psalm 22 is a vivid prophecy about the Crucifixion of Christ. Psalm 24 describes the Coming of our Lord in glory and power, presenting Him as a great King over the earth. Between the two is Psalm 23 with its green pastures and still waters. There's a famous little outline that says:

- Psalm 22 tells of the Savior's Cross.
- Psalm 23 tells of the Shepherd's Crook.
- Psalm 24 tells of the Sovereign's Crown.

Or we can think of it like this: Psalm 22 tells us of the sufferings on Mount Calvary. Psalm 24 tells us the glories of Mount Zion. Between the two we have a lovely valley with green grass, quiet waters, and grazing sheep—a pathway of righteousness leading from the Cross to the crown under the escort of the Good Shepherd.

The Lord Is My Shepherd
In his little book on the 23rd Psalm, published in 1899, the evangelist J. Wilber Chapman suggested we should learn to emphasize every word of this phrase. The Lord—literally, Jehovah—the Eternal, Self-Existent God, the King, Eternal, Immortal, Invisible. This Jehovah, this Lord is—present tense, right now, at this moment. The Lord is my—a personal pronoun; He is mine today and He is yours today. It doesn't say, "The Lord is a shepherd," or "the Lord is the shepherd," but "the Lord is my shepherd"—and what a difference that little pronoun makes. The Lord is my shepherd. Jesus called Himself the good shepherd, and Peter called Him the chief shepherd. All that an ancient, oriental shepherd was to his sheep, the Lord is, and more, to you and me.

APPROPRIATE HYMNS AND SONGS

"A Shelter in the Time of Storm," Ira D. Sankey & Vernon J. Charlesworth, Public Domain.

"Abba Father," Darlene Zschech, 1999 Hillsong Publishing Company. (Admin. in U.S. and Canada by Integrity's Hosanna! Music).

"All Who Are Thirsty," Brenton Brown & Glenn Robertson, 1998 Vineyard Songs.

"Comfort, Comfort Now My People," Catherine Winkworth, Johannes Olearius, Louis Bourgeious, Public Domain.

FOR THE BULLETIN

On March 9, 1074, Pope Gregory VII excommunicated all married Roman Catholic priests. Until then, celibacy had only been enforced from time to time and place to place. ● Giovanni de Medici, age 13, was made a cardinal-deacon of the church on March 9, 1489. Though he never became a priest, he was elected pope in 1513, taking the title Leo X. His excesses sparked the Protestant Reformation. ● On March 9, 1745, the bells for the first American carillon were shipped from England to Boston. ● On March 9, 1831, evangelist Charles Finney concluded a six-month series of meetings in Rochester, New York, during which 100,000 people were reportedly converted, including many of the city's leaders. Taverns went out of business, the theater became a livery stable, and the crime rate dropped by two-thirds. The city jail was virtually empty for the next two years. ● March 9, 1839 is the birth date of Phoebe Palmer Knapp, Methodist hymnwriter, who wrote the tune to Fanny Crosby's hymn, "Blessed Assurance." ● On March 9, 1913, Eberhard Nestle, German biblical scholar, died at 61. Nestle is primarily remembered as a Greek scholar who, in 1898, published the first edition of his Greek New Testament based on the work of leading German and British scholars. In 1904, his text was adopted by the British and Foreign Bible Society in place of the Textus Receptus, and became arguably the most widely used edition of the Greek New Testament. ● Andrae Crouch wrote "Through It All" on this day in 1971.

WORSHIP HELPS

Call to Worship
Salvation belongs to our God who sits on the throne and to the Lamb! Blessing and honor and glory and power be to Him who sits on the throne, and to the Lamb, forever and ever (from Rev. 7:10; 5:13)!

Scripture Reading Medley
The LORD is my shepherd; I shall not want. There is no want to those who fear Him. The young lions lack and suffer hunger; but those who seek the LORD shall not lack any good thing. They shall not be ashamed in the evil time, and in the days of famine they shall be satisfied. For the LORD God is a sun and shield; the LORD will give grace and glory; No good thing will He withhold from those who walk uprightly. Do not seek what you should eat nor what you should drink, nor have an anxious mind. For

all these things the nations of the world seek after, and your Father knows that you need these things. But seek the kingdom of God, and all these things shall be added to you. And my God shall supply all your need according to His riches in glory by Christ Jesus (Ps. 23:1; 34:9–10; 37:19; 84:11; Luke 12:29–31; Phil. 4:19).

Benediction
Now may the God of peace who brought up our Lord Jesus from the dead, that great Shepherd of the sheep, through the blood of the everlasting covenant, make you complete in every good work to do His will, working in you what is well pleasing in His sight, through Jesus Christ, to whom be glory forever and ever. Amen (Heb. 13:20–21).

PRAYER FOR THE PASTOR'S CLOSET

O Lord, my best desire fulfill,
And help me to resign
Life, health, and comfort to Thy will,
And make Thy pleasure mine.
—WILLIAM COWPER in
The Olney Hymns

Additional Sermons and Lesson Ideas

Cleansing Sinners
By Dr. Robert M. Norris

Date preached:

SCRIPTURE: Hebrews 1:1–4

INTRODUCTION: Do you want to hear God speak? Here the author of the Hebrew epistle reminds his hearers and us that God has spoken. God is not silent. He communicates. He means to connect with us.

1. God Has Spoken Through the Person of His Son (vv. 1–2).
2. God Has Spoken Through the Work of His Son (vv. 3–4).

CONCLUSION: I close by commending this great Person to you that you might trust in Him and love Him and worship Him. He is alive and sitting at the right hand of God with all power and authority and will one day come in great glory. He has that exalted place because He *is* Himself God the Son; and because He upholds you and me by the word of His power; and because He made a perfect purification of sins.

Honoring God's Order
By Rev. Billie Friel

Date preached:

SCRIPTURE: 1 Corinthians 14:33, 40

INTRODUCTION: Imagine a boy putting on his sweater. He begins by putting button #1 in hole #2. When he finishes, the sweater is a crooked mess, all because he started out of order. Paul writes 1 Corinthians to put a church in order that had become crooked through sin.

1. God Is a God of Order (vv. 33, 40).
2. God's Order in the Physical World. God is the Creator of all things (Gen. 1) from our bodies (Ps. 139:14) to the tiniest atomic particle.
3. God's Order in the Spiritual World. Scripture is divinely written in order of God's progressive revelation of Himself to man (Heb. 1:1–2). The church has been structured with Christ as the head, just as man is head of his household (Eph. 5:23).

CONCLUSION: Everything seems to be moving toward disorder. However, God is in charge as we come to the end of time. He is on His throne. Is your life in order (2 Kin. 20:1)?

MARCH 16, 2008

You Must Be Born Again

Date preached:

By Dr. Ed Dobson

Scripture: John 3:1–16, especially verse 3
Jesus answered and said to him, "Most assuredly, I say to you, unless one is born again, he cannot see the kingdom of God."

Introduction: Imagine if someone you trust were to call you up in a panic. Out of breath, they tell you, "Your life is in danger. Listen to me very closely. The only chance you have of survival is . . ." and then you only hear a dial tone. You would frantically call him or her back, you would worry, you would look for any clues you could find to be saved. Yet when we come to Scripture, there is no dial tone; Christ completely revealed His salvation to us. Despite all this, many here today have never even considered whether or not we are fit for heaven and saved from eternal hell. May we be honest with ourselves and ask the question: Have I ever been born again?

I. **What Does It Mean to Be Born Again (v. 3)?** We throw the term "born again" around. It's actually become ingrained in our popular language and culture to some extent, but what does it really mean? The word *again* is a Greek preposition (*anothen*) with several meanings.

A. **Start Over from the Beginning.** The word *anothen* has the meaning of completely starting over. Imagine you're the batter at a baseball game. You've just smacked the ball into the outfield. As you ran the bases, you barely missed first base with your foot, but you kept running. The infielders catch on, throw the ball to first, and guess what? You're out! What if you said to the umpire, "Oh, come on. Let me run the bases again; I'll get all of them this time!"? He would not allow it because it's such a radical request! Yet this is the meaning conveyed here by being born again. We are given a completely clean slate, a fresh start, a new beginning! I wonder how many here are burdened with the weight of your guilt. There may be many here who have not made the decision to follow Jesus and you find yourselves wishing for a new beginning. Jesus came to give us this opportunity!

    B. From Above. The word also means "from above." Later in John 3, we read about the one who is *anothen,* from above (3:31). So, to be born again means to go back to the beginning and start over, a radical serious change. But it also means to be born from above. To be born again is not turning over a new leaf. It's not making a series of resolutions. It's not joining a church. It's not something on a human level that we do. To be born again is to be born from above.

2. **Why Do We Need to Be Born Again (v. 6)?** We are flesh and flesh gives birth to flesh. What Jesus is essentially saying is that we are all sinners. The Bible says, "For all have sinned and fall short of the glory of God" (Rom. 3:23 NIV). The Bible says there is no one who is righteous, not one single person. Flesh gives birth to flesh and the problem is, in our flesh we are sinners. Yes, created by God. Yes, loved by God, but separated from God. The Bible says that the penalty of our sin is death (Rom. 6:23)—separation from God now and separation from God for all of eternity.

3. **How Can I Be Born Again (v. 16)?** To believe means to rely on something, to have confidence in something, to trust something. Faith in Christ is that point in our lives where we admit that we are sinners, where we know that Jesus died and rose again for us—but it's more than understanding who we are, it's more than understanding what Jesus did—it's taking the gift and putting it on. It is saying, "Lord Jesus, I know I'm a sinner and I want You to forgive me. Come into my life."

4. **When Should I Be Born Again?** You know what the Bible says? ". . . Behold, now is the accepted time; behold, now is the day of salvation" (2 Cor. 6:2). When God speaks, when God's Spirit moves, when the opportunity is there, that is the time to respond.

Conclusion: Have you been born again?

STATS, STORIES, AND MORE

John 3:16 may be the world's best-loved text, but no one loved it more than the nineteenth-century British evangelist, Henry Moorehouse. Henry began preaching shortly after his conversion from a life of vile wickedness, and every time he stood to preach he gave John 3:16 as his text. His sermons varied, but his text was always the same.

Once Moorehouse sent D. L. Moody a letter offering to preach for him. Moody was leaving on a trip just as Henry arrived in Chicago. "I don't think he can preach," Moody told his church leaders, "but let him try." When Moody returned, the church was astir. "He has preached two sermons from John 3:16," Mrs. Moody said. "He preaches a little different from what you do. He tells sinners God loves them."

"Well," replied Moody, "he is wrong." Moody trudged reluctantly to church that night, and Moorehouse announced his text—John 3:16. Moorehouse preached for seven nights, always from John 3:16, and his message stirred D. L. Moody to his depths. From that week, Moody's great ministry took on a deeper, softer tone.

Some years passed and Henry Moorehouse came to his deathbed at age 40. His last words were: "If it were God's will to raise me up, I should like to preach from the text John 3:16. Praise be to the Lord."

APPROPRIATE HYMNS AND SONGS

"Hosanna We Sing," Claire Cloninger & Robert Sterling, 2005 Word Music, LLC.

"Born Again," Ruth Sandberg, 1981 Ruth Sandberg.

"Rock of Ages," Rita Baloche, 1997 Maranatha Praise, Inc.

"A New Name Written Down in Glory," Charles Austin Miles, Public Domain.

FOR THE BULLETIN

On this day in A.D. 37, the Roman Emperor Tiberius, having retired to Capri, died on a visit to the mainland. He was the second emperor of Rome and his reign (A.D. 14–37) provided the political backdrop for the ministry of Jesus Christ and the birth of the church. ● On March 16, 1190, the Jews of York, England, committed mass suicide rather than submit to forced baptism. They had sought refuge in Clifford's tower after being attacked by a local mob. ● The Fifth Lateran Council, under the leadership of Pope Leo X, issued a special sale of indulgences before adjourning on this day in 1517. ● March 16, 1621, marks the birth of George Neumark, a German educator and hymnist. Twice in life he lost everything, the first time by theft and the second by fire. He is the author of, "If Thou But Suffer God to Guide Thee." ● On March 16, 1849, Reverend James E. Smith, age 100, became a father with a woman 64 years younger. ● On March 16, 1850, *The Scarlet Letter,* Nathaniel Hawthorne's novel about adultery and judgment in Puritan Massachusetts, was published. ● On this day in 1851, Spain signed a concordat with the Papacy under which Roman Catholicism became the only authorized faith. ● This is the birthday of Dr. Robert H. Bowman, cofounder of Far East Broadcasting Company, born in 1915.

WORSHIP HELPS

Call to Worship
Lord, You have been our dwelling place in all generations. Before the mountains were brought forth, or ever You had formed the earth and the world, even from everlasting to everlasting, You are God (Ps. 90:1–2).

Invitation
If you've never been born again, in just a moment I'm going to pray a prayer out loud and if you would like to give your life to Christ today, I want you to quietly, from where you're seated, in your heart to God's repeat this simple prayer after me. If you believe God has spoken to you and you'd like to receive Christ and experience a radical, from above birth in your life then repeat this simple prayer from your heart to the Lord: "Dear Lord, I admit to You that I am a sinner. Please forgive me. I believe that Jesus died and rose again for me. Come into my life, Lord Jesus. I give my life completely and totally to You, and it's my desire to follow You."

While our heads are bowed and our eyes are closed, if you prayed that prayer and you really meant it, I'd like to pray for you. I may not know you by name, but God does. While our heads our bowed, if you prayed that prayer would you just slip your hand up high so I can see it? "Lord, I pray for all persons who raised their hand for prayer. I pray that You would encourage them in their new journey. I thank You that when we invite You into our lives You come in, You forgive, You make us new, and You give us everlasting life. I pray that You would strengthen all persons who raised their hand and who prayed that prayer. In the name of Christ Jesus our Lord we pray. Amen."

Quote for the Pastor's Wall

The Bible tells us to love our neighbors, and also to love our enemies; probably because they are generally the same people.

—G. K. CHESTERTON

Additional Sermons and Lesson Ideas

Who Rules?
Date preached:

By Rev. Melvin Tinker

SCRIPTURE: Genesis 1

INTRODUCTION: Every day we see glimpses of a world gone wrong. Whether we reference Auschwitz or the Sudan, we begin to wonder if there is any way out of this chaos. Genesis 3 explains how man is responsible for all of the problems we see. Looking at Genesis 1 helps us understand God and the world as He intended us to partake of:

1. The Only God (v. 1). The writer of Genesis goes to great lengths in his language to explain that there is but one God. This is the foundational truth of Scripture.
2. The Orderly God (v. 16). God has always been a God of order. He fashioned the world as He saw fit, and everything was pronounced good!
3. The Owning God (v. 26). This world was not an accident, but a masterful work of an omnipotent Creator!

CONCLUSION: God wants to bring order into your world, for He owns it, and He owns you.

The Hannah Pathway
Date preached:

By Pastor Al Detter

SCRIPTURE: 1 Samuel 1:1–28

INTRODUCTION: When we're extremely distressed about something and it doesn't look like there's a thing in the world we can do about it, we can follow Hannah's example:

1. Assess the Situation (vv. 4–8).
2. Take Positive Spiritual Initiative (vv. 9–18).
3. Get Passionately Before the Lord (vv. 9–13).
4. Connect with a Spiritual Partner (vv. 12–18a).
5. Release the Situation to God (v. 18b).
6. Wait for God to Answer (vv. 19–20).
7. Keep Your Promises to God (vv. 21–28).

CONCLUSION: What part of the Hannah Pathway are you on? My prayer for you is—no matter what your reality—get on the Hannay Pathway. You'll come through okay if you stay with it!

When Members Leave

Today I met with a young minister who has suffered some kicks in the stomach. He's made a few changes in his church— nothing too drastic—but it's been too much for some of his older members. "It's not the same church anymore, Preacher," they've told him. "We've been here forty years, but we're leaving the church. It's not the way it used to be."

And then the inevitable: "I'm not the only one who feels this way, Pastor. People have been calling me about it."

So far my young friend has lost several trustees, a couple of deacons, a Sunday school teacher, the church pianist, and the secretary. The stress and strain is wearing on his wife, too. The mud of criticism splatters on her; and she's understandably protective of his well-being and reputation and of her own relationships.

Every pastoral couple can identify.

As it happens, last night I had a deacon's meeting in which a controversial proposal came up. We're out of space for our growing teen group; and our chapel, which is used only rarely for weddings or funerals, is near our youth classes. Our committees want to upgrade the chapel by refurbishing and keeping it traditional, but installing flexible seating so the room can handle various youth services and events. But a handful of tenured members are appalled at removing the pews they worked so hard to purchase and install in the 1960s; and I can understand their feelings. I saw a recent rerun in which Frasier Crane replaced his dad's threadbare chair with a new leather recliner. The old man was grief-stricken. He had sat in that chair during life-changing moments. Frasier dutifully pulled the old chair out of the dumpster and installed it back in his pristine living room, masking tape and all.

Furniture can have sentimental value, and it can also be symbolic. My handful of members is equating those pews with their heritage, and they feel the church is passing them by. The loss of their pews signifies, to them, their waning influence.

I'm terribly torn; we don't have any other good options for

Continued on the next page

our growing youth program, and I know our youth ministry needs the flexibility of chairs rather than a room full of rigid pews. Jesus didn't make those pews in the carpentry shop of Nazareth, and all the wood in the world can't compete with the worth of one teenager.

Some pastors wouldn't be too bothered by this. They're made of aggressive sinew, and they barrel right on, changing and innovating and facing forward with seldom a glance back. They're willing to accept casualties. They may lose some of the old-timers, but other churches will take them in; and the most important thing is reaching the lost and growing the church.

By nature I'm not that aggressive; yet people still get mad at me and I lose members, too; and I may lose one or more members over the pews, whichever way the decision goes.

I only remember one year in which no one left the church in anger. It was my second year of ministry when I was pastoring a little church in the mountains. My other twenty-nine have all had their share of casualties. Some have left because I was too progressive; others because I was too traditional. I've had people leave because they thought I was too denominational, and others because I wasn't denominational enough. Some found me too Calvinistic and others too Armenian. Some people have left because our church was too small, and others because we're too large. Seems like I'm always losing people; and it's only by the grace of God that our church has grown at all.

Of course, some of our growth has been from people who have left other churches to try ours. If I were honest, I'd say that this doesn't bother me as badly. Still, my gains are someone else's losses, and every loss hurts. All in all, this is one of the most discouraging aspects of pastoring. Today's attenders are consumer-driven, and it doesn't take much for them to leave without a backward glance. I read one survey that said a third of all current church members will be in a different church within three years.

The secret is knowing how to lose your members without losing your morale—or your mind. The Bible counsels pastors on this subject, and I'd like to offer four verses that may be of help.

2 Chronicles 1:10: *Now Give Me Wisdom*

Sometimes we lose people unnecessarily. A little wisdom, diplomacy, tact, empathy, and understanding would have saved many an upset member. Last year, during a period of exhaustion, we faced a vexing issue in our congregation, and in personal conversations I overreacted a few times, snapping at people. On one occasion, I had an acrimonious conversation with a member. But we got together to talk it over, and I explained to him the pressures of church work, the difficulties of keeping people happy, the sting of criticism, and the burdens of my heart. I also apologized for snapping at him. His attitude instantly changed, and from that day he's been one of my best supporters.

Many times members leave because we needlessly upset them. James invites us to ask God for wisdom, for we're in a work that requires the sage of Solomon.

John 6:36: *Do You Also Want to Go Away?*

Having said that, not even the wisdom of One-Greater-than-Solomon could stave off attrition. Our Lord preached one ill-received sermon and lost virtually His whole crowd. If He, possessing endless wisdom, lost members, we'll probably not do much better. A growing ministry will always be shrinking in the process of growing; and sometimes it's God's way of clearing out the logjam so that real progress can be made. I've been grateful for some occasional "blessed reductions."

2 Chronicles 25:9: *The Lord Is Able to Give You Much More Than This*

Third, remember that God is able to send replacements. Through the years, I've made it a practice, when I lose a family for some reason or another, to pray this prayer: "Lord, give me two families to replace the one that left." I've found the Lord faithful to do this, and I recommend the practice to you.

In the process, don't grow bitter or burn bridges. I've lost many families who discovered the grass wasn't greener elsewhere

Continued on the next page

HELPS FOR THE PASTOR'S FAMILY—*Continued*

after all, and who ended up back in their old seats months or years later. Sometimes people become their own replacements.

Acts 20:28: *Take Heed to Yourself*

Finally, remember what Paul told the Ephesian elders: Take care of yourself. When a leader walks into your office and says, "Pastor, I'm leaving the church," take a little time off to process the hurt. No one else understands the pain a pastoral couple feels when their ministry has been rejected by others. A relationship is lost, and you need time to process the grief. It's hard not to take these things personally, because they often center upon our actions or failures. You might need to leave the office for the afternoon, or take a day or two off. Sometimes we need some time away to heal and regain our strength.

But don't quit pressing forward or lose your vision. Churches change; and if they don't change by growing, they will change by dying. Do your best to help people adapt to healthy change, and in the process pray for wisdom. Remember the example of the Lord. Ask God to redouble His blessings. And take care of yourself.

It's not your church anyway, but His.

MARCH 23, 2008

EASTER SUGGESTED SERMON

"He's Alive (But Don't Tell Anyone)"

Date preached:

Scripture: Matthew 27 and 28:1–10, especially 28:6–7
He is not here; for He is risen, as He said. Come, see the place where the Lord lay. And go quickly and tell His disciples that He is risen from the dead.

Introduction: Last year, 65 new roller coasters opened around the world, adding to hundreds in existence. The top coaster in the world is reportedly the Kingda Ka at Six Flags in New Jersey. It goes from 0 to 138 miles an hour in four seconds and has a completely vertical drop. I know of only one more dramatic ride: Matthew 27 and 28, and the roller coaster of emotions connected with the death and resurrection of Jesus Christ. I describe it as a roller coaster because I want us to experience the ups and downs of that weekend, from the depths of horror to the heights of joy. I'd like to ask you three questions:

1. **Were You There When They Crucified My Lord (Matt. 27:35–39)?** Experience the grief. Can you imagine the sorrow of His loved ones as they gazed at His battered body exposed on the Cross? The crosses that adorn churches today are polished and smooth. But the Romans split rough wood for Calvary. It was jagged, filled with splinters, and perhaps crawling with insects. When the scourged backside of Christ was forced onto the Cross, the full weight of His body exposed Him to the tortures of the wood. He was bearing the ugly pain of sin for us (see Is. 53).

2. **Were You There When They Laid Him in the Tomb (Matt. 27:57–66)?** Experience the despair. Can you imagine the depression of that black weekend? His family and friends suffered multiple blows. Their dearest had died. He had died young and under torture before their very eyes. They had deserted Him and were overwhelmed, not only with grief, but with guilt. They had also lost their religion, for they had based their eternal destiny and spiritual hope on His Messiah-ship. Virtually everything in their lives had collapsed, and the blackness of despair had fallen over them like the edge of night.

3. **Were You There When He Rose Up from the Grave (Matt. 18:1–10)?** Experience the Joy. Can you imagine the intoxicating exuberance that dawned Easter Sunday? The Resurrection of Christ is biblically logical and theologically necessary. None of us would have invented a story like this, but as we look back on it we can see the genius of God in the plan devised from the foundation of the world. God was in Christ defeating sin and Satan, and destroying death and despair forever. No wonder the angels said, "Go and spread the news!" Can you imagine the impossibility of keeping this a secret?

Marty Halyburton's husband, Porter, was shot down during the Vietnam War, and Navy representatives came to her home to tell her he had died in action. For several days, Marty was too numb to react. Flags flew at half-staff all over town, and a grave-marker was placed in Porter's memory in the family cemetery. Eighteen months passed, and though Marty tried to adjust to her loss, it was very hard. Then one day, a group of military experts appeared again at her house, this time with dramatic news. Porter was alive, in relatively good condition, being held by the North Vietnamese. Marty's emotions leaped as if on a roller coaster. But they told her to keep the information to herself for fear of reprisals against the POWs if the news got out. It was impossible to do. How do you hide the sparkle in your eyes, the bounce in your step, the smile on your face? How do you hide the sudden transformation of your personality? How do you talk to friends without blurting out the news? In the end, the Navy realized this and made it easier by officially changing Porter's status, and Marty phoned everyone she could with the life-changing news: "He's alive!"

Conclusion: The joy of the Resurrection is irrepressible. You can't keep it hidden. We should live out that joy every day; and we can do it by giving our lives without reservation to our Lord. What Jesus Christ did was very public before the entire world, but it's very personal to each of us. In His omniscience, I believe Christ had in mind every individual in the world who needed or would ever need redemption. He was thinking of you, and today He is calling you to become His follower. He wants to forgive your sins, heal your hurts, and give you everlasting life.

STATS, STORIES, AND MORE

Go Quickly and Tell

The far-famed preacher, Robert G. Lee, told of a terrible train wreck that occurred near Kinston, North Carolina. An excursion train plunged into an open draw bridge on the Elizabeth River, and eighteen passengers were killed or drowned. An inquiry to determine the cause of the accident heard from the signal man and from the engineer. The signal man swore under oath that he had waved a red flag, signaling the train to stop. The engineer, however, swore that the flag had been white, indicating full speed ahead. The mystery was solved when the flag was recovered and presented as evidence. It was a red flag, but it had become so faded in time that it would have appeared white from a distance. "Many Christians have become like a faded flag that fails to convey God's message of warning to imperiled men," said Lee. "Oh, the wrecks that have resulted from the unfaithfulness of those whose Christianity is a faded flag."[1]

Do "dying sayings" interest you? It's intriguing to compare the final moments of Christians to those without Him. The last words of Thomas Carlyle, the famous Scottish writer, was: *I am as good as without hope . . . a sad old man gazing into the final chasm.* Compare that with the dying words of evangelist D. L. Moody: *Earth recedes! Heaven opens before me. This is no dream . . . It is beautiful! It is like a trance! If this is death, it is sweet! God is calling me, and I must go!* Easter changes the way we look at both life and death. When the Bible says that Christ is the firstfruits of those who sleep, it means He is the first of many to be resurrected. "Firstfruits" refers to the earliest ingathering of crops. It indicates there's a greater harvest coming. Jesus was the first of those to be resurrected, and because He lives, we shall live also. As Charles Wesley put it in his great hymn: "Lives again our glorious King, / Where, O death, is now thy sting? / Dying once He all doth save, / Where thy victory, O grave? Alleluia!"

—Dr. David Jeremiah

APPROPRIATE HYMNS AND SONGS

"Christ the Lord Is Risen Today," Charles Wesley, Public Domain.

"I Stand Amazed," Dennis Jernigan, 1991 Shepherd's Heart Music.

"How Deep the Father's Love for Us," Stuart Townend, ThankYou Music.

"Worthy Is the Lamb," Darlene Zschech, 2000 Hillsong Publishing.

"Up from the Grave He Arose," Robert Lowry, Public Domain.

---

[1]Robert G. Lee, *Robert G. Lee's Sourcebook of 500 Illustrations* (Grand Rapids: Zondervan Publishing House, 1964), p. 75.

FOR THE BULLETIN

Johann Sebastian Bach, two days old and the youngest in a family of German musicians, was baptized on March 23, 1685. He later became one of Christianity's greatest musicians whose life's purpose was to create "well-regulated church music to the glory of God." When he sat down to compose he often scribbled *J.J.* on his blank pages: *Jesu Juva—Help me, Jesus.* At the manuscript's end, he jotted *S.D.G.—Soli Deo Gloria*—to God alone, the glory. ● On March 23, 1743, Handel's *Messiah* opened in London. ● March 23, 1797, Missionary William Carey, concerned about his lack of converts, wrote his friend Andrew Fuller: *I am sure the work of God must prevail . . . I know there are only two real obstacles in any part of the earth, viz., a want of the Bible, and the depravity of the human heart.* ● March 23, 1839, marks the first recorded time the letters "OK" were used, meaning *oll korrect,* in the Boston *Morning Post.* ● March 23, 1891, marks the birth of radio Bible teacher, Dr. M. R. DeHaan in Zeeland, Michigan. ● On March 23, 1925, Tennessee became the first state to forbid the teaching of evolution. Teacher John Scopes ignored the ban and was prosecuted later in what became known as "The Monkey Trial." ● On March 23, 1966, the Archbishop of Canterbury, Arthur Michael Ramsey, exchanged public greetings with Pope Paul VI in Rome—the first official meeting between heads of the Anglican and Roman Catholic churches in over 400 years.

WORSHIP HELPS

Call to Worship
. . . knowing that Christ, having been raised from the dead, dies no more. Death no longer has dominion over Him. For the death that He died, He died to sin once for all; but the life that He lives, He lives to God. Likewise you also, reckon yourselves to be dead indeed to sin, but alive to God in Christ Jesus our Lord (Rom. 6:9–11).

An Ancient Hymn
We have a handful of hymns that we sing every year at Easter. But earlier eras of Christian history wrote and sang many hymns that have been lost to us. Today I'd like to choose one of them to quote (or sing or use as an antiphonal reading). It is entitled "Praise the Savior Now and Ever" and was penned by Venantius Honorius Clementianus Fortunatus (c. 530–609). You can find this in its full version and many other hymns at www.cyberhymnal.org:

Praise the Savior now and ever;
Praise Him, all beneath the skies;
Prostrate lying, suff'ring, dying
On the cross, a sacrifice.
Vict'ry gaining, life obtaining,
Now in glory He doth rise.

An Idea for Guests

Why not prepare an audio CD of your Easter service in advance for your visitors? If you have access to a recording studio, you can record portions of the liturgy, perhaps some of the music, and your pre-preached sermon. A little opening and closing music, and as your guests leave, you can hand each of them a portable version of the service for as little as two or three dollars each.

Benediction

Remind us, O Lord, that every day is Easter for the Christian, and may we live in the power of Your Resurrection all day, all week, all year, all our lives, and forever!

Additional Sermons and Lesson Ideas

The Easter Angels

Date preached:

SCRIPTURE: Matthew 28:1–10

INTRODUCTION: Just as the birth of Christ as accompanied by angels, so was His Resurrection.

1. The Angel's Mission (vv. 1–6). The body of Jesus Christ apparently returned to life unseen in the darkness of that Middle Eastern tomb, rising out of His burial shroud and physically and miraculously passed through the sealed, stone door of the tomb without the guards even knowing He was gone. As the women approached the tomb, an angel descended, touched down with an earthquake, and rolled away the stone—not so that the body of Jesus Christ could get out of the tomb, but so that the women, the guards, the disciples, and all the world could go in and see for themselves that it was empty.
2. The Angel's Message (vv. 5–7). The word *angel—angelos*—literally means *messenger*. I suppose the happiest assignment ever given to any angel was the joyful task of announcing the Resurrection of Jesus Christ.
3. The Angel's Master (vv. 8–10). The risen, reigning Christ is who we want to see! The human heart has a natural hunger that only Jesus Christ can fill.

CONCLUSION: I wonder if anyone here today has a hungry heart? The reason Christ died is so that we might live, and the reason He rose again is that we might serve a Risen Savior.

The Manifestation and Sermon of Christ After His Resurrection

Date preached:

Adapted from a message by Dr. Martin Luther

SCRIPTURE: Luke 24:36–47

INTRODUCTION: Since the Lord has commanded those who preach the gospel to be steadfast in proclaiming the Resurrection, we must dwell upon it more and more.

1. The Manifestation of Christ After His Resurrection (vv. 36–44). The disciples gathered in seclusion, afraid of the Jews and in danger of their lives. They were fearful and fainthearted. The Resurrection serves to comfort and refresh the poor, sorrowing, and terrified conscience. He stands today in the midst of the weak and fainthearted, though He is strong and mighty. He says: "Come, and learn from Me."

2. The Sermon Christ Preached to His Disciples (vv. 45–47). We preach repentance and remission of sins. Repentance is our part, signifying a change of the whole life. Remission is God's part. In Christ the sins of all the world are swallowed up. He suffered death to put away sin from us, and arose to devour it and blot it out.

CONCLUSION: Thus you have heard what the gospel is, and what repentance and forgiveness of sins are. Take heed and be His.

PRAYER FOR THE PASTOR'S CLOSET

Almighty God, do Thou grant unto us light in which to read Thy word. Thou didst write the book for us, now do Thou tell us what it means, that the heart may be won, that our whole being may go out after Thee as after a fountain of living waters. —Dr. Joseph Parker

MARCH 30, 2008

The Ring of Authority

Date preached:

By Dr. Timothy K. Beougher

Scripture: Mark 1:21–34, especially from verses 22, 27
And they were astonished at His teaching, for He taught them as one having authority . . . with authority He commands even the unclean spirits, and they obey Him.

Introduction: Power has always held fascination for human beings. For
some individuals, the pursuit of power is an all-consuming passion. As
fallen human beings, we have a tendency to worship those with power,
and to covet power for ourselves. We, however, do not have the right
to ultimate power. We see in Jesus' ministry, power as God intended
it to be used. We see power used not to call attention to itself, but to
point to the mercy of God and to call people to Him. In this passage,
the Greek word for power can be translated "the right to exercise power."

1. **Christ's Authority Expressed in His Teaching (vv. 21–22).**

    A. **Context for Christ's Teaching (v. 21).** Capernaum was a small
    town on the northwest shore of the Sea of Galilee. If you visit
    Capernaum today you can see the remains of a second-century
    synagogue which probably was built on the sight of the original
    synagogue in which Jesus preached. The synagogue was a place
    for reading the Scriptures, praying and worshiping God. In the
    synagogues, it was customary to ask visiting rabbis to read
    the Scriptures and teach, which explains why Jesus had such
    freedom to minister in the synagogues.

    B. **Content of Christ's Teaching (v. 22).** The phrase "they were as-
    tonished," literally means they were struck with panic or shock.
    The text tells us why: "He taught them as one having authority,
    and not as the scribes." When the scribes taught, they always
    appealed to other authorities beyond themselves. They would say
    something like, "According to Rabbi Gamaliel, or Rabbi Hillel,
    or Rabbi Shammai, or Rabbi Eleazar, etc." and then they would

teach. However, Jesus simply stood up and said, "This is the way it is." There was no appeal to Rabbi so-and-so. His words were absolute authority and the people could sense that. The scribes spoke *from* authority, but Jesus spoke *with* authority. As believers today, we stand in Jesus' authority as set forth the Scriptures.

2. **Christ's Authority Expressed in His Power Over Satan (vv. 23–26).** We are not told a lot about the demon-possessed man in these verses, but we do know that the light of Jesus' teaching was too much for the unclean spirits. Notice how the demon knew exactly who Jesus was, identifying Him as "the Holy One of God" (v. 24)! The phrase, "Did You come to destroy us?" in the context it is not really a question, but a statement, a rhetorical question. It could be phrased, "You have come to destroy us, haven't You?" The answer is yes (cf. 1 John 3:8)! Jesus is still in the business of delivering people from the power of the evil one. This plays out supremely in salvation, when the stronghold of sin is broken!

3. **The People's Amazement Expressed in Their Response (vv. 27–28).** These verses tell us that "immediately His fame spread throughout all the region around Galilee" (v. 28). How did this happen? People went and told others! Jesus is with us today! His authority rests with us! What implication does this have for us? We who have experienced the wonder of Christ's authority in our lives, through the power of His Word and His deeds, need to be sharing the wonder of Christ with others!

4. **Christ's Authority Expressed in Healing (vv. 29–34).** Jesus had taught in the synagogue and cast out demons; He could have claimed the right to rest after the exhausting service, but instead He gave of Himself for others. He healed Peter's mother-in-law (vv. 29–31) and even continued His ministry well into the night to help others (v. 32). Ministry can't always be done when it is convenient. People are important to God and should be important to us! Are we committed to serving others?

Application:

1. **The Importance of Regular Attendance at Worship.** Think of those who chose to stay home the day "God showed up" at church (vv. 21–22)!

We always worship God, but at times He really shows up in power! I don't want to miss that when it happens!

2. **The Priority of the Word of God.** God's Word, not experience must be our authority.

   We need to know it and to live it.

3. **Take Your Problems to Jesus!** Peter felt the freedom to share his need with Jesus, and so should we.

STATS, STORIES, AND MORE

More from Dr. Beougher—Who's Your Authority?
Four sources of authority that people tend to rely upon are:

  1. The Bible: the supreme authority.
  2. Tradition: this is the way we have always done it.
  3. Reason: it makes sense to me.
  4. Experience: it seems good based on my experience.

Throughout the centuries, Christians have held that while each of these four sources have input into our decision-making, ultimately the Bible is our source of authority. We must filter our experience through Scripture, not change Scripture to fit our experience. There comes a time when standing for the truth means going against the culture, and that isn't easy.

Paul warned believers in 2 Timothy 4:3: "For the time will come when they will not endure sound doctrine, but according to their own desires, because they have itching ears, they will heap up for themselves teachers." This describes a common occurrence: preachers and teachers who are more concerned about what other people *think* than about what God *knows*.

Could I speak very personally? James 3:1 is, to me, the scariest verse in the Bible: "My brethren, let not many of you become teachers, knowing that we shall receive a stricter judgment." I take my responsibility very seriously. I study, I pray, and I seek to be faithful to proclaim what God's Word says, not what our culture might want it to say. One day I will have to give an account of my life, and so will you for your life. As I preach, as you talk to others, we are to do so, not based on our own authority but on His authority.

APPROPRIATE HYMNS AND SONGS

"All Hail the Power of Jesus' Name," Edward Perronet, John Rippon, Oliver Holden, Public Domain.

"His Strength Is Perfect," Jerry Salley and Steven Curtis Chapman, 1988 Sparrow Song; Careers—BMG Music Pub. Inc.; Greg Nelson Music.

"All Glory Laud and Honor," John Mason Neal, Melchior Teschner, Theodulph of Orleans, Public Domain.

"The Power of the Cross," Keith Getty & Stuart Townend, 2005 ThankYou Music.

FOR THE BULLETIN

March 30, 1135, is the birthday of Moses Maimonides, Jewish philosopher, born in Spain. He is regarded as the foremost intellectual figure of medieval Judaism. ● March 30, 1533, Thomas Cranmer became archbishop of Canterbury, setting the stage for the English Reformation. ● Sicke Freerks, more commonly known as Sicke the Snyder (Tailor), was condemned on March 30, 1531, for his views on baptism. The court record reads: ". . . to be executed by the sword; his body shall be laid on the wheel, and his head set on a stake, because he has been rebaptized and perseveres in that baptism." Freeks was executed in Leeuwarden, the Netherlands. His martyrdom prompted a Dutch priest named Menno Simons to begin studying the Scriptures about baptism. Simons later renounced the Roman Catholic Church and became a leader of the Anabaptist movement in the Netherlands. ● Dr. Thomas Coke was a zealous young Anglican curate in the Parish Church of South Petherton, England, who, to the annoyance of his flock, came under the evangelical influence of John Wesley and the Methodists. On Sunday morning, March 30, 1777, following his sermon, there was an interruption in the service. It was announced that the vicar had dismissed his curate, forbidding him to preach in his church again. Suddenly the bells in the old tower burst into a discordant clanging, so that Dr. Coke was unable to respond. The next Sunday found him standing in the village marketplace, preaching in the open air. He later became one of Methodism's greatest leaders.

WORSHIP HELPS

Call to Worship

And the twenty-four elders and the four living creatures fell down and worshiped God who sat on the throne, saying, "Amen! Alleluia!" Then a voice came from the throne, saying, "Praise our God, all you His servants and those who fear Him, both small and great! And I heard, as it were, the voice of a great multitude, as the sound of many waters and as the sound of mighty thunderings, saying, Alleluia! For the Lord God Omnipotent reigns (Rev. 19:4–6)!

Kid's Talk

Before this kid's talk, find two identical boxes and place a pack of chewing gum in one, and in the other place a small stalk of broccoli (cut to similar weight as the pack of gum). Seal both boxes and write a number 1 on the first and number 2 on the second. Write down which item goes with which box on some paper and bring these materials with you. At the service, ask for three volunteers. Give one of the volunteers your sheet of paper revealing which item is in which box. Tell the other volunteers that they should shake both boxes and try to figure out which box contains the gum. The third volunteer is not allowed to shake the boxes, but receives the contents of the box he or she chooses. Before choosing a box, he or she is allowed to ask *only one* of the other two volunteers which box is correct. Allow the other children to suggest which person he or she should ask: the one with the paper containing the answer, or the one who shook the boxes and has a guess. After this exercise, explain that not everyone believes in God, so they often take guesses as to how we should live. That's why there's so much hurt in the world, because everyone wants to live by their own rules. But Jesus has given us all the answers we need about how to live and please God; it's written down in our Bibles. We should always look to the One that we know has the right answer!

Additional Sermons and Lesson Ideas

The Extraordinary Christian
By Dr. Michael A. Guido

Date preached:

SCRIPTURE: Psalm 1:1–3

INTRODUCTION: The greatest enemy of the world isn't the worst, it's the good. Don't be content to be an ordinary Christian. Be an extraordinary Christian and you'll be a happy Christian. You get a good picture of one in the first psalm.

1. The Extraordinary Christian Is Separated from the World (v. 1). Like our Lord, we should be different but not distant; consistent, not capricious. You'll never move the world if you're moved by the world.
2. The Extraordinary Christian Is Saturated in the Law of the Lord (v. 2). In what is your delight, the Word or the world?
3. The Extraordinary Christian Sends Forth His Fruit in Season (v. 3). What is the fruit of the Christian? New Christians! When is the last time you have shared the gospel, or even thought about the salvation of others?

CONCLUSION: Being extraordinary is actually quite simple: be separate from the world, saturated in the Word, and sending forth the gospel of Christ.

Getting It Right When You've Done It All Wrong
By Dr. Larry Osborne

Date preached:

SCRIPTURE: Psalm 51

INTRODUCTION: We all struggle with this thing called sin (doing what we know we shouldn't and failing to do what we know we should). We can learn from Scripture how to deal with our sin. David, in Psalm 51, shows us how to do what the Bible calls repentance:

1. Face the Facts (vv. 1–5).
2. Ask God to Change You from the Inside Out (vv. 6–12).
3. Accept God's Forgiveness (vv. 13–19).

CONCLUSION: Is there anything in your life you haven't faced up to yet? Are you running from your sin or trying to change yourself? Follow the example given here in Scripture and experience the restoration God has provided through Jesus Christ.

APRIL 6, 2008

A Constant Temptation

Date preached:

By Rev. Melvin Tinker

Scripture: Hebrews 3:1—4:16, especially 4:15–16
For we do not have a High Priest who cannot sympathize with our weaknesses, but was in all points tempted as we are, yet without sin. Let us therefore come boldly to the throne of grace, that we may obtain mercy and find grace to help in time of need.

Introduction: I wonder how many here today have close friends or relatives whom we have seen walk away from the Christian faith, whether they outright rebel or their religious fervor simply dies out. People fail to realize that the Christian faith is a journey, not instant access to perfection. When that fact is ignored or downplayed, disillusionment sets in as well as the temptation to return to our old way of life. Clearly that was the temptation facing the believers in Hebrews chapter 2:2. The root cause of this spiritual drift is a failure to take God at His Word. So our writer, with all the tenderness and compassion of a caring pastor, issues a spiritual health warning as he diagnoses the cause, consequences, and the cure for unbelief:

1. **The Cause of Unbelief (3:7–15).** The main burden of this passage is a penetrating one, namely, make sure that we who call ourselves Christians and follow Jesus do not make the same mistake as those who were called Israelites and followed Moses. The writer tells us about this mistake by quoting Psalm 95, no less than three times, so it must be important: "Today if you will hear His voice, do not harden your hearts as in the rebellion, in the day of trial in the wilderness, where your fathers tested Me, tried Me, and saw My works forty years" (Heb. 3:7–9). Now do you see the cause of unbelief? It is a hardened heart, which is a rebellious heart, one which does not know God's ways. They heard God but they did not obey God. If belief is not backed up by behavior it is only a matter of time before the belief itself evaporates like the morning mist in the noonday sun.

2. **The Consequences of Unbelief (3:18—4:13).** According to the book of Genesis, which our writer quotes in 4:4, the seventh day was

unlike any other day. All the other days were concluded with the words, "there was evening and there was morning" or some variation. However, this is not so on the seventh day. The implication is that from this point on the whole condition of the world was one of rest: not inactivity, but harmony, wholeness, pure delight, shalom. In Genesis 3 this paradise was disrupted by sin, and every ill of this world is a direct result of that. The remaining story of the Bible is about God's plan to restore that "rest." We have to make every effort to enter that rest (v. 11). There is no freewheeling into heaven and the new creation. And although we may fool others and even fool ourselves into thinking that we are believers when we are not, we do not fool God (vv. 12–13). The question that matters is not: "Did you believe? But, "Are you obediently trusting Him now?"

3. **The Cure for Unbelief (4:14–16).** We have a fantastic encouragement to press on, which is the cure for unbelief! You may be thinking: "Well, it is easier said than done. You have no idea of the pressures I am under from home, work, and friends. There are times I do have my doubts. Life is a struggle sometimes and I am just plain tired." Perhaps I don't know how you feel; but verses 15 and 16 tell us without a doubt that there is Someone who does! Jesus can fully relate to how you feel. When on earth, how did He overcome His testing? By believing and obeying God's Word. He trusted that what His heavenly Father said was true. He found His promises did hold up when all others failed. And if that Word was good enough for Him, then surely it is good enough for us. So instead of looking back, we are encouraged to look up in verse 16: "Let us therefore come boldly to the throne of grace, that we may obtain mercy and find grace to help in time of need."

Conclusion: God knows how you feel and He cares. From the funeral to the factory. From the home to the office. So do not make the mistake of abandoning Him, He so wants to hold on to you and to speak to you. The question is: Will you hear His voice today and follow Him?

STATS, STORIES, AND MORE

More from Rev. Tinker

She was a bright young woman, a keen Christian, too. She arrived at University full of zest and zeal. Later she was to lead several friends to faith in Christ. She became leader of a Bible study and was slated as the next vice president of the Christian Union. But gradually, almost imperceptibly, she began to change. Her attendance at church became erratic. In time, she started to spend as much time in the student union bar as she had previously spent in the student Christian Union. She also struck up a relationship with a non-Christian. I was asked to go and see her. When I met her, the face that had previously been bright and beaming was now sour and stressed. I gently asked her: Why? Why the change? She replied: "Melvin, I have become disillusioned. I thought that being a Christian would mean an easy life. But to be honest I have found things rather difficult. I have had real struggles and I have decided it's simply not worth it."

This is a story that has been repeated over and over; and no matter how long you are in the ministry, the pain of seeing someone slipping from the faith never lessens. Of course, there are many reasons that can be put forward as to why this sort of thing happens. But one of the main reasons is the failure to remember that Christians are on an arduous journey which begins in this world and will not be completed until we reach the next. —*Rev. Melvin Tinker*

APPROPRIATE HYMNS AND SONGS

"Guide Me, O Thou Great Jehovah," John Hughes, Peter Williams, & William Williams, Public Domain.

"He Leadeth Me," Joseph Gilmore & William Bradbury, Public Domain.

"Forever," Chris Tomlin, 2001 worshiptogether.com songs (Admin. by EMI Christian Music Pub.), Sixsteps Music.

"Let It Rise," Holland Davis, 1997, 1999 Maranatha Praise, Inc.

"You Are Holy (Prince of Peace)," Mark Imboden & Tammi Rhoton, 1994 Imboden Music (Admin. by Music Services), Martha Jo Publishing (Admin. by Music Services).

FOR THE BULLETIN

On April 6, 1415, the Synod of Constance issued what was called "the most revolutionary document in the world"—the *Sacrosancta*—declaring its own authority over popes. In the end, the popes won the dispute, but only after years of struggle. ● The artist, Raphael, died on his 37th birthday, April 6, 1520. ● On April 6, 1735, the first Moravians from Europe arrived in America as part of their great missionary advance. Invited by Governor James Oglethorpe, ten males of the *Unitas Fratrum* landed in Savannah, Georgia. ● Today is the birthday of Edmund Hamilton Sears, author of "It Came Upon A Midnight Clear." He was born in 1810. ● On April 6, 1830, Joseph Smith organized the first church of Latter Day Saints in Fayette, New York. ● James Augustine Healy, the first black Roman Catholic bishop in America, was born to an Irish planter and a slave on a plantation near Macon, Georgia, on April 6, 1830. ● The first modern Olympic Games opened in Athens, Greece, on this day in 1896. ● On April 6, 1923, athlete Eric Liddell shared his testimony with a group of about eighty men in Armadale, Scotland. "It wasn't a speech at all," someone later wrote. "It was more of a quiet chat, and in his slow clear words, Eric for the first time in his life told the world what God meant to him." It was his debut in public evangelism. Liddell later became famous as an Olympic champion and as an outspoken Christian missionary who died in 1945 during the Japanese occupation of China.

Quote for the Pastor's Wall

I knew an old minister once . . . How I envy him . . . I am listed as a famous home-runner, yet beside that obscure minister, who was so good and so wise, I never got to first base!

—Babe Ruth

WORSHIP HELPS

Call to Worship

Though the fig tree may not blossom,
Nor fruit be on the vines;
Though the labor of the olive may fail,
And the fields yield no food;
Though the flock may be cut off from the fold,
And there be no herd in the stalls—
Yet I will rejoice in the LORD,
I will joy in the God of my salvation.
The LORD God is my strength;
He will make my feet like deer's feet,
And He will make me walk on my high hills (Hab. 3:17–19).

Pastoral Prayer

Father in heaven, we beg for Your strength to endure the
journey set before us. We ask that Your Spirit would constantly
guide, convict, and comfort us. Help us not to forget that faith
in You is not temporary, but daily. Restore our strength; renew
our faith; revive our fervor. Guide us into Your rest. We pray
through Him whose name is above every name: it is in Jesus'
name we pray. Amen.

Benediction

And behold, I am coming quickly, and My reward is with Me, to
give to every one according to his work. I am the Alpha and the
Omega, the Beginning and the End, the First and the Last.
Blessed are those who do His commandments, that they may
have the right to the tree of life, and may enter through the
gates into the city (Rev. 22:12–14).

Additional Sermons and Lesson Ideas

Thank God for Pressure

SCRIPTURE: 2 Corinthians 1:1–11

INTRODUCTION: Today's world is full of pressure. Paul wrote 2 Corinthians in response to the pressures he faced. Yet, while he detailed his stress points in 2 Corinthians, he also sounded a note of triumph. The first word in the body of the book is *Praise*.

1. Pressure Leads to God's Comfort (vv. 3–4). "Praise be to God who comforts us in all our troubles." He often comforts us by giving us promises or truths from His Word in times of distress.
2. Pressure Equips Us to Comfort Others (vv. 4–5). We recycle our comfort, our verse, our insights, and our lessons from the Lord.
3. Pressure Produces Patient Endurance (v. 6).
4. Pressure Teaches Us to Rely on God Who Raises the Dead (vv. 8–9). Troubles in life drive us to the promises of God, and as we focus on the promises our faith grows stronger.
5. Pressure Generates Prayer and Thanksgiving (vv. 10–11).

CONCLUSION: What pressures have been weighing on you lately? I challenge you to make them into a prayer list, take them home, and spend some time before the Lord in praise and trust Him with the results.

The Great Problem of Loneliness
By Rev. Billie Friel

SCRIPTURE: 1 Kings 19:1–18

INTRODUCTION: Loneliness is one of the most lethal difficulties that we face. We can learn a lot about loneliness and how to handle it through the example of the great prophet, Elijah.

1. God's Physical Provision in Our Lives (vv. 1–8). After fleeing the threat on his life by Queen Jezebel (vv. 1–5), God first provided rest, food, and water for Elijah that supernaturally sustained him for 40 days and nights (vv. 5–8)!
2. God's Presence in Our Lives (vv. 11–12). By revealing Himself to Elijah, God proved His presence. God is always with us.
3. God's Purpose in Our Lives (vv. 15–16). God gave Elijah a purpose, just as He has for each of us. Get your mind off yourself and immerse yourself in service to others.
4. God's People About Our Lives (v. 18). God reminded Elijah that others still worshiped the one true God. We should all be an active part of God's family of faith!

CONCLUSION: God's physical provision, presence, purpose, and people guarantee that we are never alone.

Jars of Clay

There was a minister in New York City whose daily walk took him through a park where he regularly saw an old fellow sitting on a bench. The old man seemed forlorn and homeless. One day in a surge of compassion, the preacher handed him an envelope with ten dollars and a note saying "Never Despair."

As the preacher passed by the next day, the old man handed the envelope back. It contained sixty dollars. The old codger explained: "Never Despair was in the money paying six to one in the second race."

The old man wasn't homeless at all, but an illegal bookie. But the minister learned a lesson. We're winners whenever we make up our minds to Never Despair—though there are lots of moments when we feel a little desperate. Recent years have been tough for pastors around the world. One British pastor told me his church had been through a difficult time with two contrary opinions dividing the congregation. My friend didn't originate the problem but was caught in the middle, and it was so damaging to his nerves he had to take a two-month sabbatical.

Another pastor told me that his church had gotten into an argument about something—I never found out what—and had split, with over 200 people leaving to start another church.

At the same time I received a letter from a Midwestern pastor who made some superficial changes to the Sunday services. Afterward an elderly member asked him why he was tearing the church apart. The old man claimed a lot of people were upset. He himself had been attending the church for forty years, he said, but would not be back. The encounter took the life and spirit out of my young friend.

I've heard more stories like this in the past couple of years than ever before. We're living in times of high pressure, endless demands, and untold discouragement for those in ministry.

That's why the Lord gave us 2 Corinthians, a thirteen-chapter memoir on the stresses of ministry. It's the most autobiographical of Paul's writings. I've read 2 Corinthians many times over the past year or so because of pressures in my own pastoral work, and I've come to love the verse that says: *But we have this treasure in jars of clay to show that this all-surpassing power is from God and not from us* (2 Cor. 4:7 NIV).

The three critical words here suggest three essential attitudes we must adopt.

- ❧ Treasure: We should be happy.
- ❧ Clay: We should be humble.
- ❧ Power: We should be hopeful.

Treasure: We Should Be Happy

Let's start with the word *treasure*. We mustn't forget that Christ and His ministry are valuable assets entrusted to us. We're wealthy people, for, as verses 6 and 7 put it: *God, who said, "Let light shine out of darkness," made his light shine in our hearts to give us the light of the knowledge of the glory of God in the face of Christ. But we have this treasure . . .*

It makes a difference when we remember how rich we are. Simply put, there are two ways I can get out of bed on Sundays. Sometimes I wake up and ask myself, "Do I have the energy and ability to preach today? I needed more time to develop my sermon. I'm in a slump and need a vacation. I'm already tired, and I've not even started the day."

The other way is waking up to say, "I am preaching Christ today! I'm going to stand in the stead of God Himself so He can dispense truth and hope through me to those whom He has appointed to hear it. He has given me another opportunity to preach, and He will bless me as I faithfully do it. This is the day the Lord has made!"

When I go out on visitation, I'm tempted to think, "This is a hard job. I'm a little intimidated by this, and I'm weary. I could be spending this time with my family."

But the other way is saying: "Jesus and I are going visiting. Jesus and I are going to the hospital. Jesus and I are soul-winning.

Continued on the next page

THOUGHTS FOR THE PASTOR'S SOUL—*Continued*

Jesus and I are going to minister to that grief-stricken family. Jesus and I are going to see that shut-in. Oh, the joy and treasure of working side-by-side with Him today!"

That perspective makes all the difference. Dr. Gardiner Spring once said: "Oh, if ministers only saw the inconceivable glory that is before them, and the preciousness of Christ, they would not be able to refrain from going about, leaping and clapping their hands for joy, and exclaiming, I am a minister of Christ! I am a minister of Christ!"

Clay: We Should Be Humble

But the apostle adds a further point: *We have this treasure in jars of clay.* In Bible times, not having banks or safe repositories, people would bury their treasures in the earth or hide them in caves, often using clay jars, as we know from the discovery of the Dead Sea Scrolls. Paul uses this as an example of you and me. We are repositories for God's treasure, yet we are fragile, breakable, and easily damaged.

No matter how strong we think we are or how stoic we try to be, we are fragile people who break and are easily damaged. Perhaps you feel like a jar of clay that's been chipped, cracked, or broken. Someone has thrown a rock and shattered something inside you. Well, the benefit is that it keeps us humble. In fact, the rest of the verse makes this quite plain as we come to the third word—power.

Power: We Should Be Hopeful

The Lord could have made us vaults of steel or with chests of titanium, but He made us earthen vessels *to show that this all-surpassing power is from God.*

The word *all-surpassing* is the Greek word from which we get our English term *hyperbole*. It means *throwing beyond, excess, extraordinary amount, to an extreme degree.* The word *power* is that old classic term that occurs over 100 times in the New Testament and from which we get our English word *dynamite.* Paul used this word many times in 1 and 2 Corinthians, for example:

> ◈ 1 Corinthians 1:18—*For the message of the cross is foolishness to those who are perishing, but to us who are being saved it is the **power** of God* (NIV).

> ◈ 1 Corinthians 1:24—*But to those whom God has called, both Jews and Greeks, Christ the **power** of God and the wisdom of God* (NIV).

> ◈ 1 Corinthians 2:4–5—*My message and my preaching were not with wise and persuasive words, but with a demonstration of the Spirit's **power**, so that your faith might not rest on men's wisdom, but on God's power* (NIV).

The all-surpassing power that fuels our lives comes from an external source—from God Himself—so we can be resilient in the face of discouragement. He goes on to explain: *We are hard pressed on every side, but not crushed; perplexed, but not in despair; persecuted, but not abandoned; struck down, but not destroyed. We always carry around in our body the death of Jesus, so that the life of Jesus may also be revealed in our body. For we who are alive are always being given over to death for Jesus' sake, so that his life may be revealed in our mortal body* (2 Cor. 4:8–11 NIV).

It's God's power that keeps us going, and therefore nothing short of God can shut us down. We just do the work and trust Him with the results.

Once when an acquaintance praised Johann Sebastian Bach's rendition of a particular work, he replied, "There is nothing very wonderful about it. You have only to hit the right notes at the right moment and the instrument does all the rest."[1]

Similarly, Martin Luther once said, "I simply taught, preached, wrote God's Word . . . otherwise I did nothing . . . . The Word did it all."[2]

Several years ago when I was in one of those periods in which

Continued on the next page

---

[1] Patrick Kavanaugh, *The Spiritual Lives of Great Composers* (Nashville: Sparrow Press, 1992), p. 13.

[2] David L. Larson, *The Company of Preachers* (Grand Rapids: Kregel, 1998), p. 155.

THOUGHTS FOR THE PASTOR'S SOUL—*Continued*

I wondered if my ministry was making a difference, the thought came to me that I'm simply an extension cord, a piece of conduit, and that's all I need to be—nothing more. So I wrote a little verse entitled "I Can Do It If I'm Conduit," and perhaps it could become your prayer today:

It's not I, but it's Christ, in the pulpit today!
I'm a pipeline, a channel, a vessel of clay,
I am conduit through whom living currents are poured,
It's not I, but it's Christ, my Redeemer and Lord.

PRAYER FOR THE PASTOR'S CLOSET

O Lord,

Remit all my failings, shortcomings, falls, offenses, trespasses, scandals, transgressions, debts, sins, faults, ignorances, iniquities, impieties, unrighteousness, pollutions.

The guilt of them be gracious unto, pardon, remit, forgive, be propitious unto, spare, impute not, charge not, remember not the stain, pass by, pass over, disregard, overlook, hide, wash away, blot out, cleanse the hurt, heal, remedy, take off, remove, abolish, annul, disperse, annihilate; that they be not found, that they exist not.

Supply to faith, virtue; to virtue, knowledge; to knowledge, continence; to continence, patience; to patience, godliness; to godliness, brotherly love; to brotherly love, charity . . .

. . . that I forgot not my cleansing from my former sins, but give diligence to make my calling and election sure through good works.

Amen. —BISHOP LANCELOT ANDREWS (1555–1624)

APRIL 13, 2008

SUGGESTED SERMON

A Different King

Date preached:

By Rev. David Jackman

Scripture: Acts 17:1–7, especially from verses 3 and 7
. . . the Christ had to suffer and rise again from the dead . . . there is another king—
Jesus.

Introduction: Several years back I saw a poster that said, "Don't bother me with the facts; I've already made up my mind!" That expresses the difficulty that many of us feel when we have to contemplate change, especially when change threatens the most-loved ruts and tracks of our lives. The Christian message, however, is the message of revolutionary change! The book of Acts displays the major challenges the gospel presented to those who heard. In our passage today, we see that the gospel challenges established religion in the form of a Jewish synagogue.

Context: Thessalonica, as a port city with major Roman roads running through, was a melting pot of nationalities. The local Jewish population had proselytized many Greeks and women (cf. 17:4). Jewish teaching centered around keeping the commandments of the Old Testament, with the ultimate goal of reigning in Jerusalem with the Messiah as King. Achieving righteousness with God was simply a matter of climbing a religious ladder, following the commands and becoming good enough to be accepted. Against this backdrop, Paul drops the death charge of the gospel. Luke wants us to notice both what he says (his message) and how he says it (his method), because both are immensely powerful and both are immensely provoking. Let's look at the two as they're given in the passage:

1. **The Message (v. 3).** Paul explains and proves that the Christ had to suffer and rise from the dead. The natural response of most Jews would be the objection that the Christ was to put an end to their oppression, bring them to Jerusalem where they would reign with Him. Paul's explanation is that the Jews completely misinterpreted the message of Scripture! That's a bombshell, a highly provocative charge to these Jews. Paul explains that Christ brings together two essential ingredients, which Jews at that time kept separate. First,

the Messiah was the Suffering Servant who would suffer and die; and second He is the universal King who reigns forever in universal power. Paul showed that the Messiah does both.

2. **The Method (vv. 2–3).** Look at the verbs in these verses: Paul "reasoned" with them, "explaining" and "demonstrating." So clearly, Paul's message was a logical argument addressed to the minds of his hearers. The Christian gospel is not irrational. It transcends reason, but does not conflict with it. In our presentation of the gospel, we must always keep that in mind. Paul goes through the mind in order to activate the heart and will. That is conveyed in verse 4 in the verb "persuaded" to the point where they joined Paul and Silas. That's true conversion! If we truly believe in our minds, our hearts and wills motivate us to live according to that belief.

3. **The Response (vv. 5–7).** The remaining verses show the response of many when the gospel is preached in its true form. To those who refuse to believe, it challenges the very core of their religion. To the Jews, it assaulted the certainties of the synagogue; it challenged their complacency; and worse still it stole away their converts. Verse 5 tells us the Jews were jealous. It was too much to bear, having their proselytes converted by a renegade rabbi like Paul who preached a Messiah who was humiliated on a Roman cross. This exposes the "club" mentality of religion that is so easy for us to drift into. Once the idea that numbers are most important creeps in, we begin to bicker about particulars of our "inner circles," we become upset at transferring members, and we ostracize those who don't fit our preferences. This sets aside the gospel and introduces new "ladders" to climb. The glory of the Kingship of Jesus and the free grace of God is often set aside for arguments of church government, rituals, or any number of issues.

Conclusion: The gospel is not a matter of building a ladder to reach God, but of Jesus who climbed down the ladder to rescue us through His life, death, and resurrection. We may appeal to the kings and authorities of our day to keep our comfortable traditions in place, or we may accept the suffering of Jesus on our behalf and crown Him as King for eternity. The question is: which do we find the most persuasive?

STATS, STORIES, AND MORE

The story is told of a centenarian who, on his 100th birthday, was being interviewed by a young lady from a local television station. She wasn't getting very far because he was fairly deaf and uncooperative, but she was sent to make an interesting interview. Eventually she turned the interview to focus on his age. She said: "Well I suppose you've seen a lot of changes in the 100 years you've lived." The old man replied, "Yes, young lady, I have. And I'm proud to say I've been against every one of them!"

More from Rev. Jackman
The Jewish prophet Isaiah spoke of One who would be led like a lamb to the slaughter. He means that He will be an atoning sacrifice for sin, not just for the Jews but for the whole world. That's the only way to be right with God. He taught that God has not put up a ladder to climb to Him, but that God laid upon Jesus the sins of us all (Is. 53:6). Jesus carried our sins in His own body on the Cross; He had to suffer. But you see how that immediately pulls down the ladder of religion! It totally undermines rules for righteousness. It says you'll never be good enough for God. So, only through Jesus' suffering on the Cross and His Resurrection are we brought back into a right relationship with God. As the hymn says:

> *Bearing shame and scoffing rude,*
> *In my place condemned He stood;*
> *Sealed my pardon with His blood.*
> *Hallelujah! What a Savior!*
> —PHILLIP P. BLISS, *Hallelujah!*
> *What a Savior*, 1875

APPROPRIATE HYMNS AND SONGS

"We Will Glorify," Twila Paris, 1982 New Spring.

"Sing to the King," Billy Foote and Charles Silvester Horne, 2003 worshiptogether.com songs (Admin. by EMI Christian Music Publishing), Sixsteps Music.

"He Reigns," Peter Furler & Steve Taylor, 2003 Ariose Music (Admin. by EMI Christian Music Publishing), Soylent Tunes.

"Hallelujah Our God Reigns," Dale Garrett, 1972 Scripture in Song Maranatha Music (Admin. by Music Services).

FOR THE BULLETIN

On April 13, 1525, Reformer Ulrich Zwingli, rejecting the doctrine of transubstantiation, abolished the elaborate rite of the Mass in the Great Minster Church of Zurich in favor of the first evangelical communion service. ● On April 13, 1598, King Henry IV of France signed the Edict of Nantes, granting toleration to Protestant Huguenots. ● Jeanne Marie Bouvier de la Motte was born on this day in 1648 at Montargis, France, about fifty miles north of Paris. She later became known as Madam Guyon (pronounced Gay-yo), a celebrated French Mystic. ● On April 13, 1685, four Scottish women stood before the court at Wigtown accused of rebellion due to their Presbyterian views. They were forced to their knees for sentencing. Margaret MacLachlan, 70, was executed by drowning; Margaret Maxwell, 20, was publicly flogged; Margaret Wilson, 18, was drowned, and her sister Agnes, 13, was fined one hundred pounds. ● Handel's *Messiah* was first presented on this day in 1742, in Dublin, Ireland. ● Adoniram Judson Gordon, powerful Boston pastor and writer, was born on this day in 1836. Among his books is the moving little autobiographical volume, *When Christ Came to Church.* ● The most bitter fight in Charles Spurgeon's life was the "Downgrade Controversy" with the Baptist Union. He felt that some of the Baptist ministers were denying the basic tenets of Scripture. On April 13, 1888, five minutes before a critical session of the Baptist Union, the controversy was defused by a hastily developed plan on the part of Spurgeon's brother, James. It left no one satisfied.

PRAYER FOR THE PASTOR'S CLOSET

Now therefore, O God,
strengthen my hands.
—NEHEMIAH 6:9

WORSHIP HELPS

Call to Worship
"Hosanna to the Son of David! 'Blessed is He who comes in the name of the LORD!' Hosanna in the highest" (Matt. 21:9)!

Offertory Comments
John Wesley had three rules about money: "Make all you can. Save all you can. And give all you can." We realize that many people are no longer willing to give to a church simply because it is a church. They want to know their donation will make a difference and leave a mark on the world. I'd like to take a moment today to tell you how your contributions *are* making a difference. (Briefly describe to your congregation one of the ministries of your church, then say:) This is only one of the ministries made possible by our generously given dollars. Today as you give, ask the Lord to bless and use that gift to extend and strengthen the kingdom for Christ and His glory.

Pastoral Prayer
Lord Jesus, we thank You again for Your infinite mercy. We praise You that You, the Christ, had to suffer. We cannot take that in; we are amazed that You should condescend to come into our world to rescue us. We thank You for the Cross that spells forgiveness and reconciliation. Thank You for the risen Lord Jesus, that You have validated and vindicated Your claim through the resurrection from the dead. Thank You that today You are the King of kings and Lord of lords. So deliver us, Lord, from anything smaller than that, from any sort of "club" mentality, from all the human rules that want to obscure or confine the gospel. Send us out rejoicing in the freedom of being men and women who know the living Lord, the King Jesus. May our lives commend Him to others for Your name's sake, Amen.   —*Rev. David Jackman*

Additional Sermons and Lesson Ideas

Taming the Temper
By Dr. Michael A. Guido

Date preached:

SCRIPTURE: Various, especially Psalm 37:8

INTRODUCTION: When anger gets the best of you, it reveals the worst of you. Let's look at what Scripture has to say about anger:

1. Listen to the Command (Ps. 37:8): "Cease from anger, and forsake wrath . . ."
2. Look at the Curse (Gen. 4:4–11). Cain's anger motivated the first murder in the history of the world. God pronounced a great curse upon Cain and those who shed blood out of anger.
3. Look at the Cure:
   A. Confessing (1 John 1:9): When we confess our sins, we realize that Jesus had to pay for them. His love motivates true repentance.
   B. Committing (Ps. 37:8): Memorize Psalm 37:8; write it down; keep it close. A commitment to obey the Word of God will help you to avoid sin (Ps. 119:9).

CONCLUSION: Will you commit your life to Christ? Allow Him to tame your temper and live His life through you.

Listening to God
By Pastor Al Detter

Date preached:

SCRIPTURE: 1 Samuel 3:1–21

INTRODUCTION: The story of God's encounter with young Samuel teaches us five lessons for listening to God:

1. To Hear God, We Need a Servant's Spirit (vv. 1, 9–10). We can't be running our own lives.
2. To Hear God, We Need a Discerning Ear (vv. 4–8). We need to be able to pick out God's voice from the many voices out there.
3. To Hear God, We Need a Conducive Environment (vv. 3, 5–6, 9). We can't be in the clutter of noise and movement all the time.
4. To Hear God, We Need to Listen to God Rather Than Speak (v. 10). Most of the time, we do the talking and God does the listening. It needs to be the other way around.
5. To Hear God, We Need a Tolerance for Hard Truth (vv. 11–18). We must be willing to accept something difficult from God for what's best rather than what makes us feel good.

CONCLUSION: If we practice these five lessons, we'll hear clearly from God. Not to hear His voice on a regular basis is to court disaster.

Ten Ways to Protect Your Voice

For preachers, the little eight-inch connector between the head and shoulders is an all-important part of our body, for it contains our larynx and our livelihood. The voice is the preacher's stock-in-trade, and we should take care of it the way a reporter guards his sources or a cowboy minds his horse. Too many of us take our voices for granted, but with a little routine maintenance they can last longer, go further, and be more effective.

1. The single most important ingredient for a healthy voice is water. Good hydration is essential, and experts tell us to drink several large glasses of water each day. Water moistens the body's cells internally, and this ensures that the vocal folds (vocal cords) stay well-hydrated, which in turn reduces wear and tear as you speak. Moist vocal folds produce voicing with less effort than dry vocal folds. It's like keeping oil in your car's engine; without it, the parts rub together, creating a lot of viscosity and unnecessary wear on the motor. Two easy ways to increase your water intake are: (1) develop the practice of drinking a glass of water whenever you brush your teeth; and (2) order water when dining in restaurants.

2. It's also useful to inhale steam or vapor to moisten the vocal folds. That's the benefit of warm drinks. Many people think that hot beverages with lemon or honey help the throat directly, but the vocal folds actually don't come into contact with food and liquid when swallowing occurs. But the inhalation of steam and vapor do come into contact with the vocal folds since inhaled steam and vapor enter the lungs, passing by and contacting the vocal folds directly, and this is what soothes and calms the throat. (Since hot drinks do directly contact the throat, drinking them does benefit a sore throat, but a sore throat and damaged vocal folds are not the same thing.)

3. Lowering your caffeine intake also helps keep vocal folds hydrated. Excessive caffeine acts as a diuretic which dries out the

Continued on the next page

TECHNIQUES FOR THE PASTOR'S DELIVERY—*Continued*

vocal folds, dehydrating the cells, and may even aggravate reflux. An easy way to reduce caffeine for those who can't kick the habit altogether is to choose half-caffeinated coffee in the morning. You can either mix it yourself, or purchase specially prepared "half-caff" brands.

4. Avoid excessive and hard throat-clearing and coughing, which causes the vocal folds to bang together and will damage the mucosal (mucous) covering. Sometimes a good, hard swallow will do the trick.

5. When speaking loudly, be sure to speak from the lungs. If your throat is sore or hoarse after a sermon, it's a warning sign that you're straining your voice or tensing up when speaking. Remember that the act of speaking begins in the lungs as air is expelled and forced through the throat and out the mouth. To speak loudly, simply increase the amount of air passing out of the mouth.

6. For those suffering frequent allergies, consult a doctor or an allergist, who can tackle this problem medically. Many allergies can be treated with a system of regular injections, which saves you from taking medications that dry out your sinuses—and, in the process, dries out your throat. I'm not just talking about antihistamines. Even aspirin can result in excessive drying of the vocal folds, as can anti-reflux medications, antiviral agents, bronchodilators, central nervous system stimulants and depressives, corticosteroids, diuretics, hormones (androgen lowers the voice), and even vitamin C (excessive amounts can lead to excessive drying of the vocal folds). It's best to consult your doctor, allergist, pharmacist, or your ENT (ear, nose, and throat specialist) to find treatment options that protect your voice quality.

7. For individuals with heavy or thick mucous in the throat, it may be helpful to avoid dairy products, which ultimately can produce a thicker mucous that will sit on the vocal folds, causing an increased difficulty in voicing. This may also result in excessive throat clearing and coughing.

8. A trip to the doctor can also be crucial for your voice quality if you're suffering from reflux or GERD (gastroesophageal reflux disease), which occurs when stomach acid or fluids are regurgitated from the esophagus back into the throat. That irritates the throat and vocal folds, resulting in tenderness, soreness, and swelling. This can be caused by overeating, tight clothing around the waist, and spicy foods. Because this condition can cause direct damage to the vocal folds and throat, the public speaker must consider these problems important enough to seek medical advice sooner rather than later.

9. Don't yell, shout, scream, or holler. Reduce talking when your throat is hoarse, and don't try to hold conversations in loud places.

10. Warm up your voice before preaching. Billy Graham is famous for practicing *Yes! Yes! Yes!* in hotel rooms before preaching, to which his wife would sometimes shout *No! No! No!*

Have you ever noticed, when listening to various preachers, how different their voices are from one another? Some have deeply resonating voices that almost make the walls vibrate. Others are fast-pitched or high-toned. Some voices are gravelly, while others are velvet smooth. The Lord gave you the exact voice He wanted you to have. It's tailor-made for your ministry. No one else in the world has a voice quite like yours. So take care of it as a good steward, and it'll give you years of quality service for His glory.

APRIL 20, 2008

When Jesus Makes House Calls

Date preached:

Scripture: Acts 23:11
The following night the Lord stood by him and said, "Be of good cheer, Paul; for as you have testified for Me in Jerusalem, so you must also bear witness at Rome."

Introduction: A couple of years ago, Tony Dungy, coach of the Indianapolis Colts, suffered a tragic loss with the death of his 18-year-old son. At the same time, the Colts faltered during their final games and lost the chance to play in the Super Bowl. As players cleaned out their lockers, Dungy told them there is a difference between disappointment and discouragement. "We're disappointed by things that happen to us," he said, "but we can't let disappointment deteriorate into discouragement, and we can't let discouragement become depression." The heroes of the Bible faced the triple threat of disappointment, discouragement, and depression. In Acts 23, the apostle Paul was bewildered and disappointed. He had expected to launch a fourth missionary tour. Instead he found himself nearly killed by a mob, barely saved from scourging, and imprisoned (Acts 21—23). That's when the Lord Jesus stepped from the paradisiacal throne into the atmospherics of earth to stand beside Paul, telling him to be of good cheer. Jesus makes house calls (see 2 Tim. 4:16–17; John 16:32)! How do we cultivate a sense of the presence of Jesus in our lives?

1. **Peruse.** First, peruse this subject in the Bible, looking for verses about the omnipresence and the immediate presence of God in the universe and in our lives.

   A. **Begin with the *Omnipresent* Verses, About God's Measureless Immensity in the Universe** (see 1 Kin. 8:27; Jer. 23:23–24; Is. 66:1; and Ps. 139:7–10).

   B. **Review the *Presence* Verses** (see Ex. 33:14; Ps. 16:11; 46:1; 140:13; Acts 3:19; Heb. 6:18–19).

C. Check Out the *With Us* Verses (Is. 41:10; Gen. 28:13; Ps. 23:4; 46:7; Deut. 31:6; Matt. 1:23; 28:20; 2 Cor. 13:14).

D. Don't Forget the *Nearness* Verses (Deut. 4:7; Ps. 34:18; 73:28; 145:18; James 4:8; Heb. 10:22).

2. **Perceive.** In his book, *The Holy Spirit in Missions*, Dr. A. J. Gordon pointed out that Jesus said, "It is expedient for you that I go away; for if I go not away, the Comforter will not come; but if I go away, I will send Him unto you." Gordon said: "By Christ's ascent to the Father, and the Spirit's descent upon the disciples, the Church exchanged the presence of the Lord for His omnipresence." There's a sense in which the Holy Spirit communicates to us the presence of Jesus. Jesus Himself promised that where two or three gathered in His name, He would be there. We have an allowance to visualize this truth with sanctified imagination. Once on an airplane, I was seated with no one beside me, and as I studied my Bible I felt the Lord Jesus Himself in that empty seat, tutoring me in His Word. When I walk across a stage toward a microphone, I can sense Him walking with me as if to say, "I'll do the preaching today. All you have to do is open your mouth at the right times." Often when I'm on a visit, I sense Jesus knocking on the door with me and sitting down with the inquirer. When I retire at night, I can imagine the Lord on my bedside, hearing my prayers like a divine parent. These are not figments of my imagination; they are realities of my theology. God is described in the Bible as present but invisible (see Gen. 28:15–16). God is in this place, and we *should* know it. There's no reason we shouldn't conceptualize Him all the time.

3. **Pray.** We draw near to God in prayer (see Deut. 4:7 NIV). Come before His presence with thanksgiving (Ps. 95:2). What if you went through the day whispering out loud, "Thank You, Lord, for these socks I'm putting on, for my shoes, for my overcoat You've provided. Thank You for this job I have. Thank You for this school teacher I like. Thank You for helping me with this or that." The Bible says that He daily loads us with benefits. If we were more expressive with our thanksgiving, we'd recognize His presence more frequently. Maybe this is what the Bible means when it says, "Pray without ceasing."

Conclusion: There in his gloom and doom, Jesus came and stood by Paul and told him, "Be of good cheer." Do you know the Lord Jesus Christ as your Savior? Are you committed to Him, to do His will, to hear His voice, and to respond with faith and obedience?

Just when I need Him, Jesus is near,
Just when I falter, just when I fear;
Ready to help me, ready to cheer,
Just when I need Him most.

STATS, STORIES, AND MORE

Missionary Darlene Deibler Rose was captured by the Japanese during the war and taken to a death prison. She later wrote: "On the door of the cell before which the guard paused were written in chalk these words: *Orang ini musti mati,* 'This person must die.' The guard unlocked the door, opened it, and shoved me inside the cell. The door closed upon me, and I dropped to my knees, eyes intent upon the keyhole. When I saw the key make a complete revolution, I knew I was on death row, imprisoned to face trial and the sentence of death. I listened to the footsteps of the guard recede on the concrete walkway. When I could hear them no longer, I sank back onto my heels. My face and hands were wet with cold perspiration; never had I known such terror. Suddenly I found I was singing a song that I had learned as a little girl in Sunday School in Boone, Iowa:

Fear not, little flock,
Whatever your lot,
He enters all rooms,
The doors being shut.
He never forsakes,
He never is gone,
So count of His presence
From darkness 'till dawn. . . .

So tenderly my Lord wrapped His strong arms of quietness and calm about me. I knew they could lock me in, but they couldn't lock my wonderful Lord out. Jesus was there in the cell with me."[1]

---

[1]Darlene Deibler Rose: *Evidence Not Seen* (Carlisle, Cumbria, CA3 OQS, U.K., 1988), p. 114.

APPROPRIATE HYMNS AND SONGS

"Sing for Joy," Lamon Hiebert, 1996 Integrity's Hosanna! Music.

"Joyful, Joyful We Adore Thee," Henry Van Dyke & Ludwig van Beethoven, Public Domain.

"God Leads Us Along," George A. Young, Public Domain.

"O Worship the King," Chris Tomlin, 2004 worshiptogether.com songs (Admin. by EMI), Sixsteps Music.

FOR THE BULLETIN

In early centuries the church had excommunicated heretics, but most church leaders had opposed physical punishment. But as bureaucracy grew and heresy flourished, attitudes changed. During the 1100s and early 1200s, stronger measures evolved; and on April 20, 1233, Pope Gregory IX delegated the prosecution of heresy to the Dominican order. The Inquisitors roamed the countryside, admonishing heretics to confess. Those who didn't were brought to trial, the Inquisition serving as a special court with broad and frightening powers, including the use of torture. ● April 20, 1314, marks the death of Pope Clement V, who moved the papacy to Avignon, France. ● April 20, 1718, is the birth date of David Brainerd, colonial American missionary to the Indians of New England. He died from tuberculosis at 29, but his journal influenced hundreds to become missionaries after him. ● Women in the churches of Puritan New England helped supply the needs of pastors' families by annual "Spinning Bees." For example, in Newbury, Connecticut on April 20, 1768, young ladies met at the house of the Rev. Mr. Parsons, who preached to them a sermon from Proverbs 31:19. They spun and presented to Mrs. Parsons 270 skeins of good yarn while drinking "liberty tea." ● During the War in Vietnam, two missionary nurses, Minka Hanskamp and Margaret Morgan, were working among lepers in the predominately Muslim area of neighboring Thailand. On April 20, 1974, while in the town of Pujub to hold a leprosy clinic, they were kidnapped. Their skeletons were later found in the jungle.

WORSHIP HELPS

Call to Worship
Draw near to God and He will draw near to you. Cleanse your hands, you sinners; and purify your hearts, you double-minded. Lament and mourn and weep! Let your laughter be turned to mourning and your joy to gloom. Humble yourselves in the sight of the Lord, and He will lift you up (James 4:8–10).

Scripture Reading Medley
Your ears shall hear a word behind you, saying, "This is the way, walk in it," whenever you turn to the right hand or whenever you turn to the left. I will instruct you and teach you in the way you should go; I will guide you with My eye. Do not be like the horse or like the mule, which have no understanding, which must be harnessed with bit and bridle, else they will not come near you. Trust in the LORD with all your heart, and lean not on your own understanding; in all your ways acknowledge Him, and He shall direct your paths (taken from Is. 30:21; Ps. 32:8–9; Prov. 3:5–6).

Benediction
My heart is glad, and my glory rejoices. . . . You will show me the path of life; in Your presence is fullness of joy; at Your right hand are pleasures forevermore (Ps. 16:9–11).

Additional Sermons and Lesson Ideas

The Servant Solution
By Rev. Melvin Tinker

Date preached:

SCRIPTURE: Isaiah 49:1–7

INTRODUCTION: Several hundred years before the baby was born in Bethlehem who was given the name "Emmanuel"—God with us—a prophet caught a glimpse of Him under the inspiration of God's Spirit. Isaiah saw a figure called "The Servant" who would change the world forever.

1. The Calling of the Servant (vv. 1–3). The Lord prophesies of His special plans for this Servant. God ordained Jesus' paths before He ever stepped onto earth.
2. The Crisis of the Servant (v. 4). The mood changes in this verse; something would happen to the Servant that would cause Him to suffer. Now we know that event as the Crucifixion of Jesus!
3. The Conquest of the Servant (vv. 5–7). The Servant was to be honored in God's sight; one day kings and rulers of the world would bow down at His feet. He would bring Israel back to God and be a light to the Gentiles!

CONCLUSION: There is not a single person here in this building in whom this Servant is not passionately interested. Won't you submit your life to Him today?

Living Worthy
By Dr. Larry Osborne

Date preached:

SCRIPTURE: Philippians 1:27—2:5

INTRODUCTION: The *gospel* is the good news that we've been forgiven, adopted, and changed. A worthy Christian life is characterized by unity, courage, and change. Let's look at each:

1. What Kind of Unity Is God Looking For (1:27)? God doesn't ask for uniformity, but that we stick together despite our differences (cf. Eph. 4:3–6; 1 Cor. 12:14–27). He wants unity based upon Him!
2. What Kind of Courage Is God Looking For (1:28–29)? God is not asking us never to be afraid or discouraged, but to see every situation through the eyes of faith (cf. 2 Kin. 5:15–17; 2 Cor. 5:7).
3. What Kind of Humility Is God Looking For (2:1–5)? God doesn't ask us to have a low opinion of ourselves, but a high opinion of others. He wants us to serve others sacrificially (cf. Matt. 11:29; John 13:3–5).

CONCLUSION: Which of these areas need growth in your life? I encourage you to search the Scriptures and find key verses that will strengthen you in unity, courage, and humility.

APRIL 27, 2008

Church Building

Date preached:

By Rev. Peter Grainger

Scripture: 1 Corinthians 3:1–23, especially verses 9 and 11
For we are God's fellow workers; you are God's field, you are God's building. . . . For
no other foundation can anyone lay than that which is laid, which is Jesus Christ.

Introduction: An inadequate understanding and appreciation of the church is one of the most serious problems facing Christians in the West today. If you had been a first-century postman at the sorting office in Corinth, you would have been hard pressed to know where to deliver the letter addressed to "The church of God in Corinth." No, of course, no such thing happened. The letter that Paul, an apostle or messenger of Jesus Christ wrote to the church of God in Corinth was, as most letters were in those days, hand-delivered. But it makes an important point that we so easily miss or misunderstand today. The church is not a building but people. A church consists of people in a specific geographical location who have been called out by God to be holy and who call on the name of the Lord Jesus Christ (cf. 1 Cor. 1:2).

1. **The Growth of the Church (vv. 1–9).** Paul addresses the Corinthians as spiritual babies who need guidance. The Corinthians' factionalism and grouping around certain leaders serve as signs that they are acting on a purely human rather than spiritual basis (vv. 3–4). He explains that the church came into being because Paul planted the seed, Apollos watered, and God gave the increase (v. 6). Paul then reminds the Corinthians (and us) that every person is responsible to God for his own work (v. 8). We cannot sit back and say that God will do it whatever and so we don't need to bother. No, we are responsible and accountable. So what are you doing, and are you doing it diligently? But, when we have done it all and done it diligently, we cannot claim any ultimate credit for the life and growth of the church, for we are only doing what we were asked and giving what we have received. What are we? Only servants (v. 9).

2. **The Structure of the Church (vv. 10–15).** The first essential for any building is to lay a good foundation. Paul says that this was his role in the church in Corinth. Again he stresses it was a God-given appointment and a privileged role (v. 10). And in verse 11, he stresses that there is only one foundation for any genuine church: Jesus Christ. Have we shifted from the foundations or ignored the foundations upon which our church is laid? Let me give you a simple litmus test. How often do you hear about the Cross of Christ and how much time is spent together in teaching that builds on that foundation? Or have we, like the Corinthians, moved on from there to something more "sophisticated?" Oh, we may not deny the Bible, or doubt the deity of Christ, but we can ignore the Cross of Christ.

3. **The Function of the Church (v. 16).** In Greek, there are two words for "temple." One is the word for the temple building and all its precincts. The other is the word for the shrine or inner sanctum, the inner part where God makes Himself present—the Most Holy Place in the Old Testament temple where the High Priest alone could enter—and then only with the blood of animals as a sacrifice for sin. That's the word used to describe the church in Corinth—the temple where God is present by His Spirit. This is a mind-blowing thought then and now. Yet Paul says that God's Spirit is present and, by inference, only present when people meet together in the name of Jesus Christ, God's Son. God built this temple, Jesus Christ is its foundation and the Spirit is resident in it, whenever and wherever these people meet. Surely this should change much of our thinking about the church. To treat this temple of people lightly, or to use it as a power base for factions and personalities is desecration and invites the judgment of God!

Conclusion (vv. 18–23): So the chapter and this section conclude with a rebuke from Paul to the Corinthian Christians and us today: "don't fool yourselves." It is a call for a change in perspective about human wisdom and about human leaders. Jesus Christ alone should be the object of our praise!

STATS, STORIES, AND MORE

The Loss of Church-Focus in Our Hymns
Most of our modern songs and hymns are written in the first person
singular rather than plural. I did a quick count of a particular worship
songbook and 100 of the 1,000+ songs begin with the word "I" while 40
begin with "we." Now it is not a case of either/or but both/and. Thankfully,
God is interested in us personally and we can and should enjoy a personal
relationship with Him. But His plan has always been to call out for himself
a people and we must never forget that dimension and what it means to
be the church, the people of God. And, even where we are concerned
about the church, our horizons are too narrow, limited to our particular
church or denomination. First Corinthians 3 provides a healthy corrective.
—Rev. Peter Grainger

A Firm Foundation
In the last church in which we served, we began by meeting in a
community center. Eventually we were given (or bought at a reduced rate)
a piece of land on which to erect a church building. We formed a limited
company to subcontract out the work ourselves. The first job was to clear
the site and lay the foundations. It cost a lot of money and when it was
finished all you could see for your work was . . . nothing! If you visit the
place today, you will see a beautiful building but you will see nothing of
the foundations. Yet, without them, whatever was built on the site would
have been useless and insecure. In fact, a few months after it was
completed, we had terrible storms in the south of England, and nothing
was damaged, the house stood firm. How true this is of every group of
believers! If Jesus Christ is their foundation, the storms of trials and
hardships will not shake their faith. *—Rev. Peter Grainger*

Losing Foundational Focus
I think of a church in which I was involved in the early days of its
foundation. I visited it some years later and there was a large congregation.
I arrived half an hour after the start (after having preached somewhere
else) and there was still another hour of singing and dancing and people
falling on the floor. Someone mentioned the Cross of Jesus and one of the
leaders commented, in passing, words something like: "Yes, it's good to be
reminded of that—we don't focus on that much these days." What a sad
day that was. *—Rev. Peter Grainger*

APPROPRIATE HYMNS AND SONGS

"We Are Still the Church," Kirk Talley & Lanny Wolfe, 1986 Kirk Talley Music (Admin. by Integrated Copyright Group), Lanny Wolfe Music (Admin. by Gaither Copyright Management).

"The Church's One Foundation," Samuel John Stone & Samuel Sebastien Wesley, Public Domain.

"This Is Your House," Randy Phillips, 2002 Awakening Media Group (Admin. by Gaither Copyright Management).

"Blest Be the Tie That Binds," Johann Naegeli & John Fawcett, Public Domain.

FOR THE BULLETIN

Pollio, who lived in Gibalea (modern Vinkovce, Hungary), was hauled before a judge on April 27, 204, and asked if he was a Christian. He replied that he was a Christian and his ministry was to read God's Word at church. He was promptly burned to death. ● On April 27, 1537, Geneva's first Protestant catechism was published, based on Calvin's "Institutes." ● On April 27, 1564, leaders of Geneva tearfully gathered around the deathbed of John Calvin, who told them: "This I beg of you, again and again, that you will be pleased to excuse me for having performed so little in public and private, compared with what I ought to have done." ● On April 27, 1667, John Milton, 58, sold the copyright to his religious epic *Paradise Lost* for ten English pounds (less than $30). ● Moravian missionary, Peter Bohler, who was instrumental in the conversion of Methodist founder and evangelist, John Wesley, died on this day in 1775. ● The modern state of Israel was officially recognized by the British Government on April 27, 1950. ● Roy and Gillian Orpin were married on this day in 1961 and settled down to serve Christ in the jungles of Thailand. A year later Roy was shot by robbers and rushed to a government hospital. After asking his wife to quote the hymn "Jesus, I Am Resting, Resting," he quietly said, "How good God is!" He was 26. A few days later little Murray Roy was born.

WORSHIP HELPS

Call to Worship
"Come we that love the Lord, and let our joys be known. Join in a song with sweet accord and thus surround the throne"
—*Isaac Watts*

Welcome
Good morning and welcome to Sunday morning at our church! Someone recently said that according to the Bible, worship is something we do, not something we attend. As we sing and pray and express our thanksgiving to God, and as we present our tithes and offerings and listen to His Word, we invite you to be fully engaged with us. We're here in the presence of the living God, and He is in this very room, deserving of our worship.

Benediction
Peace to the brethren, and love with faith, from God the Father and the Lord Jesus Christ. Grace be with all those who love our Lord Jesus Christ in sincerity. Amen (Eph. 6:23–24).

Kid's Talk

Gather some pictures of church buildings and of church members meeting together. Preferably, these would not be pictures limited to North American settings. Photos of this type can easily be found on the Internet or in Christian/Missions magazines. Show the pictures to the children and explain that you are showing them different locations and people associated with churches. Ask them which one they think God cares more about, the buildings or the people who meet in them for worship. Explain that a church is a group of people, and any building will work, whether a mud hut or the open air; what's important is that people meet together to praise Jesus Christ. Lead them in a prayer for all the people in churches around the world right now.

Additional Sermons and Lesson Ideas

Confidence in God
Date preached:

By Dr. Robert M. Norris

SCRIPTURE: Hebrews 4:14—5:3

INTRODUCTION: All the inadequacies of the old priesthood point forward to something greater, to someone perfect and complete: to Jesus Christ, the perfect High Priest.

1. Jesus Provides Confidence to His People. ". . . we have a great High Priest who has passed through the heavens, Jesus the Son of God" (v. 14). God's people are given a perfect confidence of our acceptance by God because Jesus has secured it for us!
2. Jesus Is Sympathetic to Our Weaknesses. "For we do not have a High Priest who cannot sympathize with our weaknesses, but was in all points tempted as we are, yet without sin" (v. 15). Jesus was tested like we are, and does not roll His eyes at our pain or downplay our struggle with sin.

CONCLUSION: "Let us therefore come boldly to the throne of grace, that we may obtain mercy and find grace to help in time of need" (v. 16). The confession is simply our unshakable hope that God is for us and will work to bring us into His final rest and joy.

How Does It Look to You?
Date preached:

(Especially appropriate for launching a new ministry initiative, stewardship campaign, or building program)

SCRIPTURE: Haggai 1:1—2:9

INTRODUCTION: Lillian Dickson, missionary in Formosa, served a particular village needing a church building. She asked every Christian in the village to make a commitment to carry a certain number of stones each day from the river. As each person sacrificed time and effort to select appropriate stones and carry them to the building site, the church was built.

BACKGROUND: Haggai 1:1 with Ezra 1:1—5:2

1. God Will Build It (Hag. 1:2–15). The people were suffering privation because they weren't putting God's ministry first. When they changed their priorities, the Lord promised His presence, His provision, and His prosperity.
2. God Will Bless It (Hag. 2:1–9). As the work resumed on the temple, the old timers, remembering the regal temple of Solomon, grew discouraged; but the Lord promised that the temple they were building would become a place for ministry by Him who is the Desire of All Nations.

CONCLUSION: Our work is all of Him, first to last. He will build it and He will bless it. Our work is just to carry the stones.

MAY 4, 2008

God's Wake-Up Call

Date preached:

By Dr. Stephen Olford

Scripture: 2 Chronicles 7:14
If My people who are called by My name will humble themselves, and pray and seek My face, and turn from their wicked ways, then I will hear from heaven, and will forgive their sin and heal their land.

Introduction: Revival is the work of God in God's people primarily, spilling over a dynamic and redemptive witness to the world outside. I want to speak to you today on the subject of the reality of revival, now.

1. **The Problem That Hinders Revival.** "If My people . . . will turn from their wicked ways." Notice how many times the word "My" is used in this verse. If you ask the question, "Who hinders revival?" God answers "My people." The hindrance to revival in America today is the church. What is the problem? Why is heaven shut up? Glance at 2 Chronicles 6:26 to find out why the heavens have shut up and there is no rain; the answer is, "they have sinned." Deuteronomy 11:13–14 tells us that obedience to God's commandments brings rain from heaven, and that sin is failure to hear God, to love God, to serve God. Let me be practical about this: have you had your quiet time this morning? Have you heard from God today through His Word? A lack of obedience is a lack of love for God. If there's one word missing today in our evangelical circles, it's "obedience." Serving involves doing fervently and faithfully what God has commanded. Every one of us should be finding, following, and finishing God's work for our lives at every stage whether in school, seminary, shop, or in the farm.

2. **The Process That Hastens Revival (v. 14).** "If My people . . . will humble themselves, and pray and seek My face, and turn from their wicked ways." Have you ever analyzed the process of repentance? It's a movement characterized by four steps:

   A. **Brokenness.** "Humble themselves." When the writer here says we should "humble" ourselves, he's using a Hebrew word found in Judges 8:28 where we read that Midian, when she was subdued under Gideon, could no more lift their heads. This is the type of brokenness we need before God and in our nation. We know that God respects the heart broken over sin (Ps. 51:17). God relieves the broken heart and saves such as have a contrite spirit. Are you living out the concept of repentance day by day as a lifestyle? That's brokenness. Husbands and wives, parents and children, pastors and deacons, do you have a willingness to admit sin and get right?

B. **Prayerfulness.** "Pray." Of the twelve words used in the Old Testament for prayer, the word used here literally carries the connotation of self-judgment. So often we pray, "Lord send a great revival. Begin in me that I may be known as a Jonathan Edwards, George Whitefield, etc." Our motives are wrong. We so often pull out our hair because prayer is out of the government, prayer is out of school, but what bothers me is that prayer is out of the church!

C. **Earnestness.** "Seek My face." This reminds us of Jacob's wrestling match with God. After he was broken, he continued to cling to God until He blessed him. Andrew Murray in South Africa prayed for 30 years for revival, and then it came, the greatest revival South Africa has ever known. More preachers went out from South Africa than in any other time before or since.

D. **Holiness.** "Turn from their wicked ways." Are we translating the praises we sing today into everyday life? One of the biggest challenges we face is to be holy in a day of moral decay and degradation.

3. **The Promise That Heralds Revival.** "Then will I hear from heaven, and will forgive their sin and heal their land." Here we have a threefold statement of God's response:

A. **Divine Visitation.** "I will hear from heaven."

B. **Forgiveness.** "And will forgive their sin."

C. **Restoration.** "And heal their land."

Conclusion: Are you prepared to obey these principles that determine revival? Brothers and sisters, in this holy place, in this sacred moment, will you acknowledge the problem that hinders revival in your life? Will you accept the process that hastens revival in your life? Will you affirm the promise that heralds revival in your life, now?

STATS, STORIES, AND MORE

Examples of Revival from Dr. Olford

I remember as a young man in Wales, sitting down on the carpet, looking up into the face of Evan Roberts. For those of you who may not be familiar with that name, he was a man God used in such a mighty way, to initiate under His sovereignty what is known as the Welsh Revival of 1904. On September 29 of that year at a Sunday school service, a young minister was passionately preaching the Word. Throughout the sermon, every other paragraph was punctuated with these words, "Lord, bend us!" Walking out of that awesome service, young Evan Roberts' heart was broken. On his way out he kept on praying, "O, Lord, bend me, bend me!" He went out to preach and God began to pour His Spirit upon him and upon that nation. In a matter of a few months, 100,000 souls were converted. Ultimately that 1904 revival affected England, Ireland, North and South America, and Kentucky in particular in America.

In New York in Fulton Street, a man called "Jeremy Lanpher" knelt in prayer because of tremendous events taking place in 1857. It was on the twenty-third of September that he began to pray. He put a little notice out in the window that said, "Come share with me in prayer for revival." Six men joined him. His intensity in prayer scared them away. He ended up praying alone. Some returned, then more and more joined until close to 3,000 every noon were praying to God! That happened in New York, Chicago, Philadelphia, and then in practically every city of our great country. It was the greatest "layman's revival" this country has ever known. In a matter of two years, one million out of a population of 30 million people were saved!

APPROPRIATE HYMNS AND SONGS

"Come, Christians Join to Sing," Christian Henry Bateman, Public Domain.

"Revive Us Again," William MacKay & John J. Husband, Public Domain.

"Lead Me Lord," Elizabeth Goodine & Wayne Goodine, 1994 New Spring.

"I'll Lead You Home," Michael W. Smith & Wayne Kirkpatrick, 1996 Careers-BMG Music Publishing, Inc.

"Word of God, Speak," Bart Millard & Pete Kipley, 2002 Simpleville Music (Songs from the Indigo Room, Wordspring Music, LLC).

FOR THE BULLETIN

On May 4, 1493, the Spanish Pope Alexander VI issued the *Inter caeterea II*, which divided the known world between Spain and Portugal along a longitudinal line running 250 miles west of the Cape Verde Islands. ● Returning from the Diet of Worms, Martin Luther was "kidnapped" for his own protection on May 4, 1521, by the German ruler Frederick the Wise and kept at Wartburg where he translated the Bible into German. ● Gulielma Springett was born in London in 1644 and joined the Quaker movement at age 15. On May 4, 1672, she married William Penn and lived on an English estate where the couple assembled with their servants each day for worship and Bible reading. William later fled to America to escape persecution, but his wife died in England. Her last words were: "Let us all prepare, not knowing what hour or watch the Lord cometh. . . . I have cast my care upon the Lord." ● On May 4, 1737, evangelist George Whitefield penned a note to Gabriel Harris, describing the response to his open air preaching in areas around Gloucester: "People flock to hear the word of God from the neighboring villages as well as our own. They gladly receive me into their houses and I have not a hindrance to my ministerial business." ● May 4, 1784, marks the birth of Carl G. Glaser, German music teacher and writer of the tune for Wesley's "O For a Thousand Tongues."

WORSHIP HELPS

Call to Worship

If My people who are called by My name will humble themselves, and pray and seek My face, and turn from their wicked ways, then I will hear from heaven, and will forgive their sin and heal their land (2 Chr. 7:14).

Reader's Theater (May Be Used as a Responsive Reading)

Reader 1: Will You not revive us again, that Your people may rejoice in You (Ps. 85:6)?

Reader 2: Turn away my eyes from looking at worthless things, and revive me in Your way. Establish Your word to Your servant, who is devoted to fearing You. Turn away my reproach which I dread, for Your judgments are good. Behold, I long for Your precepts; revive me in Your righteousness (Ps. 119:37–40).

Continued on the next page

WORSHIP HELPS—*Continued*

Reader 3:   For thus says the High and Lofty One who inhabits eternity, whose name is Holy: "I dwell in the high and holy place, with him who has a contrite and humble spirit, to revive the spirit of the humble, And to revive the heart of the contrite ones (Is. 57:15).

Reader 1:   Let Your hand be upon the man of Your right hand, upon the son of man whom You made strong for Yourself. Then we will not turn back from You; revive us, and we will call upon Your name. Restore us, O LORD God of hosts; cause Your face to shine, and we shall be saved (Ps. 80:17–19)!

Pastoral Prayer/Invitation by Dr. Olford
Let's have a moment of stillness.

Lord, make us serious. Make us sincere. Make us courageous in this moment to fulfill the principles that determine revival. Lord, so many of us cop out of the notion of a sovereign revival in our land because we talk in generalities and not personally. You start with me, then us, then Your world. Do this thing right now, Lord, in our hearts as we respond to Your call.

I'd like those of you who really mean business on the basis of the teaching this morning to quietly stand to your feet right now. With heads bowed in this solemn moment, I'd like you to repeat after me. I'm praying it for myself; I want you to pray it for yourself aloud: Revive me, O Lord. Revive us, O Lord. Revive Your world, O Lord. Lord, rend the heavens and come down. Melt the mountains of obstruction. Send a mighty revival throughout our land for Your eternal glory, the extension of Your kingdom, and a mighty change in our national and international life.   —*Dr. Stephen Olford*

Additional Sermons and Lesson Ideas

Prayer for Revival
By Rev. Richard S. Sharpe, Jr.

Date preached:

SCRIPTURE: Psalm 85

INTRODUCTION: We live in a nation often referred to as Christian. While many claim to be Christian, their lives often don't match such a claim. That's exactly the way the Israelites lived before they were brought into captivity. Psalm 85 is a prayer for revival as the Jews returned to Israel from captivity.

1. Prayer for Favor (vv. 1–7). The psalmist recognizes that captivity and judgment were necessary and prays that the Lord would turn from His anger and grant them mercy. We, too, must admit our faults before the Lord will revive us.
2. Willingness to Hear the Lord (vv. 8–13). A failure to listen to God brings judgment, so the psalmist is willing to hear the Lord in hope of revival. If the conditions of repentance are met, the psalmist knows blessings will follow!

CONCLUSION: I ask you this week to pray over this Psalm, repent of sin, and plead with God for His favor, that He might revive your heart, this church, our nation, and this world for His sake.

The Pressure of Criticism

Date preached:

SCRIPTURE: 2 Corinthians 3:12–18

INTRODUCTION: Nobody likes to be criticized. The best strategy is to shrug it off, but occasionally, we need to answer. In 2 Corinthians, Paul is answering his critics, telling them that his message and his Savior are so glorious that he cannot help being bold.

1. Our Message Is Super-Glorious (vv. 7–11). The Old Covenant was glorious, but the New Covenant (the gospel) is super-glorious.
2. Our Message Makes Us Bold (vv. 12–13). Paul says, "Yes, when it comes to the gospel, I am assertive and bold, the reason being that I have a message that radiates with a glory far surpassing Moses' message of the Law."
3. Our Message Is Veiled to Some (vv. 14–17).
4. Our Message Is Perpetually Transforming to Others (v. 18). As we behold Jesus, the Holy Spirit performs in our hearts a perpetual work of sanctification, making us more and more like Christ, transforming us from glory to glory.

CONCLUSION: When you face the pressure of criticism, stand firm in the message of the gospel; let your light shine as Jesus transforms you from the inside out.

George Truett

Thirty-year-old George W. Truett had just been named pastor of the First Baptist Church of Dallas, and some of his men, wanting to get to know him, took him quail hunting. Among them was Jim Arnold, the city's Chief of Police. Another of the men later recounted what happened: *At 3:30 just as we were starting home, George Truett accidentally shot Capt. Arnold in the right leg, below the knee, making an awful wound. I succeeded in stopping the blood by using my suspenders as a tourniquet. Brother Truett was in agony unspeakable. Never saw the like. Arnold suffers much. Fainted several times.*

The following Sunday, Arnold died. All Dallas was stunned and Truett was devastated. He paced the floor day and night, unable to eat or sleep, muttering, "I will never preach again. I could never again stand in the pulpit."

Finally this verse came to mind, and his words began changing. As he paced, he mumbled, "My times are in Thy hands. My times are in Thy hands." Finally he collapsed in sheer exhaustion.

That night he vividly dreamed of Jesus standing by his bed. The Lord said, "Be not afraid. You are My man from now on." Later the dream came again, then a third time. At length it was announced that Truett was returning to the pulpit. Churches across Dallas dismissed services and gathered at First Baptist in support.

"When Brother Truett came into the pulpit," a member later said, "He looked terrible, his face drawn, his eyes sad. He remained silent for a long moment. You could have heard a pin drop. When he began, somehow he sounded different. His voice! I shall never forget his voice that morning . . ."

Truett remained at the First Baptist Church until his death in 1944. During his tenure, membership increased from 700 to over 7,000, with a total of 19,531 new members received and over 5,000 baptisms recorded.

He was God's man now.

MAY 11, 2008

PENTECOST/MOTHER'S DAY SUGGESTED SERMON

When Momma Ain't Happy

Date preached:

By Pastor Al Detter

Scripture: 1 Kings 17:7–24, especially from verse 24
. . . by this I know that you are a man of God, and that the word of the LORD in your mouth is the truth.

Introduction: Little cute creatures called babies make some ladies mothers. When you look at little babies, you could almost get the idea that being a mother is the easiest, happiest, most exciting job in the world. The truth is—being a mother may be the most demanding, self-sacrificing, draining, unrelenting, and thankless job in the world. No one can deny the joys that motherhood brings to a woman. But there are a lot of difficult times that come with being a mom, some downright unhappy moments. Let me introduce you to a mother who wasn't too happy. She is known as "the widow of Zarephath."

1. **What Makes Momma Unhappy (vv. 8–18).** God's judgment had fallen upon Israel due to their idolatry. Elijah was God's prophet during this time and had proclaimed God's judgment, which was evidenced by a great famine in the land. Amidst this context, we find a mother from whom we can learn a great deal. What makes mothers unhappy?

   A. **Loss of Her Spouse (vv. 9–10).** We learn that this woman in Zarephath was a widow, with whom Elijah was to stay during the famine.

   B. **Loss of Her Support (v. 12).** Elijah asked for a tiny bit of bread, but the widow had nothing left to offer. In fact, she was planning a last meal for her son and herself, having accepted the coming of death. God provided food to keep them alive, but one final blow awaited this unhappy mother.

   C. **Loss of Her Son (vv. 17–18).** After all the hardship endured, this mother saw her son get sick and die.

2. **What Makes Momma Happy (vv. 19–24).** Elijah takes the widow's son and begs the Lord to resurrect the boy. After three times of intense and physical prayer, the boy was raised to life! Notice the response of the woman when she experienced not only a restoration of happiness, but a confirmation that God was responsible and sovereign over her circumstances: ". . . by this I know that you are a man of God, and that the word of the LORD in your mouth is the truth" (v. 24).

3. **Lessons for Momma (and all of us) When We're Unhappy.** This text has some important application to all of us today when we experience unhappy circumstances:

   A. **Life Has a Way of Disturbing Our Happiness.** Like the widow, I wonder how many unhappy mothers are here today. Perhaps you've lost a spouse or a child. Maybe you're not a mother, but you are intensely unhappy with life. We have to remember that trials will come, but if we endure, God will strengthen and reward us (James 1:2–8).

   B. **God Is at Work in Ways We May Not Know or Understand.** The widow had no idea a prophet would save her life and her son's when he came to her. No matter what life may look like, we have to remember God is at work:

      1) **Crafting Change in Us.** God allows things to break into our lives that disturb us, but He will remake us!
      2) **Preparing a Connection Between People.** Elijah and the widow were living separate lives, but God ordained that they be brought together to teach them both about Himself.
      3) **Empowering Us to Make a Contribution.** The widow provided food for Elijah and Elijah saved the life of the widow's son! Everyone involved in trials can make a contribution to the Lord's work: a little flour saved a prophet's life!

   C. **Obey God Despite the Circumstances.** It seemed foolish for Elijah to stay with a non-Jewish widow, but he obeyed as did she. No matter what we think is best, we must obey the Lord.

   D. **Don't Blame God for the Losses We Experience.** When her son died, the widow immediately blamed Elijah. Elijah had nothing to do with his death. Jesus tells us that we will encounter problems in life (John 16:33).

E. **God Is Faithful Regardless of the Circumstances.** When the widow's son was resurrected, she was as happy as could be! How many of you are dealing with a wayward child or a divorce? God can turn things around!

Conclusion: Momma can't be at her peak if she's always happy—and neither can the rest of us. It's in the midst of life's searing circumstances that we make our deepest connection with God. Hang on to the lessons we spoke about today and let them be anchors for your soul.

STATS, STORIES, AND MORE

More from Pastor Detter—When Momma Ain't Happy
There are some things our mothers teach us when they aren't happy:

- Religion: "You'd better pray that comes out of the carpet."
- Time Travel: "If you don't straighten up, I'm going to knock you into next week."
- Foresight: "Make sure you wear clean underwear in case you're in an accident."
- Gymnastics: "Look at the dirt on the back of your neck."
- Osmosis: "Shut your mouth and eat your dinner."
- Envy: "There are millions of children around the world who don't have parents like you."
- Weather: "It looks like a tornado went through your room."
- The Circle of Life: "I brought you into this world and I can take you out."

Obeying Despite Circumstances
When I was in high school, I learned a huge lesson about obedience. A high school retreat was coming up and $15 was due that Sunday. All I had was $15 when God said to me, "Put it in the offering." I debated and disobeyed because I could not see how I could go to the retreat and obey God, too. We had evening church in those days. All during the service, God kept saying, "When the offering plate comes by, put in the $15!" I felt the press of God's Spirit, but I let the plate pass me by. Immediately after the service, a dear widow of little means came up to me. Her name was Mrs. Kline. She said, "All day long the Lord has been telling me to give this to you. I think you will need it for the retreat." She put some money in my hand and left. Any guesses as to how much it was? $15!! It was a gracious rebuke from God. And I found an usher in a hurry.   —Pastor Al Detter

APPROPRIATE HYMNS AND SONGS

"Faith of Our Mothers," Henri F. Hemy, Public Domain.

"For the Beauty of the Earth," Folliott S. Pierpoint & Conrad Kocher, Public Domain.

"Blessed Be Your Name," Beth Redman & Matt Redman, 2002 ThankYou Music (Admin. by EMI Christian Music Pub.).

"In Christ Alone," Keith Getty & Stuart Townend, 2001 ThankYou Music (Admin. by EMI Christian Music Pub.).

FOR THE BULLETIN

In A.D. 324, Emperor Constantine, believing the future lay in the East rather than the West, decided to move his capital from Rome to Byzantium. Before long there was a fabulous hippodrome, a prized university, five imperial palaces, nine palaces for dignitaries, 4,388 mansions, 322 streets, 1,000 shops, 100 places of amusement, splendid baths, magnificent churches, and a swelling population. It was a city that shimmered in the sunshine. The New Rome—Constantinople—was dedicated as capital of the Eastern Empire on May 11, 330. It became the center for Eastern Christianity. ● On May 11, 1682, the General Court of Massachusetts repealed two Puritanical laws, one forbade the observance of Christmas, and the second demanded capital punishment for Quakers. ● On May 11, 1816, delegates from a number of Christian organizations met in New York City to form the American Bible Society. Today the ABS has Scriptures available in over a thousand languages and annually distributes hundreds of millions of low-cost Bibles. ● The American Tract Society, the first national tract league in America, was formed in New York City on May 11, 1825. ● The first CARE packages arrived in Europe, at Le Havre, France, on this day in 1946. ● On May 11, 1949, Israel was admitted into the United Nations as the world body's 59th member.

WORSHIP HELPS

Call to Worship
Therefore by Him let us continually offer the sacrifice of praise to God, that is, the fruit of our lips, giving thanks to His name" (Heb. 13:15).

Welcome
This Sunday is both Mother's Day and the day the church recognizes Pentecost. Some might find this an unusual combination, but it's actually quite appropriate. When we think of mothers in Scripture, we often think of Mary, for all generations after her have called her blessed. Rightly so, for she bore the Christ child (Luke 1:48)! When we think of Pentecost, we think of the Holy Spirit's mighty work in the lives of believers. Mary experienced a mighty work of the Holy Spirit, as a virgin, and conceived the Son of God. Today, then, our focus is on Jesus Christ, the One born of a Spirit-filled virgin mother, born of God Himself. Let's worship Him together.

Recognition of Mothers
Ask all mothers who are members in your congregation (or visiting believers who are in good standing at their local church) to stand. Tell the congregation, "I want you to take a look at those standing here today. There's a portion of Scripture that describes the characteristics of these godly mothers and wives." Read Proverbs 31:10–31. After reading the text, remind the congregation of verse 28: "Her children rise up and call her blessed; her husband also, and he praises her."

Additional Sermons and Lesson Ideas

Keeping Your Marriage Vows (Part 1)
Date preached:
By Dr. Larry Osborne

SCRIPTURE: Various

INTRODUCTION: The seventh commandment not to commit adultery often distorts our understanding of sex and marriage. Let's look at some truths from Scripture:

1. Sex Is God's Idea (Gen. 1:28; 2:4; 1 Cor. 7:3–5).
2. Sex Outside Marriage Is a Good Thing in the Wrong Place (1 Thess. 4:3–8; 1 Cor. 7:8–9).
3. Adultery Is More Often the Sin of the Fool than the Sin of the Wicked (Prov. 6:32; 7:6–27).
4. You Can't Affair-Proof Your Marriage; You Can Affair-Proof Your Life (Gal. 5:16).

CONCLUSION: There's a hard truth here. Adultery is not the average sin; it's worse (cf. Deut. 22:22). It's the one sexual sin listed in the Ten Commandments. It can end a marriage and always comes to light. What's the answer? Live by the Spirit (Gal. 5:16). We will look at some practical examples as to how (see part 2).

Keeping Your Marriage Vows (Part 2)
Date preached:
By Dr. Larry Osborne

SCRIPTURE: Various

INTRODUCTION: You cannot affair-proof your marriage, but you can affair-proof your own life. Let's map out a practical game plan from Scripture to affair-proof our lives:

1. Never Think *It Can't Happen to Me* (2 Sam. 11—12). If a spiritual giant like David can fall, it can happen to all of us. Cockiness kills; never underestimate the power and complexity of our sexual drives.
2. Never Fight When You Can Run (1 Cor. 6:18; Prov. 5:3–8; Gen. 39:1–12; Eph. 5:3–4; Matt. 5:27–28; 15:19). Some situations to run from are: the flirt, the emotional connection, and the first sign of secrecy or shame.
3. Never Ignore God's Divine Early Warning System (Prov. 6:32–35). Take seriously your spouse's complaints, jealousies, or concerns.
4. Never Lay a Foundation Where You Can't Build a Home (Prov. 4:23; Matt. 5:27–28; 15:29). Proverbs 4:23 warns us to guard our hearts. Friendship and emotional connections to the opposite sex lay a foundation that only belongs to our spouse.

CONCLUSION: Study these Scriptures. Talk with your spouse about these principles. The one who guards against adultery guards against a foolish mistake with immeasurable consequences.

MAY 18, 2008

SUGGESTED SERMON

Be of Good Cheer! It Is I; Do Not Be Afraid

Date preached:

Scripture: Matthew 14:22–33, especially verse 27
Be of good cheer! It is I; do not be afraid.

Introduction: "Be of good cheer" is a powerful phrase. It was more than a salutation or causal greeting. It was an authoritative blessing, commandment, and promise—all rolled into one. It literally meant to take heart, to take courage, to take cheer, to deliberately eject the emotions of gloom and doom and choose instead to let the joy and strength of Jesus shine through. Some translations say: Cheer up! There's a popular television program called "Fear Factor." Well, think of this story under the title "Cheer Factor." There are four factors here that, joined together, can make us cheerful people.

1. **The Multitude Factor.** There's got to be purpose and meaning in our lives if we're going to have good cheer. For Jesus and His disciples, that meant ministering to the multitudes. Look at how Matthew tracks (4:25; 5:1; 8:1; 8:18; 9:8; 9:36; 12:15; 12:23; and 13:1ff). Those multitudes represented the millions whose lives He intended to change. For us to sustain joy and fulfillment in life, we've got to reach the multitudes. That may involve a large ministry. It might mean a small ministry which, unknown to us, will have large results. It's not enough to earn a paycheck, to enjoy a vacation, to buy a new car, to play video games, and go to movies. We're placed here to make a difference, and God intends for each of our lives to have significance.

2. **The Solitude Factor.** But there's a balance. We need frequent breaks from the multitude, time alone with ourselves and with God. Notice how Jesus safeguarded His time alone (see Matt. 13:36, 14:13, and 14:22).

3. **The Fortitude Factor.** While Jesus was up on the hillside enjoying leisure time with the Father, the disciples were in crisis, and this brings us to the third factor in having a cheerful attitude, the fortitude

factor. In Roman times, the night divided into various watches. The fourth watch comprised the hours between three and six in the morning. Jesus allowed His disciples to struggle for a prolonged period of darkness and distress. He didn't solve their problem instantly. The Lord sometimes lingers and delays and watches, as it were, from a distance, praying for us in the mountains as we struggle on the stormy sea below. He's more interested in developing our faith than He is in relieving our distress, and He wants us to be strong in grace and in faith and in Him. The Bible tells us on thirty-four different occasions to be strong. We can't be strong in our own strength, but we can be strong in His strength. We can be strong in the promises. We can be strong in grace (see Deut. 11:8 and 31:6; Josh. 1:9; 2 Chr. 15:7; Is. 35:3–4; Dan. 10:19 and 11:32; 1 Cor. 16:13; Eph. 6:10; and 2 Tim. 2:1). Jesus came to them on the water, walking across the waves, stepping on the whitecaps as though they were paving stones. And as He approached the boat, He shouted above the surf these words that have echoed through the ages down to you and me: *Be of good cheer! It is I. Don't be afraid!* Whatever your storm, whatever your gale, whatever your struggle, you have total access through His grace to those same three short, simple sentences: *Be of good cheer! It is I. Don't be afraid!*

4. **The Gratitude Factor.** How does the story end? It ends with thanksgiving, praise, worship, and awe. *Then those who were in the boat came and worshiped Him, saying, "Truly You are the Son of God."* Let's freeze-frame that picture, and let's go back one hour and freeze-frame that picture, too, when the disciples were at their moment of desperation. Put the two pictures side-by-side. Three o'clock: Exhaustion. Four o'clock: Exaltation. Three o'clock: Anguish and worry. Four o'clock: Awe and worship. The secret of great faith is knowing at three o'clock that four o'clock is coming, and reacting accordingly. It is replacing worry with worship, and doing so by faith, learning to trust Him till the storm passes by.

Conclusion: Faith is being of good cheer at three o'clock because we know Jesus will show up in His timing and make all things work together for good. That is the faith that remembers the words: *Be of good cheer! It is I. Do not be afraid!*

STATS, STORIES, AND MORE

When I was a student at Columbia Bible College, I had several mentoring sessions with Dr. H. Edwin Young, then the pastor of First Baptist Church of Columbia. One day as we sat in his office, I said, "Dr. Young, sometimes you're very hard to see. It took me a solid month to line up this appointment." He smiled and apologized for that, then he said something I've never forgotten. "Rob, I've learned that if I'm always available, I'm never available." He explained, "If I'm always available I become so drained and tired and depleted that I don't have anything to give when I am available. I need time to recharge, to replenish, to cultivate my own soul, to stay fresh for the ministry God has given me." Well, it doesn't take a month for someone to see me. I don't want to give you the wrong idea. But Dr. Young's principle is important for all of us. We need time to ourselves and time when we're shut away just with the Lord. I can't get enough of those times.
                                                            —*Pastor Robert J. Morgan*

A Closing Poem

Exhausted and frightened, they battled the rain,
The wind, the waves, enduring the strain,

Till finally their nerves could stand it no more;
and their strength was all gone and their muscles were sore.

But up on the mountain Jesus could see,
every white-capping wave on the rough Galilee.

And treading the billows like a carpet of sod,
He came to their aid with the power of God.

They worshiped Him then, with rejoicing and awe
For the marvels He did and the wonders they saw.

But better to praise Him with the storm at its worst;
By remembering His power and promises first.

—Pastor ROBERT J. MORGAN

APPROPRIATE HYMNS AND SONGS

"Come, Now Is the Time to Worship," Brian Doerksen, 1998 Vineyard Songs.

"You Are Good," Israel Houghton, 2001 Integrity's Praise! Music.

"Here I Am to Worship," Tim Hughes, 2000 ThankYou Music (Admin. by EMI Christian Music Pub.).

"It Is Well," Haratio Spafford & Philip Bliss, Public Domain.

"Great Is Thy Faithfulness," Thomas O. Chisholm & William Runyan, 1923, renewed 1951 Hope Publishing Company.

FOR THE BULLETIN

On May 18, 1291, the city of Acre fell to invading Moslem armies, signaling the end of a Christian "military presence" in the Middle East during the Crusades. ● On May 18, 1593, the Protestant Henry Bourbon of Navarre converted to Catholicism to become France's King Henry IV. Five years later, he issued the Edict of Nantes, granting Huguenots (French Protestants) religious freedom. ● Frontier evangelist, Sheldon Jackson, was born on May 18, 1834. He stood just over five feet tall, but his size, he said, allowed him to sleep anywhere. His bed was a stagecoach floor, a saloon loft, a hollow log, a teepee, a canoe. During 50 years of ministry, he traveled a million miles through the West and North. He oversaw the establishing of 886 churches. ● On May 18, 1901, while in Naples, Italy, on a trip to the Holy Land provided by his New York church, Rev. Maltie D. Babcock, 43, suddenly died of "Mediterranean fever." He is best remembered as the author of the hymn "This Is My Father's World." ● Karol Wojtyla—Pope John Paul II—was born on May 18,1920. He became the Archbishop of Krakow in 1963, and on October 16, 1978, became the first non-Italian pope since Hadrian VI in the sixteenth century. ● On May 18, 1926, popular evangelist Aimee Semple McPherson mysteriously vanished while visiting a beach in Venice, CA. She reappeared a month later, claiming to have been kidnapped. Her story was widely disbelieved. ● May 18, 1959 marks the death of pastor and popular author, F. W. Boreham.

WORSHIP HELPS

Call to Worship

But God forbid that I should boast except in the cross of our Lord Jesus Christ, by whom the world has been crucified to me, and I to the world (Gal. 6:14).

Responsive Reading

Leader: On that day David first delivered this psalm into the hand of Asaph and his brethren, to thank the LORD: Oh, give thanks to the LORD!

People: Call upon His name;

Leader: Make known His deeds among the peoples!

People: Sing to Him, sing psalms to Him;

Leader: Talk of all His wondrous works!

People: Glory in His holy name;

Leader: Let the hearts of those rejoice who seek the LORD!

People: Let the heavens rejoice, and let the earth be glad; and let them say among the nations, "The LORD reigns."

Leader: Let the sea roar, and all its fullness; let the field rejoice, and all that is in it.

People: Then the trees of the woods shall rejoice before the LORD, for He is coming to judge the earth.

All: Blessed be the LORD God of Israel from everlasting to everlasting (1 Chr. 16:7–10, 31–33, 36)!

Benediction

Acknowledge and take to heart this day that the LORD is God in heaven above and on the earth below. There is no other (Deut. 4:39 NIV).

Additional Sermons and Lesson Ideas

Who Is Jesus to You?
Date preached:
By Dr. Timothy K. Beougher

SCRIPTURE: Various

INTRODUCTION: Since the time of Jesus' birth, there have been varied interpretations of who He really is. Scripture gives us some important guidance in understanding who Jesus really is:

1. Your **Friend** who sticks closer than a brother (Prov. 18:24; John 15:13–15).
2. Your **Guide** who will show you both the pathway and the steps He wants you to follow (John 16:13–15).
3. Your **Encourager** who will give you hope even in seemingly hopeless situations (Phil. 2:1; 1 Tim. 1:1).
4. Your **Energizer** who imparts His power for life and ministry to you (Luke 10:19; Acts 1:8).
5. Your **Helper** who is on call 24 hours a day (John 14:26).
6. Your **Conqueror** who will lift you to new heights of victory and triumph (1 John 3:8; 5:4).
7. Your **Intercessor** who prays for you day and night (Heb. 7:25).
8. Your **King** who wants to make your heart a kingdom where He reigns supremely (Luke 1:31–32).
9. Your **Cleanser** who will purify, clean, and sanitize your heart as you confess and forsake any and all sin (1 John 1:9).

CONCLUSION: What an awesome Savior we serve!

Beloved Children Walking in the Light
Date preached:
By Rev. Larry Kirk

SCRIPTURE: Ephesians 5:1–4

INTRODUCTION: Paul gives three specific ways that God wants us to live:

1. Live as His Dearly Loved Children (vv. 1–2). The basis of all our actions should be the love that God has shown us and placed within us.
2. Uphold Uncompromising Sexual Purity (v. 3). Parents with high moral standards are always on the lookout to protect their children from sexual sin. How much more important to our holy God that we protect against sexual sin!
3. Reflect His High Standards of Purity in Daily Speech (v. 4). It will help us to define some words in this verse to stay away from: "Filthiness" suggests openly shameful, ugly, or filthy language. "Foolish talking" suggests senseless, crude, or stupid comments. "Coarse jesting" suggests turning a word so it takes another meaning; for example, some people find sexually suggestive ideas in almost any sentence.

CONCLUSION: Does your life reflect these high standards?

Keeping XXX Out of the Pastorate

There has never been a generation as sexually charged as ours nor as many ministers ensnared by immorality, and much of it has to do with our technology. Pornography is the primary driver of the development of much of our modern media technology, including the Internet and the proliferation of mobile and handheld devices. One expert said that all this technology has made pornography as addictive as crack cocaine.

Another said: "Sexual addiction is rapidly becoming recognized as a major social problem with similarities more well-known to alcohol and drug addiction or compulsive gambling. We are becoming accustomed to hearing about sexual scandals in our communities, in the workplace, in churches and schools, even in the White House, involving those in which we place our trust. And sometimes we experience shocking sexual discoveries in our own families, involving people we know personally."[1]

A reported 40 million American adults regularly log onto pornographic Web sites, and one survey of men attending a Promise-Keeper rally found that 53% of them had viewed pornography in the week prior to the survey.

The average age of a person's first exposure to Internet pornography was age eleven, and ninety percent of all young people ages 8 to 16 have viewed pornography online, most of them while doing homework.

Pastors are targeted by Satan; for when a preacher falls into sin, the entire church suffers reproach. Our headlines—as well as the Bible itself—are full of examples of men and women who succumbed to moral temptation with disastrous results. One man who didn't fall into sin was Joseph when he was tempted by Potiphar's wife in Genesis 39; and his story—old as it is—still gives us the abiding secrets of personal purity.

The first is to realize that it's a *spiritual* battle. Joseph's ability

Continued on the next page

[1]http://www.sexaddictionhelp.com/general.html, accessed October 17, 2006.

to resist temptation didn't just come from the fact that he was a "good boy." There's a phrase that occurs repeatedly in this chapter that explains Joseph's character.

- ❧ Verse 2: *The Lord was with Joseph, and he was a successful man.*
- ❧ Verse 3: *And his master saw that the Lord was with him.*
- ❧ Verse 21: *But the Lord was with Joseph and showed him mercy.*
- ❧ Verse 23: *The Lord was with him; and whatever he did, the Lord made it prosper.*

The battle against moral temptation in a highly immoral age is a spiritual battle that can only be won by spiritual people using spiritual means. We have to be serious about drawing near to God and walking with the Lord. You can't maintain purity for the sake of your wife, or your family, or even yourself. You've got to do it for Christ.

Maintaining your own spiritual health and vitality is all-important for the pastor. Too many of us become weary and worn, and we're vulnerable to temptation. We need a constant sense of God's presence at every moment, giving us the inner discipline of the Holy Spirit.

Second, we must control our eyes. There are two very interesting phrases in Genesis 39. Verse 6 says that Joseph was handsome in form and appearance. In other words, he was well-built and handsome. The next verse says: *And it came to pass after these things that his master's wife cast longing eyes on Joseph, and she said, "Lie with me."*

What an interesting phrase—she cast longing eyes. Sexual temptation comes to us largely through the avenue of our eyes. One of the authors of *Every Man's Battle,* confessed in the book that he had been addicted to actual hard-core pornography, but he vowed to never do that again; and he was successful in staying away from pornographic sources. But now he realized he had to face a whole new set of battles on a slightly different plane. He found himself watching movies in the motel when he traveled, movies that weren't technically pornographic but still weren't clean. He was also eyeing girls jogging along the roadside, and he found himself scanning the advertising inserts in the Sunday paper which featured certain ads. He began to realize that the sin itself had never changed, only the delivery systems. And so he committed himself to learning how to overcome these temptations as well.

Perhaps the most practical verse in the Bible on this subject is Job 31:1: "I have made a covenant with my eyes; why then should I look upon a young woman?" There was a time in Job's life when he sat down, thought it through, and made a serious commitment to control his eyes.

Proverbs 4:25 (NIV) says: *Let your eyes look straight ahead, fix your gaze directly before you.* If there's a chance the video or movie you're thinking of watching contains any images that would feed your sexual energy, don't watch it. My wife and I enjoy renting a good movie from time to time, but we almost never watch anything R-rated. And even with other movies, we have to be careful. Even pastors can become desensitized to our highly charged, immoral age, and we need to renew our commitment to purity of the eyes. Learn to ricochet your glance when things come unexpectedly into your line of vision.

With the Internet, you need multiple protections: a filtering software, an accountability partner, and perhaps a computer guru who will monitor your traffic on a regular basis.

Genesis 39:8–9 contains another of Joseph's secrets—his personal determination. It says when tempted: *But he refused . . . .* He understood that immorality was a three-fold sin. It was a sin against others, against himself, and against God: *But he refused and said to his master's wife, "Look, my master does not know what is with me in the house, and he has committed all that he has to my hand. There is no one greater in this house than I, nor has he kept back anything from me but you, because you are his wife. How can I do this great wickedness, and sin against God?"*

There's another little phrase in verse 10 that's significant. It says: *So it was, as she spoke to Joseph day by day, that he did not heed her, to lie with her or to be with her.* Continued on the next page

HELPS FOR THE PASTOR'S FAMILY—*Continued*

He had drawn his boundaries in advance, and he was determined not to sleep with her, but he also knew that he needed to avoid her altogether as much as possible. He took steps to not even be with her.

That's why pastors are advised never to make visits alone, never to counsel a member of the opposite sex alone, and in general, never to be alone with any woman who isn't a part of your own family. We can't yield even an inch. We have to be almost paranoid about being with the opposite sex.

In fact, we must run hard in the other direction, and that was Joseph's fourth secret. When all else failed, he ran as fast as he could in the opposite direction. Joseph decided he would rather lose his job and go to prison than to compromise his principles, betray his trust, disappoint his God, and mar his life.

If you're going to be victorious, you've got to be determined before God to walk with Him, to make a covenant with your eyes, to yield not an inch, and to run in the opposite direction. Pornography is a sin that can be beaten and a disaster that can be avoided.

PS: The story of Joseph in Genesis 39 is a powerful narrative for preaching about sexual purity, to men, to the youth group, or to the congregation on Sunday. Begin with some statistics about pornography in our society, either from this article or from your own research, and then read the story of Joseph. The four points are:

1. Realize this is a spiritual battle. Like Joseph, you need the Lord to be with you.
2. Control your eyes. That's what got Potiphar's wife in trouble. Make a covenant with your eyes.
3. Make up your mind to refuse to yield to temptation, whoever great. Joseph did not heed her to go to bed with her or even to be with her.
4. Run in the opposite direction. It cost Joseph a term in prison, but it saved his character and his future usefulness for the Lord.

MAY 25, 2008

SUGGESTED SERMON

When Worship Turns to War   *Date preached:*

By Dr. David Jeremiah

Scripture: James 4:1–12, especially verse 1
Where do wars and fights come from among you?

Introduction: Harry Ironside was riding home one night with his wife on a streetcar in San Francisco. He had preached five times that day and was exhausted. His wife said something to him, and he snapped at her, giving free reign to his selfish mood. When she rebuked him, he replied, "My dear, don't you realize that I have worn myself out. I have preached five times today, and I am all unnerved." His wife replied, "Well, if you think you have something to complain about, look at me. I've had to *listen* to you five times today. I'm at least as tired as you are. If I can afford to be pleasant, certainly you can." No Christian has the right to let his personal feelings lead him to quarrel with and wound others in order to gratify his own selfish mood. That was the essence of what this passage says. Worldliness is self-centeredness, and James is dealing with this problem in the church. Worldliness is evidenced just as much at a church business meeting as it is out in the carnal places and dens of iniquity.

I. **Symptoms of Worldliness Within the Church.** There are two symptoms that are easy to see.

   A. **Self-Centeredness (vv. 1–2).** Wars among us come from our desires for pleasure. We murder and covet and fight and war. Those phrases remind us that worldliness occurs in the church when individual egos run wild and people are out for their own purposes. James' point is that wherever the "self" is allowed to reign supreme, we have immediately plugged into the world's system, giving rise to wars and all kinds of problems.

   B. **Symptom of Frustration (v. 3).** These wars and fightings occur when we lust for what we cannot have. James takes it into the realm of prayer. We don't have what we need because we fail to ask, so we're frustrated. We don't have what we need because we ask in the wrong spirit, so we're frustrated. Wherever worldliness lives in the body of Christ there will be a sense of frustration in the church.

2. **Worldliness Is Spiritual Adultery (vv. 4–5).** This problem of worldliness is described as spiritual adultery. The people James was addressing had become friends with the world and enemies with God. Verse 5 says that just as a man who loves his wife is going to have a right kind of jealous heart for her, so the Spirit within us is jealous not to share us with anyone but God exclusively.

3. **Characteristics of Grace in Your Life (vv. 6–10).** The next few verses give a staccato-list of seven commands that ward off worldliness in our lives and churches. These verses tell us how we can have the characteristics of grace in our lives that will enable us to resist the pull of worldliness.

   A. **Attitude of Gracious Humility (v. 6).** God resists the proud but gives grace to the humble.

   B. **Attitude of Godly Submission (v. 7).** You have to come understanding that God's in charge and be willing to let Him be the boss. So many people I know have the Holy Spirit as the resident of their life but they haven't made Him the president of their life and they're not submitting to God.

   C. **Guard Against the Devil (v. 7).** Resist the devil and draw near to God. The devil is allergic to praise, so that's one way to resist him.

   D. **Attitude of Concern About Sin in Our Lives (vv. 8–10).** There was a day in history when the blessed Lamb of God was slain upon the hill of Golgotha. He was nailed there by everything I have done in my life that violates the holiness of God. When the world creeps back into my life and I am brought to a place of conviction about it, I must soberly confess my sin. James said, "Let your mourning replace your laughter, and let your gloom replace your joy." Sometimes we need to sober up and reflect upon our lives.

   E. **Humble Yourselves (v. 10).** Twenty-seven times the Bible indicates that when we humble ourselves we will be lifted up.

Conclusion: Through gracious humility, through Godly submission, through guarding and resisting against the devil, through drawing near to God, through confessing our sin to the Lord . . . through all these things, God's grace flows in our lives, making them resistant to the world. I do not know where you are or what it is that God is doing in your life, but I do know that James 4 calls each of us to a major decision in life, and that decision is, which world are we going to live in. If you are caught in a magnetic pull that is drawing you away from God, confess your sin. Mourn or weep. And draw near to God and He will draw near to you.

STATS, STORIES, AND MORE

More from Dr. Jeremiah
Someone has said the problem that James is dealing with is Diotrephes' Disease. Do you know what that is? In 3 John, verses 9 and 10, John said that he wrote to the church, but Diotrephes, who loves to have the preeminence, received us not. Diotrephes Disease is the disease that belongs to those who love to have the preeminence within the body, the elevation of self. I read a story recently about some children playing in the backyard who happened to be Christian children, and belonged to a Christian family. As children do on occasion, they got into a fight and were screaming and shouting. Mother stuck her head out the backdoor and said, "Kids, I want you to stop that what are you doing." They replied, "Don't worry, mom; we're just playing church."

APPROPRIATE HYMNS AND SONGS

"There Is None Like You," Lenny LeBlanc, 1991 Integrity's Hosanna! Music.

"Fill this Place," Bo Cooper & David Baroni, 1993 Sunday Shoes Music (Admin. by Brentwood Benson Music Co.).

"You and I Were Made to Worship," Chris Tomlin, Ed Cash, & Stephen Sharp, 2006 worshiptogether.com songs (Admin. by EMI Christian Music Pub.).

"O Worship the King," William Kethe & Johann Haydn, Public Domain.

"Praise Ye the Lord the Almighty," Joachim Neander, Public Domain.

FOR THE BULLETIN

May 25, 1085, marks the death of Pope Gregory VII (Hildebrand), one of the greatest popes of the Roman Catholic Church. He had been chosen by the people themselves, and his greatest desire was to reform the Roman Catholic Church. He was driven into exile, however, by Germany's King Henry IV. Gregory died brokenhearted in Salerno. ● On May 25, 1793, Rev. Stephen Theodore Badin became the first Roman Catholic priest to be ordained in the United States, in a ceremony in Baltimore. He later became a frontier missionary, and played a key role in establishing Catholicism in Kentucky, Indiana, and Tennessee. ● On May 25, 1824, the American Sunday School Union established. It began as a coalition of local Protestant Sunday school groups, uniting to promote the establishment of Sunday schools and to provide local communities with libraries and materials for religious instruction. ● When Billy Bray, a coal-miner in Cornwall, England, was converted, at age 29, he began shouting for joy. He never stopped, becoming a unique Methodists evangelist who danced and shouted his way through a lifetime of ministry. His dying word as he fell asleep on May 25, 1868, was "Glory!" ● On May 25, 1949, the Communist forces of Mao Tse-tung entered Shanghai, closing the churches and forever changing the lives of the Christians and pastors living there. One of the pastors later imprisoned was Watchman Nee.

Kid's Talk

Show the children a picture of a close friend or family member who lives far away, and perhaps a map showing their city and state. Tell them about going to see them, something like this: "Right now we are 2,000 miles away from each other, but next month I'm going to the airport and get on a plane and take off down the runway in the direction of my sweet mother. The plane will fly toward the east and get closer and closer to where she lives. Then I'll catch a cab and go right to her house. Then I'll walk up the sidewalk and through the front door and we will hug. We will go from being far away to being very close. The Bible tells us to draw near to God like that. When we draw near to God, we don't have to ride on a plane. We have to read His Word, pray to Him, remember that He is always with us, and obey Him."

WORSHIP HELPS

Call to Worship
Come, let us enter God's presence in worship. Let us enter through gates of thanksgiving. Let us come to Him with singing and grateful hearts. Come, and let us adore Father, Son, and Holy Spirit!

Scripture Reading Medley
Do not love the world or the things in the world. If anyone loves the world, the love of the Father is not in him. For all that is in the world—the lust of the flesh, the lust of the eyes, and the pride of life—is not of the Father but is of the world. . . . Demas has forsaken me, having loved this present world. . . . Again, the devil took Him up on an exceedingly high mountain, and showed Him all the kingdoms of the world and their glory. And he said to Him, "All these things I will give You if You will fall down and worship me." Then Jesus said to him, "Away with you, Satan! For it is written, 'You shall worship the LORD your God, and Him only you shall serve.'" Then the devil left Him. . . . Resist the devil, and he will flee from you. Draw near to God and He will draw near to you (1 John 2:15–16; 2 Tim. 4:10; Matt. 4:8–11; James 4:7–8).

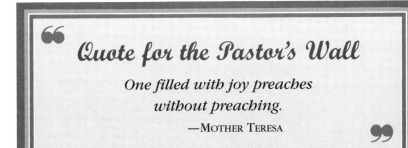

" Quote for the Pastor's Wall

*One filled with joy preaches
without preaching.*

—MOTHER TERESA

Additional Sermons and Lesson Ideas

Light Up Your Life
Date preached:

SCRIPTURE: 1 John 1:5—2:2

INTRODUCTION: The beginning of the gospel is that God is light. This seems to be referring to the intellectual and moral perfections of God. He possesses the intellectual perfection of *truth* and the moral perfection of *holiness.* Until we understand this, it's hard to appreciate our need for salvation. John gives us six implications of this, each beginning with the word *if.*

1. Don't Claim You're Perfect (v. 6). If we claim to have fellowship with Him yet walk in the darkness, we are lying.
2. Let God Forgive You (v. 7). If we walk in the light, we have fellowship with Him. The "one another" here is referring to God our ourselves as His blood cleanses us from the sins that separate us from Him.
3. Don't Think that Conversion Keeps You from Temptation (v. 8). If, as Christians, we think we're without sin, we're deceiving ourselves.
4. Confess Sins that Mar Your Fellowship with Him (v. 9). If, as Christians, we confess our sins He cleanses us.
5. Don't Hide Your Sin (v. 10). If we hide our sins, we violate His Word.
6. Remember that Christ Is Always Interceding for You (vv. 1–2). If we do sin, we have an Advocate with the Father.

CONCLUSION: Sin brings darkness. Jesus Christ brings the light back into life.

Three-Dimensional Giving
Date preached:
By Dr. David Jeremiah

SCRIPTURE: John 12:1–11

INTRODUCTION: The Bible often presents both sides of an issue so we can see it in balance. Two people are placed at opposite poles of reality in this passage—the generous Mary and the selfish Judas.

1. A Sacrificial Attitude Is Essential in Christian Giving. Mary gave to Jesus something that was very costly. The Bible tells us that we should not offer to the Lord that which costs us nothing.
2. A Servant Attitude Is Essential in Christian Giving. She came to His feet and worshiped Him.
3. A Submissive Attitude Is Essential in Christian Giving. She bathed His feet, wiping them with her hair.

4. A Scriptural Attitude Is Essential in Christian Giving. She gave to Jesus because she really believed what God had said to her through Him. She was anointing Him for His burial.

CONCLUSION: In contrast, look at Judas. He didn't care about Mary's worship nor did he care about the poor. He thought only of money. Every time the offering plate comes our way, each of us responds either like Mary or like Judas. Are you giving to God's work in a way that pleases Him?

PRAYER FOR THE PASTOR'S CLOSET

Grant unto us, Almighty God, of thy good Spirit, that quiet heart, and that patient lowliness to which Thy comforting Spirit comes; that we, being humble toward one another, may have our heart prepared for that peace of Thine which passeth understanding; which, if we have, the storms of life can hurt us but little, and the cares of life vex us not at all; in presence of which death shall lose its sting, and the grave its terror; and we, in calm joy, walk all the days of our appointed time, until our great change shall come. Amen.

—GEORGE DAWSON (1821–1876)

YOUTH SERMON

SUITABLE FOR A GRADUATION COMMENCEMENT ADDRESS OR
GRADUATE RECOGNITION SERVICE

How to Avoid Losing Your Faith

Date preached:

By Dr. Ed Dobson

Scripture: Various, especially 1 Timothy 1:18–19 (NIV)
Timothy, my son, I give you this instruction in keeping with the prophecies once made about you, so that by following them you may fight the good fight, holding on to faith and a good conscience. Some have rejected these and so have shipwrecked their faith.

Introduction: I'm thankful to God for the amazing potential sitting before me today. You now sit on the brink of opportunities to learn, grow, specialize, and develop into adults who will be out on your own. While great opportunity awaits, so does great temptation and confusion. In fact, the apostle Paul spoke to his young student and friend, Timothy, about this very issue: "Some have rejected these and so have shipwrecked their faith." Today I want to look at three reasons young people and students often abandon the faith, and three ways to avoid this pitfall.

1. **Why Young People Abandon the Faith.** While reasons may be numerous, three of the most common are:

   A. **Inauthentic Role Models.** Students look to those of us who are older as models of the faith, examples of what it means to follow Jesus. But, if in our lives there is disparity between what we believe and how we behave, the greater that disparity, the more likely it is that those who watch us will check out on God. If you have a parent or a role model who is not authentic, all I can say is to remember the ultimate example is Jesus, not us. Look for believers who are authentic and follow them.

   B. **Legalism.** By legalism I mean establishing rules and regulations that are primarily focused on external behaviors and then judging everyone else based on "your" rules for external behavior. Let me say something to the students who are graduating. I don't care how many piercings you get, I don't care what you get pierced or how you dress, what matters ultimately is your heart—your heart. And if you have a heart that is devoted to Jesus and you sincerely desire to follow the Scriptures, God will give you wisdom in sorting through your own convictions and your own preferences.

C. **Unanswered Questions.** This happens all too often. A student goes off to a state school, a university and meets a professor who is the kindest, most compassionate, loving and gentle person (what a Christian is supposed to be) that the student has ever met. The only problem is the professor is an agnostic and has sensed some "call" to mess with the faith of people who are devoted to Jesus. So they begin raising questions—questions the student isn't yet capable of answering. Often, the reaction is "I'm going to bale; I'm going to give up on the faith." When you're alone in your room or talking to a professor and all of these questions keep coming up in your mind, and you've walked to the edge of the cliff, remember that faith and doubt can both exist in the same mind and in the same heart, as long as Jesus is the Lord of that life and is trusted even with the doubts.

2. **How to Protect Your Faith.** Here are three very practical ways to protect your faith in the midst of great temptation and confusion:

A. **Make a Commitment to Community (Heb. 10:23).** The writer of Hebrews gives us a key to protecting our faith: "Let us hold unswervingly to the hope we profess, for he who promised is faithful" (NIV). Wherever you're headed, find a strong, Bible-believing church and get involved. You could also find a Campus Crusade, Navigators, Young Life, or whatever evangelical organization there is on campus. You can walk with, and pray with, encourage, and be around and be accountable to other people who share your faith.

B. **Make a Commitment to Service (James 2:14).** To hold on to your faith, unless you want a dead faith, James says put your faith into action: "What does it profit, my brethren, if someone says he has faith but does not have works? Can faith save him?" When you graduate, whether you're getting a job, going off to college, or staying locally, I would encourage you to get involved in serving other people, especially those who are marginalized, who are disenfranchised, who are on the fringes of society. Look up the homeless organization in the town where you're going. Look up the rescue missions. Make a determination, "I'm going to get involved in pouring my life into others." I've discovered something interesting over the years, that the more you get involved in pouring life into others, the less intimidating your struggles and your questions seem.

C. **Make a Commitment to Grow (1 Pet. 2:1–2 NIV).** As Peter instructed, "Therefore, rid yourselves of all malice and all deceit, hypocrisy, envy, and slander of every kind. Like newborn babies, crave pure spiritual milk, so that by it you may grow up in your salvation." Read your Bible, study it even if you have questions, even if you have doubts, even if you have struggles. Continue growing in the Word and in your faith.

Closing Prayer: *Father, I pray that this challenge would not only be for those who are graduating, but for all of us. We pray that we would all live in community with others so we can stir each other to love and good deeds. I pray that we would be involved in serving others and that we would pay attention to our own personal growth and walk. In Christ's name we pray. Amen.*

SUGGESTED SERMON

The Path of Wisdom

Date preached:

By Rev. David Jackman

Scripture: Proverbs 3:13–26, especially verse 13
Happy is the man who finds wisdom, and the man who gains understanding.

Introduction: Is God really interested in everyday life, or is He only involved in the bits that seem to be Christian? Is God involved in your everyday life? If He is, the implications are colossal. As Christians, our tendency is to retreat from the everyday world into our contained Christian groups, which can readily become a sort of Christian ghetto. It cripples our ability to build bridges to unbelievers. The wisdom literature of the Old Testament forces us to reflect upon life in God's world in the light of God's Word. The great themes of Proverbs are covered in chapter 3:

1. **Wisdom Is What You've Always Wanted (vv. 13–18).** Verse 13 begins "Happy is the man who finds wisdom, and the man who gains understanding." The verses that follow are a hymn in honor of wisdom. Wisdom is typically personified as a woman because the writer wants to make the abstract principle of wisdom personal. Finding wisdom and getting understanding is the best investment you'll ever make in life. That's the thrust in these verses. The language in verses 14–15 is taken from the marketplace with words such as "profits, silver, gain, gold, precious, rubies." The writer tells us these things cannot compare with wisdom. The possession of wisdom is the greatest treasure you can acquire. Verses 16–18 describe the rewards of wisdom with words like "length of days, riches, honor, pleasantness, peace, happy." These verses aren't intended to promise certain treasures to those who take hold of it, but they teach us a different currency, that wisdom is of greater value than all these possible blessings. Verse 18 refers to the "tree of life," a reference to the Garden of Eden, saying that wisdom is "a tree of life to those who take hold of her." What was lost at the Fall of man into sin can be, to some extent, regained on earth through the

wisdom of God and will lead us on a path to eternal life where all things will be restored.

2. **Wisdom Is How God Has Always Acted (vv. 19–20).** "The LORD by wisdom founded the earth; by understanding He established the heavens; by His knowledge the depths were broken up, and clouds drop down the dew." If we understand how something works and why, we're much more likely to use it and benefit from it. Think of all the training manuals you've used for five minutes and then tossed on the shelf. Proverbs tells us the training manual for wisdom is creation. It points to creation as the handbook of wisdom. Biblical wisdom grounds its worldview in the fact that the universe is God's creation. He is the one God over the whole world. Because it was fashioned after the wisdom of God, the world we live in isn't a random or meaningless phenomenon. The incredible complexities of this world point us to the wisdom of the Creator. This should motivate us to understand His wisdom more through His revealed Word. The wisdom God has shown us through creation and revelation guarantee us meaning in life. The wise person sets aside time and effort to discern and understand the structure of creation so as to be able to live appropriately within it.

3. **Wisdom Is Why We Can Always Live Confidently (vv. 21–26).** The thrust of these last few verses is that if we live according to God's wisdom, we will have confidence in every area of life. It imparts discretion (v. 21), gives life to the soul (v. 22), brings adornment to the neck (v. 22), allows us to walk securely (v. 23), liberates us from fear (v. 24), and protects from fear of terror (v. 25). The Lord Himself is our confidence and will keep us from error (v. 26). The faithful, covenant Lord should be the basis and the grounds for our confidence.

Conclusion: Wisdom is walking with God characterized not only by good management of our resources, but over and above that, characterized by the Lord's personal care over His people. The Lord is our confidence. There's a quiet poise and integrity to the life of someone with wisdom and understanding. Wisdom is to live in a right relationship with God the Creator, within the moral order of His world, as it's revealed in His Word.

STATS, STORIES, AND MORE

The Wisdom of God in Physical Laws of Nature
The wisdom of God is everywhere in creation from the complex inner workings of the human body to natural laws that He continually sustains by His sovereignty. Physical laws are put into place to show His continual unchanging nature and sustaining activity in creation. That's why the police in Oxford closed Magdalene Bridge one May morning. They realized that the tradition of jumping off the bridge to celebrate May Day (a tradition beloved of undergraduates) was extremely dangerous because the river was only three feet deep! Even Oxford undergraduates aren't immune to the law of gravity. *—Rev. David Jackman*

Revelation Motivates Scientific Exploration
The wise person does not think he can totally understand creation, but attempts to seek out the wisdom of God in it as much as possible, for God has revealed Himself as the Creator. That's why it was the Reformation that gave great impetus to scientific exploration. That's why at the Rutherford Laboratories in Cambridge you will find inscribed Psalm 111:2 "The works of the LORD are great, studied by all who have pleasure in them." Rutherford was saying that he was only studying what God had already put in place. All of creation shouts of God's existence, but it's only by His revelation that we can articulate and understand it fully. *—Rev. David Jackman*

The Wisdom of God
It's amazing to me that the actual proverbs section of Proverbs doesn't really begin until you get to chapter 10, which opens with a heading saying, "The proverbs of Solomon." The first nine chapters of the book are a series of images and arguments, telling us how vitally important it is to seek God's wisdom by drinking in His Word like dehydrated shipwreck victims who discover a freshwater spring on their deserted island. There is no abiding wisdom apart from God's Word, but as we store up His commandments within us and begin looking at life's events through the prism of His precepts, we begin maturing into people of sanctified common sense—which is another definition of wisdom. Dr. Paul Tournier once wrote, "The Bible . . . is a book in which [a person] may learn from his Creator the art of healthy living."

APPROPRIATE HYMNS AND SONGS

"He Knows My Name," Tommy Walker, 1996 Doulos Publishing (Maranatha Music).

"Be Thou My Vision," Irish Hymn, (c. 8th century; arr. by Donald Hustad, 1973), Public Domain.

"All I Once Held Dear (Knowing You)," Graham Kendrick, 1993 Make Way Music (Admin. by Music Services).

"Take My Life," Scott Underwood, 1995 Mercy/Vineyard Publishing (Admin. by Music Services).

FOR THE BULLETIN

One day in the second century, Justin Martyr, about 30, met an old man who told him about Christ. He was saved and immediately began telling everyone that Christ can satisfy both mind and heart. He eventually became one of the church's first apologists, and was condemned, flogged, and beheaded for his faith. His life is remembered every year on his feast day, June 1. ● James Guthrie, a Scottish Covenanter, was hanged for his faith on this day in 1661, after which his head was affixed on Netherbow Port. In coming months his little son William, sneaking away to steal glances at his father's decaying head, would run home crying, "I've seen my father's head! I've seen my father's head!" ● On June 1, 1792, at the Baptist Associational Meeting in Nottingham, England, a motion passed that "a plan be prepared against the next Ministers' Meeting at Kettering, for forming a Baptist Society for propagating the gospel among the heathens." It set the stage for the missionary endeavors of William Carey and has been called the "birthday of modern missions." ● On June 1, 1793, Henry Lyle wrote the hymn "Abide with Me." ● On June 1, 1859, Philip and Lucy Bliss were married. They were later to perish in a terrible train wreck, but not before Philip had written such popular hymns as *Man of Sorrows—What a Name!; Jesus Loves Even Me; The Light of the World Is Jesus!; Almost Persuaded;* and *Wonderful Words of Life.* ● June 1, 1972 marks the death of Chinese Christian Watchman Nee, who died in a Chinese prison for his faith in Christ.

WORSHIP HELPS

Call to Worship
I will praise Your name, O LORD, for it is good (Ps. 54:6).

Scripture Reading Medley
Where can wisdom be found? And where is the place of understanding? Man does not know its value. . . . God understands its way, and He knows its place. . . . The LORD gives wisdom; from His mouth come knowledge and understanding; He stores up sound wisdom for the upright; He is a shield to those who walk uprightly. . . . Who is wise? Let him understand these things. Who is prudent? Let him know them. For the ways of the LORD are right; The righteous walk in them. . . . Therefore whoever hears these sayings of Mine, and does them, I will liken him to a wise man. . . . The wisdom that is from above is first pure, then peaceable, gentle, willing to yield, full of mercy and good fruits, without partiality and without hypocrisy. . . . If any of you lacks wisdom, he should ask God, who gives generously to all without finding fault, and it will be given to him. . . . The Spirit of the LORD shall rest upon Him, the Spirit of wisdom and understanding, the Spirit of counsel and might, the Spirit of knowledge and of the fear of the LORD (Job 28:12–13, 23; Prov. 2:6–7; Hos. 14:9; Matt. 7:24; James 3:17 NKJV; 1:5 NIV; Is. 11:2).

Pastoral Prayer
Father, we ask that by Your Spirit You will help us to understand these things more clearly. Give us a great appetite for wisdom, a great incentive to find out more of Your wisdom, so that in all the many changing scenes of life, we may be guided by this greatest of all Your gifts: the wisdom that comes through Your Word, and that is supremely revealed to us in Your Son. Please help us to work at it, and to grow in our love and knowledge of You, through Jesus Christ we pray, Amen.

Additional Sermons and Lesson Ideas

The Creator

Date preached:

By Rev. Melvin Tinker

SCRIPTURE: Isaiah 40:12–31

INTRODUCTION: Do you ever feel discouraged about the state of the world? Isaiah did. However, in the midst of that discouragement, God revealed Himself with tremendous power.

1. God Is Beyond All Measure (vv. 12–14).
2. God Is Beyond All Comparison (vv. 18–24).
3. God Is Beyond All Rivals (vv. 25–26).
4. God Is Beyond All Praising (vv. 27–31).

CONCLUSION: We are not to judge by what we feel or see, but by the word of the living God. It is those who put their hope in him that will keep on when humanly it seems impossible.

The Voices of God

Date preached:

By Dr. Larry Osborne

SCRIPTURE: Psalm 19

INTRODUCTION: "How can I know God and His plan for my life?" That's an age old question answered in Psalm 19. As we study this ancient Psalm (written by King David), we'll discover how God reveals Himself and how He wants us to respond:

1. What God Says Through Nature (vv. 1–6). The majesty, consistency, and completeness of this world declare God's glory. It's unmistakable and only deniable by those who have turned to foolishness (Rom. 1:20–32).
2. Why We Still Need the Bible (vv. 7–11). Nature is inconclusive, however. It displays wisdom, but doesn't teach us of salvation. We need the Word of God to understand and follow Him.
3. What God Expects from Us (vv. 12–14). We are expected, based on the word of God through nature and the Bible, to repent of our sins and plea for acceptance from God.

CONCLUSION: Have you turned to God, the Creator of this world who has revealed Himself through His own Words?

JUNE 8, 2008

SUGGESTED SERMON

It's SO Not About Us!

Date preached:

By Dr. Timothy K. Beougher

Scripture: Romans 11:33–36, especially verse 36
For of Him and through Him and to Him are all things, to whom be glory forever.
Amen.

Introduction: Ptolemy was a second-century astronomer whose viewpoints dominated astronomy until the sixteenth century. He taught that the earth was the center of the universe and that everything else revolved around the earth. But in the early sixteenth century, Copernicus showed that the sun, not the earth, was the center of the universe, and that the earth revolved around the sun. This is known as the Copernican Revolution. We need a Copernican Revolution in our lives and in our church! We need to be reminded that we are not at the center of the universe: God is! We need to be reminded that it is all about God's glory! What happens when we catch a fresh vision of God's glory?

1. **We Ascribe Him Praise (v. 33a).** Romans 11:33 follows several chapters of Paul's presentation of God's Person and His plan. As Paul concludes his discussion of theology, he bursts forth in a doxology of praise. Good theology makes for good doxology. Paul recognizes that God is unlimited in His resources. God knows all there is to know. His wisdom is supreme. When we ponder the greatness of God we will praise the glory of God. Praise should be our natural response to an encounter with God. When we enter into the presence of His majesty and glory, of His holiness and love, we should stand in awe. When we catch a fresh vision of God's glory, we ascribe Him praise.

2. **We Assert His Transcendence (v. 33b).** God is beyond our comprehension. How unsearchable are His judgments, and His paths beyond tracing out! Isaiah 55:8–9 says: "'For My thoughts are not your thoughts, nor are your ways My ways,' says the LORD. 'For as the heavens are higher than the earth, so are My ways higher than your ways and My thoughts than your thoughts.'" Sometimes we

can see a part of His wondrous ways, and we can be thankful for that glimpse. But often we can't understand. We can, however, learn to trust that God knows what He's doing and that He will do what is right. What we can do is worship Him in wonder and awe. God is the transcendent One.

3. **We Acknowledge His Sufficiency (vv. 34–35).** Paul here quotes from Isaiah 40 to bring into focus God's sufficiency. Who has known the mind of the Lord? Or who has been His counselor? The expected answer to those rhetorical questions is a resounding "No one!" God is sufficient in Himself: He doesn't need advice from us in how to run the universe. It's laughable to think that anyone would presume to be God's teacher. Is there anything that God doesn't know? But how often we feel compelled to try and tell God how to do His job and get mad at Him when He doesn't do exactly what WE think is best!

4. **We Affirm His Centrality (v. 36a).** "For of Him and through Him and to Him are all things . . ." This teaches us:

   A. **God Is the Source of All Things.** "Of Him." All things originated from God. There was a time when there was nothing but God (Gen. 1:1; John 1:1–4).

   B. **God Is the Sustainer of All Things.** "Through Him." God is providentially exercising His care over the world. God maintains all things. Deism teaches that God created the world but isn't involved in it now. This is heresy! God is the Sustainer of all things (cf. Col. 1:16–17; Rom. 8:28)!

   C. **God Is the Significance of All Things.** "To Him." Everything in creation is designed to bring glory to God. Consider Isaiah 48:9–11: "For My name's sake I will defer My anger, and for My praise I will restrain it from you, so that I do not cut you off. Behold, I have refined you, but not as silver; I have tested you in the furnace of affliction. For My own sake, for My own sake, I will do it; for how should My name be profaned? And I will not give My glory to another."

5. **We Aim for His Glory (v. 36b).** "To Him be the glory forever! Amen." Living for the things of this world is shortsighted. You were made for eternity.

Conclusion: First Corinthians 10:31 reminds us: "Therefore, whether you eat or drink, or whatever you do, do all to the glory of God." It is SO not about us! Let's catch a fresh vision of the glory of God and let it transform us! Let's do everything for His glory!

STATS, STORIES, AND MORE

More from Dr. Beougher

Joni Erickson Tada, in her award-winning book, *A Step Further,* responds to the struggle she faced following the accident that left her a quadriplegic. As she questioned God's goodness and fairness in the midst of her suffering, she began to see the futility of such thinking: "What made me think that even if God explained all His ways to me I would be able to understand them? It would be like pouring million-gallon truths into my one-ounce brain. Why, even the great apostle Paul admitted that, though never in despair, he was often perplexed (2 Cor. 4:8). . . . In fact, the whole book of Ecclesiastes was written to convince people like me that only God holds the keys to unlocking the mysteries of life and that He's not loaning them all out! . . . If God's mind was small enough for me to understand, He wouldn't be God!"

"Through Him"

> *Through Him we heirs of Heaven are made;*
> *O Brother, Christ, extend Thine aid*
> *That we may firmly trust in Thee*
> *And through Thee live eternally.*
> *Hallelujah!*
> —AN ANONYMOUS SEVENTEENTH-CENTURY
> HYMN

APPROPRIATE HYMNS AND SONGS

"It Is You," Peter Furler, 2002 Ariose Music (Admin. by EMI Christian Music Pub.).

"Jesus, Lover of My Soul," Paul Oakley, 1995 ThankYou Music (Admin. by EMI Christian Music Pub.).

"The Heart of Worship," Matt Redman, 1997 ThankYou Music (Admin. by EMI Christian Music Pub.).

"Be Glorified," Louie Giglio, Jesse Reeves, and Chris Tomlin, 1999 Worshiptogether.com songs (Admin. by EMI Christian Music Pub.).

FOR THE BULLETIN

On June 8, 328, Athanasius was named Bishop of Alexandria, the highest ecclesiastical office in the East. During his 46 years as bishop, he combated heresy and fearlessly proclaimed the gospel. He was banished four times from his church and spent a total of 20 years in exile. ● The founder of Islam, Mohammed, died on this day in 632. He did not rise again. ● John Huss, the Bohemian Reformer, was sentenced to death on June 8, 1415. The night before he had suffered from toothache, vomiting, and headache, yet he defended himself using the example of St. Paul as his model. He was burned on July 6th. ● On June 8, 1794, a disciple of Rousseau named Robespierre and the French National Convention formally inaugurated a new religion. It was a form of deism, the belief that there is a God who, having created the universe, more or less disappeared. ● The German composer Robert A. Schumann was born on this day in 1819. He wrote the tune Canonbury, which became the setting for the hymn "Lord Speak to Me That I May Speak." ● President Andrew Jackson died on this day in 1845. After resisting the witness of his wife, Rachel, for many years, Jackson became a Christian after her death. To a friend he said: "I have full confidence in the goodness and mercy of God. The Bible is true. Upon that sacred volume I rest my hope for eternal salvation, through the merits and blood of our blessed Lord and Savior Jesus Christ."

Kid's Talk

Bring a five-gallon bucket, some bricks or large rocks, and labels. Ask the children to tell you what God is like. As they call out attributes and actions of God, write them down on the labels, label each brick, and put it in the bucket. Once you've filled it to be fairly heavy, ask the children if they think they can lift it. You might try yourself and show them how heavy it is. Label the bucket "Glory." Explain that the word "glory" in the Bible actually means "weight." If we were to truly understand all that God is and all He does, it's too hard for us to understand, just like the bucket is too hard for us to lift!

WORSHIP HELPS

Call to Worship
Sing to Him, sing psalms to Him; Talk of all His wondrous works! Glory in His holy name; Let the hearts of those rejoice who seek the LORD (1 Chr. 16:9–10)!

Offertory Scripture
He who sows sparingly will also reap sparingly, and he who sows bountifully will also reap bountifully. So let each one give as he purposes in his heart, not grudgingly or of necessity; for God loves a cheerful giver. And God is able to make all grace abound toward you, that you, always having all sufficiency in all things, may have an abundance for every good work (2 Cor. 9:6–8).

Benediction
Almighty Lord, we praise You for Christ Jesus, for of Him and through Him and to Him are all things, to whom be glory forever. Amen (Rom. 11:36).

Additional Sermons and Lesson Ideas

Praise the Lord!
By Joshua D. Rowe

Date preached:

SCRIPTURE: Psalm 150

INTRODUCTION: The final Psalm instructs us to praise the Lord. This is obviously its theme, as it repeats the word "praise" thirteen times, once in every line! It begins and ends with the command "Praise the Lord!" (vv. 1, 6). In between this repetition of commands, the Psalm answers important questions about praise:

1. Where? Praise the Lord Where He Is (v. 1). In the Old Testament, the sanctuary was considered the dwelling place of God. However, they also understood the omnipresence of God, so they acknowledged God's presence in the "firmament" or heavenly expanse.
2. Why? Praise the Lord for What He Does and Who He Is (v. 2). We should praise God for His "mighty acts" (what He does) and for His "excellent greatness" (who He is).
4. How? Praise the Lord with Every Instrument (vv. 3–5). Anything that helps create music to celebrate and uplift the Lord should be used to its greatest potential to do just that!

CONCLUSION: Praise the Lord (v. 6)!

A Guiding Star for the Journey of Faith
By Pastor Larry Kirk

Date preached:

SCRIPTURE: Genesis 18:16–33

INTRODUCTION: On a number of occasions, people have been lost and in danger of death, but found their way by locating the North Star. What makes the North Star so important is that it is dependable. God's righteousness is an unchanging point of reference that guides His actions, and should guide our faith:

1. God's Commitment to Righteousness Guides His Purpose for Our Lives (vv. 17–19). The Lord declares that His plans were centered around showing His own righteousness to Abraham. He wants us to see His righteousness too!
2. God's Commitment to Righteousness Guides His Judgment on Sin (vv. 20–21). God judged Sodom and Gomorrah because their sin was offensive to His own righteousness. We must keep in mind that our sin offends God's character!

3. God's Commitment to Righteousness Guides Our Faith in Him (vv. 22–33). Abraham wasn't questioning God's love and righteousness, He was exploring the meaning of God's love for righteousness. As we explore the extent of God's righteousness, we see the true depth of His character!

CONCLUSION: Put your faith in God, for only He is righteous. You can stand firm in that fact!

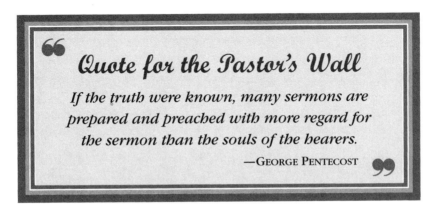

66 *Quote for the Pastor's Wall*

If the truth were known, many sermons are prepared and preached with more regard for the sermon than the souls of the hearers.

—GEORGE PENTECOST 99

Finding Time to Study

Bishop Ambrose of Milan is famous for counting among his converts the great Augustine, who was deeply persuaded by the Bishop's sermons and touched by his intensity and piety. Interestingly, however, August had little actual interaction with Ambrose. The man didn't have time to see people; he was too busy studying. His guests—including Augustine—were ushered quietly into his office and allowed to watch him while he studied, but interruptions weren't allowed.

No wonder his sermons were powerful enough to convert the young cynical, skeptical Augustine.

Some ministers have the intestinal fortitude to resist their congregation's attempts to water down their study time. Dr. Peter Grainger, pastor of Charlotte Chapel of Edinburgh, told me how one of his predecessors, Dr. Graham Scroggie, handled it. Calling his elders into the office, he threw his feet onto the desk and said, "Gentleman, you can either have my feet or my head; you cannot have both."

They wanted his head, so they gave him time to study and found others to do the footwork required for effective pastoring.

Most of our congregations wouldn't stand for such a thing today; but we still need adequate time for study. Our primary job is to feed the sheep; but the demands of today's churches make it hard to obey Paul's injunction, "Study to shew thyself approved unto God, a workman that needeth not to be ashamed, rightly dividing the word of truth" (2 Tim. 2:15 KJV).

The problem is magnified for bi-vocational pastors. Having put 30, 40, or 50 hours into another job, how can the pastor possibly find time to *tend* the flock and to *feed* it?

I'd like to throw out a scattering of ideas that have helped me over the years. Some of these suggestions will work in your setting; others won't. But perhaps scanning the list will inspire you to devote yourself afresh to standing in God's counsel and waiting for His message.

✎ *Work Your Study Time into a Set of Lifetime Habits.* When I was preparing for ministry, I was deeply influenced by preachers who recommended devoting the morning hours to study. Dr. W. A. Criswell of Dallas famously kept his study in his home, and every morning he padded there pajama-clad to study until lunch. Then he dressed, went to the church, and spent the rest of his day available to the world, as he put it. The great British scholars had this down pat. Their mornings were sacred, set apart for Bible study and sermon preparation. As a result of these influences, I began my first pastorate telling people I wanted my mornings for study, barring emergencies. Most people appreciated this habit and respected it. The morning hours might not work for you, and it may be impossible to devote 20 or 30 hours a week to studying; but find a routine that fits your schedule and make it a habit. Just an hour a day will make a difference.

✎ *Along the Same Lines, It Might Be Helpful, When Possible, to Have Your Study in Your Home, Easily Accessible and Less Interruptible.* I did this my first year of ministry, and then we needed the room for a baby nursery, forcing me to the church office. Now, 30 years later, I'm reestablishing a home study by renovating my garage. One advantage is I can keep an open Bible on my desk there, and if I have just ten or fifteen minutes—like during halftime—I can take advantage of the moments. At night when I can't sleep, my books are close at hand.

✎ *Think of Studying as Something You Do Throughout the Day at the Slightest Opportunity.* Even when I'm waiting on someone for lunch, I can scan the newspaper looking for a good sermon illustration. I often keep a book in my car in case of traffic jams, construction delays, or railroad crossings. With our portable electronic tools, we can even listen to books or lectures while walking or working out;

Continued on the next page

THOUGHTS FOR THE PASTOR'S SOUL—*Continued*

but there's one caution: Great podcasts can never replace the fine art of meditation . . . . But that's the next point.

❧ *Learn to Meditate.* Years ago, a New York attorney named Richard Storrs entered the ministry and was alarmed at hearing other pastors. As a lawyer, he'd watched the great courtroom jurists who, without notes, had waxed eloquent and won their arguments. In contrast, most ministers of that day read their sermons and the presentations were utterly boring. In 1875, Storrs delivered a set of lectures at Union Theological Seminary in which he advocated preaching without notes, and he suggested a unique study technique—walking. He said, in effect, that we should study the passage on which we're planning to preach until we've mastered the facts of it. Then we should go for a long walk and think it through until we can explain it simply, as though taking a friend through the passage point by point on the hoof. He advocated peripatetic sermon preparation. We can preach the passage simpler and with fewer notes when we let the content of the Scripture unfold naturally. What Storrs was really describing was basic biblical meditation, a missing ingredient in most sermon preparation today.

❧ *Have Bible, Will Preach.* When I was in college, I had the opportunity to spend a weekend in the home of my favorite preacher, Stuart Briscoe, and I actually slept on the little sofa-bed in his study. What surprised me was his lack of books. When I asked him about it, he told me that a preacher's widow had recently offered to give him her late husband's entire library, "but I didn't have time to go get it," he said. Well, I would certainly have gotten it because I love books. But Stuart was (and still is) almost always on the road. His terrific sermons come from his own study of the Bible without much recourse to commentaries, inspirational books, preaching aids, pulpit helps, biographies, or theological works. "Have

Bible, Will Preach," he once quipped to me. While I still use a lot of books, I've found that the Bible itself contains all I really need, and by the time I've thoroughly studied the biblical text I often don't have time for the other books that litter my shelves. If you have a Bible at hand, your study is wherever you are, morning, noon, or night. "Apply yourself wholly to the text," said Johann Albrecht Bengle, "and apply the text wholly to yourself."

- *Take Study Breaks.* Many of the British expositors took the entirety of July away from their pulpits as a month-long study sabbatical for upcoming sermons. I've never done that, but I do sometimes steal away overnight or for a few days just to immerse myself in the book of the Bible or topic I'm planning to tackle in the pulpit. Personal study retreats are good for both body, mind, and soul.

- *Preach Shorter Messages, and Fewer.* Finally, try preaching a little less, giving more study to each individual message. Recently I downloaded a sermon by John Stott and started listening to it with great interest. It was just what I needed, and Stott's exposition was flawless. To my surprise, after about ten or fifteen minutes he signed off and was finished. I shouldn't have been surprised, because Stott is known for preaching sermons that are as short as they're rich. But it reminded me that a concise, well-arranged sermon is better than a longer one that rambles.

In his classic book, *Waldon,* Henry David Thoreau described the simple pleasure of logs for the fireplace. "They warmed me twice" he wrote, "—once while I was splitting them, and again when they were on the fire!"

It's the same with good sermons—they warm us twice, once while we're preparing them and again when we preach them. Find a way of keeping your ax sharp, your arm bared, and the splinters flying.

JUNE 15, 2008

FATHER'S DAY SUGGESTED SERMON

Pleasing Father

Date preached:

By Pastor Al Detter

Scripture: Various, especially John 8:29
And He who sent Me is with Me. The Father has not left Me alone, for I always do those things that please Him.

Introduction: Today people will get cards and give greetings that say, "Happy Father's Day." For some of us, it's a happy day. For others, it's not. Some have great relationships with their fathers; for some, the memories and relationships aren't so pleasant. Our circumstances are so varied in this room when it comes to our fathers. So, I want to talk about something we can all relate to today—how important it is to please our heavenly Father. I would like to point out six specific things that please God according to Scripture.

1. **Attention.** Paul in 2 Timothy 2:4 says, "No one engaged in warfare entangles himself with the affairs of this life, that he may please him who enlisted him as a soldier." God doesn't want the cares and things of this world to distract our attention from Him. God the Father loves our attention. We must take steps daily to give Him undistracted devotion. It pleases Him.

2. **Obedience.** Jesus said in John 8:29 that He always did the things that pleased the Father. That's a remarkable statement. Doing the things that please the Father means obedience to what God tells us to do. Jesus lived a life of total obedience to the will of the Father and it was pleasing to the Father. Friends, what Jesus did must become the goal for our lives—we should always do what pleases the Father (cf. John 4:34; 5:30; 1 John 3:22).

3. **Holiness.** Unfortunately this word is quite infrequent in our vocabularies. However, it's high on God's agenda: ". . . but as He who called you is holy, you also be holy in all your conduct" (1 Pet. 1:15). Holiness is about our lifestyle, how we behave (cf. 1 Thess. 4:1; Col. 1:10). We are holy when we do what God would have us do and unholy when we disregard the commands of Scripture.

4. **Faith.** The author of Hebrews teaches an incredible truth about pleasing God: "But without faith it is impossible to please Him . . ." (Heb. 11:6). Faith pleases the Father. He loves for His children to trust Him. Faith and trust have been very hard for the children of God over the centuries. We respond very strongly to the data of what's observable around us. It affects how we live more than anything else. We live in a world where seeing is believing, but God says, "I'm pleased when you trust Me for things you can't see."

5. **Sacrifices.** Hebrews 13:15–16 teaches us, "Therefore by Him let us continually offer the sacrifice of praise to God, that is, the fruit of our lips, giving thanks to His name. But do not forget to do good and to share, for with such sacrifices God is well pleased." By giving thanks, we acknowledge that God is sovereign and working all things. By giving to others, we share the grace given to us by God. When God sees people praising Him or doing good things for others, it gives Him pleasure. So don't neglect doing good to one another, especially those who are of the household of faith (Gal. 6:10).

6. **Witnessing.** Paul tells us in 1 Corinthians 1:21: "For since, in the wisdom of God, the world through wisdom did not know God, it pleased God through the foolishness of the message preached to save those who believe." I'd love to see all of us sharing our faith with others on a consistent basis. And not just because people come to Christ, as great as that is. But because it pleases God! We need to understand that when we share the good news of Christ and when people believe, God is thrilled. And so is all heaven. Nothing could please Him more. There's nothing greater on God's heart than reaching the lost.

Conclusion: Maybe we can't always please our earthly fathers. And maybe there are some earthly fathers who aren't easy to please. But we can each please our heavenly Father. We must all remember an important truth: God doesn't love us on the basis of performance. If we please Him really good, He doesn't love us more. And if we rarely please Him, He doesn't love us less. That's part of the mystery of God's love for us. But I can't imagine living as a believer without a deep desire to please God. The joy of our hearts should be giving God pleasure.

STATS, STORIES, AND MORE

Hint for the Preacher

This sermon would be enhanced by a personal illustration or story about your desire to please someone in authority over you. Perhaps there was a time when you so very much wanted to please your dad or mom, or a teacher or coach. That's the way we should feel about pleasing our heavenly Father.

A Charles Wesley Hymn

> I want the witness, Lord, that all I do is right,
> According to Thy mind and Word, well pleasing in Thy sight.

From the Obituary Pages

There are some miscellaneous obits that occurred as the Sourcebook was going to press. Using a search engine, you could find a set of your own showing how much it means to people when they see someone whose desire is to please others:

> ❧ *His uniform and appearance was head and shoulders over the rest of us. He was easy to get along with and wanted to please everyone*—about a soldier killed in the Iraq War when his Blackhawk Helicopter went down.

> ❧ *I'll always remember how good he was and how much he wanted to please his family*—about a North Carolina salesman who died of a heart attack.

> ❧ *All his teachers liked him. He wanted to please and do his best*—nine-year-old who battled cancer.

The Advantages of Pleasing God Rather than Men
by Richard Baxter (1615–1691)

1. If you seek first to please God and are satisfied therein, you have but one to please instead of multitudes; and a multitude of masters are harder pleased than One.
2. And it is One that putteth upon you nothing that is unreasonable, for quantity or quality.
3. And One that is perfectly wise and good, not liable to misunderstand your case and actions.
4. And He is One that is constant and unchangeable; and is not pleased with one thing today, and another contrary tomorrow; nor with one person this year, whom He will be weary of the next.
5. And He is One that is merciful, and requireth you not to hurt yourselves to please Him: nay, He is pleased with nothing of thine but that which tendeth to thy happiness, and displeased with nothing but that which hurts thyself or others.

APPROPRIATE HYMNS AND SONGS

"Faith of Our Fathers," Frederick W. Faber & Henri F. Hemy, Public Domain.

"God of Our Fathers," Daniel C. Roberts & George W. Warren, Public Domain.

"My Redeemer Lives," Reuben Morgan, 1998 Hillsong Publishing.

"Blessed Be the Name," Charles Wesley, Public Domain.

FOR THE BULLETIN

On June 15, 1215, King John put his seal on the Magna Carta at Runnymede, which had been heavily influenced by Archbishop Stephen Langton. ● On June 15, 1520, Pope Leo X issued his famous *Exsurge Domine,* which began "Arise, O Lord . . . a wild boar has invaded your vineyard." The wild boar was Martin Luther who was threatened with excommunication if he would not recant his beliefs. ● On June 15, 1551, Theodore Beza took sick while at Lausanne during the plague. His worried friend, John Calvin, wrote: "I am concerned about the loss the church would suffer if in the midst of his career he should suddenly be removed by death. I hope . . . that he will be given back to us in answer to our prayers." Calvin's prayers were answered. Beza had yet a half-century to minister. ● Samuel J. Mills was dedicated to foreign missions by his mother before his birth in 1783. He was converted to Christ at age 17, and was a participant in the famous 1806 "Haystack Prayer Meeting" that helped launch America's first foreign missionary program. He died at age 35 on this day in 1818 while returning from a missionary trip to Africa. ● On June 15, 1951, missionary William C. Easton was leading a youth service in Columbia, South America. The police burst in and seized him and four young men. They were clubbed, whipped, dunked in cold water, stripped, and forced to roll in hot ashes. The next morning upon his release, Rev. Easton told the police, "I forgive you in the name of Jesus Christ."

WORSHIP HELPS

Call to Worship
The living, the living—they praise you, as I am doing today;
fathers tell their children about your faithfulness (Is. 38:19 NIV).

Reader's Theater
*This would be appropriate for a grandfather, father, and a son from
your congregation to read these Scriptures if possible. If not, an older
father, young father, and a boy would be appropriate as well.*

Grandfather: Do not forsake me, O God, till I declare your
power to the next generation, your might to all
who are to come (Ps. 71:18 NIV).

Father: Fathers, do not exasperate your children; instead,
bring them up in the training and instruction of
the Lord (Eph. 6:4 NIV).

Young Man: Children obey your parents in the Lord, for this is
right (Eph. 6:1 NIV).

Father: Fathers, do not embitter your children, or they
will become discouraged (Col. 3:21 NIV).

Young Man: Children, obey your parents in everything, for this
pleases the Lord (Col. 3:20 NIV).

Grandfather: I will exalt you, my God the King; I will praise
your name for ever and ever. Every day I will
praise you and extol your name for ever and ever.
Great is the LORD and most worthy of praise; his
greatness no one can fathom. One generation will
commend your works to another; they will tell of
your mighty acts (Ps. 145:1–4 NIV).

Benediction
You, O LORD, reign forever; your throne endures from
generation to generation (Lam. 5:19 NIV).

Additional Sermons and Lesson Ideas

Men Behaving Dadly

Date preached:

SCRIPTURE: Proverbs 4:1

INTRODUCTION: Fatherhood is an awesome concept, but there's nothing abstract about being a dad. It's a matter of everyday life, of saying and doing the right things for your kids. Here are six important techniques for behaving dadly:

1. Find Ways to Complement Your Child Often. Children tend to derive their "explanatory style" (such as optimism or pessimism) from their mothers, but their self-image is usually based on how they believe their father views them.
2. Tuck Your Child into Bed Every Night with Prayer. There's nothing that bonds father and child together more than the quiet moments at the end of the day, in the shadows of a darkened room, as you sit on the bedside and pray with your child.
3. Read Books and Deemphasize Movies and Television.
4. Memorize Bible Verses with Your Child. Your child can memorize four verses for every *one* you can learn; but make sure you're storing God's Word in their IQs.
5. Assign Chores for Your Child to Do. Children learn to be responsible by accomplishing their assigned tasks at home.
6. Go on Excursions with Your Youngster. Your children need your time, dates and opportunities when your attention is focused just on them.

CONCLUSION: Some of these things are doable, whatever the age of your child. It's never too late to behave dadly.

Understanding Our Spiritual Battle (Part 2)

Date preached:

By Dr. Larry Osborne

SCRIPTURE: Ephesians 6:10–20

INTRODUCTION: Today I want to discuss spiritual warfare. Let's look at Scripture's advice on this subject:

1. Three Traits You Need for the Battle:
    A. Truth (v. 14).
    B. Righteousness (v. 14).
    C. Peace (v. 15).

2. Three Things You'll Need in the Battle:
   A. Trust God Enough to Do What He Says (v. 16).
   B. Salvation (v. 17).
   C. Scripture (v. 17).
3. One Habit You'll Want to Practice Daily: Prayer (vv. 18–20).

CONCLUSION: We must remember that spiritual warfare isn't about avoiding pain, hardship, or injustice. It's about standing tall in the midst of life's toughest blows (Matt. 7:24–25; James 4:7; 1 Pet. 5:8–10; Heb. 10:32–39). Are you ready for the battle?

PRAYER FOR THE PASTOR'S CLOSET

I am lonely
But Thou leavest me not.
I am feeble in heart,
But Thou leavest me not.
I am restless,
But with Thee there is peace.
In me there is bitterness,
But with Thee there is patience.
Thy ways are past understanding,
But thou knowest the way for me.
—DIETRICH BONHOEFFER
(1906–1945)

JUNE 22, 2008

SUGGESTED SERMON

Courting Disaster

Date preached:

By Rev. Peter Grainger

Scripture: 1 Corinthians 6:12–20, especially verse 19
Or do you not know that your body is the temple of the Holy Spirit who is in you, whom you have from God, and you are not your own?

Introduction: The opportunities for sexual indulgence in our society are enormous. What was once practiced secretly and seen as shameful is now openly accepted. However, there's nothing unique about sexual indulgence. The Greek city of Corinth was overlooked by a 2,000-foot-high hill topped with a huge temple to the goddess, Aphrodite, which reportedly housed 1,000 sacred prostitutes. In such seemingly hostile soil, another kind of temple had come into being in Corinth: not a physical building but a group of people in whom the one true God lived by His Spirit. Writing to these Christians, Paul exhorts them not to fall back into their old lifestyle. We can learn three vital truths and three applications to keep our bodies pure.

1. **The Purpose of the Body (vv. 12–14).** Prevalent in Corinth was the idea that everything is permissible, so one can do as he wishes with his own body. Paul explains that such an inference is wrong. God is vitally concerned about what we do with our bodies. They were not designed for sexual immorality, but for the Lord. Living the Christian life is actually the life of the Spirit lived through our bodies. At the end of His life on earth, rather than casting off the body and assuming a spiritual existence, Jesus was raised! So, our bodies, too, have an eternal destiny and purpose in the resurrection. The Christian focuses not on his rights, but his responsibilities.

2. **The Power of the Body (vv. 15–18).** The Corinthians believed that the spirit of a person was on a different level than the body, so deeds of the flesh don't affect the spiritual realm. They were wrong and so are we if we hold to this idea! Paul reminds the Corinthians that their bodies are members of Christ Himself (v. 15). The word "joined" in verse 17 literally means "to glue together." For a Christian whose

body is destined for resurrection, to glue himself to a prostitute leads to self-harm and offense to Christ.

3. **The Purchase of the Body (vv. 19–20).** Rather than a Christian being free to do what he or she likes with the body (as in v. 12), Paul reminds the Corinthians and us that we no longer belong to ourselves but to God who has a different plan for our bodies. The language is that of the marketplace and the slave market in particular. The Christians, once slaves to sin, have now been purchased by God. Because we were bought, we must honor God with our bodies (v. 20). No view of the Christian's body—as a temple in which God lives by his Spirit—could be higher. No stronger reason or incentive could be given for avoiding sexual immorality.

Application:
1. **Radical Surgery (Matt. 5:27–30).** The word for "sexual immorality" includes all sexual acts outside of marriage, whether men or women. This includes the thought and the intention behind the acts that are also crucial (Matt. 5:27–28). Jesus calls for radical surgery to protect against sin: "If your right eye causes you to sin, pluck it out and cast it from you; for it is more profitable for you that one of your members perish, than for your whole body to be cast into hell" (Matt. 5:29).

2. **Radical Discipleship (Mark 8:34).** Radical discipleship means: "Whoever desires to come after Me, let him deny himself, and take up his cross, and follow Me." This means not standing up for our perceived rights, but laying them aside in the Father's service as Christ did on the Cross. Denying yourself in the area of sexual behavior is a most distinctive way this will be seen and noticed.

3. **Radical Repentance (Rom. 6:13).** If you've failed in this area of sexual purity, or any sin against the body for that matter (drugs, alcohol, self-injury, anorexia, etc.), you need to repent today. Radical repentance begins with confession of sin to God and being accountable to a mature Christian. Present yourself to the Lord as in Romans 6:13: And do not present your members as instruments of unrighteousness to sin, but present yourselves to God as being alive from the dead, and your members as instruments of righteousness to God."

Conclusion: So perhaps today is a day for radical repentance and a day for cleansing the temple and rededicating it to the service of the One who purchased it with His own blood.

STATS, STORIES, AND MORE

Stats About Youth and Sex in the Media

- In the programming most frequently watched by adolescents, 83% contains some sexual content—not just passing references but an average of 6.7 scenes that include sexual topics per hour—and 20% explicitly or implicitly portrays couples engaging in sexual intercourse.[1]

- In 2001, 30% of sexually active minority adolescent females said they had seen an X-rated movie in a theater or on videotape in the three months before the survey.[2]

- On average, children aged nine to seventeen years use the Internet four days per week and spend almost two hours online at a time. Sixty-one percent of teenagers using computers "surf the net," and 14% report "seeing something they wouldn't want their parents to know about." Sixty percent of youth report accessing chat rooms and Web sites, mainly alone.[3]

- In 1999, 22% of teen-oriented radio segments contained sexual content, 20% of which were "pretty explicit" or "very explicit."[4]

Letter to a pastor from a member after a sermon on sexual purity:

Yes, I do struggle with porn. I have for nearly thirty years. My job requires computer use. Some days that's like asking an alcoholic to man the liquor store. You have got to be prayed up every minute of every day. Your mind has to be on God and His faithfulness. And more importantly His Grace and His Mercy that are new every morning. Guilt can tear you down and send you into a downward spiral that takes weeks to get out of.

[1]Escobar-Chaves, S. Liliana, Susan R. Tortolero, Christine M. Markham, Barbara J. Low, Patricia Eitel and Patricia Thickstun, *Impact of the Media on Adolescent Sexual Attitudes and Behaviors—Executive Summary,* Pediatrics 2005;116;297–300. (Pediatrics is the official Journal of the American Academy of Pediatrics), DOI: 10.1542/peds.2005–0355B. Online Article at: http://pediatrics.aappublications.org/cgi/content/full/116/1/S1/297 accessed 1/16/2007.
[2]Ibid.
[3]Ibid.
[4]Ibid.

APPROPRIATE HYMNS AND SONGS

"Fairest Lord Jesus," Munster, Hoffman von Fallersleben's, arr. by Richard S. Willis, Public Domain.

"Rock of Ages," Rita Baloche, 1997 Maranatha Praise, Inc.

"Savior, Like a Shepherd," William B. Bradbury, Public Domain.

"Search Me, O God," J. Edwin Orr & Mark Hill, 1997 Harold Flammer Music.

FOR THE BULLETIN

The Third General Council of the church convened in Ephesus on June 22, 431, primarily to deal with the Nestorian heresy. ● Queen Elizabeth's Prayer Book was published on this day in 1559. ● America's first "Blue Laws" requiring church attendance in Virginia were enacted on June 22, 1611. Everyone was required, morning and afternoon, to attend services on the Sabbath. Penalty for the first offense was economic sanction; second offenders were whipped. ● Commentator Matthew Henry died on June 22, 1714. ● On this day in 1750, Jonathan Edwards was dismissed from his pulpit in Northampton, Massachusetts, by popular vote, after serving there twenty-three years.

WORSHIP HELPS

Call to Worship
Whoever offers praise glorifies Me; and to him who orders his conduct aright I will show the salvation of God (Ps. 50:23).

Offertory Comments
Before the offering is collected today, I would like you all to bow your heads. As we bow, I want to ask you a few questions. First, have you thought about today's offering: why you are or aren't giving, how much, and with what type of heart? I want to pause for a moment to allow you to pray over the offering you're about to give, that you might have a cheerful heart in giving, that you would give as God prompts your heart, and God would bless what you give to further His kingdom.

Suggested Scriptures
- Mark 7:20–23
- Romans 13:13
- 1 Corinthians 10:8
- 2 Corinthians 12:21
- Galatians 5:19
- Ephesians 5:3
- Colossians 3:5
- 1 Thessalonians 4:3
- Jude 1:7
- Revelation 2:14–25

Additional Sermons and Lesson Ideas

How to Replace Wrath with Mercy
By Dr. Larry Osborne

Date preached:

SCRIPTURE: Various

INTRODUCTION: Everyone thinks mercy and forgiveness are lovely ideas. That is until we have someone or something to forgive! Today we'll look at scriptural ideas for dealing with life's little (and huge) injustices.

1. I Must Genuinely Want to Be Merciful (Mark 7:6–9).
2. Give God Permission to Change the Way I Think and Feel (Prov. 19:11; Rom. 12:1–2; Eph. 4:17–24; Phil. 2:13).
3. Stop Making Excuses and Take Full Responsibility for How I Respond (Prov. 29:11; Matt. 5:23–24; 7:3–5).
4. Immediately Start Returning Good for Evil (Prov. 25:21–22; Matt. 5:43–48; Rom. 12:17, 20–21; Eph. 4:32).

CONCLUSION: "Blessed are the merciful, for they shall obtain mercy" (Matt. 5:7).

We Will Tell of God's Greatness
By Pastor Al Detter

Date preached:

SCRIPTURE: Psalm 145:3–6

INTRODUCTION: God's greatness is proclaimed in these verses and all throughout nature and Scripture. How should we respond to the greatness of God? Psalm 145 gives us three specific ways:

1. Celebration (vv. 3–4). Praise God for who He is and what He's done!
2. Meditation (v. 5). Ponder God's majesty and His wondrous works.
3. Conversation (vv. 4, 6). Pass down the praise of God to the next generation (v. 4) and tell everyone of our great God (v. 6).

CONCLUSION: Do you live and worship in light of God's greatness?

JUNE 29, 2008

SUGGESTED SERMON

Seven Steps for Trusting God as We Get Older

Date preached:

By Dr. Woodrow Kroll

Scripture: Psalm 62, especially verses 1–3
Truly my soul silently *waits* for God; from Him *comes* my salvation. He only *is* my rock and my salvation; *He is* my defense; I shall not be greatly moved. How long will you attack a man? You shall be slain, all of you, like a leaning wall and a tottering fence.

Introduction: Aging is an issue we all face, for every day takes us closer to the last day of our lives. Will God be faithful to us in the end of life as He was in the early part of life? More importantly, will we be faithful to Him? Psalm 62 gives us David's seven-step program for trusting God as we age.

1. **Wait Silently Before God Each Day (v. 1).** Spend time every day in silence before God. I'm interested in that phrase "wait silently." It's the same Hebrew term as in Leviticus 10:3 about Aaron after the death of his two sons. The older we get, the more difficult it is to get into the habit of spending time with God each day. So, if you're moving toward old age (and we all are), the first step is to wait silently before God every day. That means you're not going to complain to God when things don't go the way you think they should. You're going to hang on and let God do His work. All this depends on how much you trust the character of God (v. 5b). God is our expectation.

2. **Cling to Something that Doesn't Change (vv. 2–6).** When things are rapidly changing around you, you need to cling to something that doesn't change. It's like holding on to a bar or a tree or something when you're in the middle of a windstorm. You have to hang on to something that isn't going to change. God is our rock. As things change around you, think of His faithfulness. Cling to Him because He is the One you can trust in the middle of the storm. The storm comes in older age with regard to pain. It comes with

regard to the loss of friends or family members. The issues of age can be a great deterrent to faith, but faith can be a great deterrent to the issues of age.

3. **Don't Be Shaken in Your Faith (vv. 3–7).** Maybe you've lost the dearest on earth to you. You're living alone now and asking yourself, "Has God abandoned me? I'm worried about the kids because they don't seem worried about me." Suddenly, you find yourself shaken in your faith like an old shed tottering in the wind. Take time every day to be silent before the Lord and let Him minister to you. While you're doing that, hold on to God. Cling to Him as you would cling to a rock wall in a storm. While you're doing that, don't be shaken in your faith. That's difficult advice, but good advice. Confidence is always the antidote to the jitters. Where you're shaken in your faith, confidence in God is the answer. Verse 7 says God is our salvation, glory, rock, and refuge.

4. **Trust Him at All Times (v. 8).** Learn to trust God in every issue you face. Some of the issues we face in aging are different and more difficult than the issues we faced when we were younger. But trust God at all times. We trust God when we have confidence in His character to do what He has promised to do. Learn to trust God regardless of what comes to your life.

5. **Pour Out Your Heart to Him (v. 8).** What does this mean? We have good examples in the stories of Hannah who poured out her burden in the tabernacle, and Hezekiah who spread out a threatening letter in the temple. It means being purposeful and passionate in prayer.

6. **Don't Let Money Ruin Your Old Age (v. 10).** At verse 10, David changed the subject dramatically and began talking about money. Isn't this an aging issue? Most people think it's the lack of money that ruins their golden years, but David said, "If riches increase, do not set your heart on them" (see 1 Tim. 6:17ff).

7. **Keep Working for Heavenly Rewards (v. 12).** The last thing David has to say in Psalm 62 is, "Don't let up on earning heavenly rewards just because you're getting older." Work doesn't stop at retirement. There are still things I can do, and there is still work for me to do. As long as I'm alive and have breath, there is something I can contribute to the kingdom of God.

Conclusion: I have to make sure everything I do has eternal benefit or there's no reason for me to do it. That's why I think we start every day at the Judgment Seat and work backwards from there. God can be trusted when we're eighty or ninety just as much as when we're eight or nine or eighteen or nineteen. Those of us who walk with Him age gracefully as we prepare for our eternal reward.

STATS, STORIES, AND MORE

More from Dr. Kroll

David told us not to be moved. The word "moved" there doesn't mean I'll not be moved from this apartment to that apartment. It means "shaken." In fact, the word means "to totter." Have you ever seen an old shed? The wind comes along and you look out the window and say, "That shed is going to fall down." That's the image here. Wouldn't it be a shame to walk with God all the days of your life and come to the last years and be shaken from that faith because you don't have all the answers to the issues you face?

Someone Once Said . . .

- *It's attitude, not arteries, that determines the vitality of our maturing year.* —J. Oswald Sanders

- *The cure for age is interest and enthusiasm and work. Life's evening will take its character from the day which has preceded it.* —the blind poet and hymnist George Matheson

- *I have reached an honorable position in life because I am old and no longer young. I am a far more useful person than I was fifty years ago, or forty years ago, or thirty, twenty, or even ten. I have learned so much since I was seventy.* —Pearl Buck

- *There is a blessedness about old age that we young men know nothing of.* —Charles Spurgeon

- *You know you're getting older when it takes more time to recover than it did to tire out.* —Milton Berle

- *The first half of our lives we are romantic. The last half we are rheumatic.* —Vance Havner

- *The older we grow, the more we become like the place we're going.*

APPROPRIATE HYMNS AND SONGS

"'Tis So Sweet to Trust in Jesus," Louis M. R. Stead & William J. Kirkpatrick, Public Domain.

"Trust and Obey," James Sammis & Daniel Towner, Public Domain.

"In Christ Alone," Don Koch and Shawn Craig, 1990 Paragon Music Corporation (Admin. by Brentwood Benson).

"Indescribable," Laura Story, 2004 worshiptogether.com songs (Admin. by EMI Christian Music Pub.).

"He's Been So Good to Me," R. Douglas Little, 1978 Heartwarming Music Company.

FOR THE BULLETIN

On June 29, 48 B.C., Julius Caesar defeated Pompey at Pharsalus, becoming sole dictator of Rome. ● This is the traditional date for the crucifixion of St. Peter, who was reportedly executed upside down on June 29, A.D. 64. It is also the traditional date for the execution of the apostle Paul, perhaps in the year A.D. 67. ● Hildebrand was consecrated Pope Gregory VII on this day in 1073. He became one of the greatest popes in Christian history, a tireless advocate and reformer of the papacy. ● On June 29, 1685, the great English Puritan, Richard Baxter, was found guilty of unauthorized preaching and was confined to the Tower of London where he remained for eighteen months, during which time he continued writing. An early biographer wrote, "He continued his imprisonment nearly two years, during which he enjoyed more quietness than he had done for many years before." ● The first American Missionary society was organized on June 29, 1810—the American Board of Commissioners for Foreign Missions, in Bradford, Massachusetts, by the Congregationalists. ● On June 29, 1875, the first session of the famous Keswick Convention (pronounced Kes'-ick) convened in Keswick, England. The annual summer conference, still going on today, emphasized the Victorious Christian Life, the indwelling and fullness of the Holy Spirit, and the priority of global missions.

WORSHIP HELPS

Call to Worship
Trust in Him at all times, you people; Pour out your heart before Him; God is a refuge for us (Ps. 62:8).

Pastoral Prayer Based on Psalm 62
Almighty God, our souls find rest in You alone. You are the source of our salvation and the secret of our strength. You are our rock, our fortress, our center of stability in a changing world. Lord, we face many foes each day; some are humans who taunt us. Others are societal changes that threaten us. Others are circumstances in life that cause us to tremble and, but for Your grace, to totter. But our souls find rest in You alone, and because You are our rock, we shall not be shaken. Teach us to trust in You at all times, to pour out our hearts to You, to rely on You rather than on riches. Keep us faithful through all the seasons of life, and trusting You for those eternal rewards for which, by faith, we are working. We pray in Jesus' name. Amen.

Kid's Talk

If you have pictures of your grandparents, show them to the children. Ask them what they call their grandfathers and grandmothers, and what they like best about them. Tell them that some people are young (like you) and some are older (like your grandparents). Older people are usually wiser. They may not be as athletic, but they have maturity and strength. Advise the children to ask their grandparents about days gone by, and to respect them.

Additional Sermon and Lesson Ideas

And Now in Conclusion

Date preached:

SCRIPTURE: Hebrews 13

INTRODUCTION: Many of the writers of the New Testament letters came to the end of the scroll on which they were writing, and they still had a lot they wanted to say. So they started giving brief, abbreviated snippets of advice, almost like the book of Proverbs, and thus we have some of our richest morsels. Hebrews 13 is a good example.

1. Be Hospitable (vv. 1–3). To strangers, to those in prison.
2. Be Holy (v. 4). Marriage must remain sacred and the marriage bed pure.
3. Be Happy (vv. 5–6). We have God's very presence; what more could we need? His promises are better than our portfolios.
4. Be Humble (v. 7). Let your leaders mentor you; learn from them.
5. Be Sound in Faith (vv. 8–10). Right in the middle of all this practical advice, the writer gives the Bible's most definitive declaration of the immutability of Christ.
6. Be Busy in Faith (vv. 11–16).
7. Be Supportive at Church (vv. 17–19).

CONCLUSION: We can't do these things on our own, so the writer ends by asking the God of peace to equip us with everything good for doing His will and to work in us what is pleasing to Him.

The Landmark of Christ's Atonement

Date preached:

By Dr. Woodrow Kroll

SCRIPTURE: Romans 5:6–8

INTRODUCTION: Atonement is a word we don't often use in English, but the landmark of the Bible is there is only one way to God, and that's the way provided for you through Jesus Christ His Son. The death of Jesus Christ purchased for you:

1. Justification (Rom. 5:16–18). Justification means that God treats you as if you had never sinned.
2. Redemption (Eph. 1:3–7). Redemption means the release of a prisoner through the payment of a price.
3. Reconciliation (Eph. 2:11–13 and Col. 1:15–22). We were at war with God; Jesus' blood brought us together, reconciled us, two warring partners. This also provides the basis for reconciliation with other people.

4. Substitution (Rom. 5:18). Jesus died in place of us. He died as a substitute for us. This is central to the Christian faith, a landmark that cannot be moved!

CONCLUSION: There are two things we Christians need to do every time we think about salvation. One is thank God because we are recipients of God's grace. Secondly, take seriously the fact that we have friends and relatives who are not where they need to be with relationship to the grace of God.

PRAYER FOR THE PASTOR'S CLOSET

A Hard Day's Prayer

Dear Father,

In spite of everything, I thank You for calling me to this work, and I praise Your name for success amid failure, conversions among the hardened, and a few kind words from my friends to offset the gossip of my critics. Save me from obsessing over my foes or from thinking I'm a martyr because of low approval ratings. Don't just keep me faithful; make me joyful. Relieve my anxieties, increase my confidence, and use me despite myself. Keep me from leaving this work a minute too early, or from staying a day too long. In all I do, help me work heartily as unto You, offering the work of my hands and heart as a sweet savor humbly rendered. Anoint me with Your blessings, though delayed or unseen, for You have promised that my labor in You is not in vain, and I am taking You at Your Word.

In Jesus' name. Amen.

JULY 6, 2008

SUGGESTED SERMON

The Almost Forgotten Beatitude

Date preached:

Scripture: Acts 20:35

. . . remember the words of the Lord Jesus, that He said, "It is more blessed to give than to receive."

Introduction: In many Bibles, the words of Jesus are in red. Most of these are found in the Gospels, but there is a famous sentence from the lips of Christ that isn't found in Matthew, Mark, Luke, or John; but years later, as the apostle Paul spoke to the Ephesian Church in Acts 20, he quoted this sentence. We could call it *the almost-forgotten beatitude*. There are many Beatitudes in the Bible (when a sentence begins with the words *Blessed is . . .* or *Blessed are . . .*). The word *blessed* occurs forty-two times in the Gospels. But only once in the Bible does the phrase "more blessed" occur. By reading this verse carefully, we can see that Jesus was really describing two blessings in life.

1. **The Blessing of Receiving.** "Receiving" is our primary job as human beings. It is very us-like. God created us as recipients. He is the Source, the Supply, the Great Giver, the Endless Provider who gives:

    A. **Universal Blessings.** God causes the sun to shine and the rain to fall on the just and on the unjust. The world of nature and the entire cosmos was created for our pleasure. In Genesis 1, the Lord made the heavens and the earth for our use. He created the stars above our heads and the ground beneath our feet. He did it to provide a home for Adam and Eve, and for you and me. He gives us richly all things to enjoy.

    B. **Daily Blessings.** He meets all our needs. "The LORD is my shepherd; I shall not want." Jesus told us not to worry about our temporal needs for our heavenly Father knows we have need of all these things. He supplies all our needs out of the riches of His glory.

C. **Spiritual Blessings.** Ephesians 1:3 tells us to praise the God and Father of our Lord Jesus who blesses us in the heavenly realms with every spiritual blessing in Christ. Second Peter tells us that God's divine power has given us everything we need for life and godliness through our knowledge of Him who has given us His very great and precious promises.

D. **Eternal Blessings.** The Lord has given us eternal life through our Lord Jesus Christ (John 3:16). Our primary role in life is to be the recipient of God's goodness and grace. What could be greater? What could be more wonderful than that? What could possibly be "more blessed?" Only one thing. Jesus said, "It is more blessed to give than to receive."

2. **The Blessing of Giving.** Why is it more blessed to give than to receive? When we receive, we are acting like ourselves; but when we give, we are acting like God. Receiving is us-like. Giving is Christlike. Having an attitude of giving allows us to move into the divine realm and do something that God Himself delights to do. In his book, *None of These Diseases,* Dr. S. I. McMillen discusses the life of John D. Rockefeller. As a young man, Rockefeller was strong and husky, and when he entered business he drove himself like a slave. He was a millionaire by age 33. By 43, he controlled the largest business in the world. At 53, he was the world's richest man. But he developed a disease called alopecia. His hair fell out and his digestion was so bad he could only eat crackers and milk. Someone said: "An awful age was in his face. He was the oldest man I have ever seen." One night, unable to sleep, Rockefeller realized he couldn't take a thin dime into the next world. Everything was sand castles, doomed by the inevitable tide. Money was not a commodity to be hoarded, but something to be shared. The next morning, he lost no time transforming his money into blessings for others. He established the Rockefeller Foundation to channel his fortune to needed areas. He gave hundreds of millions to universities, hospitals, mission work, and underprivileged people. The focus of his life changed from *getting* to *giving.* The result is that he did not die at age 53; he lived to be 98. Whether or not Rockefeller was a born-again believer, he did discover one of the moral laws God placed in the universe: Giving is good for us. It enriches our lives.

Conclusion: He has blessed us with abundance, and from His hand we've received all we have. Now may He bless us by prompting our hearts to give all that is needed for His work, remembering the words the Lord Jesus Himself said: *"It is more blessed to give than to receive."*

STATS, STORIES, AND MORE

God has given us blessings above and below. Above us are the stars. In one publication, a scientist was asked how many stars are in the universe. He replied that no one has any idea how many stars are in the heavens. The usual way to determine the number of stars in the universe, he explained, is to consider how many stars are in the Milky Way, then to multiply that number by our best guesstimate at the number of galaxies in the universe. We suppose there are about 400 billion stars in the Milky Way, although there could be as many as 600 billion. Multiply that by the number of galaxies there are in the universe. But that presents a problem, for we have never found the edges of the cosmos. Astronomers believe there must be billions of galaxies. So you have to multiply billions of stars by billions of galaxies—and it boggles our minds.

But there are marvels beneath our feet, too. Scientists tell us that each shovelful of dirt we dig up holds more living things than all the human beings ever born. Lots of microscopic species are still waiting to be identified and named. The world of worms, bugs, insects, and fungi is as mysterious as the depths of space. Billions of stars above our heads, and billions of creatures of infinitesimal size in just a shovel of dirt beneath our feet. This is our Father's world, and God created it all for us.

APPROPRIATE HYMNS AND SONGS

"Count Your Many Blessings," Johnson Oatman Jr. & Edwin O. Excell, Public Domain.

"Free," Kirk Franklin, 2000 Kerrion Publishing/Lilly Mack (BMI).

"Showers of Blessings," Daniel Whittle & James McGranahan, Public Domain.

"Ancient of Days," Gary Sadler & Jamie Harvill, 1992 Integrity's Hosanna! Music.

FOR THE BULLETIN

On July 6, 1415, Bohemian Reformer John Huss, refusing to recant his beliefs before the Council of Constance, was found guilty of heresy, condemned, and taken to the outskirts of the city to be burned. His last words: "God is my witness that the evidence against me is false. I have never thought nor preached except with the one intention of winning men, if possible, from their sins. In the truth of the gospel I have written, taught, and preached; today I will gladly die." ● July 6, 1535, also marks the execution of Sir Thomas More, lord chancellor of England. He was beheaded in the Tower of London for refusing to recognize Henry VIII as supreme head of the Church of England following the king's split with Rome. ● The death of England's King Edward VI (Protestant son of Henry VIII) on this day in 1553 put the Protestant movement at risk. His half-sister, Mary Tudor, rose to the throne, intent on reestablishing Catholicism throughout the land. Known to history as "Bloody Mary," she unleashed a terrible persecution against Protestants, which was later chronicled by John Foxe in his *Book of Martyrs*. Over 300 Protestant leaders were burned at the stake, including Thomas Cranmer, Hugh Latimer, and Nicholas Ridley. ● July 6 is the birthday of William M'Kendree (1757), first American-born bishop of the Methodist Church, and of John Sammis (1846), author of "Trust and Obey." ● Francis and Edith Schaeffer were married on this day in 1935.

PRAYER FOR THE PASTOR'S CLOSET

Often I become weary with reading and hearing many things. You are all that I want and desire. Let all teachers be mute and all creation keep silence before You. Speak to me, You and You alone.

—THOMAS À KEMPIS

WORSHIP HELPS

Call to Worship

> *Glory to God on high,*
> *Let praises fill the sky!*
> *Praise ye His Name.*
> —JAMES ALLEN (1761)

Scripture Medley

This medley of Scripture reading is from the famous devotional, *Daily Light*, published by Jonathan Bagster in the 1870s. It's the reading for the evening of October 7, and is reprinted below in the King James Version.

> *O Lord GOD, . . . with thy blessing let the house of thy*
> *servant be blessed for ever. . . . Thou blessest, O LORD,*
> *and it shall be blessed for ever . . . The blessing of the*
> *LORD, it maketh rich, and he addeth no sorrow with it.*

. . . remember the words of the Lord Jesus, how he said, It is more blessed to give than to receive. . . . When thou makest a feast, call the poor, the maimed, the lame, the blind: and thou shalt be blessed; for they cannot recompense thee: for thou shalt be recompensed at the resurrection of the just. . . . Come, ye blessed of my Father, inherit the kingdom prepared for you from the foundation of the world: for I was an hungred, and ye gave me meat: I was thirsty, and ye gave me drink: I was a stranger, and ye took me in: naked, and ye clothed me: I was sick, and ye visited me. . . . Blessed is he that considereth the poor: the LORD will deliver him in time of trouble. . . . The LORD God is a sun and shield . . . (2 Sam. 7:28–29; 1 Chr. 17:27; Prov. 10:22; Acts 20:35; Luke 14:13–14; Matt. 25:34–36; Ps. 41:1; 84:11 KJV).

Benediction

Lord, teach us to be good receivers of all Your blessings, and teach us to be even better givers, remembering this week the words of our Lord, that it is more blessed to give than to receive. In Jesus' name. Amen.

Additional Sermons and Lesson Ideas

Lust and Self-Control
By Dr. Larry Osborne

Date preached:

SCRIPTURE: Various

INTRODUCTION: If ever our society considered an idea out of date, it would be the idea that repressing our sexual drives is a good thing. We seem to think that unfulfilled or repressed desires and drives inevitably leads to great harm, yet nothing could be further from the truth. When lust gains the upper hand, it's deadly. Let's look at some principles about lust and self-control:

1. Temptation Is Not a Sin (Matt. 5:27–28; Heb. 4:15).
2. Lust and Immorality Are Neither Private Nor Victimless (Num. 14:18; 1 Cor. 6:15–20).
3. Lust and Immorality Seldom Barge into Our Lives; They Usually Sneak In (1 Kin. 11:1–14, 23–43; Prov. 7:6–27; Rom. 1:21–28; also compare 2 Pet. 2:7–8 with Gen. 19).
4. Self-Control and Sexual Purity Flow from Wisdom, Not Willpower (1 Cor. 10:13; Gal. 5:22–23; 2 Pet. 1:5–6).
5. The Key to Maintaining Self-Control and Sexual Purity Is Avoiding Temptation, Not Resisting Temptation (Prov. 5:1–23; 7:6–27; Matt. 5:27–30; 2 Tim. 2:22).

CONCLUSION: It's only when self-control reigns that true emotional, physical, sexual, and spiritual health are possible.

Jesus the Shepherd
By Rev. Melvin Tinker

Date preached:

SCRIPTURE: John 10:1–21

INTRODUCTION: There are three things about Jesus, the shepherd leader, which marks Him out from all the other leaders the world has ever known or will know.

1. Jesus Is the Shepherd Who Knows His People (vv. 1–6).
2. Jesus Is the Shepherd Who Nourishes His People (vv. 7–10).
3. Jesus Is the Shepherd Who Dies for His Sheep (vv. 11–18).

CONCLUSION: The final three verses show the two responses we can have to Jesus the Shepherd. We will either be offended by Him and insult or reject Him (vv. 19–20). Or, we may believe Him because of His words and works (v. 21)!

Rev. Gardiner Spring

For an incredible sixty-three years, Dr. Gardiner Spring pastored the famous Brick Presbyterian Church of New York City. He began his professional life as a lawyer, but was called to the ministry through the preaching of another man. You may want to dig out his life's story for yourself; it abounds in great lessons and illustrations. But to whet your appetite, here is Rev. Spring's obituary, which appeared in the *New York Times,* on August 20, 1873.

Rev. Gardiner Spring

Rev. Gardiner Spring died on Monday, in this city, at the advanced age of eighty-nine. His father was Rev. Samuel D. Spring, a warm supporter of the Revolution, and a chaplain in the army in 1775 when Benedict Arnold made his celebrated attack on Quebec . . . (and) also an intimate personal friend of President Madison.

Rev. Gardiner Spring was born on the 24th of February, 1785, in Newburyport, Mass., and was the oldest member of his family. In his autobiography he makes particular reference to himself as a willful, selfish boy who would brook no control. With growing years he observed that these qualities developed themselves in some instances in a form of deceit, and with deep humiliation he remarked that in manhood and even in old age he had struggled against the dominant and cherished sins of his boyhood. He was by nature as he himself declared, a child of wrath, and he often wondered at the mercy of Providence that kept him out of hell. That his parents did not share with him the opinion which he entertained of himself, is established by the fact that they designed him for the ministry.

The rudiments of education were imparted to him in the grammar school of his native town, but he was also placed under the charge of Chief Justice Parsons, who acted in the capacity of a private tutor. In his fifteenth year he entered Yale College, where he became the class-mate of John C. Calhoun, and was one of the oldest graduates of that celebrated institution, for he delivered the valedictory address at the Commencement exercise in 1805. He did not then appear to incline toward the Church, and on leaving college pursued the studies of law in the office of Judge Daggett, in New Haven. The principal portion of his time, however, was occupied in teaching, and he established an English school in the Bermuda Islands, where he passed fifteen months.

He was admitted to the Bar in 1808, and commenced practice under favorable auspices, but he subsequently abandoned the profession against the wishes of his wife, whom he married in 1803, and declared his intention of becoming a minister. This sudden change he himself attributed to the effect of a sermon preached by Rev. John Mason, in New Haven, from the text, "To the poor the gospel is preached." He described the impression the discourse produced as miraculous; he could not restrain from tears, and from that moment he followed the ministry with zeal and piety.

He spent one year at Andover Theological Seminary, and in the year 1809 was ordained. After receiving calls from several New England parishes he preached in Cedar-street Church in the following spring, and in the same year, by unanimous call, was invited to the pastorate of the old Brick Church in Bookman Street in this city. Dr. Spring frequently received calls of higher trust and responsibility, including the presidencies of Dartmouth and Hamilton Colleges, but he did not desire to abandon his first field of labor, and during the sixty-three years of his pastoral care of that church he was regarded as second to no preacher

Continued on the next page

in this city. His congregation removed to Murray Hill in 1851, and in the following year he accepted as his associate Rev. Wm. G. T. Shedd.

Dr. Spring's style of preaching was vigorous, simple, and always interesting. He ignored everything vapory, florid, or whatever might produce transient excitement, basing his preaching altogether on the simple truth, as enunciated by Christ. He was an industrious author, and his works, among others, included "The Attraction of the Cross," "The Mercy Seat; or Thoughts Suggested by the Lord's Prayer," "First Things," "The Glory of Christ," "The Power of the Pulpit," "Short Sermons to the People," "The Obligations of the World to the Bible," "Memoirs of the Late Hannah L. Murray," "The Restoration of Israel," "Dissertation on the Rule of Faith," "The Doctrine of Election," "Essays on Christian Character," "The Mission of Sorrow," "Fragments from the Study of a Pastor," "The Bible, Not Man," "Pulpit Ministrations; or, Sabbath Readings, &c.," "Personal Reminiscences, &."[1]

A deeper review of Spring's life demonstrates a profound respect for the office of preaching. Dr. Spring once said that every preacher should "preach as though he were in sight of the cross and heard the groans of the Mighty Sufferer of Calvary."

The Lord is present in our preaching, he said. "It was the Savior's voice by whom this message is uttered. He bows the heavens and comes down. He walks amidst the golden candlesticks. When His ministers speak His name, He is with them; when His people meet together, He is there. He will be sanctified in them that come nigh to Him, and before all the people He will be glorified.[2]

---

[1] I am indebted to http://www.shilohonline.org/articles/spring/spring_obit.htm, which credits Mrs. Hope V. Hatch of Syracuse, NY for locating and providing this obituary.
[2] Quoted by David L. Larson, *The Company of Preachers* (Grand Rapids: Kregel Publications, 1998), p. 448.

JULY 13, 2008

SUGGESTED SERMON

Stop Passing the Blame

Date preached:

By Joshua D. Rowe

Scripture: James 1:13–15, especially verse 13
Let no one say when he is tempted, "I am tempted by God"; for God cannot be tempted by evil, nor does He Himself tempt anyone.

Introduction: One of the hardest things for us to do as humans is admit our own faults. How many times have you been confronted for a mistake and passed the blame? Maybe even this week you made a mistake at work and, when confronted, you blamed circumstances, a customer, or a coworker instead of owning up to it. The worst possible way to pass the blame is when we blame our holy, righteous God for our own sin. In James 1:13–15, James instructs believers not to blame God for their temptations and precisely why this is unacceptable.

1. **When You're Tempted, Don't Accuse God (v. 13).** "Let no one say when he is tempted, 'I am tempted by God' . . ." Perhaps when you hear this command you wonder how this message is applicable to those who understand that God is not responsible for evil. I'm afraid we are guiltier than we realize. We must take into account the context of these verses. James assumes a life filled with trials as we read in 1:1–12. When we face trials, aren't we more likely to pass the blame? In verses 13–15 specifically, James has in view a trial that leads to our sin. When our sin is found out, don't we naturally pass the blame? Don't blame God! That's the main thrust of these verses and should be taken seriously in our lives.

2. **Accusing God for Temptation Denies His Blamelessness (v. 13).** ". . . For God cannot be tempted by evil, nor does He Himself tempt anyone." Suppose I came to you and told you, "You know, my boss at work is really tempting me to look at pornography." Immediately you would think two things: first, you would think my boss has a problem with pornography himself, and second that he is actively encouraging me to do the same. Suppose I continued, "Yes, you see, he gave me a new computer and an office with a door that

shuts . . . what does he expect?" Obviously you would realize my ignorance. A boss dispenses resources for the good of the company, not for the personal indulgences of the individual. We show the same ignorance when we imply that God is tempting us. We bring God down to a human level, denying His righteousness and associating Him with sin! James is interested in upholding the righteousness of God. Your understanding of the gospel can stand or fall based on the principle that God cannot be tempted and doesn't tempt anyone: "For He made Him who knew no sin to be sin for us, that we might become the righteousness of God in Him" (2 Cor. 5:21).

3. **Accusing God for Temptation Denies Our Sinfulness (vv. 14–15).** James gives us a realistic view of temptation, which causes us to take a healthy responsibility for our own sinful temptations. We learn first that we must:

A. **Recognize the Nature of Temptation (v. 14).** "But each one is tempted when he is drawn away by his own desires and enticed." This defines the source of temptation as individual ('each one') and internal ('by his own desires'). We tend to act as if temptation is external and corporate, blaming everything and everyone else but ourselves!

B. **Recognize the Process of Temptation (vv. 14b–15).** ". . . drawn away by his own desires and enticed. Then, when desire has conceived, it gives birth to sin; and sin, when it is full-grown, brings forth death." The language here is purposely scandalous. James is speaking in reproductive language: "desires, enticed, conceive, give birth, full-grown, bring forth." The fact that James points out this pattern that we recognize from our own experience: it can serve to give us an important warning. This should motivate us to cut sin off at its root: our own lust/evil desires.

Conclusion: Now that we've had a bit deeper look at this passage, I hope you can identify and proactively respond to specific areas where you struggle with the ideas of these verses. Maybe you need to repent because you often accuse God of tempting you indirectly by His sovereign control. Maybe you realize that you just have a hard time owning up to sin. You always point to stress, pressure, responsibilities, situations, and other people as the source of your temptation. You need to own up to these tendencies and depend more fully on the Spirit of God to resist. I would encourage you to identify any such issue and repent.

STATS, STORIES, AND MORE

Accusing God Indirectly

As a young boy, I remember my parents' divorce vividly as it impacted me very deeply. My father approached me one day, saying, "Josh, you seem different since this divorce. You used to be much more lighthearted. You don't joke around or smile as much. It really seems to be getting to you deeply." After this conversation, I remember being in my back yard wondering why I was this way. I knew that it was because of my parents' divorce, but on a deeper level, I knew that God was the only One who could prevent that divorce. As I began to "logically" think about God's ultimate control, I became increasingly angry. I lifted my fist up to heaven and yelled, "This is *Your* fault. *You* made me this way!" I'm thankful for the forgiveness of God for my ignorance, but doesn't this demonstrate our own thinking so often? When trials come, when sin occurs, we tend to blame God. We need to be trained by Scripture to think differently.

—Joshua D. Rowe

The First Excuse in History

The first sin that was ever committed was immediately followed up by an excuse: "And he said, 'Who told you that you were naked? Have you eaten from the tree of which I commanded you not to eat?' The man said, 'The woman *whom You gave* to be with me, she gave me from the tree, and I ate'" (Gen. 3:11–12 NASB, emphasis added). Adam suggests that if God wouldn't have given him Eve, he never would have sinned. By logical deduction, Adam implied that God was somehow responsible for Adam's temptation and sin! This situation is all too familiar in our own lives.

The Snare of Temptation

The sexual language of James 1:14–15 is reminiscent of Proverbs 7, especially verses 21–23: "With her enticing speech she caused him to yield, with her flattering lips she seduced him. Immediately he went after her, as an ox goes to the slaughter, or as a fool to the correction of the stocks, till an arrow struck his liver. As a bird hastens to the snare, he did not know it would cost his life." The idea that James and the writer of Proverbs is getting across is that sin, like sexual activity, brings both pleasure and reproduction. We might experience temporary delight in sin, but, according to James and the writer of Proverbs 7, we won't like its offspring which is ultimately death!

APPROPRIATE HYMNS AND SONGS

"The Lord's Prayer" (Matt. 6:9–13); Albert Hay Malotte, 1976 by G. Schirmer, Inc.

"Thou Art Worthy," Pauline Mills & Tom Smail, 1975 by Fred Bock Music Company.

"The Potter's Hand," Darlene Zschech, 1997 Hillsong Publishing.

"How Great Is Our God," Chris Tomlin, Ed Cash, & Jesse Reeves, 2004 worshiptogether.com songs (Admin. by EMI Christian Music Pub.).

FOR THE BULLETIN

On Wednesday evening, July 13, 1099, the Crusaders attacked the Muslim-held city of Jerusalem with shouts of "God wills it!" After two days of furious fighting, the city fell, and Crusaders rushed through the city, killing and looting. ● On July 13, 1234, St. Dominic, founder of the Dominicans, was canonized. ● On this day in 1587, Manteo became the first Native American baptized as a Protestant. He was declared to be Lord of Roanoke. One week later, Virginia Dare became the first white child to be born and baptized in North America. Shortly thereafter, the entire colony disappeared in one of American history's greatest mysteries. ● Scottish Puritan Samuel Rutherford, exiled to the city of Aberdeen for his preaching, wrote to his congregation in Anwoth on July 13, 1637, describing how he felt at being removed from his pulpit: "Next to Christ, I had but one joy, the apple of the eye of my delights, to preach Christ my Lord; and they have violently plucked that away from me. It was to me like the poor man's one eye; and they have put out that eye, and quenched my light in the inheritance of the Lord." ● Irish Episcopal clergyman, Thomas Kelly, was born on July 13, 1769. He wrote 765 hymns, the best known being "Praise the Savior, Ye Who Know Him." ● On July 13, 1960, the wife of C. S. Lewis, Joy, died. Lewis later wrote about this in *A Grief Observed*.

WORSHIP HELPS

Call to Worship
Let them shout for joy and be glad, who favor my righteous cause; and let them say continually, Let the LORD be magnified, who has pleasure in the prosperity of His servant. And my tongue shall speak of Your righteousness and of Your praise all the day long (Ps. 35:27–28).

Benediction
You are the temple of the living God. As God has said: "I will dwell in them and walk among them. I will be their God, and they shall be My people." Therefore "Come out from among them and be separate, says the Lord. Do not touch what is unclean, and I will receive you. I will be a Father to you, and you shall be My sons and daughters, says the LORD Almighty" (2 Cor. 6:16–18).

Kid's Talk

Arrange a special Kid's Talk with children who have been converted and baptized in your church. Gather those children around you and ask them to share why they put their trust in Jesus. After allowing them to give their testimonies, use this as a challenge to the congregation and read Matthew 18:1–5: "At that time the disciples came to Jesus, saying, 'Who then is greatest in the kingdom of heaven?' Then Jesus called a little child to Him, set him in the midst of them, and said, 'Assuredly, I say to you, unless you are converted and become as little children, you will by no means enter the kingdom of heaven. Therefore whoever humbles himself as this little child is the greatest in the kingdom of heaven. Whoever receives one little child like this in My name receives Me.'"

Additional Sermons and Lesson Ideas

When You're Concerned for Your Children

Date preached:

SCRIPTURE: Job 1

INTRODUCTION: Some people think a parent's job is nearly finished when the children are grown, but there's never a time when parents aren't concerned for their children, and sometimes the concerns grow greater as our children grow older. Job was a remarkable father who can teach us what to do when we're worried about our youngsters, whatever their age.

1. Be Blameless and Upright (v. 1). Our children's greatest anchor, stability, and legacy are found in the moral character of their parents.
2. Pray Earnestly (vv. 2–5). Job apparently didn't feel too good about his children's feastings, and so he covered the occasions with special prayer.
3. Ask God for a Hedge Around Your Home (vv. 9–10). Satan was unable to touch Job's family because of a hedge of divine protection.
4. Trust God When Things Don't Go Well (vv. 18–22). Even when it appeared God had not answered his prayers for his children, Job trusted and worshiped.

CONCLUSION: By the end of the book, Job's first set of children were in heaven, and he was enjoying his second set on earth. God blessed his home and his family; and the Lord will do the same with yours.

Stay Away from Trouble

Date preached:

By Pastor Al Detter

SCRIPTURE: Proverbs 1:10–19

INTRODUCTION: Scripture warns us against keeping the wrong company.

1. When the Wrong Crowd Pressures You to Do Wrong, Don't Accept Their Invitation (vv. 10–14).
   A. Pressure (vv. 11–14). Notice the recurrence of "us" and "we." Peer pressure is not a new phenomenon!
   B. Plot (vv. 11–12). The wrong crowds know exactly what they will do, and it's not pretty!
   C. Purse (vv. 13–14). This type of crowd entices you based on what will be gained by doing evil.
2. Stay Away from the Wrong Crowd (vv. 15–19).
   A. Their Agenda Is Evil (v. 16).
   B. They Are Oblivious to Danger (v. 17).
   C. They Destroy Their Own Lives (vv. 18–19).

CONCLUSION: What kind of company are you keeping around you? Parents, do you set a high standard for your children's choice of friends?

JULY 20, 2008

SUGGESTED SERMON

The Biblical Bishop

Date preached:

By Dr. Melvin Worthington

Scripture: 1 Timothy 3:1–7, especially verse 1
This is a faithful saying: If a man desires the position of a bishop, he desires a good work.

Introduction: In view of 1 Timothy 3:1–7, it should be noted that the word "bishop" in the New Testament is most often understood to equate to the office of a pastor or church leader. The message today challenges me very deeply. I hope that you will hold me to the standards of Scripture. But further than that, I wonder if anyone here feels called to preach! As a church, we are responsible to identify people such as these verses describe, encourage their gifts, and send them into the ministry! Beyond that, these are qualities that we should *all* exhibit in our lives. So, it's important that all of us be attentive to the qualifications of a biblical bishop or pastor.

1. **Personal Credentials.** Pastors must be godly, possessing and practicing the Christian virtues. They should be of irreproachable character demonstrating truth, honesty, and general uprightness (v. 2). They must be *gentle* (v. 3). Paul reminds Timothy that the servant of the Lord must not strive but be gentle to all (2 Tim. 2:24–26). Gentleness is not a sign of weakness but a necessary ingredient for the pastor who, without it, is lacking in sound personal credentials.

2. **Public Credentials.** The profile of pastor includes their public integrity. They must have the reputation of integrity among those who are not Christians if they are to reach them (v. 6). The pastor's family life must outwardly demonstrate a commitment to Christ. He should have but one wife (v. 2) with children who are reverent and submissive (vv. 4–5). A pastor's public testimony is a passport behind closed doors in the community. No amount of ability, accomplishment, achievement or activity will substitute in the eyes of the lost for the moral integrity of the pastor. Without integrity pastors are destitute in a world of towering needs.

3. **Practical Credentials.** Pastors *superintend* their local churches. They are not to arrogantly dictate to their congregations, but to lead them in the ways of God and take the oversight (1 Pet. 5:2). The pastor *shepherds* the flock, watches lovingly over them, and serves the local church. There is no contradiction when the pastor is charged to both superintend and serve (v. 5). The greatest in the kingdom is still a servant. The pastor *speaks* to the congregation as a preacher and teacher (v. 2) with responsibilities to preach and pray. Pastors speak to the saints from the Word of God, and they speak to the Sovereign in prayer about the saints. The good pastor will be characterized as a student of the Word of God (2 Tim. 2:15). A call to pastor includes the call to study. The pastor is a *soldier* who leads his congregation in battle with courage, consecration, consistency, and concern. The pastor fights the good fight of faith, follows the Lord Jesus, and flees the entanglements of this world. Pastors organize, operate, and observe their congregations with the vigilance needed in the spiritual battle. The pastor is a *sensitive* person (v. 6), and not arrogant or abrasive. We should laugh with those who laugh and weep with those who weep. No problem or need is insignificant.

4. **Professional Credentials.** Consider the pastor's professional credentials:

   A. **Approval.** Whether it's the local church or a denominational ordaining council that is charged with responsibility for ordaining ministers, it is evident that these must be approved by peers and parishioners.

   B. **Accountability.** The Scriptures teach the principle of ministerial accountability. All ministers must be accountable for their doctrine and deportment, not only to God but to those who ordained them.

Conclusion: The pastor-teacher is a divine gift to the church. The ideal pastor engages in a teaching ministry, feeding the saints on expository preaching, giving them the rich food of the Word of God, thereby prompting the church's internal development and outward expansion. Is God calling you to become a pastor? Is He bringing to mind someone in this very congregation who fits the description, but needs your acceptance and encouragement? As a church, let's seek out those that God would call to pastor others! And let's all live above reproach whatever our personal calling before God and ministry.

STATS, STORIES, AND MORE

From Oswald Chambers in his book *Disciples Indeed*

- The Call is the inner motive of having been gripped by God—spoilt for every aim in life save that of disciplining men to Jesus.
- *One man or woman called to God is worth a hundred who have elected to work for God.*
- *If a man is called to preach the gospel, God will crush him till the light of the eye, the power of the life, the ambition of the heart, is all riveted on Himself. That is not done easily. It is not a question of saintliness, it has to do with the Call of God.*

How Dr. George Truett Was Called to Preach

George Truett (1867–1944) was converted to Christ at age 19 after hearing a sermon based on Hebrews 10:38: *The just shall live by faith.* The following Wednesday night, his pastor encouraged him to share his testimony, and the crowd was amazed at the power and passion of his words. From that time, many people encouraged him to enter the ministry. His primary vocational interest, however, was teaching school. Whenever asked to speak at church services or evangelistic meetings, he demonstrated remarkable ability. He was once introduced with the words, "Brethren, this is George Truett, and he can speak like Spurgeon. George, tell them what the Lord has done for you . . ." Still Truett worked at school teaching and toyed with the idea of studying law. One Saturday, he heard that a special business meeting was going to be held at his church that night. He arrived to discover that the church was meeting to vote to ordain him into the ministry. The oldest deacon present rose to his feet and said, "I move that this church ordain brother Charles Truett to the full work of the gospel ministry." Truett, 23, rose to protest, but the church would have none of it. He later recalled, "There I was, against a whole church, against a church profoundly moved. There was not a dry eye in the house . . . one of the supremely solemn hours in a church's life. I was thrown into the stream, and just had to swim."

APPROPRIATE HYMNS AND SONGS

"All That Thrills My Soul Is Jesus," Thoro Harris, 1959 Nazarene Publishing House.

"Shine on Us," Michael W. Smith & Deborah D. Smith, 1996 Milene Music Inc. and Deer Valley Music.

"Draw Me Nearer," Diane Sheets, 2004 Word Music, Inc.

"I Lift My Eyes Up," Brian Doerkson, 1990 Vineyard Songs Canada (Admin. by Vineyard Music Global Worldwide).

FOR THE BULLETIN

During the first millennium of Christianity, two centers of gravity emerged—Rome and Constantinople. In the mid-eleventh century, Michael Cerularius became patriarch of Constantinople, and Pope Leo IX, head of the Church of Rome. Leo sent Humbert to Constantinople, where he excommunicated Michael Cerularius. Four days later, on July 20, 1054, Cerularius responded by excommunicating the pope and his followers. This became the Great Schism, separating the Western Church (Catholic and Protestant) and the Eastern Church (Orthodox). ● Peter Lombard, Latin theologian and intellectual, died on July 20, 1164. ● On July 20, 1648, the Westminster Larger Catechism was adopted by the General Assembly of the Church of Scotland at Edinburgh. ● Jonathan Edwards and Sarah Pierpont were married on this day in 1726. ● Rev. Samuel Langdon, noted pastor in Portsmouth, New Hampshire, resigned from his pulpit to become a chaplain to patriot troops during the American Revolution. His journal for July 20, 1775, says: "This has been one of the most important and trying days of my life. I have taken leave of my people for the present and shall at once proceed to the American camp at Boston and offer my services as chaplain in the army. . . . The scene in the house of God today has tried me sorely." How silent, how solemn, was the congregation, and when they sang the sixty-first Psalm—commencing, "When overwhelm'd with grief / My heart within me dies"—sobs were heard in every part of the building." ● Hymnwriter Charles Tindley died on this day in 1933. He is the author of "We Shall Overcome" and "Stand by Me."

WORSHIP HELPS

Call to Worship
I will praise You, O LORD, with my whole heart; I will tell of all Your marvelous works. I will be glad and rejoice in You; I will sing praise to Your name, O Most High (Ps. 9:1–2).

Scripture Reading
We give no offense in anything, that our ministry may not be blamed. But in all things we commend ourselves as ministers of God: in much patience, in tribulations, in needs, in distresses, in stripes, in imprisonments, in tumults, in labors, in sleeplessness, in fastings; by purity, by knowledge, by longsuffering, by kindness, by the Holy Spirit, by sincere love, by the word of truth, by the power of God, by the armor of righteousness on the right hand and on the left, by honor and dishonor, by evil report and good report; as deceivers, and yet true; as unknown, and yet well known; as dying, and behold we live; as chastened, and yet not killed; as sorrowful, yet always rejoicing; as poor, yet making many rich; as having nothing, and yet possessing all things (2 Cor. 6:3–10).

Offertory Comments
Today I want to encourage those of you who have been giving regularly. It's such a temptation to hold back our tithe when times get difficult. However, even the Philippians, who were not known to be wealthy people, gave to the ministry of Paul. Notice what he says in response: ". . . I am full, having received . . . the things sent from you, a sweet-smelling aroma, an acceptable sacrifice, well pleasing to God. And my God shall supply all your need according to His riches in glory by Christ Jesus." When we give to the Lord's ministry, we can rest assured He will supply all our needs!

Additional Sermons and Lesson Ideas

Envy and Gratitude
By Dr. Larry Osborne

Date preached:

SCRIPTURE: Various

INTRODUCTION: Envy is a dangerous poison. When it barges into our life, we can easily justify its presence—unaware that it's rotting our soul and every relationship it touches. On the other hand, its antidote, gratitude, is a life-giving elixir. Even in the darkest of circumstances it has the amazing ability to bring joy and hope to everything it touches.

    1. Envy Should Be Removed from Our Lifestyles Because:
        A. Envy Destroys Our Health (Prov. 14:30).
        B. Envy Destroys Our Relationships (James 3:16; 4:1–2).
        C. Envy Destroys Our Walk with God (Rom. 1:21–32; Gal. 5:19; 1 Thess. 5:18; Heb. 12:28).
    2. Gratitude Should Be Built into the Fabric of Our Life and Outlook Despite Our Circumstances (Dan. 6:10; Phil. 4:6–7; Col. 3:15–17).

CONCLUSION: Are you living an envious life or a grateful one?

Prayer: What, Why, Where, When
By Dr. Michael A. Guido

Date preached:

SCRIPTURE: 1 Timothy 2:1–8

INTRODUCTION: Just as a wingless bird is a monstrosity to nature, a prayerless person is a monstrosity in the realm of the spirit.

    1. The Procedure of Prayer (v. 1). We are to pray with (1) Supplications, made out of a sense of need; (2) prayers, a wonder that was only used in the Bible with reference to God; (3) intercession, praying for others; (4) and don't forget about thanksgiving.
    2. The People of Prayer (vv. 1–2, 4). Pray for everyone (v. 1), specifically for government officials and authorities (v. 2).
    3. The Purpose of Prayer (vv. 2, 4). God desires all to be saved. We are to pray for peace and for the salvation of others.
    4. The Place of Prayer (vv. 5, 8). With Jesus at the right hand of God as our mediator, we can be anywhere (v. 8) and pray in spirit and truth.
    5. The Prerequisites of Prayer (v. 8). We must lift up our hands, symbolizing dependence upon God and submission to Him.

CONCLUSION: Does your prayer life follow the biblical model?

JULY 27, 2008

SUGGESTED SERMON

Settled Out of Court

Date preached:

By Rev. Peter Grainger

Scripture: 1 Corinthians 6:1–11, especially verse 2
Do you not know that the saints will judge the world? And if the world will be judged by you, are you unworthy to judge the smallest matters?

Introduction: One of the anomalies of being a church minister is that you are reckoned in the eyes of the law to be working for God rather than any human agency or employer. In a case brought by a Methodist minister in 1984 which went to final appeal in the High Court, the Master of the Rolls declared in their judgement: "Ministers of religion owe their allegiance to God rather than to a terrestrial authority" (The Methodist Conference *v.* Parfitt, 1984). Paul teaches that disputes between believers/churches must always be settled out of court. Attempting to use the public court system to reconcile our disputes has four dire consequences:

1. **It Trivializes Our Future Destiny (vv. 1–4).** In regard to the matter of settling disputes, Paul focuses on the future settling of all disputes—the final judgment of the world. Although Christians have no business judging the world now, they will have a prominent role in judging the world in the future! We will judge the world (v. 2) and even angels (v. 3). Paul goes on to say, if these Corinthian "saints" are going to judge the world—including the magistrates in Corinth—surely they can sort out some minor dispute between one another (v. 4)! The recourse of most Christians should not be the legal process. While this is necessary and appropriate in cases where the law of the land is broken and where vulnerable people are threatened or abused (child or spousal abuse, etc.), there are many other areas where we need to recapture the sense of outrage and shame that Paul felt, the strategy that he advocated, and the future perspective which underlies it. Churches should deal with disputes between members.

2. **It Compromises Our Christian Integrity (vv. 5–6).** A Christian church is a community of reconciliation—people from all sorts of

backgrounds who have been reconciled to God through His Son, Jesus, and made one through the indwelling Holy Spirit who lives within each Christian and among Christians when they meet together. Paul seeks to shame the Corinthians, whom as we have seen, prided themselves on their wisdom which was one of their buzzwords. It is a source of shame when it is not resolved within the church (v. 5). Where there are unresolved disputes, where Christians who fall out are not being reconciled, it is a source of shame. Not only is it a source of shame internally, it's a source of scandal when exposed to the world (v. 6)!

3. **It Reveals Our Misplaced Priority (vv. 7–8).** People embark on legal enterprises in the hope that they will win. In Corinth, there are no real winners (whatever the courts may rule) for one good reason: both parties are Christians. If they are Christians, claiming their rights, winning a verdict, or gaining money from another Christian should not be the most important thing. In the case of the Christian who has been "wronged" or "cheated," it is better to lose out rather than retaliate in kind and do damage to a brother! God's reputation must come first; if that means my reputation suffers, then I can leave that with God.

4. **It Questions Our Real Identity (vv. 9–11).** Paul asks a rhetorical question: "Do you not know that the unrighteous will not inherit the kingdom of God?" (v. 9). Paul infers that such things like deliberately cheating and defrauding someone falls into the category of "wicked." This calls into question the spiritual standing of any such person and their inheritance-rights into God's kingdom! So, in the list that follows, "thieves" and "covetous" are included (v. 10). Paul mentions that the Corinthians once lived this way, but now should be living transformed lives (v. 11). Taking other believers to court for personal gain or vengeance calls into question whether this transformation is authentic.

Conclusion: If you are a Christian, then you cannot afford to be in any kind of dispute with another Christian, especially within the same church. You need to be reconciled with your brother or sister despite whether it involves a legal case. If you are the wronged party, be willing to forgive and ask the Lord to remove any bitterness from your heart. If you are the one who has wronged another then seek forgiveness. This is the time and this is the place.

STATS, STORIES, AND MORE

Getting Along
Once there was a Chinese prince who died and was given a glimpse of both heaven and hell. First he was escorted to hell, where he found tables laden with various foods and delicacies, but the people were sitting there angry and frustrated, quarreling with each other. They were not permitted to pick up the food with their fingers, and they couldn't feed themselves because the chopsticks they were given were ten feet long. Then the prince was taken to heaven. Again he found a beautiful banquet, and again only 10-foot chopsticks. But here the people were happy and content, for they sat on opposite sides of the tables, each one feeding the person across from him.

Problems in the Church?
When the church began on earth, the pastor was being executed as a criminal; the chairman of the board was out cursing and swearing that he had never even been a part it. The treasurer was committing suicide. Most of the rest of the board members had run away. And about the only ones who showed any signs of faithfulness were a few ladies from the women's auxiliary.

Lawsuits in the Popular Culture
According to Wikipedia, the classic lawsuit in English literature is Jarndyce v. Jarndyce in Charles Dickens' novel, *Bleak House.* The case proceeds over decades, enriching regiments of attorneys and bleeding the assets being fought over until nothing is left for the beneficiaries. In our modern entertainment, the legal system is the basis for countless television shows and movies, from Perry Mason to Boston Legal. While attorneys are often the target of disparaging jokes, the public can't seem to get enough of them.

APPROPRIATE HYMNS AND SONGS

"Sweeter," Israel Houghton, Melease Houghton, & Cindy Cruse-Ratcliff, 2003 Integrity's Praise! Music, Lakewood Ministries Music and My Other Publication Company.

"You Are God," James Katina, Joe Katina, John Katina, Jesse Katina, and Samuel Katina, 1999 Maroon Dogg Music, Inc./Emack Music, Inc.

"How Great Thou Art," Carl Boberg, Public Domain.

"Rejoice the Lord Is King," Charles Wesley & John Darwall, Public Domain.

FOR THE BULLETIN

Today marks the death of Pope St. Celestine I in A.D. 432. He fought heresy, supported Augustine of Hippo, and perhaps sent St. Patrick to Ireland. ● Donald Cargill was a powerful Scottish Presbyterian preacher when such were outlawed. On July 10, 1681, Scottish troops burst into the house where Cargill, James Boig, and Walter Smith were sleeping. The men were rousted from bed and taken to prison. Soon, two others joined them. All were condemned. At the scaffold Cargill put his foot on the ladder, turned, blessed the Lord with uplifted hands, and said, "The Lord knows I go up this ladder with less fear, confusion, or perturbation of mind than ever I entered a pulpit to preach." Five good men were martyred in Edinburgh on "that never-to-be-forgotten bloody day—July 27, 1681." ● On July 27, 1926, British Methodist leader, William Sangster, was ordained at Wesley Chapel in York. In 1939, Sangster assumed leadership of London's Westminster Central Hall. During his first worship service he announced to his stunned congregation that Britain and Germany were officially at war. He quickly converted the church basement into an air raid shelter, and for 1,688 nights Sangster ministered to the various needs of all kinds of people. ● The parents of German Christian Dietrich Bonhoeffer, who was killed by the Nazis at Flossenberg Prison, heard of their son's death while listening to a radio broadcast of a memorial service from London on this day in 1945. The speaker said, "We are gathered here in the presence of God to make thankful remembrance of the life and work of his servant, Dietrich Bonhoeffer, who gave his life in faith and obedience."

Quote for the Pastor's Wall

Never think of giving up preaching!
The angels around the throne
envy your great work.

—ALEXANDER WHYTE

WORSHIP HELPS

Call to Worship

Oh, magnify the LORD with me, and let us exalt His name together (Ps. 34:3).

Scripture Medley

Have all the workers of iniquity no knowledge, who eat up my people as they eat bread, and do not call on the LORD? . . . You call on the name of your gods, and I will call on the name of the LORD; and the God who answers by fire, He is God. . . ." If we ask anything according to His will, He hears us. And if we know that He hears us, whatever we ask, we know that we have the petitions that we have asked of Him. . . . Ask, and it will be given to you; seek, and you will find; knock, and it will be opened to you. For everyone who asks receives, and he who seeks finds, and to him who knocks it will be opened. For what man is there among you who, if his son asks for bread, will give him a stone? Or if he asks for a fish, will he give him a serpent? If you then, being evil, know how to give good gifts to your children, how much more will your Father who is in heaven give good things to those who ask Him! . . . Arise, call on your God . . . (taken from Ps. 14:4; 1 Kin. 18:24; 1 John 5:14–15; Matt. 7:7–11; Jon. 1:6).

Invitation

If you are not a Christian then, whatever you may have done and whatever your lifestyle, God can cleanse you from your sin, make you holy, and put you right with Himself. The work of Jesus assures you of this. As you look around this congregation, know that no one is better than anyone else for we all came to the same place: the level ground at the foot of the Cross. Will you come today?   —*Rev. Peter Grainger*

Additional Sermons and Lesson Ideas

Four Reasons to Trust God with Daily Needs
Date preached:

SCRIPTURE: Deuteronomy 1:19–33

INTRODUCTION: Many of us are intellectually persuaded of the truthfulness of Christianity and have personally trusted Christ as Savior. But on a daily basis, we struggle with trusting God with everyday needs. In Deuteronomy 1, Moses recounted the story of the twelve spies (Num. 13—14) and gave four reasons to trust God with our burdens.

1. We Should Trust God Because of His Commands (v. 21). "Do not fear or be discouraged" (v. 29). "Do not be terrified or afraid." God has commanded us to trust Him.
2. We Should Trust God Because of His Promises (v. 30). "The LORD your God, who goes before you, He will fight for you." The battle is the Lord's, and He promises we will be more than conquerors through Him who loved us.
3. We Should Trust God Because of His Past Faithfulness (v. 31). "In the wilderness . . . you saw how the LORD your God carried you, as a man carries his son."
4. We Should Trust God Because of His Personalized Care (vv. 32–33). "Your God . . . went in the way before you to search out a place for you to pitch your tents, to show you the way you should go."

CONCLUSION: Instead of fretting about it, try faith-ing it. Trust God with your daily cares.

The Church Is Your Family
Date preached:
By Joshua D. Rowe

SCRIPTURE: 1 Timothy 5:1–3

INTRODUCTION: Churches in our modern culture are rapidly growing more individualistic. Jesus' body was never meant to function as individual units doing their own thing. We need to return to an understanding of the church as a family!

1. Your Fathers (v. 1a). Older men should be treated as fathers. No one should be harsh, rebuking older men. We are to "appeal to him as a father" (NASB).
2. Your Brothers (v. 1b). Younger men should be treated as brothers and respected as such.
3. Your Mothers (vv. 2a–3). Older women should be treated as mothers (v. 2), since they play a mothering function at home and/or in the church. In this category would fall widows, who deserve honor (v. 3).

4. Your Sisters (v. 2b). Younger women should be treated as sisters. The phrase is added here, "in all purity." The purity of a sister in Christ must be highly exalted and protected by the church family.

CONCLUSION: Are you still concerned only about what you "get out of church" every Sunday? Why don't we shift our focus to consider our time at church "family time?"

PRAYER FOR THE PASTOR'S CLOSET

Refresh our bodies, we pray Thee, with quiet and comfortable rest; but especially let our souls be refreshed with Thy love. We humbly pray Thee, for Christ's sake. Amen. —MATTHEW HENRY

AUGUST 3, 2008

Partial Obedience

Date preached:

By Rev. Richard S. Sharpe, Jr.

Scripture: 1 Samuel 15:1–23, especially from verse 22
Has the LORD as great delight in burnt offerings and sacrifices, as in obeying the voice of the LORD? Behold, to obey is better than sacrifice, and to heed than the fat of rams.

Introduction: Anyone who has children knows what partial obedience is. We can send our children to clean their rooms and they come out after a couple of minutes and say it's all done. When we check, we find they've taken all the toys off the floor and thrown them into the closet; and that's their idea of cleaning. The Lord gives us commands to obey. We think that we can just obey part way and the Lord will be happy. Saul discovered the hard way that the Lord doesn't want partial obedience. As we look into this text, we learn what He expects from His people.

1. **The Orders (vv. 3–5).** God was not vague in His command: "Now go and attack Amalek, and utterly destroy all that they have, and do not spare them. But kill both man and woman, infant and nursing child, ox and sheep, camel and donkey." These people had not given the Israelites help when they were traveling from Egypt to the Promised Land of Canaan. The Lord waited until they had conquered the land of Canaan and established a king before He sent them on this mission. The orders were plain. We might think it's cruel of God to have all the people of a nation killed, but the Lord knew what the descendants of this nation would do in the future if they stayed alive (Esth. 3:1). God, then, was more merciful to cut off the offspring of a rebellious nation than to allow them to continue to reproduce. They had passed "Redemption Point." In any case, God knows every detail, and we can only guess at why He commanded as He did, but there's no guessing as to whether it was the right thing!

2. **The Battle (vv. 5–9).** King Saul went to the valley outside the city of Amalek. He told the Kenites to leave the area before the battle because they had treated the Israelites well when they came out of

Egypt. The Kenites left. Saul slew some of the Amalekites, but he took the king of the Amalekites, Agag, captive. They also saved the best of the sheep and other animals ". . . and were unwilling to utterly destroy them. But everything despised and worthless, that they utterly destroyed." They didn't obey the command. They saved the best of the animals and the king of the Amalekites.

3. **The Confrontation (vv. 10–23).** Samuel was told of the Lord to go to King Saul. He told Samuel, I greatly regret that I have set up Saul as king, for he has turned back from following Me (v. 11a). It grieved Samuel so much that he cried to the Lord all night (v. 11b). Samuel rose early in the morning and went to Saul. Saul claimed to have kept the command of God by winning the battle. What Saul didn't realize is that God wasn't interested in who won; He was interested in His will being done! Saul claimed he had saved the cattle to sacrifice to the Lord. Samuel's response is an excellent lesson for us, "Has the LORD as great delight in burnt offerings and sacrifices, as in obeying the voice of the LORD? Behold, to obey is better than sacrifice, and to heed than the fat of rams" (v. 22).

Conclusion: This historical account in the history of Israel has a lesson for us to learn. The Lord has not changed between Testaments. He is the same. He wants us to obey His commands on a regular basis. Samuel compares rebellion against the commands of the Lord with witchcraft and stubbornness against the commands of the Lord with idolatry.

After accepting Christ as our Savior, we are to live in a manner that is pleasing to the Lord. That life would include obeying the commands He has given us. Are we obeying the commands we find in the Word of God? Are we attending church on a regular basis? Are we tithing to the Lord on a regular basis? Are we witnessing to others about our Lord on a regular basis? Are we manifesting the fruit of the Spirit to each other on a regular basis?

STATS, STORIES, AND MORE

Incomplete obedience always boomerangs, and the sins we secretly tolerate in our lives can rise up when we least expect it and ravage us. One man told of a boa constrictor he had for a pet. His family had taken it in when just a baby snake and had raised it. It had become the family pet, and they had a cute name for it. But one day, he walked into the nursery to find that the boa constrictor had coiled around the child and was squeezing the life from the baby. It took all the man's strength to pull it away and, in the nick of time, to save his child. He said, "We had thought it a cute thing, a pet; we thought we could control it, but it nearly ruined our lives." I wonder if someone here today is tolerating some habit you think you can control. Ephesians 4:27 says, "Do not give the devil a foothold" (NIV).

Ron Handley, the head of Fellowship of Christian Athletes, speaking at a conference in New Mexico, said that the subtlety of sin and of compromise is so great that he meets with a group of friends each Monday and they ask each other these ten questions:

1. Have you spent daily time in Scriptures and in prayer?
2. Have you had any flirtatious or lustful attitudes, tempting thought or exposed yourself to any explicit materials that would not glorify God?
3. Have you been completely above reproach in your financial dealings?
4. Have you spent quality time with family and friends?
5. Have you done your 100% best in your job, school, etc.?
6. Have you told any half-truths or outright lies, putting yourself in a better light to those around you?
7. Have you shared the gospel with an unbeliever this week?
8. Have you taken care of your body through daily physical exercise and proper eating and sleeping habits?
9. Have you allowed any person or circumstances to rob you of your joy?
10. Have you lied to us on any of your answers today?[1]

---

[1] http://www.donelson.org/pocket/pp-980816.html, accessed February 1, 2007.

APPROPRIATE HYMNS AND SONGS

"You Are Worthy of My Praise," David Ruis, 1991 Maranatha Praise Inc.

"In the Secret (I Want to Know You)," Andy Park, 1995 Mercy/Vineyard Publishing.

"Through It All," Andrae Crouch, 1971 Manna Music, Inc.

"Because We Believe," Jamie Harvill & Nancy Gordon, 1996 Mother's Heart Music (Admin. by ROM Admin.).

"Sanctuary," John Thompson & Randy Scruggs, 1982 by Full Armor Pub. and Whole Armor Pub.

FOR THE BULLETIN

On Friday, August 3, 1492, Columbus and his 52-member flagship *Santa Maria* crew weigh anchor for a voyage from Palos, Spain, seeking passage to "India." Two smaller ships, the *Nina* and the *Pinta*, accompany him. ● Holy Roman Emperor Charles V convened a church council in Augsburg in 1530 to address the Catholic-Protestant conflict that was tearing apart his empire. This proved to be the last Protestant attempt for acceptance by the church. They presented a statement of their beliefs which became known as the Augsburg Confession. On August 3, 1530, the Catholics issued their own statement, the *Confutio*, in response to the Augsburg Confession. ● On August 3, 1553, Mary, daughter of Catherine of Aragon entered London to begin a harsh five-year reign in which hundreds of Protestants were burned at the stake. ● August 3, 1858, marks the birth of Maltbie D. Babcock, American Presbyterian clergyman, remembered as author of the song, "This Is My Father's World." ● On August 3, 1966, Ernie Fowler, missionary to Columbia, South America, was vacationing with his family in the high mountains near the Venezuelan border. While hiking, he was shot and killed by bandits in front of his children.

WORSHIP HELPS

Call to Worship
"Draw near to God and He will draw near to you. Cleanse your hands, you sinners; and purify your hearts, you double-minded. . . . Humble yourselves in the sight of the Lord, and He will lift you up" (James 4:8, 10).

Responsive Reading (Ps. 118:25–29)

Leader: Save now, I pray, O LORD;

People: O LORD, I pray, send now prosperity.

Leader: Blessed is he who comes in the name of the LORD! We have blessed you from the house of the LORD.

People: God is the LORD, And He has given us light;

Leader: Bind the sacrifice with cords to the horns of the altar.

People: You are my God, and I will praise You; You are my God, I will exalt You.

Everyone: Oh, give thanks to the LORD, for He is good! For His mercy endures forever.

Benediction
And now, O Lord GOD, You are God, and Your words are true, and You have promised this goodness to Your servant. Now therefore, let it please You to bless the house of Your servant, that it may continue before You forever; for You, O Lord GOD, have spoken *it,* and with Your blessing let the house of Your servant be blessed forever (2 Sam. 7:28–29).

Additional Sermons and Lesson Ideas

Avoiding Personal Contamination

Date preached:

SCRIPTURE: 2 Corinthians 6:14—7:1 (NIV)

INTRODUCTION: Our society is concerned about contaminated water, soil, vegetables, etc. God is concerned about soul contamination.

EXPOSITION: The first word of verse 1, "Since . . . ," refers back to chapter 6. Paul warns the church about being unequally yoked with false teachers, which would contaminate the church. He quotes a series of Old Testament promises relating to God's holy presence among us, then says: "Since we have these promises, dear friends, let us purify ourselves from everything that contaminates . . ." That verse (7:1) gives us three strategies for a noncontaminated life:

1. Claim His Word. *Since we have these promises. . . .* This refers to the Old Testament promises quoted at the end of chapter 6, which Paul himself evidently used to remain pure in life. Bible verses can counter any temptation we face.
2. Cleanse Your Life. *Let us purify ourselves. . . .* Often the Bible uses this word to refer to God's purifying us. Here the onus is put on us. We have to decide to remain pure.
3. Come of Age in Your Christian Experience. *Perfecting holiness out of reverence for God.* Keep growing, perfecting your sense of personal holiness. As we grow stronger in Christ, we're increasingly victorious over sin.

CONCLUSION: You can live a noncontaminated life by mastering the truths of this passage.

Sez Who?

Date preached:

By Rev. Melvin Tinker

SCRIPTURE: Romans 1:16–32

INTRODUCTION: Yale Law Professor Arthur Leff talks about "the grand sez who?" He argues that if there is no God, no transcendent source of value, then there is no universally accepted source of authority. Genocide is wrong? Sez who? You wouldn't object to killing a thousand ants would you, so why not a thousand people? Paul tells us exactly who has the final say as to what's right and wrong; and He has the power to judge.

1. The Problem of Judgment (vv. 18–23). Everyone is under condemnation for doing as they please rather than submitting to God.

2. The Signs of Judgment (vv. 24–32). God's wrath is displayed by His allowing people the consequence of their own actions; this will eventually lead them to hell for eternity.

3. The Solution to Judgment (vv. 16–17). The gospel (Good News) of Jesus Christ is salvation from this judgment for everyone who believes!

CONCLUSION: Are you living by the principle of "sez who?" or have you submitted to Christ that you may be judged righteous in Him?

PRAYER FOR THE PASTOR'S CLOSET

O God, without Thee we are not able to please Thee; mercifully grant that Thy Holy Spirit may in all things direct and rule our hearts; through Jesus Christ our Lord. Amen. —BOOK OF COMMON PRAYER

AUGUST 10, 2008

SUGGESTED SERMON

Be of Good Cheer: I Have Overcome the World

Date preached:

Scripture: John 16:33
These things I have spoken to you, that in Me you may have peace. In the world you will have tribulation; but be of good cheer, I have overcome the world.

Introduction: Loren Bailey, a soldier in Iraq during the last war, wrote home about his experiences, saying: "We got hit by an Improvised Explosive Devices (IED) today. My brothers-in-arms, Iekar (eye-car) and Kohail, were walking out to inspect a civilian car when it exploded. They both were blown back about 100 feet or so. The hilarious part is when they got up, they started yelling and laughing. Iekar came back screaming, "Yee-Haw! I'm still alive! Praise God Almighty, I'm alive!" He had the biggest smile in the world on his face. When he got back, he asked me to help him do something. I said sure, and he asked if I would pray to God for thanksgiving with him." Loren, a new Christian, ended his letter by thanking God for the opportunity to pray with an Iraqi and by saying, "Jesus has been the BEST companion over here. He listens to my every prayer and answers me every morning with renewed strength and a clear mind."

We're in the combat zone of life, faced with satanic IEDs and demonic snipers every day. Jesus said, "In this world you will have tribulation, but be of good cheer, for I have overcome the world." We can have a peace that passes all understanding. The Upper Room Discourse of our Lord is found in John 13—17, and the last sentence of His last sermon gives us several principles for inner peace.

1. **In Me You May Have Peace.** This is arguably the most powerful phrase in the Bible—*in Me*. It was Paul's theme. He used the phrase "In Christ" about 100 times. It refers to union with Him. Suppose I saw a bottle on the shore. Unscrewing the top, I walked over to the sea, filled the bottle up with water, screwed on the top, and tossed the bottle into the surf. The water would be in the bottle, and the bottle would be in the water. When we confess Jesus Christ as Lord,

He comes to live within us by the living water of the Holy Spirit, and we are in Christ.

2. **These Things I Have Spoken** . . . Our sense of inner peace grows from trusting His words. What did Jesus mean by "these things?" In the broadest sense, we can claim the entirety of the Word of God. In another sense, Jesus was thinking of all the teachings He had given His disciples since He called them by the shore of Galilee. Specifically, "these things" refer to the Upper Room Discourse. John 13—17 are remarkable chapters because Jesus spoke them in an atmosphere of incredible tension, yet His message was one of supernatural peace. (Review the key verses and promises found in John 14, 15, and 16.)

3. **In the World You Will Have Tribulation.** John 16:33 goes on to issue a warning. Our inner peace, which is based on our union with Christ and grows as we trust His words, will be assaulted by the world. Jesus promises that we'll have problems in the world. Opposition. Persecution and satanic attacks. Misunderstandings, hurts, heartaches, and things that challenge your faith.

4. **But Be of Good Cheer. I Have Overcome** . . . But Jesus did not end His teachings there. Here is the last thing He said before His prayer in chapter 17, the concluding sentence of three years of ministry, the last syllables of the last sermon He preached prior to Calvary: BUT BE OF GOOD CHEER; I HAVE OVERCOME THE WORLD. He was saying: "I've come into the world and lived here for thirty-three years without sinning so I can serve as an innocent, sacrificial victim whose blood can atone for the sins of the world. I am going to lay down my life willingly and I will take it up again. The grave cannot hold Me, death cannot keep Me, and I'm going to burst from the tomb like a fist through cardboard. I have overcome the world."

Conclusion: If Jesus Christ has overcome the world, He can overcome your anxieties and make all things work together for good in your experiences. He is the great Overcomer, whatever tribulations we face. Our peace is in Him. It's reinforced by His words. It's assaulted by the world, but He says to you in His last *ex cathedra* utterance: *Be of good cheer. I have overcome the world.*

STATS, STORIES, AND MORE

Amy Carmichael, in one of her prescient observations from Scripture, pointed out that Jesus did not say, "These things I have spoken to you, that in your circumstances you might have peace." He did not say, "These things I have spoken to you that in the love of others you might have peace." He said: "In Me!" D. L. Moody once said that if he saw a man in a cellar, shivering some from the cold and dampness and trying to see in the dim light, he would say to him, "Come on up, out into the sunshine. It's warm and bright up here." But suppose the man said, "No, I'm trying to see if I can make my own light down here, and I am trying to work up a warm feeling." That's where a lot of people are today. They're in the cellar of life, trying to generate a little light and trying to work up a warm feeling when what they really need is the light and the warmth of the sunlight of Jesus Christ. He said, "In Me you will have peace." So our peace comes from being in union with Christ.

Lucky Dog
Missionary C. T. Studd once traveled to China on a ship whose captain was an embittered opponent of Christianity. When he learned Studd was on board, the captain lit into him. Instead of arguing with him, Studd put his arm around the captain and said, "But, my friend, I have a peace that passeth all understanding and a joy that nothing can take away." The captain finally replied, "You're a lucky dog," and walked away. Before the end of the voyage, he became a rejoicing believer in Jesus Christ.[1]

APPROPRIATE HYMNS AND SONGS

"Lord I Lift Your Name on High," Rick Founds, 1989 Maranatha Praise, Inc.

"Mighty Is the Power of the Cross," Chris Tomlin, Sean Craig and Jesse Reeves, 2004 Ariose Music/Praise Song Press/worshiptogether.com songs.

"Still," Reuben Morgan, 2002 Reuben Morgan/Hillsong Publishing.

"Crown Him with Many Crowns," Matthew Bridges, George J. Elvey, & Godfrey Thring, Public Domain.

---

[1]Norman P. Grubb, *C. T. Studd, Cricketer and Pioneer* (London: Religious Tract Society, 1933), pp. 52–53.

FOR THE BULLETIN

The Roman siege of Jerusalem began in April, A.D. 70, immediately after the Passover, when Jerusalem was filled with strangers. Captured Jews were crucified at a rate of 500 a day, crosses encircling the city. Daily temple sacrifices ceased July 17, all hands being needed for defense. The Romans, using catapults and battering rams, finally broke through the walls. The Jews fled to the temple for refuge. Titus had reportedly wanted to spare the edifice, but his soldiers would not be restrained. A firebrand was hurled through the golden gate and exploded like a bomb. The temple became an ocean of fire. It was August 10, the same day of the year, it was said, in which Solomon's earlier temple had been destroyed by Babylon. ● Laurentius of Rome, a deacon, was slowly roasted to death for his faith on this day in A.D. 258. ● A German churchman, Poppo, bishop of Brixen, was elected as Pope Damasus II, but died 23 days later, perhaps by poison, on August 10, 1048. ● Alexander VI was elected pope on this day in 1492. He was one of history's worst. ● Halley's comet appeared in the August skies in 1531, and the Swiss Reformer, Ulrich Zwingli, saw it as a sign of war and of his own death. While walking in a graveyard on August 10, 1531, he told a friend, "It will cost the life of many an honorable man and my own. The truth and the Church will suffer, but Christ will never suffer." ● On August 10, 1854, Charles Spurgeon's sermons began being published weekly. ● Missionary Robert Moffat died on this day in 1883.

WORSHIP HELPS

Call to Worship

I will praise the LORD according to His righteousness, and will sing praise to the name of the LORD Most High (Ps. 7:17).

Hymn Story: There Is a Name I Love to Hear

Frederick Whitfield was born on a cold January day in 1829, in tiny Threapwood, England, population about 250. He attended college in Dublin, Ireland, and devoted his life to pastoral ministry in the Church of England. His greatest legacy is this hymn about the name of Jesus, written when he was a student. Generations of Christians have loved "There Is a Name I Love to Hear" with its peppy refrain: "O how I love Jesus, / O how I love Jesus, / O how I love Jesus, / because He first loved me."

You might be interested to know that while Whitfield wrote the *verses* to this hymn, he didn't compose its famous chorus.

Both the simple words and the nimble tune of "O How I Love Jesus" are American inventions of unknown origin. They floated around like orphans, attaching themselves to various hymns in the nineteenth century. One hymnologist found 42 occurrences of this chorus in early songbooks. Even such stately hymns as "Amazing Grace" and "Alas! And Did My Savior Bleed" were occasionally sung to this lighthearted melody, with "O How I Love Jesus" used as the refrain. But when "O How I Love Jesus" was finally wedded to Whitfield's "There Is a Name I Love to Sing," it was a marriage made in heaven. We've been singing it ever since.[2]

Benediction

Almighty Lord, You love us, and Your love casts out fear. May we rejoice in Your love this week, being of good cheer, being glad of soul and spirit, and sharing the hope of Jesus with all we meet. In Jesus' name. Amen.

---

[2]Adapted from the editor's book, *Then Sings My Soul: Book 2*. Both volumes of *Then Sings My Soul* contain 150 hymn histories that will enhance worship services year-round.

Additional Sermons and Lesson Ideas

When Life Gets Ugly
By Dr. Larry Osborne

Date preached:

SCRIPTURE: Various

INTRODUCTION: Life can be tough; sometimes it gets downright ugly. When it does, many of us aren't sure what to think or how to respond. In today's study, we'll find out as we explore one of God's great promises and His escape plan for life's toughest valleys.

1. Perspective (Ps. 13; 73; Acts 14:22; 1 Pet. 1:6–7). Life's toughest trials are normal, natural, and sometimes necessary. Perspective sees the big picture, remembers God's blessings, and trusts even when confused.
2. Integrity (Heb. 5:7–8; 1 Pet. 2:21–23). Integrity does the right thing even when it doesn't seem to work.
3. Focus (2 Cor. 1:3–5; Rom. 8:28; Heb. 12:11). We must hold to the promise that God always works everything out for the good.

CONCLUSION: When life gets ugly, hold fast to scriptural perspective, integrity, and focus.

The Difficulties of Discipleship
By Joshua D. Rowe

Date preached:

SCRIPTURE: Luke 9:57–62

INTRODUCTION: Who sets the pace of your life as you follow Christ? Do you obey Him only when life is acceptable to you? Do you obey when it's convenient? Do you ever reconsider whether you want to follow Him? Jesus warns us against this:

1. Don't Expect a Luxurious Life (vv. 57–58).
2. Don't Defer Obedience (vv. 59–60).
3. Don't Look Back (vv. 61–62).

CONCLUSION: When Jesus calls us to be His disciples, we are to surrender to Him fully, obey Him immediately, and follow Him unreservedly. The blessings that will follow make the difficulties of discipleship fade away.

Suggestions for the Public Reading of Scriptures

"Until I arrive, give attention to the public reading of Scripture," wrote Paul in 1 Timothy 4:13 (NRSV). The public reading of Scripture is a compelling act of grace for the church, and it should be done skillfully, reverently, and meaningfully. On the one hand, the public Scripture-reader isn't an actor artificially reciting lines so as to draw attention to his or her voice or to contrive an emotional response. On the other hand, the words of Scripture have a power and charm that can never be equaled by the greatest playwrights in the world, and the humblest voice reading Scripture is greater than the noblest actor reading Shakespeare.

But our humble voices should do it faithfully and with forethought. Too many preachers and worship-leaders read a passage with inadequate preparation, often as nothing more than a transition in the order of service or as an introduction for a song or sermon. The public reading of God's Word should be a highlight in the service rather than merely a segue or filler; and it requires as much practice and preparation as any other element of worship. Here are six simple suggestions for effective public Bible reading.

1. **Choose a translation that has both clarity and cadence.**

2. **Practice in advance.** It's often helpful to pencil-in appropriate accent marks, breaks, pauses, and underscores to aid in the reading. Pay attention to inflictions. Make sure your voice conveys the pronunciation found in the passage. If the sentence is a question or an exclamation, convey that by the inflection of your voice. Remember that every vocal reading of Scripture is an interpretation of the text. By emphasizing certain words and dramatizing certain phrases, you interpret and convey the meaning of the text. Visualize the scene in your own mind. Hear Pilate disdainfully spit out the words, "What is truth?" Hear Jacob moan, "All these

Continued on the next page

things are against me." Let your voice convey naturally the emotions of the text, and choose in advance what words to emphasize. Make the appropriate notations in the text you are using.

3. Make sure you have mastered the pronunciation of difficult words. Practice them until they come to you as naturally as your own name. Learn to read distinctly, sounding out every consonant so as not to mumble.

4. Read through the passage in advance until you have "learned" it. It's not necessary to memorize it; but it's important for the stream of words to cut a channel in your brain so they can flow smoothly. You want to be able to occasionally make eye contact with the audience; in fact, the more eye contact the better. Learn to hold the Bible with one hand and with the other hand use a finger to guide your eye through the reading. Otherwise, having looked up at the audience, you might lose your place when you glance back down at your Bible.

5. Decide in advance how you will enter and exit the passage. Compose an opening line, such as, "Since Sunday is the first day of the week, the day in which our Savior rose from the dead, it is always appropriate to remind ourselves of the events of that first Easter. Let me read it to you from John's Gospel, chapter 20." Sometimes the passage ends itself quite nicely; other times it helps to say: "May the Lord add His blessings to the reading of His Word." Or perhaps something more original, such as, "With this passage ringing in our ears, let's pause for a time of quiet prayer."

6. Occasionally Read an Extended Portion. One Sunday night I was low on sermons and just didn't have anything fresh to offer. I decided to simply read through the entire book of 1 Thessalonians from the New International Version, reading as meaningfully as I could. Some verses I read slowly to let the words sink in; other verses I read at a faster clip, because it seemed that Paul was rushing with excitement as he wrote it. Occasionally I would add a word of explanation or a comment, but for the most part, I just read the letter as though I were reading it to the original recipients who had gathered to hear it as it had just come fresh from their beloved apostle. I was surprised at how the letter moved me as I read it, and at how attentive the church was. The kicker was when I got to the very end of the letter and read these words: "I charge you before the Lord to have this letter read to all the brothers." It dawned on me that in all my years of ministry, I had never until that night obeyed that injunction from the Lord.

Our job is preaching; yet nothing we say can ever match the familiar but infallible words of our Bibles. So until He arrives, give attention to the public reading of Scripture.

AUGUST 17, 2008

SUGGESTED SERMON

A Fresh Vision for Revival

Date preached:

By Dr. Timothy K. Beougher

Scripture: Isaiah 6:1–8, especially from verse 3
Holy, holy, holy is the LORD of hosts; the whole earth is full of His glory!

Introduction: We all can go through times of spiritual decline and disobedience. When we find ourselves "stuck" in a rut of sinfulness, we need revival! There are numerous instances of revival in the Bible that we could study, but I have selected Isaiah 6 as a description of revival, because revival usually begins in the heart of one individual before it spreads. Isaiah 6 provides a paradigm for us to better understand that truth.

1. **Our Need for a Fresh Touch from God (Is. 6:1a).** The context of revival in Isaiah 6 was, "In the year that King Uzziah died . . ." Isaiah's vision was prompted by a crisis: King Uzziah's death. After a long reign of peace and prosperity, the king had died. Now there was uncertainty. This uncertainty drove Isaiah to seek God. Isaiah knew he needed a fresh touch from God. Do you sense your need for a fresh touch from God this morning? That is the starting point: a sense of need.

2. **God as He Really Is (Is. 6:1b–4).** We don't have time to examine every aspect of Isaiah's vision, but two things are readily apparent:

   A. **God Is on the Throne: He Is Sovereign (v. 1b).** God was not worried about the death of Israel's leader; it didn't catch Him by surprise. He was on the throne! He is still there today! The circumstances of life may be falling apart around you, but God is on the throne! He is in control! Some of you may need to be reminded of that today. You need to "be still and know that He is God" (Ps. 46:10).

   B. **God Is Holy (vv. 2–4).** Great as the realization that God is on the throne, that was not the most prominent realization that gripped Isaiah. It was God's holiness that captivated him. Note the actions of the seraphs: even these angelic beings must cover their faces in the light of God's holiness. The foundations shook, showing the awesome holiness of God. Think about this for a minute: inanimate pillars, posts made out of stone, tremble in the presence of God, and yet some people's hearts are so hard, that they remain motionless in God's presence.

3. **Our Sinfulness and Need for Cleansing (v. 5).** We can only see ourselves correctly after we have seen God. We can no longer compare ourselves to others, but only to His holiness. Isaiah, in chapter 5, pronounced woes on other people six different times. Now all he can say is "Woe is me" (v. 5). When we find ourselves in the presence of a holy God, we become aware of even the smallest sin. Things that have long been tolerated or excused as "little things" are openly admitted to be sin that must be dealt with. They must be confessed and repented of so God's cleansing can come.

4. **God's Gracious Provision (vv. 6–7).** God does not reveal Himself to destroy us, but to cleanse us just as the angel touched a coal from the altar to Isaiah's mouth and pronounced him forgiven. What if you've really messed up? Don't despair! Don't try to hide it, but confess your sin and remember that the blood of Jesus Christ washes you as white as snow (Is. 1:8). God removes your sin from you as far as the east is from the west (Ps. 103:12).

5. **We Hear God's Voice (Is. 6:8a).** When our sin is confessed and our hearts are right, we can now hear God's voice with a new sensitivity. As with Isaiah, God wants us to hear His call to service. We live in a dying world that needs to be revived!

6. **We Respond with Joyful Obedience (v. 8b).** And I said, "Here am I! Send me." You can never be the same after an encounter with God. Your life will change. The realization that your sins are forgiven will make you eager to respond in gratitude to the Lord's call! Isaiah doesn't know anything about his mission, but none of that matters. He is available to God to be used however God chooses. Are you at that point this morning? Are you ready to yield yourself to God wholeheartedly?

Conclusion: The dare of revival is to ask God to search us and see if there is anything offensive to Him in our lives (Ps. 139:23–24).

STATS, STORIES, AND MORE

Dr. Stephen Olford on Revival

"Our Christian churches today are riddled with people who sit in church and are either regenerate or totally disobedient to the hearing of God's Word and the loving of God's person. When I was a student in London I attended the ministry of the great G. Campbell Morgan on a number of occasions. And I heard him say in very simple terms: 'Revival is a sovereign work of God.' We can no more manipulate revival than we can the breezes on the tops of the trees. Wind blows where it wishes and we can't tell where it comes from or where it's going. So is the work of God in revival and in regeneration. However, you, God's people, must be sensitive to that wind so that when God blows from heaven, that wind catches the sails of our little box and takes us across the seas of His eternal purposes.

"God laid upon me a great burden when I went to Calvary Baptist Church and we started every Friday evening a half-night of prayer from 7 P.M. to 12 A.M. For 14 years there was never a break. I attribute to the glory of God what we saw and the miracles that took place in the city of New York to that half-night of prayer.

"One of my prayers that hangs in my study on the right side of my desk is from the heart of Robert M'Cheyne, one of my heroes. . . . He was known not for only his poetry, preaching, or passion for souls, but his purity of life. When he died and his papers were sorted out, it was found that his daily prayer was: 'O, God, make me as holy as a saved sinner can be!' "

APPROPRIATE HYMNS AND SONGS

"Be Thou My Vision," Irish Folk Melody; Mary E. Byrne, Public Domain.

"Did You Feel the Mountains Tremble," Martin Smith, 1994 Curious? Music U.K. (Admin. by EMI CMG Pub.).

"Rescue the Perishing," Fanny Crosby & William Doane, Public Domain.

"My Jesus I Love Thee," William Featherstone & Adoniram J. Gordon, Public Domain.

FOR THE BULLETIN

The Second Nicea Council, convoked by the Empress Irene to end the Iconoclastic Controversy, met on this day in the church of the Holy Apostles at Constantinople, but was immediately broken up by iconoclastic soldiers. ● Pope Julius II, who laid the cornerstone of St. Peter's Basilica, was seized by violent illness on this day in 1511. For three days he hovered near death, but as his successor was about to be chosen he surprised (and disappointed) his cardinals by recovering. ● On August 17, 1635, Richard Mather arrived in Boston. An English Puritan and staunch defender of congregational church government, he is remembered as the father of Increase Mather and the grandfather of Cotton Mather. ● When the British monarchy was reinstated in 1660, a series of new laws stifled religious liberty. The Act of Uniformity, for example, required ministers to use *The Book of Common Prayer* as a format for worship. Many non-Anglicans refused, and in August 17, 1662, over 2,000 of England's finest ministers preached their "farewell sermons" and were ejected from their pulpits. ● August 17, 1761, is the birthday of William Carey, "Father of Modern Missions." ● August 17, 1780, is the birthday of George Croly, author of "Spirit of God, Descend Upon My Heart." ● On August 17, 1809, Thomas Campbell founded the Disciples of Christ Church. ● Radio Bible teacher Theodore Epp was converted on this day in 1927 after listening to a sermon from Ephesians 1.

Quote for the Pastor's Wall

Good sermons usually have a long history. They mature slowly. They are not made between Sundays. A week is too short a time for an idea to germinate, grow, blossom into full bloom. . . . The preacher will have scores of sermons . . . slowly maturing. His question is not what to preach, but only what to preach next.

—DR. RAYMOND CALKINS

WORSHIP HELPS

Call to Worship
Search me, O God, and know my heart; try me, and know my anxieties; and see if there is any wicked way in me, and lead me in the way everlasting (Ps. 139:23–24).

Scripture Reading Medley
He who covers his sins will not prosper, but whoever confesses and forsakes them will have mercy. . . . For You, Lord, are good, and ready to forgive, and abundant in mercy to all those who call upon You. . . . As far as the east is from the west, so far has He removed our transgressions from us. . . . Let Your hand be upon the man of Your right hand, upon the son of man whom You made strong for Yourself. Then we will not turn back from You; revive us, and we will call upon Your name. Restore us, O LORD God of hosts; cause Your face to shine, and we shall be saved (from Prov. 28:13; Ps. 86:5; 103:2; 80:17–19)!

Invitation
Are you feeling a load of guilt because of some unconfessed sin in your life? Confess it to God right now; claim His cleansing power. We are barren and unfruitful and out of fellowship with our Lord because we do not confess our sins. God's examinations are painful but necessary for us. Will you acknowledge that truth this morning? Open up your heart to the searchlight of the Word of God. Prayerfully allow the Holy Spirit to do His work of conviction in your heart. As God convicts you of something, confess it to Him, turn from it, and receive His forgiveness and cleansing.

Additional Sermon and Lesson Ideas

Forget Not His Benefits
By Joshua D. Rowe

Date preached:

SCRIPTURE: Psalm 103:2–5

INTRODUCTION: We often (and appropriately) focus on the difficulties that may face us in our Christian walk. However, it's equally important to spend time reflecting on the benefits that we have in the Lord. David reminds us in Psalm 102 not to forget His benefits:

1. He Forgives Your Sins (v. 3a).
2. He Heals Your Diseases (v. 3b).
3. He Redeems Your Life from Destruction (v. 4a).
4. He Crowns You with Grace and Mercy (v. 4b).
5. He Satisfies You with Good Things (v. 5a).
6. He Renews Your Strength (v. 5b).

CONCLUSION: Bless the LORD, O my soul, and forget not all His benefits (v. 2).

Fishers of Men
By Dr. Michael A. Guido

Date preached:

SCRIPTURE: Luke 5:1–11

INTRODUCTION: All around us are boys and girls, men and women, who are perishing. You and I, Christian, must be expert fishermen if they are to be saved. The principles of catching fish point us to the truths of catching men!

1. The Preparation: Wash Your Net—Repent of Your Sins (vv. 1–2).
2. The Plan: Launch Out and Do It Now (v. 4).
3. The Performance: With All Your Heart (v. 5).
4. The Payment: God's Way Brings Results (vv. 6–7).

CONCLUSION: My friend, you will make the proper preparation, won't you? Will you confess your sins and be cleansed? You have heard His command to launch out into the deep and let your net down. Now it's time for action!

AUGUST 24, 2008

SUGGESTED SERMON

Tearing Down or Building Up?

Date preached:

By Dr. David Jeremiah

Scripture: Romans 15:2
Let each of us please his neighbor for his good, leading to edification.

Introduction: If you read the headlines, you become discouraged because everywhere you turn, people are tearing down integrity, truth, purity, honesty, respect, and hope. The apostle Paul talked about times like this in 2 Timothy 3:1–4. But I want to talk to you about something better. The word *edification* is a Bible term made up of two words. One word is *oikos* which means "house." And the other word is *domeo* which means "to build." It is often used in the Bible of the literal process of building a house. Our Lord, who was a carpenter by profession, knew how to do this. The Bible tells us that just like a building is built up, we must build up the body of Christ through how we function with one another, how we treat one another, and how we encourage one another. When you walk out into the world, you walk into an environment that automatically tears you down. You come to church to get built back up again. According to 1 Corinthians 3:9, we are God's building. We build it up externally through evangelism, and we build it up internally by strengthening, encouraging, and ministering to the members of the body so they have the strength to go on and serve God in a world that is hostile to everything we believe. How do we build one another up?

1. **Edification Is Not About Yourself; It Is About the Saints (1 Cor. 10:23–24).** It's important to learn to build ourselves up (Jude 20); but when we see the word "edification" in the Bible, the major emphasis is on building others up. I'm called to build you up. You're called to build me up. We can become experts at tearing down and criticizing; yet we are to build one another up (see 1 Cor. 14:4; 1 Thess. 5:11; Eph. 4:29).

2. **It Is Not What You Profess, It Is What You Pursue (Rom. 14:19).** If I were to ask you today how many of you are builder-uppers and how many of you are tear-downers, most would say, "I'm a builder. I'm positive." But building up is something you've got to work at. I'm amazed how easily I can get into a conversation with friends and later realize how sarcastic or critical I was of someone. It's easy to say things offhand and tear people down. Romans 14:19 tells us to pursue the things that make for peace by which one may edify another. We have to do it intentionally. It won't happen accidentally.

3. **It Is Not About How Much You Know; It's About How Much You Care (1 Cor. 8:1).** Knowledge puffs up, but love builds up. There's an old adage that says no one cares how much you know until they know how much you care. Edification isn't about how smart you are, nor about how many courses you've taken in school or seminary. Edification starts primarily in the heart where you look out and see people and love them.

4. **It's Not About Your Gifts; It's About Your Goals (1 Cor. 12:31—13:1).** I believe everyone has a spiritual gift. But once you know what your gift is, don't forget what it's for (see 1 Cor. 14:26). There's a sense in which our spiritual gift ought to be incidental; it's what you do with it that counts.

5. **It's Not About Your Wisdom; It's About His Word (Eph. 20:32).** How do you get built up enough so you can build up somebody else? My friends, it's this Book. Read the Bible. If you're not in the Word of God, I can almost promise you, you are experiencing being torn down by others, and you are in the process of tearing others down. The Word of God is the fuel to help you be a builder.

Conclusion: Let me ask you a question. What does Jesus want us to do this week? I think He wants us to be builders, edifiers, people who are committed to strengthening the body. Let me just say this to you. I need you! I need your strength, I need your help, I need your encouragement. And I know that you need that from one another. Ask God first of all to build you up through His Word so you then can have a ministry in building them up in the things of the Lord.

STATS, STORIES, AND MORE

More from Dr. Jeremiah
When geese migrate, they can be seen flying in a V-shaped formation. To us on the ground, it is a thing of beauty; but to the geese it is essential for survival. If you watch them, you will observe that at certain intervals relative to the strength of the wind, the lead bird who is doing the most work by breaking the force of the wind against him will drop off and fly at the end of the formation. It's been discovered that the flapping wings create an uplift of air, and the effect is greater at the rear of the formation. So the geese take turns uplifting one another. By cooperating and working together, the geese achieve long migrations that otherwise would be exceedingly difficult for even the strongest. It is in a similar manner that God has called us as His people. As believers in Christ, we are to lift one another up through prayer. We are to share material means and heart to heart friendship in caring. And we can go further into godliness than we ever would be able to if we attempt our pilgrimage all alone.

APPROPRIATE HYMNS AND SONGS

"Who Can Satisfy My Soul Like You," Dennis Jernigan, 1989 Shepherds Heart Music, Inc.

"Majesty (Here I Am)," Martin Smith & Stuart Garrard, 2003 Curious? Music UK (Admin. in U.S. by EMI CMG Pub.).

"Rise Up, O Men of God," William Merrill & William Walter, Public Domain.

"Lift Him Up," Johnson Oatman Jr. & B. B. Beall, Public Domain.

FOR THE BULLETIN

Mt. Vesuvius erupted on August 24, A.D. 79, burying the Italian towns of Pompeii and Herculaneum. ● On August 24, 410, Barbarian invaders stampeded across Europe, trampling everything in their path. Roman legions, unable to defend their 10,000-mile frontier, collapsed; the intruders penetrated Italy to the gates of Rome itself. The Eternal City fell to Alaric and his swarms. For three days Rome was plundered. This represented the fall of the western Roman Empire. ● The second volume of the Gutenberg Bible was bound on this day in 1456, making the Bible the first full-length book to be printed using movable type. ● Today is the birthday of the Countess of Huntingdon, born Selina Shirley Hastings in 1707. She became a great benefactor and supporter of the Wesleys and of George Whitefield, selling her jewels to help promote the gospel. ● Isaac Backus, American Baptist minister and champion of freedom of religion, was born on August 24, 1741; and William Wilberforce, evangelical leader who led the crusade against slavery in the British Empire, was born on August 24, 1759. ● On August 24, 1891, Thomas Edison patented his motion picture camera. ● Pastor and devotional writer, E. M. Bounds, died on August 24, 1913, at his home in Washington, Georgia, at age 78. He is chiefly remembered for his powerful volumes on prayer. He wrote, "Prayer is no fitful, short-lived thing. It is no voice crying unheard or unheeded in the silence. It is a voice which goes into God's ear, and it lives as long as God's ear is open to holy pleas, as long as God's heart is alive to holy things."

Kid's Talk

Today's subject is an excellent one for children. Tell the youngsters of a time when someone said something that hurt your feelings or that upset you when you were a child. Explain that children often say hurtful things to one another, and read a simple paraphrase of Ephesians 4:29. You might even have that verse printed on a card to give to each of the children to memorize.

WORSHIP HELPS

Call to Worship

Let no corrupt word proceed out of your mouth, but what is good for necessary edification, that it may impart grace to the hearers (Eph. 4:29).

Scripture Reading

But concerning the times and the seasons, brethren, you have no need that I should write to you. For you yourselves know perfectly that the day of the Lord so comes as a thief in the night. For when they say, "Peace and safety!" then sudden destruction comes upon them, as labor pains upon a pregnant woman. And they shall not escape. But you, brethren, are not in darkness, so that this Day should overtake you as a thief. You are all sons of light and sons of the day. We are not of the night nor of the darkness. Therefore let us not sleep, as others do, but let us watch and be sober. . . . For God did not appoint us to wrath, but to obtain salvation through our Lord Jesus Christ, who died for us, that whether we wake or sleep, we should live together with Him. Therefore comfort each other and edify one another, just as you also are doing (1 Thess. 5:1–11).

Additional Sermon and Lesson Ideas

Marriage Sizzle

Date preached:

SCRIPTURE: Hebrews 13:4–9

INTRODUCTION: This little paragraph gives us three ingredients of a spicy marriage.

1. Sex (v. 4). The reference to the "marriage bed" is a clear reference to having a sexual relationship that is exclusive, enjoyed only within the bonds of marriage.
2. Simplicity (v. 5). Be content with what you have. It's not how much you have but how much you enjoy that enriches a home.
3. Spirituality (vv. 5–6). The Greek here is emphatic: "Never, never will I leave you; never, never, never will I forsake you." Because the Lord is present in our home, we have a priceless environment that removes fear and reassures us that the Lord is our helper.

CONCLUSION: These are three *essential* qualities to a good marriage—the physical, the financial, and the spiritual—and they can make a marriage sizzle.

Morning and Evening Songs

Date preached:

By Rev. Charles Haddon Spurgeon

SCRIPTURE: Psalm 92:1–4

INTRODUCTION: The second verse of this Psalm alludes to the offering of the morning and evening sacrifices; so we should never wake in the morning without thinking of our Lamb of God, nor fall asleep at night without turning our eyes anew to Him.

1. Morning Worship (v. 2a). There cannot be a more suitable time for praising God than in the morning. Every morning is a sort of resurrection. The psalmist suggests that the best topic for praise in the morning is God's lovingkindness, as we arise from our beds to face a new day.
2. Evening Worship (v. 2b). At night, we declare His faithfulness. Yes, I know we're tired; but we should never be too tired to praise Him for His faithfulness, for we have had another day's experience of it. Notice the word "every." Every single night, we should rejoice in His faithfulness as we retire to bed.

CONCLUSION: Dear friends, each one of you can say of yourselves, as well as of this church, that God has been faithful to you. Tell it to your children. Tell it to your neighbors. Declare His lovingkindness in the morning and His faithfulness every night.

How to Take a Vacation

Ruth Bell Graham once observed in a private conversation that most people don't know how to take a vacation, as evidenced by the fact that the average vacationer comes home more exhausted than when he left.

Ruth worked hard at planning vacations in which husband Billy could recharge his batteries and come back mentally, physically, and spiritually refreshed. On one occasion, this led to her packing a series of Bible-study tapes by Stuart Briscoe who, though he didn't know, went with the Grahams to the beach and preached every afternoon to the world's most famous evangelist.

No one needs breaks more than pastors. The nature of our work is exhausting on many levels; and if we don't take needed getaways, our work will suffer. When we're worn out, we can't preach as well, nor do we react wisely to problems. We become irritable and discouragement-prone. Our inner resources become depleted just as our bodies grow tired. The Lord intends for us to have interruptions from the stress, just as He Himself withdrew to the desert for solitude and once told His disciples to come apart for awhile to rest. It's important to:

Take a day off. Work on your hobbies.

Take frequent breaks. Since preachers don't often get weekends off, it's necessary to find a way for the pastoral couple to have some mini-honeymoons throughout the year. Maybe you need a couple's retreat regularly—with only one couple enrolled on the registration form. Don't feel guilty leaving the kids entrusted to a close friend or family member. It's occasionally necessary to keep the most fundamental relationship in the home in a healthy condition. If you plan your getaway for the weekend, that has the added benefit of releasing you from a week's sermon preparation; but whether a Monday through Wednesday, or a Friday through Sunday, take a long weekend-like break from time to time.

Take advantage of conferences. Sometimes when I'm tired, I find a pastor's conference to attend. The church is happy that I'm staying up-to-date, and I've learned that I don't have to attend all the sessions. I choose what I want, rest all I can, and enjoy being out of the daily grind for a few days.

Take an annual vacation. We also need an annual break that gives us more extended time away. In Britain, many pastors take off an entire month during the summer, allowing them the leisure to study in advance for future sermon series. In my case, I usually take two weeks off at once, though on a handful of occasions I've taken a three-week break. To my surprise, the church survived.

Vacations have been necessary for me, because I'm a workaholic, as are many pastors. Sometimes it takes a full two or three weeks before we even want to think about returning to the grind.

Money tight? Throw up a tent somewhere, find a bargain, or in the worst case go home to your folks and stay with family members (a plan that has its pros and cons). In our case, we occasionally took long trips by car or plane; but many times we stayed close to home, while pretending we weren't. Going on a long trip, after all, can be counterproductive because of the stress of traveling. Even by air, it's nerve-racking due to the long lines, inconvenient stops, missed flights, lost luggage, security checkpoints, uncomfortable seats, and surly passengers, of which sometimes I'm one.

But whether near or far, find a place and when you get there enjoy all the S's: Sun, Sleep, Sweating, Swimming, Studying, and . . . well, there are others. And don't forget to rediscover the Bible. Take along a spiritual classic, and read it just as you want to. I've invited some very distinguished fellows to join me on vacation, and they have all obliged—Martyn Lloyd-Jones, John Calvin, Thomas à Kempis, Oswald Chambers, and J. Sidlow Baxter, to name a few. I'm happy to report that none of them snored.

Take a hymnbook, too, and your journal. Let the Lord replenish your soul, and make it a time of personal renewal.

It's a bit harder to rest on a trip if you have a van full of energetic children, but remember that nothing builds memories like a vacation. The other fifty weeks of the year, the kids have to

Continued on the next page

HELPS FOR THE PASTOR'S FAMILY—*Continued*

share you with the church—and the church gets the lion's share of your time. For two weeks, love those kids with all our heart and with all your time. But try to do it without leaving yourself exhausted.

Finally, don't overspend. Traveling is expensive, but there are ways of taking breaks on a budget. Study Web sites that offer cheap vacations, and take advantage of off-season rates, campgrounds, and proffered cabins in the woods. Begin with the end in mind. As you plan your vacation this year, ask yourself: What could we do that would really bring us back home rested, refreshed, and ready to plunge back into the work? Then work backwards from there. My wife and I have often found that planning a trip is almost as relaxing as actually taking it. When we're feeling worn out, we just start talking about how much fun we're going to have on vacation, and the anticipation of it lightens our loads.

Blessed is the church whose pastor is an expert in taking vacations.

AUGUST 31, 2008

SUGGESTED SERMON

Cultivating Our New Life in Jesus

Date preached:

By Dr. Ed Dobson

Scripture: Colossians 3:1–17, especially verse 10
. . . and have put on the new man who is renewed in knowledge according to the image of Him who created him.

Introduction: Part of the Christian walk is to put to death certain things, taking radical action against that which is unholy in our lives. On the positive side, we are to cultivate our new life in Christ. Paul, in Colossians 3:10 tells us we must be renewed, or strengthened, built up, renovated. This verb is present tense, conveying an ongoing action, a daily renewal. So how does the Holy Spirit bring about this process in our lives? Let's look at three ways we are renewed:

1. **Renewal and the Word of God (vv. 10, 16).** In verse 10, Paul says, ". . . put on the new man who is renewed in knowledge . . ." This word knowledge is interesting: it's the word knowledge attached to the preposition "upon." The idea is: knowledge upon knowledge upon knowledge upon knowledge. Where does that knowledge come from? Verse 16 tells us, "Let the word of Christ dwell in you richly in all wisdom . . ." The word for "dwell" means to be at home in you. It's to walk in, sit down in the den, and put your feet on the coffee table. God transforms us as we invite His Word into our life—not closing off rooms of our life where God's Word cannot go—but inviting God's Word into our life to take up residence.

2. **Renewal and the Character of Jesus (vv. 12–14).** Paul begins this verse, "Therefore, as the elect of God, holy and beloved, put on . . ." and lists a series of qualities found in Jesus Christ. At the end of these qualities, Paul says, "But above all these things put on love, which is the bond of perfection" (v. 14). The word "bond" is a medical term used for ligaments that hold the parts of your body together. When the ligaments don't work, you limp, your knee gives way. When our lives are not filled with the love of Christ, we walk

with a spiritual limp; things give way in our life. Love binds together all of these virtues that reflect the character of Jesus.

3. **Renewal and the Objective (v. 17).** What's the purpose of the process of renewal? Paul tells us in verse 17: "And whatever you do in word or deed, do all in the name of the Lord Jesus, giving thanks to God the Father through Him." We should speak and act in the name of the Lord Jesus. Perhaps you're wondering, "Now what does that mean? When I leave church do I go eat lunch in the name of Jesus? When I golf later this week, do I swing in the name of Jesus?" Here are three simple and practical ideas of what it means to do everything in the name of Jesus:

   A. **I Am a Representative of Jesus.** Whatever company you work for you probably have a card with your company, your name, your title, etc. The card says "I represent 'X' company." Yes, you work for them, and there is a degree to which you represent them, but as a follower of Jesus I ultimately represent Jesus Christ. To do everything in the name of Jesus is to remember I am the representative of Jesus.

   B. **I Am in the Place of Jesus.** I am to speak and act as if Jesus Himself were doing it. I not only represent Jesus, but there is a sense in which my hands are, in fact, the hands of Jesus touching people. My mouth is the mouth of Jesus speaking to people. My feet are the feet of Jesus. My mind is the mind of Jesus.

   C. **I Live for the Honor of Jesus.** We are to live for Jesus' honor by calling attention to Him, not ourselves. What does it mean to honor Christ as we gather? Our attention is drawn to Jesus. Our conversations should attract people to Jesus. Our behavior should be pointing people to Jesus, not ourselves, not our religion, not our church, but ultimately to our Jesus.

Conclusion: Are you paying attention to God's Word? Are you paying attention to Godly character? Are you paying attention to Jesus? Our prayer is that whatever we do this week in word or deed we would do it in the name of our Lord Jesus Christ.

STATS, STORIES, AND MORE

More from Dr. Dobson

You never get old enough in your Christian journey where you don't need to learn. Some time ago, my dad and I were talking. He said, "You know, I was reading the book of Ephesians, Eddie. I've preached through that, I've read over that, and I noticed something I had never noticed in the book of Ephesians. In fact, I got the main points of a good sermon out of it." And I listened to all the main points. I said, "Well, Dad, you have a sermon, you need a place to preach it, don't you?" He said, "Yep!" So the next Sunday night he preached. Here's my Dad who gets up early every day, spends a couple of hours reading and praying—he has done that all of his spiritual life. He has preached faithfully all of his life, and he was still fired up and pumped up about discovering more knowledge built upon more knowledge that has opened up the truth of Ephesians in a way that he had never noticed before. Let God's Word dwell in you richly day by day.

There was a man in my congregation named Dave who contracted HIV when he was living a gay lifestyle. He came to know Christ and I'm so thankful for a Jesus who changes lives. God forgave David and he began a brand new life in Christ. He ended up meeting Kathy and they got married and had children, but Dave continued to live with the aftermath of the choices he made, namely, HIV. It has been a courageous battle. When I went to see him at the end of the battle, he recognized me, in fact, said a couple of words. We read his favorite passages of Scripture together. As I began to pray with him I pulled down the blanket and I took his hand and there on his right hand was a red bracelet: WWJD—What Would Jesus Do? David's joy was that soon he would see Jesus personally, but the captivating focus of his life since he came to know Jesus was: What Would Jesus Do? It means to act in the place of Jesus.   —Dr. Ed Dobson

APPROPRIATE HYMNS AND SONGS

"Hands and Feet," Bob Herdman, Charlie Peacock, Mark Stuart, Tyler Burkum, & Will McGiniss, 1999 Up in the Mix Music (Admin. by EMI Christian Music Pub.).

"Set My Soul Afire," Eugene Bartlett, 1965 by Albert E. Brumley & Sons.

"The Lord Is My Shepherd," James Montgomery & Thomas Koschat, Public Domain.

"Amazing Grace (My Chains Are Gone)," John Newton, Chris Tomlin, & Louie Giglio, 2006 worshiptogether.com songs/Sixsteps Music.

FOR THE BULLETIN

On August 31, 1688, John Bunyan, author of *Pilgrim's Progress,* died. On his deathbed, battling high fever, Bunyan rambled in tortured, fractured words; but even these were collected and published as *Mr. Bunyan's Dying Sayings.* ● August 31, 1820, marks the birth of Anna Bartlett Warner, author of the children's hymn, "Jesus Loves Me." ● Missionary Sarah Judson, second wife of missionary Adoniram Judson, was a devout Christian, a hymnist, and the mother of eleven children. She and Adoniram (whose first wife, Ann, had died in 1826) were married in 1834. She went to work translating Christian works into the Burmese language. Suffering from exhaustion, she and Adoniram left for America in June, 1845. Sarah died en route on August 31, 1845. ● August 31, 1861, is the birthday of Jesse Brown Pounds, author of the hymns, "Anywhere with Jesus," "I Know that My Redeemer Liveth," and "The Way of the Cross Leads Home." ● Evangelist J. H. Sullivan was holding a revival service at Pine Log Methodist Church in Pine Log, Georgia, but the response to the meetings was disappointing. During the last service, Sunday night, August 31, 1886, Sullivan prayed, "Lord, If it takes it to move the hearts of these people, shake the ground on which this old building stands!" Almost immediately, the building shook perceptibly. Many of those present rushed to the altar to pray for repentance. This became known as the "Earthquake Revival." It was later learned that the tremors they had felt were marginal shock waves from the great earthquake which demolished much of Charleston and the coastal area of South Carolina. ● On August 31, 1937, missionary Isabel Kuhn set sail for China.

Kid's Talk

Are any of you children having a birthday today? I know someone who is! Her name is Anna Warner, and she is in heaven now. She was born on this day, August 31, in the year 1860, in Long Island, New York. Her father was a wealthy lawyer in New York City, but a terrible time came and he lost his wealth. Anna started writing stories and verses to make money. Can anyone guess what her most famous poem was? It was turned into a children's song, and I wonder if you would sing it with me in honor of Anna Warner's 148th birthday? It is "Jesus loves me, this I know, for the Bible tells me so."

WORSHIP HELPS

Call to Worship

The LORD on high is mightier than the noise of many waters, than the mighty waves of the sea. Your testimonies are very sure; holiness adorns Your house, O LORD, forever (Ps. 93:4–5).

Sermon Idea

In the bulletin or on a separate note sheet, list the qualities in Colossians 1:12–14 with a blank next to them. During point #2 of the above sermon, have the congregation do this exercise. "I want you to think of a scale 0–10. The 10 represents that quality as Jesus manifested it. One or zero means it's a quality that is seldom true in your life. Five would be average." Then read verse 12 aloud, slowly, offering some help understanding the terms. Have the congregation rank themselves and put the sheet in their Bibles as a reminder this week to pray over and work through the qualities they need to improve upon.

Benediction

And whatever you do in word or deed, do all in the name of the Lord Jesus, giving thanks to God the Father through Him (Col. 3:17).

Additional Sermons and Lesson Ideas

A Word Fitly Spoken
Date preached:

SCRIPTURE: Proverbs 25:12

INTRODUCTION: It's easy to damage a marriage by wagging your tongue. Couples begin disagreeing, then arguing, then yelling, then name-calling; and the marriage is badly damaged. Proverbs 25:12 talks about the word "fitly spoken." The Hebrew word for "fitly" is used only here in the Old Testament, and experts suggest two different meanings.

1. The Well-Timed Word. The first idea behind "fitly" has to do with timing. The idea would be saying something at the right time. Think of how masterfully Jesus did this. There are times when husbands and wives need to keep their mouths closed; we don't always have to interject our opinion. There are other times when we need to speak up, especially with words of affection, tenderness, and affirmation.
2. The Well-Turned Word. Other Hebrew experts believe this word was connected to the idea of a wheel, such as a potter's wheel. The idea would be a well-turned word, one that was smooth and skillful and wise. Wise words come from a wise heart, and God wants to give us wisdom.

CONCLUSION: Both ideas are important. We need to say the right words, and we need to say them at the right time. A word fitly spoken is like apples of gold in settings of silver.

Heroes of Violence
Date preached:
By Pastor Al Detter

SCRIPTURE: Proverbs 3:32–35

INTRODUCTION: In today's world, TV, movies, video games, and so many avenues of entertainment focus around violence. The "heroes" are often violent, vengeful people. If it's not bloody, it doesn't sell! It's a day of road rage and highway shootings. The book of Proverbs teaches us these "heroes" are on the wrong path.

1. God Will Get Close to the Nonviolent Person (v. 32).
2. God Will Bless Nonviolent Homes (v. 33).
3. God Will Help the Nonviolent Person in Times of Trouble (v. 34).
4. God Will Reward the Nonviolent Person with Honor (v. 35).

CONCLUSION: Don't let violence attract you. Stay calm when attacked. Bless the people around you and pray for those who persecute you. These types of people are the real heroes.

SEPTEMBER 7, 2008

SUGGESTED SERMON

Useful to God

Date preached:

By Dr. Stephen Olford

Scripture: 1 Corinthians 2:1–5, especially verses 1–2 (NASB)
And when I came to you, brethren, I did not come with superiority of speech or of wisdom, proclaiming to you the testimony of God. For I determined to know nothing among you except Jesus Christ, and Him crucified.

Introduction: Two major concerns lie within my heart of increasing pressure in these terrifying and terminal days in which we're living. We lack two elements in preaching across our land that deeply concern me. One is spirit anointed preaching of God's Word and secondly, preaching in evangelistic work. There is no doubt about it. Paul was concerned about this himself as he spoke of his own work as a preacher. Let's look at the profile of a preacher as outlined in this portion of Scripture:

1. **The Preacher Has a Message to Proclaim (vv. 1–2).**

    A. **The Person of Christ (v. 2).** "For I determined to know nothing among you except Jesus Christ . . ." This teaches us that we are to preach two things: the humanity of Jesus and the divinity of Jesus. We should preach the Virgin Birth of Christ, the spotless life of Jesus, the gracious words of Jesus, the mighty deeds of Jesus, the saving death of Jesus, the literal resurrection of Jesus, the present session of Jesus as He sits at God's right hand. We must preach Jesus as the Christ, the anointed Prophet, Priest, and King.

    B. **The Passion of Christ (v. 2).** "For I determined to know nothing among you except Jesus Christ, and Him crucified." All of Scripture, every ounce of our faith, all our convictions and actions as believers would be completely and utterly useless were it not for the foundational, pivotal, and historical truth of the crucifixion of Jesus Christ and His resurrection that followed. Thus, the preacher must proclaim Christ crucified.

2. **The Preacher Has a Manner to Portray (vv. 3–4).** Paul's description of a preacher includes three very clear characteristics:

   A. **Humility (v. 3).** True preaching involves a conscious attitude of total dependence upon God. Pride, self-confidence, and arrogance God Himself will resist. We may impress congregation with charisma, intellectual powers, or rhetorical gifts, but what God will bless is the Christlike humility and simplicity.

   B. **Simplicity (v. 4).** Paul says that he spoke "not in persuasive words of wisdom." It's amazing how Jesus constantly focused on the simplicity of children. He taught that to enter heaven, we must have faith like a child (Mark 9:13–17).

   C. **Christlike Authority (v. 4).** It wasn't until Jesus stood on the banks of the Jordan to present Himself as the Messiah that He was anointed with the Spirit. All four Gospel writers describe that incident with the Spirit descending upon Him like a dove. He was anointed with the Holy Spirit! Do you have the authority of the Word of God in the words that you speak? It can only come through His Holy Spirit?

3. **The Preacher Has a Motive to Project (v. 5).** The single motive of the preacher of the gospel is to create by the power of the Holy Spirit in the believing heart a saving faith in Jesus Christ and a steadfast faith in Jesus Christ. The biggest breakdown in human faith at home and abroad is the lack of steadfast faith.

Conclusion: So we have seen Paul's profile of a preacher. While it's true that some are called to the ministry of preaching the Word of God occupationally, every one of us is called to preach the gospel of Jesus Christ. Nothing less than this constitutes what God expects from you and me as we go to our respective homes and workplaces. How do you measure up to the profile of a preacher?

STATS, STORIES, AND MORE

More from Dr. Olford
Billy Graham once shared with me shortly after the event in which Dr. Karl Barth, the famous theologian, came to this country on a lecture tour. Before returning to his homeland, he felt the discussion was at an end and was saying farewell. "Just a moment," said Billy Graham, "I want to ask you one more question: Will you tell me the greatest discovery you've ever made in your life?" The old scholar bowed his head and then finally looked up with tear-filled eyes and replied: "Jesus loves me, this I know, for the Bible tells me so." There is power in simplicity!

I agree with John Owen who held that the sin of the Old Testament was rejection of God the Father, the sin of the New Testament was rejection of God the Son, and the sin of our day is rejection of God the Spirit. There's such a spectrum when it comes to an understanding of the Spirit: on one end is the sin of exclusion as some say: "Don't speak about the Spirit or you will be considered a charismatic!" At the other end of the spectrum is the sin of extremism, the unbelievable distortions that have now gathered around the person and work of the Holy Spirit. Let's get back to biblical balance! You'll never be a prophet of God until you know the holy anointing of the Holy Spirit.

APPROPRIATE HYMNS AND SONGS

"Take Up Thy Cross and Follow Me," B. B. McKinney, 1964 Broadman Press.

"Friend of God," Israel Houghton & Michael Gungor, 2003 Integrity's Praise! Music & Vertical Worship Songs.

"What a Friend We Have in Jesus," Joseph Scriven & Charles Converse, Public Domain.

"Shout to the North," Martin Smith, 1995 Curious? Music UK.

FOR THE BULLETIN

Roman troops overran Jerusalem on September 7, A.D. 70, destroying the Jewish temple which had been completed only six years before. The retaining wall, left standing, is today called the "Wailing Wall." ● On September 7, 1159, Cardinal Orlando Roland was proclaimed Pope Alexander III, but he wasn't well received by Holy Roman Emperor Frederick II, who immediately named a rival pope, Octavian, who moved into the Vatican, leading to a war among European powers. ● Queen Elizabeth I was born on September 7, 1533, to King Henry VIII and Anne Boleyn (who was beheaded three years later). ● Count Nicolaus von Zinzendorf was a devout believer who helped launch the Moravian missionary advance of the 18th century. As a young man, he carefully studied what the Bible said about marriage, and after much prayer, he proposed to the young Countess Erdmuth Dorothea von Reuss. The two were married on September 7, 1722. ● On September 7, 1785, Robert Raikes helped found the Sunday School Society of London. ● On Sunday, September 7, 1807, Robert Morrison, 25, became the first Protestant missionary to arrive in China. ● Arthur F. Tylee, a brilliant missionary to Brazil from Worcester, Massachusetts, and his wife, Ethel, set out to evangelize the warlike Nhambiquaras. On October 27, 1930, their little mission station was attacked. Arthur and baby Marian were killed. Ethel returned to the United States to spend the rest of her life telling her story in churches and colleges, appealing for more workers for the unreached. She passed away on this day in 1955.

WORSHIP HELPS

Call to Worship

Praise the LORD! For it is good to sing praises to our God; for it is pleasant, and praise is beautiful (Ps. 147:1).

Invitation/Pastoral Prayer

In consideration of what we have learned about the profile of a preacher, I would like you all to stand as I ask you three questions. With everyone's head bowed, if this is the type of preacher of the Word of God you wish to be, I want you to answer aloud. Answer so that your neighbor as well as the agents of heaven can hear: "By the Grace of God, I will."

1. Have You the Message of a New Testament Preacher?
   By the Grace of God, I will.

2. Have You the Manner of a New Testament Preacher?
   By the Grace of God, I will.

3. Have You the Motive of a New Testament Preacher?
   By the Grace of God, I will.

Let us pray: Father in heaven, Holy Son, Holy Spirit, triune God, we bring these responses to You solemnly, sacredly, significantly, in this holy moment. We pray that this may not just be the language of idleness or the reactions of the emotional feelings, but the true commitment of our minds, our hearts, our lives, our all. For Your glory alone, for the extension of Your kingdom to the ends of the earth, and as a testimony to the whole world, hear our prayers and accept this morning in Jesus' name.

Benediction

I, therefore, the prisoner of the Lord, beseech you to walk worthy of the calling with which you were called, with all lowliness and gentleness, with longsuffering, bearing with one another in love, endeavoring to keep the unity of the Spirit in the bond of peace (Eph. 4:1–3).

Additional Sermons and Lesson Ideas

But as for Me . . .
Date preached:

SCRIPTURE: Psalm 73 (NIV)

INTRODUCTION: Self-pity is one of our most destructive attitudes. It makes us depressed, withdrawn, and miserable. Psalm 73 is a case-study of self-pity and recovery.

1. "But as for Me" (vv. 1–16). The writer begins, "Surely God is good . . . but as for me . . ." His theology tells him God is good, but experience says otherwise. He is oppressed while the ungodly is basking in popularity and money (vv. 4–12). He doubts his faith and is troubled (vv. 12–16).
2. "Till I Entered the Sanctuary" (v. 17). Going to the temple, he just saw the grandeur of his God and gained a new perspective. We must enter the sanctuary of God's Word and gain His perspective if we're going to overcome self-pity.
3. "But as for Me" (vv. 18–28). Now he repeats his opening phrase, but with a new attitude. "But as for me, it is good to be near God." His self-pity turned to praise when he thought of the transience of the wicked (vv. 18–23), and at his own enjoyment of God's presence (v. 23), guidance and glory (v. 24), precious companionship (vv. 25–26), and nearness (vv. 27–28).

CONCLUSION: When we enter the sanctuary and turn our eyes on the Lord, we replace self-pity with praise, and confusion with thanksgiving.

Financial Integrity
Date preached:
By Dr. Larry Osborne

SCRIPTURE: Various

INTRODUCTION: The temptations and trappings of both poverty and wealth are nothing new. Scripture gives us some excellent advice on how to gain integrity in our finances:

1. Commit to Living Within Your Means (Prov. 12:9; 13:7; 21:17, 20; 22:7; Heb. 13:5).
2. Practice Generosity (2 Sam. 24:24–25; Prov. 3:9–10; 11:25–26; 22:9; Hag. 1—2; 1 Cor. 16:1–2; Eph. 4:28; 1 Tim. 6:18).
3. Always Leave Something on the Table (Prov. 22:16; Lev. 19:9–10).
4. If Forced to Choose, Always Pick Poverty over Dishonesty (Lev. 19:35; Prov. 10:2; 11:1; 13:11; 19:22).

CONCLUSION: Commit yourself to financial integrity!

SEPTEMBER 14, 2008

SUGGESTED SERMON

Sure Thing: How to Be Certain of Heaven

Date preached:

Scripture: Hebrews 10:22

Let us draw near with a true heart in full assurance of faith, having our hearts sprinkled from an evil conscience and our bodies washed with pure water.

Introduction: We live in an insecure world, and unexpected events could occur any moment that would change our lives forever. In his book, *The West's Last Chance,* Tony Blankley of the *Washington Times* points out that human history tends to unfold with sudden, unexpected changes of course. "King Darius of Persia never imagined—even as he faced Alexander at the Battle of Issus in 333 B.C.—that within three years he would be dead, His Achaemenid Dynasty ended, and the great hegemonic Persian Empire crushed and conquered. . . . American farmers in 1860 never dreamed that within months their husbands, sons, and brothers would be killed in battle and that America would be transformed by continental war. And Londoners in the summer of 1939 . . . never expected that forty thousand of their fellow Londoners would soon lie dead in the streets from German bombing. . . ."[1] We live uncertain lives. But as Christians, we know God is in control, nothing happens outside His knowledge, and underneath are everlasting arms. Our lives are hidden with Christ in God (Col. 3:3), and we have absolute assurance of our eternal salvation. The earth may shake, the mountains may fall, the stars may roll from their sockets, and the nations may collapse—but through Christ we are eternally safe, secure, and blessed. We're to draw near with full assurance of faith. The truth of personal assurance of salvation is taught throughout the Bible, but let me show you four passages that are especially reassuring.

1. **Test Yourselves (2 Cor. 13:5–6).** In this passage, the Bible tells us to examine ourselves as to whether we are in the faith. In His Sermon on the Mount, Jesus warned that some people mistakenly think they are going to heaven because of their good lives and

---

[1]Tony Blankley, *The West's Last Chance* (Washington, D.C.: Regnery Publishing, Inc., 2005), p. 22.

religious acts (Matt. 7:21–23). It's important to realize that we are qualified for heaven, not through our own good works or merits, but purely on the basis of the sacrificial death and resurrection of Jesus Christ. If we have received Him by grace through faith, we are qualified for heaven on the basis of His shed blood. Then you can "know that Jesus Christ is in you," as Paul put it in this passage. So we should examine and test ourselves, asking, "Have I committed my life to Jesus Christ by faith and am I trusting His grace alone for my eternal salvation?"

2. **Nothing Can Separate Us (Rom. 8:31–39).** The eighth chapter of Romans ends with a doxology of praise for the unfailing security of God's love, telling us that if God is for us, no one can stand against us; nothing can separate us from His love.

3. **Nothing Can Pry Us from His Hand (John 10:25–29).** In John 10, Jesus paints a wonderful picture of the Good Shepherd giving us abundant life. The terminology of this passage breathes assurance with every sentence. In verses 25–29, Jesus states emphatically, "My sheep hear My voice . . . I give them eternal life, and they shall never perish; neither shall anyone snatch them out of My hand . . . no one is able to snatch them out of My Father's hand."

4. **Theses Are the Facts (1 John 5:11–13).** In 1 John 5, we have one of the Bible's premiere texts offering full assurance of eternal life. The words in verse 11, "This is the testimony," are sometimes rendered, "These are the facts—God's facts, eternal facts, indisputable and immutable facts." God HAS given us eternal life in His Son, and those who have the Son HAVE eternal life. No ifs, ands, or buts. These biblical truths are written that we might KNOW that we have eternal life (v. 13).

Conclusion: If you struggle with knowing for certain that you're going to heaven, you can ARM yourself with assurance in three ways:

> A = Ask yourself: Have I sincerely asked Jesus Christ to forgive my sins? Am I trusting His blood for eternal salvation? If not, it's important to do so today (2 Cor. 6:2).
>
> R = Realize that doubting your salvation is an insult to the Lord. It's questioning His faithfulness to His promises. Tell God you're sorry for doubting His integrity, and ask Him to strengthen your faith.

M = Memorize one of the passages we've read today, meditate on it whenever you're tempted with fear, and appropriate the promises of God's Word. *For by this we know that we are of the truth, and shall assure our hearts before Him* (1 John 3:19).

STATS, STORIES, AND MORE

The newspapers reported last year about a twenty-one-year-old German tourist who wanted to visit his girlfriend in the Australian metropolis of Sydney, but he landed more than 8,000 miles away near Sidney, Montana. It turns out he had mistyped his destination on a flight booking Web site. Dressed for the Australian summer in T-shirt and shorts, Tobi Gutt left Germany on Saturday for a four-week holiday. Instead of arriving "down under," Gutt found himself on a different continent and bound for the chilly state of Montana. "I did wonder, but I didn't want to say anything," Gutt told the newspaper. "I thought to myself, you can fly to Australia via the United States." Gutt's airplane ticket routed him via the U.S. city of Portland, Oregon, to Billings, Montana. Only as he was about to board a commuter flight to Sidney—an oil town of about 5,000 people—did he realize his mistake. The hapless tourist, who had only a thin jacket to keep out the winter cold, spent three days in Billings airport before he was able to buy a new ticket to Australia with 600 euros in cash that his parents and friends sent over from Germany.

It's possible to think you're heading toward one destination while all the time heading in the opposite direction. Many people on earth today think they're traveling to heaven, but they have the wrong ticket to the wrong destination. They don't realize it, and they have a false assurance of salvation. Are you sure you're on the right route?

APPROPRIATE HYMNS AND SONGS

"The Solid Rock," Edward Mote & William Bradbury, Public Domain.

"I Know That My Redeemer Liveth," Jessie Pounds & James Fillmore, Public Domain.

"Heaven Awaits," Kevin Lawson & Michael Puryear, 2003 Cedarstone Music; March Madness Music.

"Indescribable," Laura Story, 2004 Worshiptogether.com songs; Sixsteps Music; Gleaning Pub.

FOR THE BULLETIN

Cyprian was a pagan rhetorician who became a Christian in approximately A.D. 246. He gave himself to diligent Bible study, and two years later was appointed Bishop of the city of Carthage in North Africa. He fled Carthage during the Decian persecution, but continued pastoring the people through his epistles. He returned in 251. During the persecution of Emperor Valerian, however, he was arrested. On September 14, 258, he was beheaded. ● Jerusalem's Church of the Holy Sepulcher was consecrated on this day in A.D. 335. ● One of the greatest preachers in Christian history died on this day in A.D. 407. He was John of Antioch, known as Chrysostom, which means "Golden-mouthed." ● On September 14, 1224, Francis of Assisi, while on spiritual retreat, has a mystical experience that leaves him with the "Stigmata"—the marks of Christ on his hands, feet, and side. ● Dante Alighieri, author of *The Divine Comedy,* died on September 14, 1321. ● On September 14, 1741, German composer George Frederick Handel, 56, finished composing "The Messiah." He wrote the score, start-to-finish, in only 24 days. ● September 14, 1735, is the birthday of Robert Raikes, founder of the Sunday school. ● Georgetown attorney, evangelical Christian, and Sunday school leader, Francis Scott Key, was inspired to write "The Star Spangled Banner" on September 14, 1814, after it became clear that the American forces at Fort McHenry had withstood a 25-hour bombardment by the British. ● On September 14, 1927, Bob Jones University opens in South Carolina with 88 students.

WORSHIP HELPS

Call to Worship

I am persuaded that neither death nor life, nor angels nor principalities nor powers, nor things present nor things to come, nor height nor depth, nor any other created thing, shall be able to separate us from the love of God which is in Christ Jesus our Lord (Rom. 8:38–39).

Hymn Story: The Solid Rock

Edward Mote was born on January 21, 1797, in London. His parents, innkeepers, wouldn't allow a Bible in their house, but Edward heard the gospel as a teen and came to Christ. He became a skilled carpenter, the owner of his own cabinet shop. "One morning," he recalled, "it came into my mind as I went to labor to write a hymn on the 'Gracious Experience of a Christian.' As I went up to Holborn I had the chorus: *On Christ the solid Rock I stand / All other ground is sinking sand.* In the day I had four first verses complete, and wrote them off.

In 1852, Edward, 55, gave up his carpentry trade to pastor the Baptist Church in Horsham, Sussex, where he ministered 21 years. He resigned in 1873, in failing health, saying, "I think I am going to heaven; yes, I am nearing port. The truths I have been preaching, I am now living upon and they'll do very well to die upon. Ah! The precious blood." He passed away at age 77.[2]

Benediction

Dismiss us, Lord, with the gracious gift of Your love, the abiding presence of Your Spirit, and the full assurance of our salvation through faith in Jesus' name.

[2]Adapted from the editor's book, *Then Sings My Soul*, a recommended resource giving 150 hymn stories for use in public worship services.

Additional Sermons and Lesson Ideas

The Christian's Compass
By Dr. Melvin Worthington

Date preached:

SCRIPTURE: John 20:30–31; 1 John 5:10–13; Proverbs 30:5–6; 2 Timothy 3:15–17

INTRODUCTION: The Bible provides guidelines for salvation, sanctification, separation, stewardship, and service. It's an objective compass. Chafer notes, "Since we depend upon the Bible alone for the knowledge of the most vital facts of our existence there is every reason to contend for the divine accuracy of God's Word and to be grateful that it is "God-breathed" and therefore not merely as fallible as its human writers, but as infallible as its divine author."

1. The Subject of the Scriptures: The supernatural person, the sovereign purpose, the sufficient provision, and the supreme precepts for living.
2. The Sufficiency of the Scriptures: The Scriptures are sufficient for salvation, sanctification, stewardship, and service. The Scriptures are profitable (2 Tim. 3:16), powerful (Heb. 4:12), pure (Ps. 19:8), precious (Ps. 119:72), purposeful (John 20:31), practical, and personal.

CONCLUSION: For it is the God who commanded light to shine out of darkness, who has shone in our hearts to give the light of the knowledge of the glory of God in the face of Jesus Christ (2 Cor. 4:6).

The Pearl of Patience
By Charles Haddon Spurgeon

Date preached:

SCRIPTURE: James 5:11

INTRODUCTION: When we are called on to exercise any virtue, we need to call in all the helps which the Holy Spirit has bestowed on us. The example of Job is a great help in developing the pearl of patience.

CONTEXT: This verse is preceded by a triple call to patience: We're to be patient unto the coming of the Lord, as the farmer waits for his crops, and to be patient and establish our hearts (vv. 7–8). We're also to be patient with others (v. 9). In learning to do this, we're directed to the example of Job (vv. 10–11).

1. Patience Is Not an Unheard-Of Virtue: You have heard of the patience of Job. . . . We know his story. (Review Job's history.)
2. Patience Is Not an Unreasonable Virtue: It leads to blessing, for God is compassionate and merciful (v. 11). The Lord was actually blessing Job by all his tribulation. Untold blessings were coming to the grand old man while he seemed to be losing it all.

CONCLUSION: Job by his trials and the grace of God was lifted up into the highest position of usefulness. He was useful before his trial as few men have been, but now his life possesses an enduring fruitfulness that blesses multitudes every day. Brothers and sisters, we do not know who will be blessed by our pains, by our bereavements, by our crosses, if we have patience under them.

Daily Strength for Daily Needs

Before *Streams in the Desert* and *My Utmost for His Highest*, there was *Daily Strength for Daily Needs*, a popular book of 365 devotional readings designed to feed the deeper soul. I came across it in a used book store years ago. My copy has these words inscribed on the inside: "Christmas Greetings from your friend, JBG, December 25th, 1914." It had been published in Boston the previous year.

The compiler, Mary W. Tileston, possessed a masterful grasp of the great spiritual writers of Christian history, and each page contains a Scripture verse, a hymn, and one or more excerpts by great devotionalists, such as the English churchman E. B. Pusey, the German hymnist Gerhard Tersteegen, the irrepressible poet Frances Ridley Havergal, the French mystic Francois de la Mothe Fenelon, and the Catholic giant, F. W. Faber.

This is sturdy stuff, and each day's entry is something akin to a T-bone steak. This isn't a devotional for those wanting pablum; and, to tell the truth, some of the entries seem a little tedious to me. But I'd rather wade through a ponderous paragraph that strengthens my soul than a fluffy one that tickles my ears.

Frequently the readings do both. My favorite entry is for January 14th, where the verse for the day is 2 Samuel 15:15: "Thy servants are ready to do whatsoever my Lord the king shall appoint." The day's hymn is a priceless stanza I'd never seen before by the great hymnist, Anna L. Waring, who was evidently one of Tileston's favorites. It says:

> I love to think that God appoints
> My portion day by day;
> Events of life are in His hand,
> And I would only say,
> Appoint them in Thine own good time,
> And in Thine own best way.

Continued on the next page

CLASSICS FOR THE PASTOR'S LIBRARY—*Continued*

I've memorized that bit of verse, and now frequently use it in sermons. There follows an extended quotation from Havergal about the importance of doing day-by-day exactly what the King appoints for us.

On the bookshelf over my desk, sitting right beside *Daily Strength for Daily Needs,* is another book, *Great Souls at Prayer,* also compiled by Mary W. Tileston. It's another daily devotional, and on every day's page is a prayer—or two or three, depending on their length—composed by a cast of characters spanning fourteen centuries. This compact volume allows you every day to offer a prayer written by St. Augustine, Jeremy Taylor, E. B. Pusey, Samuel Johnson, George Dawson, or George Matheson, to name a few.

Who, then, was Mary W. Tileston? With the help of a close friend who's also a great librarian and researcher, I found bits and pieces of this woman's life, but the process was complicated by there being two Mary W. Tilestons—mother and daughter.

The elder Mary was born in 1843, into a sophisticated home where she was raised among writers, philosophers, educators, and poets. Her father, Caleb Foote, owned and edited the *Salem Gazette,* and Mary grew up with an in-depth knowledge of the Bible, the Apocrypha, and the works of the Catholic Fathers.

Years later, the 1880 census of Concord, Massachusetts, finds Mary, 36, living on Monument Street, where she's married to John Tileston, age 45, who was listed as a farmer. The children are Mary W., 13; Margaret, 12; Roger, 10; Amelia, 7; and Wilder, 5, who was to become a far-famed obstetrician and gynecologist at Yale.

In 1893, Mary's book, *Daily Strength for Daily Needs,* was published in Boston, and the title page lists her as the editor of a previous book that I don't presently have, *Joy and Strength for the Pilgrim's Day.*

Library records also show that she wrote a biography of Caleb and Mary Wilder Foote, a Unitarian minister and his wife who were probably her grandparents. All in all, she apparently compiled and edited twenty-five books.

In 1901, the younger Mary traveled to Lyndhurst Hall in Hampstead, England, to enroll in the missionary training school there. Of some thirty students, Mary was the only one from outside England. The next we hear from her, she is back in America, living in a boarding house on Walnut Street in Philadelphia. Her occupation was listed as "Deaconess—Episcopal Church." She apparently never married.

According to the 1930 census, the younger Mary, then 63, returned to Massachusetts to live with her ailing mother. The elder Mary's obituary appeared in the Brookline Chronicle-Citizen on July 5, 1934, and it simply said: "Mrs. Mary W. Tileston, widow of John B., died at home 43 Allerton Street in her 96th year. Born at Salem, daughter of Caleb and Mary (White) Foote, and was married to Mr. T. in 1865. . . . She was the author of several books and also wrote a collection of nursery rhymes. . . . Surviving are one daughter, Mary W. Tileston, and a son, Dr. Wilder Tileston, who is a professor at the Yale Medical School."

If you have more information on the Tilestons, I'd be interested in seeing it. In the meantime, scour the used book stores for Mary's remarkable books. After all, we all need *Daily Strength for Daily Needs*.

SEPTEMBER 21, 2008

SUGGESTED SERMON

Wild at Heart

Date preached:

By Dr. Kevin Riggs

Scripture: Various passages from Mark, especially Mark 1:12–13
Immediately the Spirit drove Him into the wilderness. And He was there in the wilderness forty days, tempted by Satan, and was with the wild beasts; and the angels ministered to Him.

Introduction: The call to discipleship is a call to meet God in the wilderness. The call is not for the timid, scared, or weak at heart. The call is for adventure. The call is a call to be wild at heart.

Context: Running through Mark's Gospel is a wilderness theme. John the Baptist was a man of the wilderness—"clothed with camel's hair and with a leather belt around his waist, and he ate locusts and wild honey" (1:6). We are told that John came "baptizing in the wilderness" (1:4). Immediately following Jesus' baptism, Jesus was sent into the wilderness to be tested (1:12–13). It is only after Jesus exited the wilderness that He began His public ministry. But throughout His ministry, Jesus retreated back to the wilderness. He often went to deserted places to pray (Mark 1:35; 6:45), to minister (Mark 1:45), or to teach His disciples (Mark 6:31–32; 9:2). The mentioning of wilderness, mountainsides, and solitary places, is not a coincidence, but rather they are intentional. Why is the "wilderness" important?

1. **The Wilderness Is a Place of Deliverance.** The central redemptive event in the Old Testament was God's deliverance of His people from Egyptian bondage. After centuries of slavery, God used Moses to call His people out into the wilderness. Now, John calls people out into the wilderness to receive deliverance from their sins. Deliverance is found in the wilderness. Deliverance is found in the good news that God has once again entered history to free people from their bondage.

2. **The Wilderness Is a Place of Worship.** Moses asked Pharaoh to let the Israelites go so they could go into the wilderness to worship God. Jesus went into the wilderness to be tempted by Satan, and at

the end of forty days, Mark records that "angels ministered to Him" (1:13). Do you feel like you are alone in the wilderness? Do you feel dry and parched, spiritually? Does it seem God has abandoned you? He hasn't. He has called you into the wilderness to be alone and worship Him. It is in the wilderness, as you worship, that your strength will be renewed.

3. **The Wilderness Is a Place of Testing.** In the wilderness, Jesus was tempted by Satan. Mark does not report the victory of Jesus over Satan, nor does he report the end of the temptation. Mark understands that Jesus was tempted by Satan throughout His ministry, and He did not win the decisive victory over Satan until Easter morning. God allows us to go into the wilderness to be tested so that we may overcome through the Spirit of Christ.

4. **The Wilderness Is a Place of Danger.** Jesus was in the wilderness with "wild animals." In the wilderness, Jesus confronted the horror, the loneliness, and the danger, of being in the wild. God calls us to meet Him in the wilderness, and that is a dangerous call. It may cost you your life. It most definitely will cost you your dreams and aspirations. Following Jesus is following Him to the Cross, and that's dangerous.

5. **The Wilderness Is the Place We Are Called to Live.** The moment you asked Jesus to come into your life and forgive you of your sins, you were delivered from your bondage. As a follower of Jesus you have the promise of a future hope, but it has not yet come. Right now you are caught in the present—the wilderness—and God is with you in the wilderness. You have been called to live out your faith in the here and now, facing the dangers, facing the testing, worshiping God, because He has delivered you from your sins.

Conclusion: The call to discipleship is a call to meet God in the wilderness! It is a call to be wild at heart; to meet Him in the here and now; and to walk with Him in the everyday, hard reality of life. Jesus did not come to give you paradise on earth. He came to deliver you from your past, and to give you what you need to live in the present, while you are ". . . looking for the blessed hope and glorious appearing of our great God and Savior Jesus Christ" (Titus 2:13).

STATS, STORIES, AND MORE

🔖 *I am always best when alone; no place like my own study; no company like good books, and especially the book of God.*
—Matthew Henry[1]

🔖 *I know of no way to recover that which we have lost other than to cultivate the practice of being more frequently alone with Him.* —J. Wilber Chapman

🔖 *It is a difficult lesson to learn today—to leave one's friends and family and deliberately practice the art of solitude for an hour or a day or a week. . . . And yet, once it is done, I find there is a quality to being alone that is incredibly precious.*
—Ann Morrow Lindberg in *Gift from the Sea*

🔖 *There is a lordly solitude which both giants and geniuses seem to find essential.* —Victor Hugo[2]

🔖 Seek a convenient time to retire unto thyself, and meditate often upon God's lovingkindness. . . . The greatest saints avoided the society of men, when they could conveniently, and did rather choose to live to God in secret. —Thomas à Kempis

🔖 *We are a peculiar people who somehow feel that the final measure of a person's spirituality is to be gauged by their capacity to go, go, go . . . for God. On the contrary, our Father calls us to come apart and spend some time in solitude with him.* —W. Phillip Keller[3]

Quiet Spots
How tough is it in America to find a quiet spot? According to experts:

🔖 The hum of power lines can be heard upward of two miles.

🔖 A chain saw cuts the quiet for more than five miles.

🔖 Road noise can travel eight to ten miles.

🔖 A coal-fired power plant can be heard as far as fifteen miles away.

🔖 A major airport can cast a "noise shadow" longer than fifty miles.

---

[1]Wilber Smith *Chats from a Minister's Library* (Grand Rapids: Baker Book House, 1951), p. 164.

[2]Quoted by Charles Connell, *World-Famous Exiles* (Feltham, Middlesex, Great Britain: Odhams Books, 1969), p. 78.

[3]W. Phillip Keller, "Solitude for Serenity and Strength," in *Decision Magazine*, August/ September, 1981, p. 9.

APPROPRIATE HYMNS AND SONGS

"Draw Me Close," Kelly Carpenter, 1994 Mercy/Vineyard Pub.

"Jesus Draw Me Close," Rick Founds, 1990 Maranatha Praise. Inc.

"Hungry," Kathryn Scott, 1999 Vineyard Songs.

"Healing Rain," Martin Smith, Matt Bronleewe & Michael W. Smith, 2004 Curious? Music UK; Word Music; Smittyfly Music; Songs from the Farm (Windswept Pacific Music Ltd.).

FOR THE BULLETIN

September 21, 1452, is the birthday of Girolamo Savonarola, Florentine preacher and Italian reformer, who was martyred in 1498. ● Martin Luther published his German translation of the New Testament on this day in 1522. ● John Coleridge Patteson, great-nephew of poet, Samuel T. Coleridge, was an Oxford athlete and scholar who became an Anglican missionary in the South Pacific. On September 21, 1871, he anchored alongside an island, saying, "Any one of us might be asked to give up his life for God, just as Stephen in the Bible. . . . It might happen today." Closing his Bible, he went ashore and was met by a barrage of arrows. He was in his mid-forties. ● Ancel Allen, graduate of Moody Bible Institute, began working with a missions organization called "Air Mail from God," which dropped Christian literature from low-flying airplanes to unreached tribes in Mexico. On September 21, 1956, his plane disappeared. It was later found with his body inside, riddled with bullets. ● According to the Far East Broadcasting Company, political terrorists invaded FEBC's radio station in Zamboanga, the Philippines, on September 21, 1992, and shot three people to death. The executions were carried out after numerous threats had been made to the station about continued broadcasts to the Tausug-speaking people. The dead were: Greg Hapalla, himself a Tausug, was a Christian pastor with the Christian and Missionary Alliance. Greg Bacabis was one of the radio technician-operators. A third person, Ambri Asari, was a local fisherman who was there to tape a public service announcement.

WORSHIP HELPS

Call to Worship
Many, O LORD my God, are Your wonderful works which You
have done; and Your thoughts toward us cannot be recounted to
You in order; if I would declare and speak of them, they are
more than can be numbered (Ps. 40:5).

Pastoral Prayer
Lord, we come together today in the name of Jesus Christ to
exalt and worship You. We thank You for coming to this world
and overcoming it, that we might come to know You and Your
victory. Lord Jesus, we know that You can identify with our
temptations, our trials, and our terrors. Yet, when You faced
these, You overcame. We find ourselves in the wilderness, but
not alone. May Your Spirit guide us, may Your angels minister
to us, and may we be victorious for Your sake, Amen.

Benediction
Do not put your trust in princes, in mortal men, who cannot
save. When their spirit departs, they return to the ground; on
that very day their plans come to nothing. Blessed is he whose
help is the God of Jacob, whose hope is in the LORD his God, the
Maker of heaven and earth, the sea, and everything in them—
the LORD, who remains faithful forever (Ps. 146:3–6 NIV).

Additional Sermons and Lesson Ideas

The Gospel Will Be Heard
Date preached:

By Rev. Mark Hollis

SCRIPTURE: Acts 16:16–40

INTRODUCTION: The gospel message is met with obstacles, but God turns them into opportunities.

    1. Satan Sends Obstacles (Acts 16:16–24).
        A. Unwanted Publicity (vv. 16–18). Without an accompanying trans-formation of life the slave girl's message was neither good public-ity nor a welcome witness.
        B. Unjust Accusations (vv. 19–21). While Christianity was not an officially recognized religion by the Romans, the owners' real con-cern was that they were losing money.
        C. Unlawful Punishment (vv. 22–24). It was illegal to beat a Roman citizen without a trial.
    2. God Turns Obstacles into Opportunities (vv. 25–40).
        A. Captive Audience (vv. 25–28). The jailer and the other prisoners formed a captive audience to hear the gospel of Christ!
        B. Miraculous Conversion (vv. 29–34). The hardened jailer humbly came to faith along with his entire household!
        C. Released and Exonerated (vv. 35–40). To have the magistrates escort Paul and Silas from the jail was tantamount to a public declaration of their innocence and a vindication of their message.

CONCLUSION: God turns obstacles into opportunities.

Patience in Hardship
Date preached:

By Joshua D. Rowe

SCRIPTURE: Psalm 40:1–4

INTRODUCTION: When you encounter trials in life, do you ever feel like you're sinking? Do you feel as if it will never end? David recounts a similar experience in Psalm 40, which demonstrates the amazing restoration that comes when we patiently seek God's help by faith. He begins, "I waited patiently for the LORD . . ." (v. 1a). The result:

    1. The Lord Will Hear Your Cry (v. 1).
    2. The Lord Will Restore You (v. 2).
        A. He Will Rescue You from Sinking (v. 2a).
        B. He Will Establish You Firmly (v. 2b).
    3. The Lord Will Enable You to Praise Him (v. 3).
        A. Your Praise Will Be to God Alone (v. 3a).
        B. Your Praise Will Turn Others to Trust the Lord (v. 3b).

CONCLUSION: "Blessed is that man who makes the LORD his trust, and does not respect the proud, nor such as turn aside to lies" (v. 4).

SEPTEMBER 28, 2008

SUGGESTED SERMON

Prepare the Way with Readiness

Date preached:

By Rev. Todd M. Kinde

Scripture: Matthew 24:36–44, especially verse 44
Therefore you also be ready, for the Son of Man is coming at an hour you do not expect.

Introduction: When I was a kid in grammar school the teacher had us make a little paper bell with 25 paper chain links. We took our bells home and hung on our bedroom walls to tear off a link each night counting down the days until Christmas. While we have marked on our calendars the celebration of Christmas, the coming of God in human flesh, and while we can count the days with a measure of certainty until then, we must admit that we do not know when Christ will come again! We are to be ready at all times as Jesus teaches in Matthew 24:36–44.

1. **Ready When We Feast (vv. 37–39).** Placing ourselves in the mindset of the prophets and the patriarchs, we read that the day and hour of the coming of Christ will be as in the days of Noah (v. 37). When we imagine the days of Noah, we most likely think of a dark, grossly immoral, and pagan culture. But this is not how the days are described here. They are described as really quite normal and even mundane. The first type of activities that characterize the day of Christ's coming is that of eating and drinking and marriage. There is the celebration of marriage and the building of households. There is food and wine to enjoy. In the early parts of chapter 24 we would see the cataclysmic signs—the destruction of Jerusalem, the abomination in the temple, the great betrayal, and strange signs in the sky—all of which were fulfilled in the year A.D. 70. But over the surface of all this and in the centuries which have followed is the reality that life goes on. Eat, drink, and get married. We ought to enjoy these things but not caught up in these things.

2. **Ready When We Work (vv. 40–42).** The next type of activity to describe the day of Christ's coming is regular, ordinary work. We

will be laboring in the fields or grinding away at the mill to make flour for bread and porridge. While we are about providing for our families and our daily bread, just going about the chores of survival and life, then will Christ come. This honors the occupations of us all. Discipleship requires faithful stewardship of our calling and work. You have your calling, a noble and worthy occupation. No, what we do may not seem like much. It may not be all that exciting, but it is our calling from God. And we are to be faithful stewards of His call. This takes great courage.

3. **Ready When We Sleep (vv. 43–44).** The third type of activity we find is that of sleeping. I suppose the verse is referring to something broader than just sleeping; it is really the day-to-day management of the household. At the end of the day things are buttoned up and rest is needed for the next day when we arise to do it all over again. Life goes on and we need rest. But there is the time when trouble arrives. The thief comes when we least expect it or when we are least prepared and most vulnerable. The coming of the Lord will be a surprise. But the prepared and the ready will look beyond the daily routines and the semblance of normalcy to detect His coming. They will be ready. They may be surprised at His timing but they will not be caught off guard.

Conclusion: The end times will be normal and life goes on despite the interruptions. What we need to be aware of for ourselves is that the time may not be so much characterized by the immorality as it is by its normalcy. And because life is normal it will be easy to be too casual with God (2 Pet. 3:4). Mary and Joseph will get married and travel for the census and pay taxes. The shepherds will be doing their work out in the field. The town will be sleeping that night. And suddenly Christ comes (Luke 14:17–21). As the business of life continues, are you ready for the coming of Christ? To get ready you must repent of your sins, believe on Christ Jesus, and live a new life of hope in His coming.

STATS, STORIES, AND MORE

More from Rev. Kinde
My mother has recently experienced the reality of an unexpected thief. She had been out on her daily rounds and sensed that she should break her normal routine and return home for some reason. As she walked up to the front door she noticed that the door knob was smashed. She walked around the side of the condo and saw in the window a man stacking things by the door. She turned to the neighbors, called the police, and began to write down the license plate number of the strange pick-up truck. The man walked out of the house and saw Mom's car in the drive and kept walking to his pick-up truck lowered the tailgate so as to hide his license plate and drove off. Jesus' return will be as unexpected as a thief standing at your door when you return home. Are you ready?

Second Coming Quotes

> Has not our Lord Jesus carried up our flesh into heaven and shall He not return? We know that He shall return.   —John Knox

> I ardently hope that amidst all these internal dissentions on earth Jesus Christ will hasten the day of His coming.
> —Martin Luther

> The Spirit in the heart of the true believer says with earnest desire, Come, Lord Jesus.   —John Wesley

> We must hunger after Christ until the dawning of that great day when our Lord will fully manifest the glory of His kingdom.
> —John Calvin

> Many times when I go to bed at night I think to myself that before I awaken Christ may come.   —Billy Graham

> The coming again of Jesus Christ and the end of the age occupies some 1,845 Scriptural verses.   —John Wesley White

> We are not just looking for something to happen, we are looking for Someone to come! And when these things begin to come to pass, we are not to drop our heads in discouragement or shake our heads in despair, but rather lift up our heads in delight.
> —Vance Havner

> Their eschatology saved them from utter despair.
> —W. R. Estep about the Anabaptists during intense persecution[1]

---

[1] W. R. Estep, *The Anabaptist Story* (Nashville: Broadman Press, 1963), p. 193.

APPROPRIATE HYMNS AND SONGS

"Days of Elijah," Robin Mark, 1996 Daybreak Music, Ltd.

"Everyday," Joel Houston, 1999 Joel Houston/Hillsong Publishing.

"When He Shall Come," Almeda Pearce, 1962 by Almeda J. Pearce.

"Hallelujah! We Shall Rise," J. E. Thomas, Public Domain.

FOR THE BULLETIN

Today marks the murder of good King Wenceslas, subject of the famous Christmas Carol. Wenceslas, who received a good Christian education from his grandmother, and ruled Czechoslovakia (Bohemia) in the 10th century. His brief reign was marked by peacemaking and concern for the poor. He was assassinated by his mother and brother, who fiercely opposed Christianity. ● Lemuel Haynes, Congregationalist preacher and the first known black pastor of a white congregation in America, passed away on this day in 1833. His tombstone reads: "Here lies the dust of a poor hell-deserving sinner, who ventured into eternity trusting wholly on the merits of Christ for salvation." ● On September 28, 1884, Joseph Parker announced to his London congregation that he was planning to preach straight through the Bible. ● In Atlanta on this day in 1895, three Baptist groups merged to form the National Baptist Convention, today the largest African-American denomination in the world. ● Evangelistic song-leader and personal evangelist, Charles M. Alexander, conducted his last service, a Young People's meeting in Birmingham, England, on Tuesday, September 28, 1920. He was promoting the Pocket Testament League which had been started by his wife, Helen Cadbury, of Cadbury Chocolate fame. Alexander broke new ground in evangelical music with the inclusion of the improvisational piano style during his evangelistic meetings. At the same time, Alexander was sanctifying the piano for use in church. He led the singing for the evangelistic crusades of D. L. Moody, R. A. Torrey, and J. Wilber Chapman. He died of a heart attack. ● C. S. Lewis was converted on September 28, 1931. ● On September 28, 1938, evangelist John R. Rice began publishing *The Sword of the Lord*.

WORSHIP HELPS

Call to Worship
Oh, give thanks to the LORD, for He is good! For His mercy endures forever (1 Chr. 16:34).

Word of Welcome
(With a little planning, this can work well, especially in a smaller church. Before the service, send out a notification or volunteer sign-up sheet for your members who are willing to have guests over for a meal after the service.)

It's so wonderful to have the people of God gathered together in the name of Jesus Christ. I would like to welcome all of you here today. We are especially excited about any of you who are guests still checking out this church. I would like to ask all of you who are our members who signed up to welcome guests into their homes to stand. If you are new here, all those who are standing have expressed interest in inviting you to eat with them, whether at a restaurant or in their homes. Simply introduce yourself to them after the service and they will ask you if you want to join them.

Responsive Reading

Leader: But as for you, speak the things which are proper for sound doctrine: that the older men be sober, reverent, temperate, sound in faith, in love, in patience. . . .

People: The older women likewise, that they be reverent in behavior, not slanderers, not given to much wine, teachers of good things—

Leader: . . . that they admonish the young women to love their husbands, to love their children, to be discreet, chaste, homemakers, good, obedient to their own husbands, that the word of God may not be blasphemed.

People: Likewise, exhort the young men to be sober-minded, in all things showing yourself to be a pattern of good works . . .

Leader: . . . in doctrine showing integrity, reverence, incorruptibility, sound speech that cannot be condemned, that one who is an opponent may be ashamed, having nothing evil to say of you (taken from Titus 2:1–8).

Additional Sermons and Lesson Ideas

A Game Plan for Witnessing
Date preached:
By Dr. Larry Osborne

SCRIPTURE: 1 Peter 3:15–16

INTRODUCTION: When we've been blessed by good fortune, the most natural response is to share the good news with those we're closest to. Yet, for a variety of reasons, many of us struggle when it comes to sharing the great things God has done in our life. Scripture presents a way that is both natural and powerful.

1. Walk the Talk (vv. 15–16). Peter instructs, ". . . sanctify the Lord God in your hearts . . . having a good conscience . . ."
2. When Asked, Tell Your Story (v. 15). Your story is why you're a Christian and what God's done for you: ". . . be ready to give a defense to everyone who asks you a reason for the hope that is in you . . ."
3. Treat Everyone with Respect (vv. 15–16). Peter tells us to share our story "with meekness and fear." We should not be pushy and arrogant, but humble and respectful.

CONCLUSION: Are you ready to give a reason for the hope that is in you?

The Trap of Cynicism
Date preached:
By Rev. Melvin Tinker

SCRIPTURE: Mark 6:30–44

INTRODUCTION: I am sure that you have seen them and you have most certainly heard them. Maybe you are standing at a bus stop when one of them sidles up to you with the opener "Buses, hopeless. We should never have gotten rid of trams if you ask me." Scripture grants an eye-opening example of why we should avoid the trap of cynicism in our spiritual lives.

1. An Impossible Situation (vv. 30–37). Not only did the disciples doubt that Jesus could feed the enormous crowd, they exclaimed that it would take eight months' wages to buy food (v. 37).
2. The Divine Provision (vv. 38–41). Jesus saw the disciples' lack of faith and used the situation to demonstrate His power and provision.
3. The Abundant Blessing (vv. 42–44). Jesus not only provided enough food for everyone, but twelve baskets full were left over after feeding 5,000 people with five rolls and a couple of fish!

CONCLUSION: What situations are you in that seem impossible? Won't you trust Jesus to turn them into lessons of His power and provision?

OCTOBER 5, 2008

SUGGESTED SERMON

Does a Godly Home Guarantee Godly Kids?

Date preached:

By Dr. Larry Osborne

Scripture: Proverbs 22:6
Train up a child in the way he should go, and when he is old he will not depart from it.

Introduction: Often in Christian circles, we find ideas that are presented as truths, but upon further study of the Scripture, we learn otherwise. One such myth is the subject of our lesson today: "Does a Godly Home Guarantee Godly Kids?" I realize this can often be a touchy subject, but I know that you would rather know the truth now than to bank on a false reality.

1. **Where'd We Get that Idea (Prov. 22:6)?** This verse reads, "Train up a child in the way he should go, and when he is old he will not depart from it."

    A. **What We Think It Says:** "If we raise a child correctly, he will come back to God eventually."

    B. **What It Actually Says:** "If we raise a child according to his bent, he won't turn away." The phrase, "in the way he should go" in Hebrew does not mean a way that is spiritually correct. It has the idea of "according to his bent." In other words, if your child is a piano player don't shove a bat in his hands. It's a natural way to encourage the talents and gifts of each individual child. We often think that our children come with a blank slate, that we can teach them precisely how to behave and they will follow our lead. Many times this myth is debunked when we have a second and third child: Personalities are unique to each child. The verse teaches us that a child raised according to his natural tendencies will not turn away; it never promises that a rebellious child will turn back!

C. **The Forgotten Distinction:** This is a Proverb, not a Promise. Proverbs explain the way life *usually* works; they aren't universal statements. A promise is the way God always responds.

2. **Why This Is a Devastating Myth:**

   A. **It Produces Needless Guilt.** When we assume complete responsibility for our children's decision to turn from Christ, we assume a great deal of guilt as well.

   B. **It Produces Foolish Pride.** If and when our children turn out right, we may think we did it!

   C. **It Produces a False Hope.** If our children rebel against Christ, we often cling to Proverbs 22:6 as if we know some day that child will repent and be restored to Him. The enemy would love for us to have false hope, for it sets the stage for us to be disappointed with God.

3. **What the Bible Actually Says:**

   A. **Rebellion Happens Even in the Best of Environments (Gen. 1—3).** Everyone is born with the sin nature. No one has to train his child how to be selfish; it's natural. In Genesis 1—3 we see the perfect environment with the perfect Father, and even Adam and Eve without a sin nature. What do they do? They break the rule!

   B. **Everyone Is Responsible for Their Own Actions (Ezek. 18:1–32).** There is nothing we can do to absolutely guarantee someone will or won't come to Christ; it's a choice each individual makes.

   C. **We Can Have Lots of Influence; We Don't Have Any Power (Prov. 21:30–31).** Don't think I'm teaching that we should just give up and let whatever happens, happen. We should take every opportunity to influence our children, and it will contribute to their lives and decisions.

Application: Increasing Your Odds of Success. Although you can't do anything to 100% guarantee how your children will turn out, we can learn some principles that will certainly increase our odds of success:

   A. **Work on Having a Great Marriage (Eph. 5:33).**
   B. **Adapt to Their Unique Bent and World (Prov. 22:6).**

C. Don't Be Unreasonably Strict (Eph. 6:4; Col. 3:21).

D. Don't Embarrass Them with Your Religious Zeal (Eccl. 7:16–18).

E. Don't Defend Them Even When They're Wrong (1 Sam. 2:22–26; 3:12–13).

Conclusion: A godly home doesn't guarantee godly kids, nor does an ungodly home guarantee ungodly kids. My call to all of us is: Let's use our influence well, pray hard, stay encouraged, but let's not beat ourselves up or puff ourselves up over the results.

STATS, STORIES, AND MORE

More from Dr. Osborne

I used to have a sermon series before Nancy and I had any kids called: "Ten Rules for Raising Godly Kids." Then my son Nathan came along and it became "Ten Suggestions for Raising Good Kids." When my daughter Rachel came along, it became "Five Ideas that Might Help." My son Josh came along and I think I renamed it something like, "Three Tips for Surviving Parenthood."   *—Dr. Larry Osborne*

B. F. Skinner was a psychologist who came up with the idea of "behavioral modification." The idea is that we are born as blank slates. Thus, you can set up the environment as you wish, and you can control the outcome of the individual. He did experiments on animals and people. He had the idea that we should pass laws about how children are raised so that eventually society would have a culture of people who were all "good." That's not a real popular theory these days because psychologists now are swinging the other way, believing we're so genetically predisposed we have no freedom to choose. Neither is the healthy or Scriptural understanding of human responsibility.

APPROPRIATE HYMNS AND SONGS

"A Christian Home," Barbara B. Hart & Jean Sibelius, 1965 by Singspiration Music/ASCAP and Breakaft and Hartel Music.

"O Perfect Love," Dorothy Gurney & Joseph Barnby, Public Domain.

"Household of Faith," Brent Lamb & John Rosasco, 1983 Straightway Music.

"Gentle Shepherd," Gloria and William Gaither, 1974 by William Gaither.

FOR THE BULLETIN

On October 5, A.D. 59, Saint Paul celebrated the Jewish Day of Atonement while sailing into dangerous waters as a prisoner headed to Rome (Acts 27:9). Shortly afterward he warned the ship's crew they were headed toward disaster. ● October 5, 1056, marks the death of Holy Roman Emperor Henry III, a deeply religious man who supported reform of the church throughout his empire. When he died, he left the throne to his six-year-old son. ● Another Holy Roman emperor, Charles V, came to power in the middle of the Protestant revolution. He vigorously sought to resolve the differences between Catholics and evangelicals, calling the Diet of Augsburg in 1530, and spending the next 15 years seeking peace between the groups. On this day in 1556, he retired, frail and depressed, to the monastery of Yuste, where he quietly passed the last two years of his life. ● October 5, 1600, is the birthday of Puritan Thomas Goodwin, English Nonconformist preacher. ● John Gerard, a Catholic who was tortured for his faith in the Tower of London during the reign of Queen Elizabeth I, climbed through a hole in the roof of Cradle Tower on October 5, 1597, threw a rope over the side, and slid down it, mutilating his hands. He labored secretly in England, then in Rome until he passed away at age 73. He is one of an elite handful of people who outwitted the Tower of London. ● October 5, 1703, is the birthday of Jonathan Edwards. ● On October 5, 1744, David Brainard began his work among the Indians. ● William Carey was baptized on October 5, 1783.

WORSHIP HELPS

Call to Worship

Prepare your hearts for the LORD, and serve Him only. . . . Serve the LORD with gladness . . . Serve wholeheartedly, as if you were serving the Lord, not men, because you know that the Lord will reward everyone for whatever good he does (1 Sam. 7:3 NKJV; Ps. 100:2; Eph. 6:7–8 NIV).

Scripture Reading

Wives, submit to your own husbands, as to the Lord. For the husband is head of the wife, as also Christ is head of the church; and He is the Savior of the body. Therefore, just as the church is subject to Christ, so let the wives be to their own husbands in everything. Husbands, love your wives, just as Christ also loved the church and gave Himself for her . . . So husbands ought to love their own wives as their own bodies; he who loves his wife loves himself . . . Children, obey your parents in the Lord, for this is right. 'Honor your father and mother,' which is the first commandment with promise: 'that it may be well with you and you may live long on the earth.' And you, fathers, do not provoke your children to wrath, but bring them up in the training and admonition of the Lord (Eph. 5:22—6:4).

Pastoral Prayer

Father, help us be men and women who grow in the wisdom of raising our children in the nurture and instruction of the Lord; but keep us from the pride of thinking that the outcome is ours. Help us do our part, and we ask You to do Yours; for with us is the possible, but You alone can do the impossible. And the impossible is what we need. In Jesus' name, Amen.

Additional Sermons and Lesson Ideas

Moses' Miracles
By Dr. Melvin Worthington

Date preached:

SCRIPTURE: Exodus 5—18

INTRODUCTION: The miracles of Moses are a powerful testimony to the power of God. In the ten plagues God attacked and defeated certain gods of the Egyptians. Following the tenth plague Pharaoh insisted that the children of Israel leave his land. The God of Israel proved to be greater than all the gods of the Egyptians.

1. The Remarkable Plagues (Ex. 5—12).
   A. The Refusal of Pharaoh (Ex. 5)
   B. The Reassured People (Ex. 6).
   C. The Reaffirmed Purpose (Ex. 7:1–13).
   D. The Recorded Plagues (Ex. 7:14–25).
2. The Rapid Pursuit (Ex. 13—14).
   A. The Exit of the People (Ex. 13).
   B. The Execution of Pharaoh (Ex. 14).
3. The Resounding Praise (Ex. 15).
4. The Revealed Pathway (Ex. 16—18).

CONCLUSION: Moses led the nation of Israel out of Egyptian bondage by God's amazing and almighty power. This feat is a testimony to the way God can use an individual who gives allegiance to Him. Moses serves as an example for us to emulate in the service of our God.

Jars of Clay

Date preached:

SCRIPTURE: 2 Corinthians 4:7–12

INTRODUCTION: Many people have grown discouraged over the pressures of church life and church work. That's why the Lord gave us 2 Corinthians. Three words in verse 7 can change our attitude.

1. Treasure: We Should Be Happy. We have discovered the treasure of knowing Christ and making Him known, so we should be happy.
2. Clay: We Should Be Humble. We are God's depository for His treasure, yet we are fragile and breakable and easily damaged.
3. Power: We Should Be Hopeful. The all-surpassing power is from God. If His power keeps us going, nothing short of Him can shut us down.

CONCLUSION: Exchange discouragement for the attitudes of happiness, humility, and hopefulness.

OCTOBER 12, 2008

Not "What's Wrong" But "What's Right" with the Church

Date preached:

Scripture: Hebrews 10:19–25

Therefore, brethren, having boldness to enter the Holiest by the blood of Jesus, by a new and living way which He consecrated for us, through the veil, that is, His flesh, and *having* a High Priest over the house of God, let us draw near with a true heart in full assurance of faith, having our hearts sprinkled from an evil conscience and our bodies washed with pure water. Let us hold fast the confession of *our* hope without wavering, for He who promised *is* faithful. And let us consider one another in order to stir up love and good works, not forsaking the assembling of ourselves together, as *is* the manner of some, but exhorting *one another*, and so much the more as you see the Day approaching.

Introduction: The *Times of London* recently ran an article on difficulties facing congregations in the United Kingdom. The article opened with a paragraph about the condition of many Anglican congregations: "Churches in Britain are a 'toxic cocktail' of bullying and terror, as parish priests struggle to lead congregations dominated by neurotic worshipers who spread havoc with gossip and manipulation." The article said that "peace and love are in desperately short supply in the pews," and that increasing numbers of clergy are succumbing to a new illness, dubbed "Irritable Clergy Syndrome." Well, we can all be irritable at times, but we need to focus on what's right with the church. I believe with all my heart that when churches are healthy and functioning as God intends, they're the most wonderful environments on earth for worshiping God, for maintaining our morale, for caring for others, for learning the truths of the Bible, for growing to be better people, and for raising our families in the nurture of the Lord. One of the best paragraphs in the Bible on this is Hebrews 10:19–25. This passage begins with a premise, and then presents a threefold plan.

"'Evil-Minded Parishioners Making Life Hell for Clergy," by Ruth Gledhill in The Times On-Line, December 9, 2006, accessed on December 11, 2006, at http://www.timesonline.co.uk/article/0,,2-2494814,00.html.

1. **The Premise of Our Church: We Are Friends with God (vv. 19–21).** Verses 19–21 present the premise of this passage—we can live in God's direct presence. When Moses led Israel out of Egypt, they stopped at Mount Sinai where God gave a detailed set of plans for the tabernacle. The innermost room was the Holy of Holies where God resided in terms of His localized presence among His people. Only one person entered this room—the High Priest, and only entered once a year on the Day of Atonement. Here the High Priest would bring the sacrificial blood of atonement. The multitudes of Israelites were undoubtedly curious to see what was inside that room. Aren't you curious to know what certain places are like? Imagine visiting the very room that served as God's earthly headquarters on earth! Yet it was off-limits to everyone except the High Priest. But when Jesus died on the Cross, the veil split in two, as though an invisible hand ripped it apart (Matt. 27:51). Hebrews 10 explains that Jesus is our High Priest. By His blood, He made it possible for us to be reconciled to God. We can enter God's presence now through faith, into the Holy of Holies. We can boldly go where no one could go before. That's the premise of this passage. That's the premise of our church.

2. **The Plan for the Church: We Are Partners with God (vv. 22–25).** The second half of this paragraph gives the implications of this as it relates to the church. We are partners with God in the building of His work. Notice the three "Let us" phrases in these verses.

   First, verse 22: *Let us draw near with a true heart in full assurance of faith, having our hearts sprinkled from an evil conscience and our bodies washed with pure water.* Since we're friends of God, let's stay close to Him with hearts that are true (not hypocritical), confident of our faith, reveling in the purity Christ imparts.

   Second, verse 23: *Let us hold fast the confession of our hope without wavering, for He who promised is faithful.* Let's cherish our doctrine and maintain its integrity, and let's trust God to keep the promises of His gospel.

   Third, verses 24–25: *And let us consider one another in order to stir up love and good works, not forsaking the assembling of ourselves together as is the manner of some, but exhorting one another, and so much the more as you see the Day approaching.* In other words, let's be faithful to becoming positive influences in our local congregations, devoted to faithful attendance and to a consistent ministry of love and good works. I read of a pastor who, worried that things weren't going well in his church, asked a deacon, "What's wrong with our church? Is it ignorance or apathy?" The deacon replied, "I don't know and I don't care!" Well, we do care, and we do care about one another.

Conclusion: It's easy to complain. After all, we're made up of people of varying levels of maturity from many backgrounds and with diverse opinions. But let's take the biblically positive approach. We're called to live in the very presence of God Himself, and we can boldly enter the Holy of Holies and be friends of God. So let's draw near to Him each day. Let's hold firmly to our faith. And let's consider one another, how we can stimulate each other to love and good works.

STATS, STORIES, AND MORE

Clarence Macartney once told of a man who dreamed of a city filled with splendid and notable buildings: Great granite temples of finance and commerce where business was transacted, marble halls where university classes met, and ornate homes for the people of that city. Along the roadside was a humble structure into which men and women were coming and going. A hundred years passed in his dream, and the man found himself in the same city, but the buildings had been torn down and rebuilt. They were even taller and more impressive. Yet in the middle of them was the same small white structure into which people were coming and going with joy on their faces. A thousand years passed in the man's dream, and again he saw the same city. It was a complete transformation, for the old buildings had vanished and new buildings with new architecture and new grandeur had taken their places—all except that little frame building along the road into which men, women, and children were coming and going with joy and satisfaction on their faces. "What is that building?" he asked a stranger in his dream. "That building?" said the stranger. "That represents the church, the house of God. Cities and societies rise and fall, but the church remains steadfast through the ages to assist God's people along the road of life."[2]

---

[2]Clarence Edward Macartney, *Macartney's Illustrations* (New York: Abingdon-Cokesbury Press, 1945), p. 61.

APPROPRIATE HYMNS AND SONGS

"Look What the Lord Has Done,"Mark David Hanby, 1974 Exaltation Music.

"Let It Rise," Holland Davis, 1997, 1999 Maranatha Praise! Music.

"Lord You Have My Heart," Martin Smith, 1992 ThankYou Music.

"Grace Flows Down," David E. Bell, Louie Giglio, and Rod Padgett, 2000
worshiptogether.com songs; Sixsteps Music.

FOR THE BULLETIN

On October 12, 539 B.C., King Cyrus launched an invasion against Babylon, leading to the fall of the Babylonian Empire as recorded in the fifth chapter of Daniel. ● Claudius became Roman emperor in A.D. 41 at age 50, as is referred to in Scripture. He lowered taxes, extended the empire into Britain and Mauritania, and refused to be worshiped as a god. But the latter years of Claudius were marred by intrigue, much of it centered around his wife, Agrippina, who wanted to secure the throne for her son, Nero. On October 12, of A.D. 54 she fed Claudius mushrooms with a potent pinch of poison. He suffered 12 agonizing hours before dying. ● On October 12, 1285, 180 Jews, refusing baptism in Munich, Germany, were set on fire. ● At 2 A.M. on October 12, 1492, Christopher Columbus discovered a new world. ● Edward VI was born at Hampton Court to King Henry VIII and Jane Seymour on this day in 1537. He inherited the throne from his father at age 10, and tilted the nation toward the Protestant cause. He was a sickly young man, and died in his teens from consumption or perhaps from overmedication. The throne passed to the Catholic Mary I ("Bloody Mary"), under whose reign 300 Protestants were slain. ● October 12, 1845, marks the death of Elizabeth Fry, a Quaker, famous as a prison reformer in Britain. ● After a torrential morning rain, the sun broke out and 2,400 Roman Catholic bishops began a long procession through St. Peter's Square toward the Basilica of St. Peter's to open the Second Vatican Council on October 12, 1962.

WORSHIP HELPS

Call to Worship
Jesus Christ is the same yesterday, today, and forever. . . .
Therefore by Him let us continually offer the sacrifice of praise
to God, that is, the fruit of our lips, giving thanks to His name
(Heb. 13:8, 15).

Suggested Scriptures
- Psalm 122
- Matthew 16:17–20
- Ephesians 4:1–6

Offertory Story
A Baptist preacher received a call from a woman who was upset
over the death of her cat, Homer. She wanted the preacher to
conduct a funeral service for Homer. The Baptist explained that
this was a little out of his line and referred her to his friend, the
Presbyterian preacher. The Presbyterian recommended her to the
Episcopalian, and on to the Methodist. Finally she came back to
the Baptist preacher, saying, "I'm planning to give $5,000 to the
church that will perform this service." The Baptist minister said,
"Well, now, why didn't you tell me Homer was a Baptist cat in
the first place?" Well, we don't perform many of those services
here; we just rely on the regular tithes and offerings of our people,
and the Lord is faithful to meet our needs.

Benediction
We ask You, who have begun a good work in us, to carry it on to
completion. Bless us and make us a blessing. Use us and make
us useful this week for Your kingdom. In Jesus' name, Amen.

Additional Sermons and Lesson Ideas

Staying Secure in an Insecure World

Date preached:

SCRIPTURE: 2 Corinthians 1:12–23

INTRODUCTION: We should plan our days as carefully as possible, yet we don't know what a day may bring forth (James 4:13–15). In 1 Corinthians 16:5–7, Paul told the Corinthians he planned to visit them, adding *if the Lord permits.* When he changed his plans, the Corinthians accused him of inconsistency. He replied that even though his schedule changed, he was operating in good faith (2 Cor. 1:12–17). Then he went on to give two sources of consistent security.

1. We Have the Promises of God in Our Hands (vv. 18–20): *For no matter how many promises God has made, they are "Yes" in Christ. And so through him the "Amen" is spoken by us to the glory of God* (NIV). Find a promise meeting your need. Will God keep it? He says, "YES!" and you say "AMEN!" Many of these promises are in 2 Corinthians (3:5; 3:18; 4:17; 5:1; 6:16—7:1; 9:6–11; 12:9).
2. We Have the Presence of God in Our Hearts (vv. 21–22). We have the treasures of eternity awaiting us in heaven. Till then, God has given the Spirit as a deposit, guaranteeing what is to come (5:1–5).

CONCLUSION: Life is uncertain and we should say, "If the Lord permits." Yet we can live securely because we have the promises of God in our hands and the Spirit of God in our hearts.

Deity Described
By Dr. Melvin Worthington

Date preached:

SCRIPTURE: 2 Samuel 7:18–29; 2 Chronicles 6:12–21, 40–42; Isaiah 6

INTRODUCTION: The description of God in the Scripture is more than sufficient for all our mental and emotional wants. He is described in the light of His authority, activity, and attributes. No other book gives the complete picture of God who created the world.

1. The Authority of God. He's described as "The Almighty." The name Almighty is used over fifty times to identify God. Almighty means "one who is mighty" or "who has all power" (Ex. 6:3; Ruth 1:20).
2. The Activity of God. He created, controls, contains, and consummates.
3. The Attributes of God. His nonmoral attributes include His omnipresence—He is everywhere (Ps. 139:7–12; Acts 17:27; Rom. 10:6–8), His omniscience—He knows all things (Ps. 147:5; Prov. 15:3, 11; Jer. 23:23; Matt. 10:30), His omnipotence—He is all powerful (Gen. 17:1; Job 42:2; Jer. 32:17; Matt. 91:26), and His immutability—He never changes (Ps. 33:11; 102:26; Mal. 3:6; Rom. 11:26; Heb. 1:12; James 1:17).

CONCLUSION: The authority, activity and attributes of God describe Him in simple, sufficient, specific, and sublime terms. The God who created the world loves the human race and has provided eternal redemption for all who will receive Christ as their Savior

OCTOBER 19, 2008

An Unfailing Inheritance

Date preached:

By Rev. Robert M. Norris

Scripture: Hebrews 9:15

And for this reason He is the Mediator of the new covenant, by means of death, for the redemption of the transgressions under the first covenant, that those who are called may receive the promise of the eternal inheritance.

Introduction: God desires to communicate with His people and in so doing He chooses to accommodate Himself to our understanding. Yet like His grace, when He speaks, God's use of language is very bold indeed. When speaking about the return of His divine Son, Jesus Christ, He compares Him to a "thief" and His return will be like "a thief in the night." In the verses which we have before us, the writer uses very bold language as he introduces the comparison between the "New Covenant" and a last will and testament.

1. **God Wrote a Will to Leave His Possessions to Another.** God is immortal; He cannot die. But the incredible truth is that He wills to experience death so as to destroy death from the inside and deliver those who are enslaved to death. For the immortal to experience death, He takes on the flesh-and-blood human nature as His own and in that nature experiences death. God wrote a last will and testament because He intended to experience death in the death of His Son, through the human nature that He took on in the Incarnation. This truth should serve to establish our faith and deepen our security and our assurance in God, because He wrote this will in eternity past. From all eternity God willed to pass on His "eternal inheritance" to you by grace. The death that is required for the heirs to come into their possession is over and done. There does not need to be another one.

2. **God Appointed an Executor.** A will usually specifies the executor, and it can never be the dead person who executes his own will! Yet here the same person who dies to put the will in force is also the executor of the will. When our author calls "Jesus, the Mediator of the New Covenant, the last will and testament," it means not only

that He is the One whose death releases all the inheritance of God for us, but also that once that inheritance is released He secures it and applies it to us. He does this because by His resurrection from the dead and His installation at the right hand of the Father on high as the High Priest of all the good things to come, He is made the Executor. Jesus makes sure that we, the heirs, gain the inheritance!

3. **God's Last Will and Testament Displays His Love.** When we ask who receives the inheritance, the answer immediately is given to us: "That those who are called may receive the promise of the eternal inheritance" (v. 15). Those who receive the inheritance are those who are called by God. God's last will and testament is not left to chance. God not only wrote the will, and He not only put it in force by the death of His own Son, and He not only raised His Son to be the executor of that will, but He is also today calling people out of darkness and death and unbelief to become fellow heirs with His Son.

Conclusion: The pressing question for each one of us to answer this morning is: Are you an heir and listed in God's last will and testament? The inheritance of God is not left to an uncertain, indistinct, and unknown groups of men and women. The Father loves His children, "His own." It is for these that Christ has shed His blood and tasted death. It is to His children that He leaves the inheritance. Does He bequeath to you the eternal inheritance? Open your spiritual ears to the voice of your Shepherd, and your spiritual eyes to the glory of your God, and believe.

STATS, STORIES, AND MORE

Yes, But It's Nothing Compared to Our Royal Inheritance in Christ
According to news reports, Britain's Prince William is expected to inherit an annual allowance of at least $320,000 from the estate of his mother, Princess Diana. The young royal will inherit the money when he turns 25 (in the summer of 2007). The money has been held in a trust fund since the princess was killed in a Paris car crash in 1997. William will effectively become financially independent when he begins receiving the yearly sum on his birthday on June 21. The prince is currently supported by his father, Prince Charles, who receives $18 million a year from his Duchy of Cornwall estate. The late princess left $27 million to her two sons, William and his younger brother Harry, 22.

Eleven million dollars of the legacy was taken in inheritance tax, but the value of the remaining sum has risen due to investments and is now conservatively estimated at $25 million, producing an income of at least $645,000 a year to be split between the princes. When he turns 25, William will also be able to take control of his share in his mother's global image rights, which are believed to be the most valuable part of her legacy. . . . William currently earns a salary of $28,308 as a second lieutenant with the Household Cavalry, serving in the Blues and Royals regiment with his brother, Harry.[1]

APPROPRIATE HYMNS AND SONGS

"And Can It Be," Charles Wesley & Thomas Campbell, Public Domain.

"You Are My King," Billy Foote , 1996 worshiptogether.com songs.

"You Are God Alone," Billy Foote & Cindy Foote, 2004 Billy Foote Music; Integrity's Hosanna! Music.

"How Deep the Father's Love for Us," Stuart Townend, 1995 ThankYou Music.

"'Prince William to Inherit Trust Money at Age 25" by Maira Oliveira—All Headline News Reporter, January 15, 2007 at http://www.allheadlinenews.com/articles/7006142219, accessed January 29, 2006.

FOR THE BULLETIN

George Abbot was born on this day in 1562. He became an Oxford scholar whose Puritan leanings brought him into conflict with others at the university. In 1604, he was named as one of the translators of the King James Bible, and in 1611, he became Archbishop of Canterbury. ● Jacob Arminius, the theologian who sought to soften the stronger points of Calvinism, died at age 49 on October 19, 1609. ● On Saturday, October 19, 1698, the Christian and mathematician, Blaise Pascal, by conducting experiments at the French volcanic mountain, Puy-de-Dome, determined that atmosphere has definite weight, and that the level of mercury varies in different altitudes and in different weather. His conclusions virtually invented the barometer. ● On Sunday night, October 19, 1856, 12,000 people streamed into London's Surrey Hall and an additional 10,000 overflowed into the surrounding gardens to hear Charles Spurgeon preach. The services started, but as Spurgeon rose to pray, someone shouted "Fire! Fire! The galleries are giving way!" There was no fire, but the crowd bolted in panic, and in the resulting stampede seven people were trampled to death. Twenty-eight more were hospitalized. The young preacher, reeling in shock, was literally carried from the pulpit to a friend's house where he remained in seclusion for weeks. ● October 19, 1912, marks the death of Mrs. A. R. M'Farland, first missionary to Alaska. Her husband, a Presbyterian home missionary, had died in May, 1876, while church-planting among the Nez Perces Indians in Idaho. Moving to Portland, Oregon, Mrs. M'Farland heard of explorations in Alaska. She sensed God's calling her there, and labored there from 1877 to 1897. ● October 19, 1921, is the birthday of Bill Bright, founder of Campus Crusade for Christ.

Kid's Talk

Bring objects or pictures of items you or a family member of yours owns as inheritance; use it as an object lesson. For example: "This is my great-grandfather's pocket watch. I used to play with it when I was a child. Before he went to heaven, he wrote down that he wanted me to have it. He's with Jesus now, and he left this watch to me. It's called an inheritance. Well I want to tell you today about an inheritance that we can all share if we trust in Jesus. You see, because God loved Jesus so much and because Jesus lived a perfect life, God gave Him the entire world as His inheritance! When Jesus died and then rose again, He made it possible for us to share with Him in this inheritance. If you trust Jesus and obey Him throughout your life, you will eventually inherit a restored, perfect world alongside Jesus!

WORSHIP HELPS

Call to Worship
When my soul fainted within me, I remembered the LORD; and my prayer went up to You, into Your holy temple. Those who regard worthless idols forsake their own Mercy. But I will sacrifice to You with the voice of thanksgiving; I will pay what I have vowed. Salvation is of the LORD" (Jon. 2:7–9).

Offertory Comments
Today we will look at Hebrews 9:15, which I would like to read now: "And for this reason He is the Mediator of the new covenant, by means of death, for the redemption of the transgressions under the first covenant, that those who are called may receive the promise of the eternal inheritance." Before we give our offerings today, I would like all of us to take a moment to meditate on the words of that verse and consider the unbelievable inheritance made available to us through Jesus Christ.

Additional Sermons and Lesson Ideas

Rejoice in All of Life's Circumstances
By Rev. Mark D. Hollis

Date preached:

SCRIPTURE: Philippians 1:1–11

INTRODUCTION: Paul was in prison. His good friend Epaphroditus came to visit and almost died there. Yet in those circumstances he wrote a letter centered on the theme of joy.

1. Paul's Greeting (vv. 1, 2). The word "all" occurs seven times in the first two chapters of Philippians.
2. Paul's Memories and Prayer (vv. 3–6). The word "joy" occurs five times in the book and "rejoice" nine times.
   A. Thankfulness (v. 3).
   B. Joy (v. 4).
   C. Partnership (v. 5).
   D. Confidence (v. 6).
3. Paul's Affection (vv. 7–8). Paul's affection for these believers was like that of Christ.
   A. You Share in God's Grace (v. 7).
   B. I Long for You (v. 8).
4. Paul's Prayer (vv. 9–11). Paul's requests reflect the fruit of God's work within.
   A. Abundant Love (v. 9a).
   B. Knowledge and Depth (v. 9b).
   C. Discernment (v. 10a).
   D. Purity (v. 10b).
   E. Fruit of Righteousness (v. 11).

CONCLUSION: Rejoice! God will complete the work He began in you.

Tithing Is Not a Four-Letter Word
By Dr. Kevin Riggs

Date preached:

SCRIPTURE: 1 Corinthians 16:2

INTRODUCTION: All of God's commands are there for our personal benefit, so here are some practical reasons why you should T.I.T.H.E.

   T—Total dependence on God.
   I—Increased blessings from God (Mal. 3:10).
   T—Take your relationship with Christ seriously.
   H—Heart for the ministry of your church.
   E—Exalt Christ.

CONCLUSION: Tithing is a biblical principle that shows your total dependence on God, insures increased blessings from God, demonstrates that you take your relationship with Christ seriously, proves you have a heart for the ministry of your church, and results in your exalting Christ in your life.

John Brown

The mid-1680s is remembered as the *Killing Time* in Scotland. Royal regiments martyred Scottish Presbyterians at will. Despite the danger, Presbyterian John Brown fell in love with Isabell Weir. He proposed to her, but warned that he would one day seal his testimony with blood. Isabell replied, "If it be so, I will be your comfort. The Lord has promised me grace." They were married in a secret glen by the outlawed minister, Alexander Peden. "These witnesses of your vows," said Peden, beginning the illegal ceremony, "have come at risk of their lives to hear God's word and his ordinance of marriage." The vows were spoken, then Peden drew Isabell aside, saying, "You have got a good husband. Keep linen for a winding-sheet beside you; for in a day when you least expect it, thy master shall be taken."

The Brown home soon included two children. It was happy, filled with prayer and godly conversation. Fugitive preachers were hidden and cared for there. But on May 1, 1685, John rose at dawn, singing Psalm 27, to find the house surrounded by soldiers. The family filed onto the lawn. The commander, Claverhouse, shouted to John, "Go to your prayers; you shall immediately die." Kneeling, John prayed earnestly for his wife, pregnant again, and his children. Then he rose, embraced Isabell, and said, "The day is come of which I told you when I first proposed to you."

"Indeed, John. If it must be so, I can willingly part with you."

"This is all I desire," replied John. "I have no more to do but to die." He kissed his children, then Claverhouse ordered his men to shoot. The soldiers hesitated. Snatching a pistol, Claverhouse placed it to John's head and blew out his brains. "What thinkest thou of thy husband now, woman?" he snarled. Isabell, fixing Claverhouse in her gaze, told him she had never been so proud of him. Claverhouse mounted his horse and sped away, troops in tow. Isabell tied John's head in a napkin and sat on the ground weeping with her children until friends arrived to comfort them.

OCTOBER 26, 2008

SUGGESTED SERMON

The Persistence of Grace

Date preached:

By Rev. Larry Kirk

Scripture: Jonah 3:1–5, especially verse 2
Arise, go to Nineveh, that great city, and preach to it the message that I tell you.

Introduction: In the closing minutes of class at the seminary, we discussed whether one could ever say that God was judging a nation or a city when catastrophe strikes. The previous Sunday, Hurricane Katrina had hit New Orleans; the following Sunday was the anniversary of September 11. Some students seemed confident these things are God's judgments; others were just as convinced that we cannot know that. We ran out of time before we ended the discussion. Well, anyone can indulge in speculation. For Christians, the only trustworthy foundation for our faith is revelation. What Jonah learned about judgment and grace is useful for us in all of life.

I. **God's Grace Is Persistent (vv. 1–2).** Notice how Jonah 3 begins: "The word of the LORD came to Jonah the second time . . ." Why did God send Jonah to Nineveh? The answer is because of His grace and compassion. Part of the message of Jonah is how out of touch we can be with the heart of God. Jonah wanted to wipe Nineveh off the map, but God wanted Nineveh to experience His grace. The last words in the book are a question from God: "Should I not pity that great city" (4:11)?

A. **God's Persistent Grace Is Available to the Sinful.** The prophet Nahum describes the sins of Nineveh. "Woe to the bloody city! It is all full of lies and robbery. Its victim never departs" (Nah. 3:1). Nahum 3:4 indicts the people of Nineveh for violence, lust, prostitution, and witchcraft. The book of Jonah tells us that He had concern, compassion, grace, and abounding love for Nineveh.

B. **The Persistence of God's Grace Is Not Speculation; It Is Revelation.** God does judge sin, but not all suffering is judgment. God's people are not exempt from the natural calamities that affect all people in a fallen world (cf. Rom. 8). God's people are called to show kindness to those who suffer, without regard to what they deserve.

C. **The Grace of a Holy God Is Central to the Bible's Story.** Not just one or two cities deserve judgment but the whole world, the city of mankind, and everyone in it (Rom. 3:1–20). What is God's response? Ultimately what He does is that He sends not just a reluctant prophet but His own Son. In John 3:17 the Scripture says, "For God did not send His Son into the world to condemn the world, but that the world through Him might be saved." Christ came not just with a call to repentance but with an act of redemption. In our place on the Cross, Christ actually suffered the judgment we deserve. The same grace and abounding love that sent Jonah to Nineveh sent Jesus to die and rise again for you and me.

2. **God's Grace Calls Us to Repentance (vv. 4–5).** "So the people of Nineveh believed God, proclaimed a fast, and put on sackcloth, from the greatest to the least of them."

A. **Repentance Involves Both Faith and Humility Toward God (v. 5).** Notice verse 5. "So the people of Nineveh believed God." They declared a fast, an act of humility, and they put on sackcloth. In putting on sackcloth, you were humbling yourself before God and submitting yourself to Him. That's the response we all need to bring to God. It doesn't matter what you have suffered, or lost, or done, or failed to do.

B. **Repentance Is Not Just for Sinful Unbelievers, But for Self-Righteous Saints.** That's part of the story. Against the backdrop of the sinful city stands the self-righteous prophet. He also needs repentance. Jonah 3 begins: ". . . the word of the LORD came to Jonah the second time . . ." (v. 1). These almost exactly parallel the opening words of the book. God is telling Jonah he needs to start over again. He was self-righteous and self-centered. There is persistent grace for Jonah.

Conclusion: Maybe you've got forty days, forty weeks, months, years? I don't know. But there comes a time when your heart is hardened or the season of grace is gone or the kids are grown up or the marriage is over. Or you've died. It is too late one way or another. Maybe these were your forty minutes. I don't know. We all need to pray, "Lord, search me and know me and show me anywhere and everywhere I need to repent. Give me the grace to respond in glad obedience to Your Word to me today."

STATS, STORIES, AND MORE

Nineveh was a wild riverside city of the ancient world. It was the "Big Easy" of Assyria. It was built on a great river, the Tigris. Like New Orleans, it had a bad reputation, but God was concerned for the well being of that city, and God wanted to show compassion to its people. Hurricane Katrina week was supposed to have been a special week. Every Labor Day weekend for the last 33 years has been special to New Orleans. They even had a special Web site with a letter of welcome from the mayor. It was going to be Southern Decadence XXXIV, also known as Gay Mardi Gras. The official Web site calls it a celebration of gay life, music, and culture. But Southern Decadence XXXIV has been postponed. Was New Orleans a sinful city? Yes. No one should deny that. Does that mean that God lost all grace and compassion for that city? No. You may be sure that God has concern, compassion, grace, and abounding love for New Orleans. And that's good news, because that means He has concern, compassion, grace, and abounding love for people like us and cities like ours. —*Pastor Larry Kirk*

APPROPRIATE HYMNS AND SONGS

"Were It Not for Grace," David Hamilton & Phil McHugh, 1997 Bridge Building Music, Inc.; Dayspring Music LLC; Gentle Ben Music; Randy Cox Music.

"Amazing Grace," John Newton, Public Domain.

"Grace Greater Than Our Sins," Julia H. Johnston & David B. Towner, Public Domain.

"Wonderful Grace of Jesus," Haldor Lillenas, 1946 Hope Publishing Company.

FOR THE BULLETIN

On October 26, 431, the Council of Ephesus drew to a close. This was the third General Church Council, summoned in the hope of settling the Nestorian controversy. ● October 26, 1466, marks the birth of Desiderius Erasmus in Rotterdam, Holland. After studying and teaching in the leading universities of Europe, he increasingly believed the church stood in need of reform. His Greek New Testament (1516) became one of the classics of Christian history and showed scholars (particularly a monk named Martin Luther) what the church should really be and teach. ● On October 26, 1529, Thomas More was named Lord Chancellor under King Henry VIII. More was a deeply religious man who opposed Protestants and refused to recognize King Henry as head of the Church of England. Henry imprisoned him in the Tower of London and later had him beheaded. ● October 26, 1751, marks the death of Puritan pastor, author, and hymnwriter, Phillip Doddridge, a prolific writer whose best-known work was *The Rise and Progress of Religion in the Soul.* He died at age 58, at the height of his ministry, from tuberculosis. Among his hymns is "O Happy Day." ● October 26, 1813, is the birthday of Henry T. Smart, British organist who wrote the music for "Lead On, O King Eternal" and "Angels from the Realms of Glory." ● The International Red Cross was organized in Geneva on this day in 1863. ● The noted Bible teacher, R. A. Torrey, died on October 26, 1928. ● Mother Teresa founded her first Mission of Charity in Calcutta, India, on this day in 1950.

WORSHIP HELPS

Call to Worship

[Jesus] said to Thomas, "Reach your finger here, and look at My hands; and reach your hand here, and put it into My side. Do not be unbelieving, but believing." And Thomas answered and said to Him, "My Lord and my God" (John 20:27–28)!

Reader's Theater

Reader 1: Who can this be, that even the wind and the sea obey Him (Mark 4:41)! Or who shut in the sea with doors, when it burst forth and issued from the womb; when I made the clouds its garment, and thick darkness its swaddling band; when I fixed My limit for it, and set bars and doors; when I said, This far you may come, but no farther, and here your proud waves must stop (Job 38:8–11)!

Reader 2: He sends out His command to the earth; His word runs very swiftly. He gives snow like wool; He scatters the frost like ashes; He casts out His hail like morsels; who can stand before His cold? He sends out His word and melts them; He causes His wind to blow, and the waters flow (Ps. 147:15–18). O Lord God of hosts, who is mighty like You, O Lord? Your faithfulness also surrounds You. You rule the raging of the sea; when its waves rise, You still them (Ps. 89:8–9).

Additional Sermon and Lesson Ideas

Prayer: Three Mistakes We Don't Want to Make
By Dr. Larry Osborne

Date preached:

SCRIPTURE: Various

INTRODUCTION: In today's study, we'll discover three of the most common mistakes people make when talking to God in prayer. We'll follow along as Jesus explains the difference between the kind of prayer that moves the heart and the hand of God and the kind that bounces off the ceiling.

1. The Mistake of the Hypocrite (Matt. 6:5–6; Mark 12:38–40). This type of praying to impress others actually intimidates others and dismisses the biblical pattern. Jesus doesn't forbid public prayer (cf. Dan. 6:10–11; John 17:1–26), but forbids the prideful type.
2. The Mistake of the Uninformed (1 Kin. 18:20–40; Prov. 1:28–31; Matt. 6:7–13; Acts 12:1–17; James 4:3–8). The uninformed think they can manipulate God with ritual and repetition. Jesus knows we need to pray and persist (Matt. 6:12–15; 1 Pet. 3:7), but the motive again is key.
3. The Mistake of the Unmerciful (Matt. 6:12–15; Mark 11:24–25; 1 Pet. 3:7). The unmerciful think they can presume upon God's mercy. It's a big mistake to assume God doesn't mean what He says (Matt. 18:21–35).

CONCLUSION: Pray with a pure heart out of genuine desire for God's will to be done.

The Source of Salvation
By Rev. Robert M. Norris

Date preached:

SCRIPTURE: Hebrews 5:4–10

INTRODUCTION: The preacher who is the author of the sermon that we know as the epistle to the Hebrews had one great desire for his congregation, and that was that they should fall more deeply in love with Jesus Christ. Let's look together at the source of our salvation, Jesus Christ.

1. We Are Shown Christ's Worth: "So also Christ did not glorify Himself to become High Priest, but it was He who said to Him: You are My Son, today I have begotten You (v. 5).
2. We Are Shown Christ's Eternity: You are a priest forever (v. 6).
3. We Are Shown Christ s Purity: Though He was a Son, yet He learned obedience by the things which He suffered (v. 8).

CONCLUSION: And having been perfected, He became the author of eternal salvation to all who obey Him (v. 9). Are you living a life of obedience to Jesus?

Tackling Life with Confidence
Date preached:

Scripture: 2 Corinthians 5:1–8, especially verses 6 and 8
So we are always confident . . . We are confident, yes.

Introduction: If you go down to your favorite bookstore, you could come home with a shopping bag containing these books: *Confidence: How Winning Streaks and Losing Streaks Begin and End; How to Develop Self-Confidence and Influence People; Ultimate Secrets of Total Self-Confidence; How to Have Confidence and Power in Dealing with People; The Confident Woman; Raising Confident Boys; Raising Confident Girls; Ten Days to More Confident Public Speaking; A Guide to Confident Living; The Confident Coach's Guide to Teaching Soccer; How to Be Your Own Therapist: A Step-by-Step Guide to Building a Confident Life,* and *Bombproof Your Horse: Teach Your Horse to Be Confident, Obedient, and Safe, No Matter What You Encounter.* All of us want to tackle life with confidence—we want that for ourselves and for our children, our students, and even for our horses. Well, if you want to know the ultimate secrets to total self-confidence, then read 2 Corinthians. Paul uses the words *confident* and *confidence* twelve times here. He's a man who has been rejected, ridiculed, beaten, battered, criticized, and vilified. But his opponents were totally stymied when it came to shaking his confidence. He said, "I know, I am confident, I am always confident."

1. **Confident People Think a Great Deal About Heaven (4:17—5:4).** Verse 1 is really the direct continuation of the previous paragraph, which, in our Bibles, is at the end of chapter 4. In life we have momentary troubles, like little weights on one side of the scale. But we are heirs of life in Christ with all that comes with that—the new heavens, the new earth, the New Jerusalem, the new order of things—and when that's on the other side of the scale, there's no comparison. So we fix our eyes on what is unseen. Whenever we're tempted to lose heart, we think about heaven. Our bodies are merely tents that will collapse at some point, but we have an eternal house in the heavens, not made by human hands. Paul tells us our bodies are like tents, temporary dwellings. At some point we loosen the

cords, pull up the stakes, collapse the tent, and pack it away. We long for our heavenly dwelling; and when we think about heaven, it gives us confidence in the future.

2. **Confident People Draw on Inner Resources (5:5).** God Himself is preparing us for the experience of putting on immortality and eternal life; and as a down payment guaranteeing what is to come, He has given us the inner resources of the Holy Spirit. (See Stats, Stories, and More.)

3. **Confident People Want to Please Christ (5:6–10).** The third mark of confident people is a desire to please Christ. Some time ago, I was driving to a speaking engagement and I became disoriented on the road and wondered if I was taking the right route. I didn't have very much time to spare, and I felt a sense of panic. I tried to call someone on my cell phone, but couldn't get anyone. I tried to read my directions as I drove, but couldn't make heads or tails of them. This frustration rose up inside me until suddenly I saw a familiar landmark. My confidence returned because I knew I was on the right road after all. When our goal in life is to please the Lord, it inspires confidence because we know we're on the right road. And the great thing about pleasing Him is that we can do it on both sides of the grave. *So we make it our goal to please Him, whether we are at home in the body or away from it.*

Conclusion: Many of us struggle with self-doubt, shyness, and a sense of inferiority. But the Bible says: *If God be for us, who can be against us.* In the closing moments of this message, I want to ordain each of you to preach a little sermon to yourself. I can't be around you twenty-four hours a day to preach to you all the time, and many of my sermons aren't what you need anyway. I want to deputize you and show you how to preach to the hardest congregation of all—yourself. Confident people preach to themselves from the truth of God's Word. They remind themselves of His promises. So here's your sermon: *I am full of confidence today because:*

- *God the Father has a house for me in the heavens, not built by human hands.*
- *God the Spirit lives within me as a divine deposit.*

> ❧ God the Son gives meaning to my life as I seek to please Him whether in life or death.

And if the whole of the Trinity is for me, who can be against me!

STATS, STORIES, AND MORE

I don't have time to review everything the New Testament says about the inner working of the Holy Spirit, but let me give you some thumbnails. The Bible teaches that the Holy Spirit enters into our hearts at the moment of conversion, He proceeds from the Father in accordance with the promise of the Son, and He goes to work, recreating the attitudes and personality of Jesus Christ in and through our lives. He forms Christ within us. He edifies us. He sanctifies us. He bears within us the fruit of love, joy, peace, patience, kindness, goodness, faithfulness, gentleness, and self-control. He fills us with Himself and empowers us for service. He reproves and exhorts and helps us with our infirmities. He guides us into all truth and illumines us as we study the Scripture. He bestows spiritual gifts for ministry, and enables us to live in victory and to work with effectiveness. If we fully appreciated the powerful indwelling presence of Jesus Himself within us by means of His Holy Spirit, don't you think we'd be confident people as we go through life? We need Jesus Christ for our *eternal* life and we need the Holy Spirit for our *internal* life.

APPROPRIATE HYMNS AND SONGS

"The Lord Is My Strength," Dennis Jernigan, 1993 Shepherd's Heart Music (Admin. by Dayspring Music, Inc.).

"Hallelujah (Your Love Is Amazing)," Brenton Brown and Brian Doerksen, 2000 Vineyard Songs (Admin. in North America by Music Services).

"There Is Strength in the Name of the Lord," Phil McHugh, Gloria Gaither, and Sandi Patti Helvering, 1986 by River Oaks Music Company, Gaither Music Company, and Sandi's Song Music.

"Lord Most High," Don Harris and Gary Sadler, 1996 Integrity's Hosanna! Music.

FOR THE BULLETIN

On November 2, 1164, Archbishop Thomas Becket, 45, left England to begin a six-year, self-imposed exile in France, having been condemned by his erstwhile friend, King Henry II. ● While a student, John Calvin became leader of the Protestant (evangelical) group in Paris. When Nicholas Cop was elected president of Paris University, he asked Calvin to help him write his inaugural speech. The two men overstated the case, attacking Catholic doctrines in sharp tones, and a melee ensued. On November 2, 1533, Calvin escaped through a window by bedsheets and fled Paris disguised as a farmer. ● November 2, 1834, is the birthday of Harriett Eugenia Buell, author of the hymn, "I'm a Child of the King." ● Absalom Backus (A. B.) Earle, a New York preacher, struggled with periodic bouts of darkness and doubt, but by perseverance and prayer he began to experience victory. On November 2, 1862, he was in his room alone, pleading for the fullness of Christ's love, "when all at once a sweet, heavenly peace filled all the vacuum in my soul, leaving no longing, no unrest, no dissatisfied feeling in my bosom. . . . For the first time in my life, I had the rest which is more than peace." He went on to hold 39,330 services, travel 370,000 miles, lead 160,000 souls to Christ, and earn a total of $65,520 for his 64 years of ministry. ● In a letter dated November 2, 1917, British foreign secretary, A. J. Balfour, wrote: "HM government views with favor the establishment in Palestine of a national home for the Jewish people. This Balfour Declaration led to the establishing of Israel in 1948.

PRAYER FOR THE PASTOR'S CLOSET

Gracious God, remember us, we beseech Thee, in our word this day. If it be Thy will, give unto us a prosperous day. May all our word be well done. May we turn out nothing half-done. May we glorify Thee by honest good work; for the sake of Him who completed His word for us, even Jesus Christ our Lord. Amen. —J. H. JOWETT

WORSHIP HELPS

Call to Worship

You, LORD, in the beginning laid the foundation of the earth, and the heavens are the work of Your hands. They will perish, but You remain; and they will all grow old like a garment; like a cloak You will fold them up, and they will be changed. But You are the same, and Your years will not fail (Heb. 1:10–12).

Scripture Reading

I charge you therefore before God and the Lord Jesus Christ, who will judge the living and the dead at His appearing and His kingdom: Preach the word! Be ready in season and out of season. Convince, rebuke, exhort, with all longsuffering and teaching. For the time will come when they will not endure sound doctrine, but according to their own desires, because they have itching ears, they will heap up for themselves teachers; and they will turn their ears away from the truth, and be turned aside to fables. But you be watchful in all things, endure afflictions, do the work of an evangelist, fulfill your ministry (2 Tim. 4:1–5).

Pastoral Prayer

Great heavenly Father, we praise You for making Yourself known to us! We ask that You preach the Word through us. We know that You have raised up for Yourself prophets and preachers from the bold, from the timid, from the rich, and from the poor. Lord, You called simple fishermen to be the greatest preachers the world has ever known. Now Lord, we ask that You would be pleased to raise up preachers from this very room to take the gospel to the world. We ask it in Jesus' name and for His sake, Amen.

Additional Sermons and Lesson Ideas

Good Timing/God's Timing

By Rev. Melvin Tinker

Date preached:

SCRIPTURE: Mark 6:45–53

INTRODUCTION: Today we're looking to Scripture at the issue of what we expect when we obey Jesus. The disciples simply did as they were told. Jesus made the disciples get into the boat, so they did. What was the result of their obedience? One of the most terrifying nights of their lives! But also, it was one of the most instructive.

1. The Absence of Jesus (vv. 45–48). Jesus left the disciples alone and all of the sudden a great storm bursts, the boat bounces, and the disciples begin to wonder why Jesus is taking so long! Jesus was teaching them to trust.
2. The Nearness of Jesus (vv. 48–50). Jesus neared the disciples as He walked on the water, but they were afraid rather than having faith. He was stretching their faith.
3. The Presence of Jesus (vv. 50–51). Jesus calmed the waves and told the disciples not to be afraid. God proved Himself to them: they could trust Him when He wasn't visible, and when He showed up differently than they expected.

CONCLUSION: And you know much of the Christian life is precisely that. Most of my life is spent rowing: getting out of bed, praying, reading the Bible. The lesson is very simple. Don't bail out. Don't give up. Don't lay down the oars! He is still the God of the waves.

Pulling Yourself Together

Date preached:

SCRIPTURE: 2 Corinthians 6:3–10 (NIV)

INTRODUCTION: A man said to a psychiatrist, "I need help. I keep thinking I'm a curtain." The doctor said, "Well, pull yourself together." We've got to learn to pull ourselves together under pressure. In the passage the apostle Paul listed almost forty personal traits. The first section described his hardships. The second section described his positive attitude. The third part of the list described the paradoxes he faced in ministry. From this we can learn that Christ wants us to be realistic about life's hardships, optimistic about His power, and active in changing the world.

1. Be a Realist: Accept the Difficult (vv. 4–5): *We commend ourselves . . . in endurance, troubles, distresses, beatings, imprisonments, riots, hard work, sleeplessness, hunger . . .*

2. Be an Optimist: Accentuate the Positive (vv. 6–7): *In purity, understanding, patience and kindness; in the Holy Spirit and in sincere love; in truthful speech and in the power of God; with weapons of righteousness in the right hand and in the left.*

3. Be an Activist: Accomplish the Impossible (vv. 8–10): . . . *genuine, yet regarded as impostors; known yet unknown; dying yet living; beaten but not killed; sorrowful yet rejoicing; poor yet making many rich; having nothing yet possessing all things.*

CONCLUSION: A realist, an optimist, and an activist once met. They are you.

Farewell Sermons

Preached by the Ejected Non-Conformist Ministers of 1662 to Their Congregations on the Day of Their Ejection

On August 17, 1662, nearly 2,500 of England's finest ministers were ejected from their pulpits. The catastrophe began two years earlier when the British monarchy was restored under King Charles II. A series of new laws was passed by the Cavalier Parliament aimed at discouraging non-conformity to the Church of England and stifling religious liberty. The Act of Uniformity, for example, required all ministers to use *The Book of Common Prayer* as a format for worship. Many non-Anglicans refused, and as a result they were forbidden to preach.

When the law went into effect on St. Bartholomew's Day in 1662, over 2,000 pastors rose to their pulpits throughout England to address their congregations for the final time. Many of these were renowned Puritans whose love for the Lord and His Word penetrated their sermons as light pervades the noonday sky.

Within a year of the Great Ejection, two volumes of these "Farewell Sermons" were published in London, including the prayers offered before and after the sermons, and messages preached in both morning and evening services. In 1816, the publishing firm of Gale and Fenner in London reprinted twenty-four of these messages, and more recently Soli Deo Gloria Publications printed a well-bound replica of that original edition. There's also a Banner of Truth edition containing nine Farewell Sermons.

As I've read these messages, I've wondered what I would have done or said had I been placed in similar straits. It's a relevant question, because the shadow of persecution is hovering over the Christian world now more than ever; and even in the western world, it's not unforeseeable that future laws will present similarly difficult dilemmas for preachers of God's Word.

These farewell messages are both practical and poignant, and if you're familiar with English Protestant history, you'll recognize the names of these faithful men. Among them, for example, was my favorite Puritan, Thomas Watson of Cambridge, who preached his "Farewell Sermon" on August 17, 1662. Here's an excerpt of what he told his grieving congregation on that black-lettered day:

> *I have exercised my ministry among you for sixteen years and have received many demonstrations of love from you. I have observed your reverent attentions to the word preached. I have observed your zeal against error; and as much as could be expected in a critical time, your unity. Though I should not be permitted to preach to you, yet shall I not cease to love and pray for you; but why should there be any interruption made? Where is the crime? Some say that we are disloyal and seditious. Beloved, what my actions and sufferings for his majesty have been is known. I desire to be guided by the silver thread of God's word and of God's providence. And if I must die, let me leave some legacy with you before I go from you, some counsel.*
>
> *First, keep your constant hours every day with God. Begin the day with God, visit God in the morning before you make any other visit; wind up your hearts towards heaven in the morning and they will go the better all the day after! Oh turn your closets into temples; read the scriptures. The two Testaments are the two lips by which God speaks to us; this will make you wise unto salvation. Besiege heaven every day with your prayer, thus perfume your houses.*

Watson proceeded to give his listeners 19 more "directions" then he ended, saying:

> *I have many things yet to say to you, but I know not whether God will give me another opportunity. My strength is almost gone. Consider what hath been said, and the Lord will give you understanding in all things.*

Farewell Sermons not only gives us insights into the powerful and practical theology of the Puritan age, but it reveals the pulse-beat of a handful of dedicated men of God who loved their flocks and honored their Lord, and would not be cowed by an earthly king. Their voices would not be stilled. These messages are a window into times not unlike our own, when the preaching of the Word was politically unpopular but desperately needed. The valor of the Ejected Preachers will inspire all of us who know their stories and heed their sermons.

NOVEMBER 9, 2008

Living for the Glory of God

Date preached:

By Dr. David Jeremiah

Scripture: John 17:1–5, especially verse 1
Father, the hour has come. Glorify Your Son, that Your Son also may glorify You.

Introduction: When Jesus offered His Priestly Prayer in John 17, perhaps the most important word is the little term *AS* (vv. 2, 11, 14, 16, 18, 21, 22, 23). God treats us *as* He treats Christ.

    A. We Have the Same Life as Christ Has (v. 2).
    B. We Have the Same Security as Christ Has (v. 11).
    C. We Have the Same Hostility from the World as Christ Has (vv. 14, 16).
    D. We Have the Same Mission as Christ Has (v. 18).
    E. We Have the Same Unity as Christ Has with the Father (vv. 21–22).
    F. We Have the Same Glory as Christ Has with the Father (v. 22).
    G. We Have the Same Love as Christ Has from the Father (v. 23).

Jesus' relationship to the Father is the pattern for our relationship to Him. If we will be to Jesus what Jesus is to the Father, then Jesus will be to us what the Father is to Jesus.

1. **Jesus Lived by Divine Purpose (v. 2).** His purpose was to give eternal life for all given Him by the Father. John 17 speaks seven times of our having been given to Him by the Father. The love-gift of God to the world is Christ, and the love-gift of Christ to the Father are Christians. The pressure never got in His way because His mind was fixed on the goal. Don't get caught up in side issues. Keep your mind fixed on what God has ordained for you.

2. **Jesus Lived by Divine Power (v. 2).** The power to accomplish His purpose was delegated to Him from the Father. All authority was given to Him, even as He sends us out as His disciple-makers (see v. 28).

3. **Jesus Lived by Divine Plan (v. 1).** When Jesus said, "Father, the hour is come," He was tapping into a current of thought about His "hour" seen repeatedly in John's Gospel.

A. **Nothing Should Distract You (John 2:4).** In John 2:4, Jesus told His mother, "My hour has not yet come." It wasn't a rebuke or a refusal to deal with the problem at hand. But Jesus was saying, "The time for Me to be submissive to the authority of man is not here yet, though I will do what you asked right now." Not even a marriage could distract Him. Most of us start out to accomplish something, then things come along; before we know it, the goal gets lost. When you have God's purpose in your mind, nothing can distract you.

B. **Nothing Should Destroy You (John 7:30).** Those seeking to harm Christ couldn't, for His time had not yet come. When you live according to God's plan, nothing can destroy you. Our lives are immortal until our work is done.

C. **Nothing Should Discourage You (John 12:27).** This is sort of a pre-Gethsemane experience. Though troubled, Jesus didn't let His overwhelming anguish dissuade Him from the task.

D. **Nothing Should Disappoint You (John 16:32).** Jesus said, "The hour is coming . . . that you will be scattered. . . . Yet I am not alone, because the Father is with Me." Sometimes you feel you're the only one who understands what God wants you to do. But you cannot be disappointed.

E. **Nothing Should Defeat You (John 17:1).** As the hour approached, the goal was in sight, the purpose was before Him, and this was His hour of glory. He could not be defeated because He had a purpose from God, and the plan was on schedule. Verse 4 is an epitaph on His life: "I have finished the work You gave Me to do." Our goal is not to find out how much work we can do. It's to find out the work God has given us to do.

Conclusion: Are you bold and courageous enough to find out what God wants you to do? Have you a purpose clearly in mind? Are you willing to submit that purpose to the empowering of the Holy Spirit and then stay on schedule to see that done? Some of you young people are in college. You may get discouraged and want to quit. God says, "Here is My plan and purpose for you. You'd better stay on schedule, My friends." God has that purpose fixed for you out there. He wants you to accomplish it. Stay on schedule.

STATS, STORIES, AND MORE

More from Dr. Jeremiah
I remember hearing Dr. J. Vernon McGee some years ago talk about a man who had been studying the doctrine of predestination. He became so entrenched by the idea of God's sovereignty protection that he told McGee, "You know pastor, I'm so convinced that God is keeping me no matter what I do, that I believe I could step out in the busiest traffic at noon time and if my hour had not come, I would be perfectly safe." McGee replied, "Mister, if you step out in traffic at high noon, your hour *has* come." You can get really out of perspective if you're not careful; but that is not what this is all about. Let me personally illustrate it. When I first began to preach across the country in different places in conferences and began to fly a lot, I had a sense of kind of fear. I would begin to think that I might never see my children again. I might never see my wife again. I don't know how to explain that. I don't think it's abnormal. I have talked to a lot of men who have gone through it. But it became a very uncomfortable experience for me. One day, I was sharing that with a friend, and he gave me a statement I will never, ever forget. He said, "Remember this, Jeremiah. God's man living in the center of God's will is immortal until God is through with him." I never thought about that before. I wrote that in my Bible and it solved my problem.

APPROPRIATE HYMNS AND SONGS

"To God Be the Glory," Fanny Crosby & William Doane, Public Domain.

"We Will Glorify the King of Kings," Twila Paris, 1982 by Singspiration Music/ASCAP.

"Glory to the King," Darlene Zschech, 1997 Hillsong Publishing.

"Yours Is the Kingdom," Joel Houston, 2005 Hillsong Publishing.

FOR THE BULLETIN

John Knox, leader of the Scottish Reformation, performed his last public act on Sunday, November 9, 1572. His health had failed, and his once trumpeting voice could barely be heard during his sermons. A successor had been chosen at his church, St. Gile's Cathedral in Edinburgh, and at his installation Knox preached his last sermon, pointing out the mutual duties of a minister and a congregation. The following Tuesday, he was seized by a violent cough and declined rapidly. On Friday, November 14th, he rose from bed, thinking it was Sunday. He wanted to dress and go to church and preach. On Monday, November 24, he asked his wife to read from the passage "where I first cast my anchor"—John 17. About 11 o'clock that evening, he passed away. ● November 9, 1865, is the birthday of John "Praying" Hyde, missionary to India. ● Amy Carmichael arrived in India on this day in 1895, ill, but determined to serve Christ as a missionary of the Church of England Zenana Missionary Society. She remained in that land until her death in 1951, founding the Dohnavur Fellowship which ministered to abused children in India, and writing devotional classics. ● On November 9, 1938, Nazi thugs in Germany unleashed a campaign of terror against the Jews. As the police stood passively by, German mobs broke windows of houses and stores and brutalized Jews. There were 267 synagogues plundered, 7,500 shops wrecked, 91 Jews killed, and 20,000 arrested and sent to concentration camps. It was afterward known as "Kristallnacht" ("Crystal Night") because of the thousands of broken windows.

PRAYER FOR THE PASTOR'S CLOSET

Grant us, O Lord, to pass this day in gladness and peace, without stumbling and without strain; that, reaching the eventide victorious over all temptation, we may praise Thee, the eternal God, Who art blessed, and doest govern all things—world without end—Amen.

—MOZARABIC SACRAMENTARY, before A.D. 700

WORSHIP HELPS

Call to Worship

> *Infinite God, to Thee we raise*
> *Our hearts in solemn songs of praise,*
> *By all Thy works on earth adored,*
> *We worship Thee, the common Lord;*
> *The everlasting Father own,*
> *And bow our souls before Thy throne.*
> —CHARLES WESLEY

Pastoral Prayer

Heavenly Father, in a purposeless world in which billions of people are hopelessly seeking significance apart from You, we praise You for giving meaning to our lives, hope to our days, and purpose to our steps. You have given us work to do, souls to save, men to help, women to encourage, and children to nurture. You have commissioned us as disciples and as apostles, sending us to become blameless and harmless, children of God without fault in the midst of a crooked and perverse generation among whom we shine as stars in the world, holding forth the word of life. Now, Lord, may this service of worship bless Your heart and encourage ours, that we may bless and encourage others outside these walls this week. We pray in Jesus' name. Amen.

Offertory Comments

In his book, *All for the Master,* Daniel J. Celia said that once upon a time he used a particular strategy for helping couples manage their finances. He asked his clients to make a list of all their bills, then to place them in order of importance. Inevitably the first priority was their mortgage payment, followed by their car payment. He then suggested their IRA or Retirement plan were even more important and should top the list. After he became a Christian, he realized there was something even more important. "Knowing what I know now and having received the grace of God, I understand the first thing of that list ought to be God, not ourselves. . . . God should be first in our giving, not last."[1]

---

[1] Daniel J. Celia, *All for the Master* (Nashville: World Publishing, 2006), p. 54.

Additional Sermons and Lesson Ideas

State of Readiness

Date preached:

SCRIPTURE: Luke 12:35–40

INTRODUCTION: Military experts work day and night to keep America's armed forces at a high state of readiness. How about you? Are you living in the State of Readiness? Sixteen times in the Bible we find the phrase, *Be ready*. It first occurs in Exodus 19, when the children of Israel were to "be ready" for the Lord's descent onto Mount Sinai. In the New Testament, we should:

1. Be Ready to Give an Answer to Those Asking About Our Hope (1 Pet. 3:15).
2. Be Ready for Every Good Work (Titus 3:1).
3. Be Ready to Give Generously (1 Cor. 9:3, 5).
4. Be Ready to Preach the Word In and Out of Season (2 Tim. 4:2).
5. Be Ready for Christ to Come Again (Matt. 24:44).

CONCLUSION: If the Boy Scott motto is "Be Prepared," the Christian's motto is "Be Ready." We can never take a break from our Christianity nor relax our spiritual vigilance. Be ready to share, to give, to preach, to work. Most of all, be ready for Christ's return. It might be today!

Ready to go, ready to stay, ready my place to fill,
Ready for service, lowly or great, ready to do His will.
—CHARLES D. TILLMAN (1903)

Be Thankful Anyway

Date preached:

SCRIPTURE: 1 Corinthians 1:4–9

INTRODUCTION: Do you have frustrations in life right now? The apostle Paul had one headache after another with his premier church in Greece, the Corinthians. He wrote a letter discussing all their problems, and it was very taxing and trying to him. But true to form, his disposition was one of thanksgiving, and he began the letter with this paragraph of praise. Every verse is a separate item of thanksgiving.

1. God's Grace, Even in the Lives of Those Who Are Frustrating You (v. 4).
2. Being Enriched in Everything by Him (v. 5).
3. The Testimony of Christ in Us (v. 6).
4. Our Spiritual Gifts (v. 7).
5. The Soon Appearing of Christ (v. 8).
6. God's Faithfulness and Fellowship (v. 9).

CONCLUSION: This week, don't be cast down. Learn the secret of thanking God anyway.

NOVEMBER 16, 2008

SUGGESTED SERMON

My Attitude Toward the Church

Date preached:

Scripture: Colossians 1:3–5, especially verse 3
We give thanks to the God and Father of our Lord Jesus Christ, praying always for you . . .

Introduction: Lots of people disdain the church. A few weeks ago, a noted professor of Islamic law at Al-Imam University in Saudi Arabia gave an interview in which he said that those who worship Christ, Son of Mary, should be hated; and he said that when a Muslim hates a Christian, it is a "positive hatred." But it's not just a problem overseas. Our American government is bending over backward to prohibit freedom of speech to Christians in public areas. And the entertainment industry is pushing an increasingly anti-Christian and anti-church agenda. Jesus warned we would be hated by all nations for His name's sake. If, then, this world is predisposed to hate the church, what should our own attitude be? We know the church better than anybody, and we know that there's no perfect church. But with all its flaws and failures, we should be thankful for the presence of the church in this world. Notice how the apostle Paul worked this out for himself in Colossians. A doctrinal problem had developed in the church, and Paul was concerned enough to write this letter, stressing the importance of maintaining theological purity in the church. Yet he opened by saying that his overarching attitude toward the church in Colossea was thanksgiving.

1. **I'm Thankful for the Church's Faith (v. 4: ". . . since we heard of your faith in Christ Jesus . . .").** Paul wasn't necessarily commending the church for its *great* faith. In fact, later in the book he admonished them to develop their faith (1:22ff and 2:5ff). Paul was just thankful that in a secular city on the eastern flanks of the Roman Empire, there was a church representing Jesus. It wasn't the size of their faith, but the very existence of their faith that thrilled him. This cannot be said of every church today. Many churches in America have become so liberal in their beliefs that the historic faith of Christianity has been abandoned. But in other parts

of the world, Christians are so committed to their Lord and His message they are braving great persecution; and there are more Christians on earth today than ever before. Christianity is spreading more rapidly than ever, despite Islamism, secularism, and liberalism. And I'm thankful for the faith of those who believe in Jesus.

2. **I'm Thankful for the Church's Love (v. 4: ". . . and of your love for all the saints").** This is a hallmark of the church. There's a story of a ship that wrecked in the South Pacific. A handful of sailors survived, but they were marooned without weapons in an area infamous for cannibalism. As they crept through the jungle, they suddenly relaxed and smiled. They saw a church building in the clearing. "Come on, boys!" said one of them. "There's a church here!" I grew up in church; and I know misunderstandings arise, people come and go, feelings get hurt, opinions differ. But every church I've ever known has been characterized by loving people who really cared for each other, and I'm thankful.

3. **I'm Thankful for the Church's Hope (v. 5: ". . . the hope which is laid up for you in heaven").** When we become a part of God's family, our sense of "home" and of "citizenship" changes. We start looking for a heavenly home, and we are citizens of a new kingdom. In Ichabod Spencer's book, *A Pastor's Sketches,* he told of being called to the bedside of a dying woman. Her bedroom filled with friends who had gathered to see her die. Making his way through the crowd, he could see she was in the last agonies of death. She was bolstered up in her bed, gasping for breath, almost suffocated by asthma. Rev. Spencer said, "You seem to be very sick." "Yes," she said, "I am dying." "And are you ready to die?" he asked. She lifted her eyes to him and said very earnestly, "God knows . . . I have taken Him at His Word . . . and . . . I am not afraid to die." Rev. Spencer quoted Scriptures to her and prayed for several minutes; and then he turned to leave, but she reached out and caught his hand. Gasping for breath, she said, "I wanted to tell you . . . that I can . . . trust . . . in God . . . while I am dying. You have often told me . . . He would not forsake me. . . . And now I find it is true. I am at peace. I die willingly and happily." In a few minutes, Spencer left the solemn room. However, the woman did not die. She recovered and lived for many more years. But no one ever forgot the dying testimony of the woman who didn't die. She said, "I have taken the

Lord at His Word. I can trust God while I'm living and while I'm dying. He will never leave me or forsake me."[1]

Conclusion: The Colossian church wasn't perfect and neither is this one or any one; but Paul was thankful for their faith, love, and hope. Down through the chronicles of the history of the church, there have been problems—but the church has always been characterized by faith, love, and hope. And I'm thankful for that. Do you have faith in Jesus Christ? Is your life characterized by His love? Do you have His hope?

STATS, STORIES, AND MORE

We see faith, hope, and love trio-ed together repeatedly in Scripture, and they seem to be the mark by which a church is measured, and by implication, by which a Christian is measured. Notice these other references (NIV):

- 1 Corinthians 13:13 says, "And now these three remain: *faith, hope,* and *love.* But the greatest of these is love."

- 1 Thessalonians 1:3 says, "We continually remember before our God and Father your work produced by *faith,* your labor prompted by *love,* and your endurance inspired by *hope* in our Lord Jesus Christ."

- Romans 5:1–5 says, "Therefore, since we have been justified through *faith,* we have peace with God through our Lord Jesus Christ, through whom we have gained access by faith into this grace in which we now stand. And we rejoice in the *hope* of the glory of God. Not only so, but we also rejoice in our sufferings, because we know that suffering produces perseverance; perseverance, character; and character, hope. And hope does not disappoint us, because God has poured out His *love* into our hearts by the Holy Spirit, whom He has given us."

- Galatians 5:5–6: "We eagerly await through the Spirit the righteousness for which we *hope.* For in Christ Jesus . . . the only thing that counts is *faith* expressing itself through *love.*"

- Ephesians 1:15–18: "For this reason, ever since I heard about your *faith* in the Lord Jesus and your *love* for all the saints, I have not stopped giving thanks for you, remembering you in my prayers. . . . I pray also that the eyes of your heart may be enlightened in order that you may know the *hope* to which he has called you . . ."

---

[1] Ichabod Spencer, *A Pastor's Sketches* (Vestavia Hills, AL: Solid Ground Christian Books, 2001), p. 58.

APPROPRIATE HYMNS AND SONGS

"A Glorious Church," Ralph E. Hudson, Public Domain.

"The Family of God," Gloria & William Gaither, 1970 by William Gaither.

"Bind Us Together," Bob Gillman, 1977 ThankYou Music.

"Give Thanks," Denny Cagle, 1981 Between the Lines Music.

FOR THE BULLETIN

Augustine, sixth-century missionary to the British Isles, was ordained as the first Archbishop of Canterbury on November 16, 597. ● Saint Hugh of Lincoln was a noble bishop who, due to the death of his mother when he was eight, was raised in a convent. He later became abbot of an English monastery, and his reputation as a wise and holy man spread widely. In 1185, he was made Bishop of Lincoln. He denounced the mass persecution of Jews in England, and was fearless in making his case before both mobs and civil authorities. He died on this day in 1200 in London. ● Ever wonder why September (Sept = seven) is the ninth month, October (oct = eight) is the tenth month, etc.? On November 16, 1621, the Vatican adopted a new calendar which made January 1 the beginning of the calendar year, instead of March. ● November 16, 1662, is the birth of Samuel Wesley, Sr., father of John and Charles. ● On November 16, 1895, as Samuel Francis Smith, 88, hurried to catch a train to fulfill a preaching engagement, he collapsed and died. Years before, while translating a patriot German hymn, he had been inspired to write the words of the hymn: "My Country 'tis of Thee." ● On November 16, 1903, missionaries Wiley and Eunice Glass arrived in China. There was no one to meet them, and they didn't know the language.

WORSHIP HELPS

Call to Worship
Then Melchizedek king of Salem brought out bread and wine; he was the priest of God Most High. And he blessed him and said: Blessed be Abram of God Most High, Possessor of heaven and earth (Gen. 14:18–19).

Offertory Comments
What do the following people have in common? Mr. Welch of Welch's Grape Juice; Mr. J. C. Kraft of Kraft Cheese Corporation; Mr. Henry P. Crowell of Quaker Oats; Wallace Johnson, founder of Holiday Inns; J. C. Penney of J. C. Penney Stores; and John D. Rockefeller, Sr. The one thing they all had in common was that they all tithed. That doesn't mean tithing will make you rich, but all these people demonstrate the understanding that what they had was because of God's blessing.

Scripture Reading Medley
Now you are the body of Christ, and members individually. You are God's field, you are God's building. You are a chosen generation, a royal priesthood, a holy nation, His own special people, that you may proclaim the praises of Him who called you out of darkness into His marvelous light; who once were not a people but are now the people of God, who had not obtained mercy but now have obtained mercy. Do you not know that you are the temple of God and that the Spirit of God dwells in you? Therefore let no one boast in men. For all things are yours: whether Paul or Apollos or Cephas, or the world or life or death, or things present or things to come—all are yours. And you are Christ's, and Christ is God's (1 Cor. 12:27; 3:9; 1 Pet. 2:9–10, 1 Cor. 3:16, 21–23).

Additional Sermons and Lesson Ideas

The Mercy of God

Date preached:

By Rev. Billie Friel

SCRIPTURE: Psalm 86

INTRODUCTION: When counting your blessings, do not forget the mercy of God. It's mentioned over 340 times in the Bible. Note these four points about God's Mercy:

1. The Attribute of Mercy (vv. 5, 15). Mercy is described as good, full of compassion, gracious, longsuffering, and abundant in mercy. God is merciful because He is good and He is good because He is merciful.
2. The Accessibility of Mercy (vv. 5, 13). God's mercy is "abundant"— beyond bounds, overflowing, having no limits. The river of God's mercy never dries up.
3. The Appropriation of Mercy (v. 5). Even though God's mercy is accessible and available to all, the ones who benefit from this gift are those who call upon Him.
4. The Appreciation of Mercy (vv. 12–13). Because of God's great mercy, David exclaimed, "I will praise You, O Lord my God, with all my heart, and I will glorify Your name forevermore. For great is Your mercy toward me, and You have delivered my soul from the depths of Sheol.

CONCLUSION: Are you merciful? Because God is merciful we must practice mercy (Matt. 5:7) and proclaim God's mercy to others (Mark 5:19).

Rejoice! God Is in Control

Date preached:

By Rev. Mark Hollis

SCRIPTURE: Philippians 1:12–18

INTRODUCTION: Like an army victoriously advancing in spite of enemy obstacles, the gospel goes forward undaunted by the attacks of Satan.

1. The Advance of the Gospel (vv. 12–14). In all the circumstances of life, God accomplishes His plan through His people. Paul's chains led to the gospel being preached:
   A. To the Palace Guard (vv. 12–13).
   B. Through the Believer's Courage (v. 14).
2. The Preaching of Christ (vv. 15–18). Methods, messengers, and even motives are not as important as the Message itself.
   A. Some Preach Out of Envy and Rivalry (vv. 15, 17).
   B. Others Preach with Goodwill (vv. 15–16).
   C. Praise God! Both Preach Christ (v. 18).

CONCLUSION: How is God at work in the circumstances of your life? Where do you need to say, "I really don't care about methods, messenger, or motives; I just praise God that Christ is preached?" Is the proclamation of Christ the central theme of your life?

NOVEMBER 23, 2008

Unity and Humility

Date preached:

By Rev. Todd M. Kinde

Scripture: Philippians 2:1–11, especially verses 2–3
Fulfill my joy by being like-minded, having the same love, being of one accord, of one mind. Let nothing be done through selfish ambition or conceit, but in lowliness of mind let each esteem others better than himself.

Introduction: There is greater enjoyment in shopping when all the wheels of the shopping cart turn the same way. Joy is that sense of purpose and accomplishment. It's the sense of attaining goals to complete a mission. When the wheels of your cart are going in various directions you'll be frustrated, and your joy will be squelched by the disunity of the wheels. It takes but one wheel to diminish the joy of shopping! Paul was concerned for the Church of Philippi, for they were in danger of losing the fundamental Christian perspective of joy. Furthermore, the lack of unity in the church was preventing Paul from experiencing joy as fully as he should. Lack of unity in any local church will prevent you and I from experiencing full joy.

1. **Our Joy Is Inaugurated When We Are United with Christ (v. 1).** The theme of joy has been introduced in 1:4 and continued in 1:18 and 1:25. This joy was the result of partnering for the sake of the gospel. With the prospect of suffering for Christ, Paul turned to mention the resources that are available in Christ to persevere in the Christian life. The resources available from the Triune God include: encouragement in Christ, comfort from love, fellowship in the Spirit, affection and sympathy (2:1). These are the results of union with Christ. Union with Christ comes by faith in His atoning work on the Cross, making us right with God; and that is the beginning of joy.

2. **Our Joy Is Completed When We Unite with One Another (v. 2).** Here Paul made his main statement: Complete my joy by being what you should be. Manifest the fruit of your union with Christ. Bear the realities of encouragement, comfort, fellowship, affection, and sympathy in your lives. The counterparts of verse 1 now appear

in verse 2—of the same mind, having the same love, of one flesh, of one mind. Pictured here is a union of mind and soul much like that of a husband and wife. It is an organic union. It is a holistic union of mind and flesh (1 Cor. 12:12–13; Eph. 4:1–7).

3. **Our Unity Is Strengthened Through Humility (vv. 3–4).** In our wedding services we often give the exhortation that, "What God has joined together let no man put asunder." This quote comes from Matthew 19:6. In our text today, verses 3–4 say the same thing. Do not do anything to destroy or undermine the unity you have in the Spirit. Paul recognized that the key to joy consists in shifting our attention away from ourselves and onto the needs of others. Verse 3 emphasizes the inner motives. Our motive ought to be driven by a perspective that values others higher than self. Verse 4 emphasizes the outer actions that flow out of the inner motive. If your motive is self-advancement, then you will do things for your own interest. If your motive is driven by humility then you will look to the interest of those above you.

4. **Our Humility Is Rooted in the Mind of Christ (vv. 5–11).** The basis of our humility is demonstrated in the mind of Christ (v. 5). He is the source of true humility because it is an attribute of God. Verses 6–11 form an ancient hymn of the New Testament church. The hymn is composed of two main sections: One of humility and one of exaltation (vv. 6–11). Paul's main purpose in quoting this hymn was, however, to present us with the mind of Christ so that we might model our manner of life after His. A mind of humility like Christ's will promote unity in Christ.

Conclusion: As long as you assert your rights, as long as you seek exaltation, as long as you are full of self, the church will have disunity and you will have incomplete joy. Just as it is only one wheel which will steer the cart wrong, it is but one person full of self which diminishes the joy we are to have in serving Christ. If there's no joy in a marriage . . . a friendship . . . in worship . . . in work . . . in ministry . . . in being with God's people . . . we need to rediscover the starting place, which is good, old-fashioned humility.

STATS, STORIES, AND MORE

An Old Puritan Quote

> ➦ In the primitive times, there was so much love among the godly as set the heathen a-wandering; and now there is so little, as may set Christians a-blushing.   —Thomas Watson[1]

A Church Conference
Someone has imagined the Carpenter's tools holding a conference. Brother Hammer presided. Several suggested he leave the meeting because he was too noisy. Replied the Hammer, "If I have to leave this shop, Brother Screw must go also. You have to turn him around again and again to get him to accomplish anything."

Brother Screw then spoke up. "If you wish, I'll leave. But Brother Plane must leave too. All his work is on the surface. His efforts have no depth."

To this Brother Plane responded, "Brother Rule will also have to withdraw, for he is always measuring folks as though he were the only one who is right."

Brother Rule then complained against Brother Sandpaper, "You ought to leave too because you're so rough and always rubbing people the wrong way."

In the midst of all this discussion, in walked the Carpenter of Nazareth. He had arrived to start His day's work. Putting on His apron, He went to the bench to make a pulpit from which to proclaim the Gospel. He employed the hammer, screw, plane, rule, sandpaper, and all the other tools. After the day's work when the pulpit was finished, Brother Saw arose and remarked, "Brethren, I observe that all of us are workers together with the Lord."[2]

APPROPRIATE HYMNS AND SONGS

"Thank You," Dennis Jernigan, 1991 Shepherd's Heart Music, Inc.

"Sing for Joy," Lamont Heibert, 1996 Integrity's Hosanna! Music.

"Joyful, Joyful We Adore Thee," Henry Van Dyke & Ludwig van Beethoven, Public Domain.

"Great Is Thy Faithfulness," Thomas Chisholm & William Runyan, 1951 Hope Publishing Company.

---

[1]Thomas Watson, *Gleanings From Thomas Watson* (Morgan, PA: Soli Deo Gloria Publications, 1995), p. 87.
[2]Leslie B. Flynn, *19 Gifts of the Spirit* (Wheaton, IL: Victor Books, 1974), p. 28.

FOR THE BULLETIN

November 23, 1596, marks the beginning of Japan's Kirishtan Holocaust when nearly 100,000 Japanese Christians were murdered (some estimates set the number at closer to a million). In A.D. 1549, when Francis Xavier, the Jesuit missionary, arrived in Japan, he met some people who had known of Christ from ancestral sources. Many of these responded with enthusiasm to become Christians, and within a year 10,000 people were following Christ. Eventually an estimated three million became part of the Kirishtan movement, and this time was dubbed "The Christian Century." But at the end of the sixteenth century, the government unleashed a persecution against the church which decimated organized Christianity. It began on November. 23, 1596, when 26 indigenous Japanese Christians were arrested in Kyoto. On the following February 5, they were crucified on a hill outside Nagasaki. The youngest was twelve years old. ● On November 23, 1654, the French mathematician, Blaise Pascal, committed his life to Christ while reading John 17. He jotted his impressions on a parchment: "From about half-past ten in the evening until about half-past twelve, FIRE! God of Abraham, God of Isaac, God of Jacob, not of the philosophers and scholars. Certitude. Feelings. Joy. Peace. This is eternal life, that they might know thee, the only true God, and the one whom Thou hast sent, Jesus Christ. Pascal sewed the paper inside his coat lining and often in moments of temptation slipped his hand over it to press its message into his heart. ● On November 23, 1873, D. L. Moody opened his evangelistic campaign in Edinburgh, Scotland. ● Hymnist and Baptist minister, Robert Lowry, died on November 23, 1899.

WORSHIP HELPS

Call to Worship
But He gives more grace. Therefore He says: "God resists the proud, But gives grace to the humble." Therefore submit to God. Resist the devil and he will flee from you. Draw near to God and He will draw near to you. Cleanse your hands, you sinners; and purify your hearts, you double-minded. Lament and mourn and weep! Let your laughter be turned to mourning and your joy to gloom. Humble yourselves in the sight of the Lord, and He will lift you up (James 4:6–10).

Continued on the next page

WORSHIP HELPS—*Continued*

Responsive Reading

Men: Likewise you younger people, submit yourselves to *your* elders. Yes, all of *you* be submissive to one another, and be clothed with humility.

Women: For "God resists the proud, but gives grace to the humble."

Men: Therefore humble yourselves under the mighty hand of God, that He may exalt you in due time, casting all your care upon Him, for He cares for you.

Women: Be sober, be vigilant; because your adversary the devil walks about like a roaring lion, seeking whom he may devour.

Men: Resist him, steadfast in the faith, knowing that the same sufferings are experienced by your brotherhood in the world.

Women: But may the God of all grace, who called us to His eternal glory by Christ Jesus, after you have suffered a while, perfect, establish, strengthen, and settle you.

Everyone: To Him be the glory and the dominion forever and ever. Amen (taken from 1 Pet. 5:5–11).

Suggested Scriptures

- Psalm 18:27; 25:9; 45:4; 147:6; 149:4
- Proverbs 3:34; 6:3; 11:2; 15:33; 18:12; 22:4
- Matthew 11:29
- Luke 22:26–27
- John 13:13–17
- 1 Peter 3:8

Additional Sermons and Lesson Ideas

The Mind of Christ
Date preached:
By Rev. Todd M. Kinde

SCRIPTURE: Philippians 2:6–9

INTRODUCTION: We can make five observations about the mind of Christ from the ancient New Testament hymn Paul quotes in these verses. He teaches us what humility means:

1. Humility Is to Submit (v. 6; cf. John 5:36–37; Heb. 5:7).
2. Humility Is to Serve (v. 7; cf. Matt. 20:26–28).
3. Humility Is to Obey (v. 8; cf. Luke 22:42; John 4:34; Heb. 5:8).
4. Humility Is to Die (v. 8; cf. Rom. 5:6–8; Eph. 5:25–26).
5. Humility Is to Wait (v .9; 1 Pet. 2:21–23).

CONCLUSION: "Humble yourselves in the sight of the Lord, and He will lift you up" (James 4:10).

Taming the Tongue
Date preached:
By Dr. Michael A. Guido

SCRIPTURE: James 3:1–14

INTRODUCTION: The old country doctor I met when I first came to Metter, Georgia, always began his examination by saying, "Let me see your tongue." That's a good way to start this sermon on Taming the Tongue:

1. The Tongue Has Power to Bid: The Bit and the Rudder (vv. 3–4).
2. The Tongue Has Power to Blight: The Fire and Animal (vv. 5–8).
3. The Tongue Has Power to Bless: The Fountain and Tree (vv. 9–12).

CONCLUSION: Won't you let the Lord Jesus control and change your speech to be glorifying to Him?

Philipp Jacob Spener and Hans Nielsen Hague

Lutheranism was born of Martin Luther's mighty zeal in the 1500s, but a century later it had sunk into cold and weary formalism. In the 1600s God raised up other giants to rekindle the flames and extend the Reformation into a new phase.

P. J. Spener, burdened for his church, opened his home for prayer and Bible reading. That simple act sparked a spiritual renewal across Germany, since called Pietism. The Pietist movement swept over Continental Europe, emphasizing inner spirituality, home meetings, mission involvement, hymn singing, and social work (particularly with orphans). Reaching into Scandinavia, Pietism touched 25-year-old Hans Nielsen Hague.

Hans had grown up in rural Norway, learning many crafts from his industrious parents. He was a skilled cabinetmaker, carpenter, blacksmith, and beekeeper. He had also known the words of Scripture and the songs of the hymnbook since infancy. On April 5, 1796, as he worked outdoors and sang the hymn, "Jesus, I Long for Thy Blessed Communion," he was abruptly caught up in a dramatic experience. His mind felt suddenly exalted and his heart overflowed with God's Spirit. The love of Christ blazed in his soul. He sensed a deep hunger for Bible study and a compelling urge to proclaim the gospel.

Hans ran home and shared his experience with his family, then with his church. He then set out to tell others, traveling for eight years and 10,000 miles throughout Norway by foot, ski, and horse. He preached to crowds large and small, emphasizing repentance, conversion, and true revival. His message sparked renewal everywhere. Occasionally local pastors, fearing his zeal and popularity, opposed him, and he was arrested ten times. But most bishops and pastors eventually thanked God for his ministry.

Having finished his preaching tour, Hans applied himself to commerce and became the owner of paper mills, a salt factory, a trading company, and a fleet of ships. He used his position in the business world to spread his message there. He passed away at age fifty-three, using his final breaths to exhort his wife, "Follow Jesus." He is today called the "Father of Scandinavian Pietism."

Regardless of our age and occupation, we can experience perpetual revival, and our constant exhortation is to follow Jesus. From age to age, from generation to generation, and from person to person, this is our timeless task.

NOVEMBER 30, 2008

FIRST SUNDAY OF ADVENT   SUGGESTED SERMON

Religion or Relationship?

Date preached:

By Dr. Timothy K. Beougher

Scripture: Mark 2:18—3:6, especially 2:27–28
And He said to them, "The Sabbath was made for man, and not man for the Sabbath. Therefore the Son of Man is also Lord of the Sabbath."

Introduction: I wonder how many people we turn off to the gospel by arguing about religious concepts rather than sharing the truth of Jesus Christ's love and mercy to save us from the wrath we deserve. I wonder how many of you got ready for church without so much as a thought of who you were coming to worship. Mark 2:18—3:6 highlights the difference between religion and a relationship in three encounters Jesus had with a group of Pharisees. There is all the difference in the world between religion and relationship.

1. **Religion Creates Confinement; Jesus Brings Celebration (vv. 18–22).** Several times in the Scriptures we see the Pharisees coming to Jesus to try and trip Him up in something He would do or say. The immediate issue was fasting. In other words, while the Pharisees were fasting, Jesus was feasting; and that was too much for them! This group of self-righteous religious leaders questioned Jesus to trap Him. Jesus answered them directly and brilliantly (2:19–20). He called attention to a wedding, to the most joyous occasion known to humanity. Jewish weddings were a festive occasion, filled with laughter and joy. Central to the celebration was the nonstop feasting. It would be unthinkable in that context to create an environment of drudgery and sorrow. Jesus reminds us that He has come not to make us miserable, but to give us abundant life. Knowing Jesus does not bring drudgery, but celebration; not sorrow, but joy! As Jesus continued His discussion with the Pharisees, He turned from this illustration to two other analogies which get to the root of the problem (vv. 21–22). The Pharisees were in effect "old wineskins." They could not handle the new life Christ offered.

2. **Religion Creates Burdens; Jesus Brings Blessings (vv. 23–28).** The Pharisees not only made regulations concerning fasting, they also

had carefully prescribed how one must act on the Sabbath. They had a list of do's and don'ts that had to be followed religiously. The fact that the disciples were "harvesting" the grain before eating it was too much for them. On any ordinary day, this was freely permitted (Deut. 23:25). However, the Pharisees had added rule upon rule about the Sabbath and expected Jesus to immediately rebuke His disciples. Jesus answered them using their own weapon. He cited the story found in 1 Samuel 21:1–6. David was fleeing for his life when he came to the tabernacle in Nob. He needed food and there was none there except the consecrated bread, or the showbread, which could only be eaten by a priest. Yet in his time of need, David took and ate that bread. Jesus showed that the Old Testament Scriptures themselves supplied precedent in which human need was a greater priority than religious ritual. He said, "The Sabbath was made for man, and not man for the Sabbath" (2:27). God created the Sabbath not to make us miserable; but to make our lives better.

3. **Religion Produces Oppression; Jesus Prizes Others (Mark 3:1–6).** Verse 2 tells us the Pharisees watched Jesus closely. The Pharisees sat in the front rows of the synagogue so they could be seen by all. Why is that important? Jesus knew they were watching Him! They were not there to worship God; but to watch Jesus and try and trip Him up. The oppressive regulations set up by the Pharisees could not accept Jesus' healing of this man's withered hand on the Sabbath. To them, healing was work, and work on the Sabbath was unacceptable, regardless of how necessary or beneficial it might be. The Pharisees had set up elaborate regulations concerning medical practices. For example, medical attention could only be given if a life was in danger. A fracture could not be attended to until the next day. A cut finger could be bandaged with a plain bandage but not with ointment. The Pharisee's tradition had become stifling. These traditions were elevated above human need, even above the Word of God. The ironic thing was that in religiously keeping that tradition, they were actually keeping themselves and others from doing what God wanted them to do. They became insensitive to human need.

Conclusion: Do we see following Christ as a burden or a blessing? Is our life attractive to others?

STATS, STORIES, AND MORE

More from Dr. Beougher
Josh McDowell is a well-known Christian apologist. A former agnostic, his two-volume apologetic work *Evidence that Demands a Verdict* has sold hundreds of thousands of copies. In an appendix in Volume 1, Josh McDowell shares his testimony of his pilgrimage from agnosticism to Christianity. While he was a university student, he went and sat down at a table in the student union with six other students and two faculty members. Josh had noticed this group that met regularly at this table, and he was intrigued by something he saw in their lives. He sat down and began visiting with the female student next to him, "Tell me, what changed your lives? Why are your lives so different from the other students and professors? Why?" Josh said that woman looked him right in the eye and said two words he never thought he would hear as part of the solution to *any* problem, especially at a university. She said, "Jesus Christ." McDowell said he responded, "Don't give me that garbage. I'm fed up with religion; I'm fed up with the church; I'm fed up with the Bible. Don't give me that garbage about religion."

She shot back at him, "Mister, I didn't say religion, I said Jesus Christ." McDowell summarized the remainder of their discussion that day: "She pointed out something I'd never known before, Christianity is not a religion. Religion is humans trying to work their way to God through good works. Christianity is God coming to men and women through Jesus Christ, offering them a relationship with Himself."[1]

APPROPRIATE HYMNS AND SONGS

"O Come, O Come Emmanuel," Thomas Helmore & Henry Sloane Coffin, Public Domain.

"Come, Thou Long-Expected Jesus," Charles Wesley & Rowland Hugh Prichard, Public Domain.

"All I Once Held Dear," Graham Kendrick, 1993 Make Way Music.

"Breathe on Me, Breath of God," George Croly & Frederick Atkinson, Public Domain.

---

[1] Josh McDowell, *Evidence That Demands a Verdict* (Campus Crusade for Christ, 1972), p. 373.

FOR THE BULLETIN

On November 30, 30 B.C., Cleopatra, queen of Egypt, committed suicide. ● On November 30, 722, Boniface was consecrated bishop. He was the English "Apostle to the Germans." ● On November 30, 1215, the Fourth Lateran Council convened for the final time. This was the council that first defined the term "Transubstantiation" with reference to the Lord's Supper. ● Following the death of Protestant King Edward VII, his half-sister, Mary Tudor, rose to the throne. On this day in 1554, she restored Roman Catholicism to England. Hundreds of Protestants perished, as chronicled in John Foxe's *Book of Martyrs.* ● John Bunyan was baptized on November 30, 1628. ● The hymn "Jesus Calls Us O'er the Tumult" is sung for the first time on this day in 1852. ● John Clough sailed from Boston as a rookie missionary to India on November 30, 1842. He and his wife were placed on a discouraging station called "Forlorn Hope," in the area of Telugu, but as John faithfully preached the gospel, conversions multiplied. Fifteen months later two Indian preachers stood in a river and began baptizing the converts. When they grew weary, other preachers relieved them. By five o'clock 2,222 had been baptized, and the baptisms continued for two more days. ● James Gilmore, a lonely, single missionary in China, asked God to give him a wife, "and a good one, too." Seeing a picture of an attractive young lady back in England, he immediately wrote to her, proposing. Though Miss Emily Prankard had never heard of Gilmore, upon receiving his letter she felt a leading to accept. In time, she sailed for China, and on November 30, 1874, the two met for the first time. They were married and had a very successful lifetime of marriage and ministry together.

WORSHIP HELPS

Call to Worship

But we see Jesus, who was made a little lower than the angels, for the suffering of death crowned with glory and honor, that He, by the grace of God, might taste death for everyone (Heb. 2:9).

Benediction

Lord, send us out today as Your children, as those who care more about loving and serving You than exalting ourselves. May You keep us from filling our lives with religious ritual rather than a relationship with Jesus Christ. Bless us in Jesus' name, Amen.

Kid's Talk

Among your church's Christmas decorations, consider setting up a table with a nativity set. Beginning with the first Sunday of Advent, place Joseph and Mary some distance away from the manger scene. Place the wise men far away as well. Each Sunday of Advent, have a Kid's Talk and read, little by little, the Christmas story from Scripture. As the weeks progress, move the characters closer to the manger, explaining the long trip Mary and Joseph took as did the wise men to see Jesus. The final Sunday of Advent or your Christmas Eve service, place the nativity scene as it normally is seen and emphasize that God worked everything together perfectly so that Christ would be born according to His plan.

Additional Sermons and Lesson Ideas

The Power of Significant Relationships
By Dr. Larry Osborne

Date preached:

SCRIPTURE: Various

INTRODUCTION: If we want to survive and thrive spiritually, accountability is one of the most important and powerful tools we have available. Unfortunately, it's also one of the most misunderstood and neglected spiritual tools. Today we want to look at how these relationships provide four powerful advantages that "lone rangers" will never have.

1. Positive Peer Pressure (Prov. 13:20; 27:17; Heb. 10:24–25).
2. Help in Times of Trouble (Eccl. 4:9–12; Gal. 6:2; 1 Cor. 10:13; 2 Cor. 7:5–7).
3. Motivation to Tell the Truth and Hear the Truth (Prov. 28:23; Eccl. 4:13; Eph. 4:15, 25).
4. Help in Resisting Sin (1 Cor. 5:9–13; Gal. 2:11–14; 2 Thess. 3:14–15).

CONCLUSION: Where and who in your life provides accountability?

Jacob's Journey
By Dr. Melvin Worthington

Date preached:

SCRIPTURE: Genesis 25—50

INTRODUCTION: A significant portion of Scripture is devoted to the life of Jacob. He's the father of the sons which constitute the Twelve Tribes of the nation of Israel. His life is a mix of faith and failure.

1. The Birth of Jacob (Gen. 25; 32:28; 35:10). His *names* are recorded (Gen. 25; 32:28; 35:10). His *nature* is also recorded. He was a plain man, an upright man, steady and domestic, affectionate, his mother's favorite, dwelling in tents, staying at home, minding the flocks, and household duties. He was a plain, passionate, and preferred man.
2. The Brother of Jacob (Gen. 25). Esau means rough. He was a wanderer, wandering abroad in keen quest of game, a man of the field, wild, restless, self-indulgent, and seldom home in the tent. He was a hunter, a heartless and haughty man.
3. The Birthright of Jacob (Gen. 25). He sought it (Gen. 25), he schemed for it (Gen. 27), he stole it (Gen. 27), and he secured it (Gen. 27).

CONCLUSION: We can learn from Jacob not to do the right thing the wrong way.

DECEMBER 7, 2008

The Brutal Facts of Life

Date preached:

By Dr. Kevin Riggs

Scripture: Mark 6:14–29, especially verse 20
Herod feared John, knowing that he was a just and holy man, and he protected him. And when he heard him, he did many things, and heard him gladly.

Introduction: Do you remember when you first realized life was not going to be easy? I can remember going to my great-grandfather's funeral when I was six years old. Do you remember when you realized the awful truths of life? What was the occasion? How did you respond? How does it affect you now?

Context: Mark stops the flow of his Gospel to insert the cruel beheading of John the Baptist. He hints at this story in Mark 1:14. But his Gospel concentrates on the ministry, travels, and works of Jesus. Why does Mark include this sad story? One reason is to tie John the Baptist with the Old Testament prophet, Elijah. A second reason is because of its connection to the coming death of Jesus. A third reason is to encourage Mark's readers. They were being persecuted and fed to the lions by Emperor Nero. Being reminded of this event would bring them strength and encouragement. We, too, can learn a lot about the brutal facts of life through this story.

1. **Life Is Not Fair.** For some reason we have been taught that if you play by the rules and do what is right, then everything will work out. The brutal fact is that many times doing the right thing gets you in more trouble than doing the wrong thing. Simply put: *Life is not fair, deal with it.* Herodias hated John the Baptist and wanted to kill him (v. 19). "Then an opportune day came . . ." (6:21). Herodias has been planning, scheming, and waiting. She wanted her marriage certificate to be written on the back of his death warrant. Herodias set it up so that her own daughter, Salome, performed a seductive dance before her father-in-law (6:22a). Aroused and drunk, the king said, "Ask me whatever you want, and I will give it to you . . ." (6:22). Salome immediately went back to her mother

and inquired what she should ask for. The answer her mother gave to tell Herod was John the Baptist's head on a platter (vv. 24–25).

2. **There Is Real Evil in the World.** If you would have asked me six years ago if I thought beheadings still occurred in today's world, I would have said "No." But oh, how things have changed! Since 9/11 and the war on terror, beheadings have been a regular report on the nightly news. Evil is real because Satan is real. The sooner you realize this, the better off you will be. Simply put: *Evil is real, protect yourself.* Once Herod heard Salome's request he sobered up and was "exceedingly sorry" (6:26). He did not want to fulfill his vow, but he had to. He had given his word. He gave the order and John the Baptist's head was brought to him on a platter (6:26–28).

3. **Good People Can Be Easily Persuaded to Go Along with Evil.** I don't mean Herod was good, and I am not implying the daughter was good. In this situation, however, Herod did not want to execute John. He liked John, but he gave into the pressure instead of using his influence to thwart the evil plan. It's easier to persuade people to do wrong than it is to do right. The Bible warns, "The heart is deceitful above all things and beyond cure. Who can understand it?" (Jer. 17:9 NIV). Simply put: *You are not above doing evil, so keep yourself pure.*

Conclusion: One of the reasons Mark included this story was because of its connection with the death of Jesus! John the Baptist was the forerunner of Jesus the Messiah; and in the same way John suffered and died, so Jesus must suffer and die. In other words, John's death is a prequel to Jesus' death. Thus, if John's death shows us the reality of evil, Jesus' death and resurrection show us that the victory over evil has been won. John was overcome by evil. Jesus overcame evil, and so can you and I.

STATS, STORIES, AND MORE

Life Isn't Fair
John F. Kennedy once summed up his philosophy about life and about political office in one brilliant phrase: "Life isn't fair, but the government should be."

Other "Life Isn't Fair" Quotes

> *Life isn't fair; it's just fairer than death, that's all.*
> —William Goldman in *The Princess Bride*

> *Life isn't fair. Get used to it.*
> —Bill Gates to high school students at Mt. Whitney High School in Visalia, California

> *Life isn't fair, but it evens out.* —Philosophy of an optimist

> *I know life isn't fair, but why couldn't it just once be unfair in my favor?"* —Christy Murphy

> *Life isn't fair, but it shouldn't cheat this much!*

> *Life isn't fair, but God is good.* —Philip Yancey

Peer Pressure
Becoming a Christian often means exchanging friends. It's not that we don't love our old friends and want to win them to the Lord. We just have to be careful about falling back into unhealthy patterns of peer pressure, and that can lead to some momentary loneliness. That's when we rediscover the sweetness of God's presence. Arthur Flake, who inspired the Southern Baptist denomination to emphasize Sunday school work, shared this testimony in his book, *Life at Eighty as I See It:* "When I first became a Christian, I lived in New York City; and did I feel lonely! I had to give up the crowd I was running with and form new friendships. I was advised by the man who led me to Christ to read the Bible. After business hours I would go to my room and read my Bible often for hours at a time; and though I did not understand all I read, and still do not, I did understand much that I read, and it made me feel that I was not alone but that I had a dear Friend who cared for me. Today I read the same identical verses and chapters I read then. Although I have read many of them literally hundreds of times, they are, I believe, sweeter today than they were then. What other book can one read with such results?[1]

---

[1] Arthur Flake, *Life at Eighty as I See It* (Nashville: Broadman Press, 1944), p. 97.

APPROPRIATE HYMNS AND SONGS

"Of the Father's Love Begotten" Prudentius, Public Domain.

"O Come All Ye Faithful," John F. Wade & Frederick Oakeley, Public Domain.

"Signs of Life," Steven Curtis Chapman, 1996 Sparrow Song; Peach Hill Song.

"The First Noel," English Carol, Public Domain.

FOR THE BULLETIN

The prophet Zechariah received a vision from God on this day in 518 B.C., as recorded in Zechariah 7:1. ● On December 7, 43 B.C., the Roman orator Marcus Tullius Cicero was executed. ● December 7, 374, St. Ambrose, 34, was ordained and consecrated as Bishop of Milan. He had never considered the ministry. As governor in Milan, he was seeking to guide the city toward a replacement for its deceased bishop. When the populace couldn't agree on a suitable candidate, a child's voice was heard, "Let Ambrose be bishop!" The crowd took up the cry, and Ambrose was drafted against his will. He gave himself to his task, however, with all his heart and became a powerful church leader, and was largely responsible for Augustine's conversion. ● The great Irish missionary hero, Columba, was born on December 7, 521. With 12 companions, he established himself on Iona, a bleak, foggy island just off the Scottish coast. He built a crude monastery that soon became a training center for missionaries, one of the most venerable and interesting spots in the history of Christian missions. From Iona, Columba made missionary forays into Scotland, converting large numbers. An entire tribe of pagans, the Picts, were won to the faith. ● December 7, 1807, marks the death of William Carey's deranged wife, Dorothy. ● On December 7, 1941, Japanese planes attacked the American naval forces at Pearl Harbor, Hawaii. Missionary activity around the world was disrupted, and missionaries in China were particularly endangered, especially the children at the MK boarding school in Chefoo.

WORSHIP HELPS

Call to Worship

> O come, all ye faithful, joyful and triumphant,
> Come and behold Him, born the King of angels;
> O come, let us adore Him,
> Christ the Lord
> > —from *O Come, All Ye Faithful,*
> > JOHN F. WADE, 1743

Advent Scripture Reading

Now [John the Baptist's] father Zacharias was filled with the Holy Spirit, and prophesied, saying: "Blessed is the Lord God of Israel, for He has visited and redeemed His people, and has raised up a horn of salvation for us in the house of His servant David, as He spoke by the mouth of His holy prophets, who have been since the world began, that we should be saved from our enemies and from the hand of all who hate us, to perform the mercy promised to our fathers and to remember His holy covenant, the oath which He swore to our father Abraham: to grant us that we, being delivered from the hand of our enemies, might serve Him without fear, in holiness and righteousness before Him all the days of our life. And you, child, will be called the prophet of the Highest; for you will go before the face of the Lord to prepare His ways, to give knowledge of salvation to His people by the remission of their sins, through the tender mercy of our God, with which the Dayspring from on high has visited us; to give light to those who sit in darkness and the shadow of death, to guide our feet into the way of peace." So the child grew and became strong in spirit, and was in the deserts till the day of his manifestation to Israel (Luke 1:67–80).

Benediction

The LORD will save me, and we will sing . . . all the days of our lives in the temple of the LORD (Is. 38:20 NIV).

Additional Sermons and Lesson Ideas

The Glorious King

Date preached:

By Rev. Melvin Tinker

SCRIPTURE: Psalm 45

INTRODUCTION: Today, we're looking at a song specially composed for a royal wedding, a wedding which will be seen not by an audience of several million, but by an entire universe. This is a royal marriage in which the promises made will be delivered with absolute certainty. It is the marriage between the King of creation and His people, or to put it in New Testament terms between Jesus and His Bride, the Church.

1. The Stature of the King (vv. 2–5).
2. The Supremacy of the King (vv. 6–9).
3. The Bride of the King (vv. 10–17).
   A. A Break with the Past (v. 10).
   B. A Submission in the Present (v. 11).
   C. A Focus on the Future (vv. 12–17).

CONCLUSION: So let me end by asking: have you accepted the invitation to the wedding? This is the King who invites you, who bled for you, who died for you and who is now enthroned in such dazzling splendor that even the angels have to hide their faces, but which He wants to share with you.

How to Tell God You Love Him

Date preached:

By Dr. Al Detter

SCRIPTURE: Various

INTRODUCTION: God created us to love Him. If we learn to do this well, we fulfill the greatest commandment (Matt. 22:37). Let's look at some practical ways to do this:

1. Spend Time with God:
   A. In Scripture (John 17:17).
   B. In Prayer (John 10:27).
   C. In Song (Ps. 66:8; 95:1; 147:7).
2. Obey God (John 14:15, 21).
3. Love Other Believers (1 John 3:10, 23; 4:20).
4. Don't Make God Jealous (Ex. 20:5; 34:14; Ps. 86:11; Matt. 10:37).

CONCLUSION: There are dozens more ways to tell God we love Him, but these are prominent ones that can truly express our love to Him.

Ten Commandments for Ministry Survival

By Dr. Kevin Riggs

1. **Thou shalt not let others steal thy joy.** Joy is a fruit of the Spirit and is determined by my relationship with Jesus Christ. Allowing others to steal my joy amounts to saying joy comes from people instead of God.

2. **Thou shalt not gripe and complain when people act like people.** Jesus saw people as sheep scattered without a shepherd. What shepherd would scorn his sheep for acting like sheep? When people whine and grumble they are acting like people— doing what comes naturally. The purpose of ministry is to enable people to do what comes supernaturally. If people acted like Jesus wanted them to act I would be out of a job. (NOTE: I am a "people" and I hope others will forgive me when I act like one.)

3. **Thou shalt keep a positive attitude in all things.** My attitude determines my altitude. I cannot control what happens to me, but I can control how I respond. Remaining positive does not mean I ignore reality. It does mean I know God is in control, the church is His church, and He will make sure everything works to the good of those who love Him.

4. **Thou shalt work with the willing while praying for the obstinate.** Most people follow without complaining. Obstinate people are in the minority but if permitted can take the majority of my time. If a captain waits for everyone to get on board the ship, the ship will never leave dock.

5. **Thou shalt not take personal criticisms personally.** Honest criticism is not personal and is extremely helpful. Destructive criticism has a personal tone. Taking personal criticisms personally does nothing to help me, nor the person giving the criticism. By not taking it personal I will be able to see more objectively and not allow the seeds of bitterness to grow in my life.

6. Thou shalt place personal integrity above professional success. My integrity is all I have and if I lose it I have lost everything. At times it is tempting to do things, or not do things, based on how I think it looks to others. It is tempting to compare my ministry with others' ministries, feeling jealousy or pride based on perceived "success."

7. Thou shalt stay focused on Christ. This one thing will keep me from violating #6. It is Christ I am serving and it is to Him I will give an account. Nothing else matters but His opinion of me.

8. Thou shalt not allow discouragement to distract thyself from duty. Discouragement is the job-hazard of ministry. There will be days when I do not feel like getting out of bed. There will be times when I do not feel like continuing. It is important that during those times I work even harder, not allowing my momentary weakness to dictate my pastoral duties.

9. Thou shalt not bring ministry problems home. My wife and family are my most important ministry. The home is to be a safe-place, a place to relax, and a place to rejuvenate for the next day. Home is not the place to discuss the difficulties and struggles of ministry. God called me into ministry, not my wife and kids.

10. Thou shalt remember thy self-worth is in thy walk with Christ not in thy work for Christ. Jesus cared for me as a person before He cared for me as a pastor. I am a success, not because of my achievements but because of His accomplishment. If my walk with Him is what it should be, I am a success even when I feel like a failure.

DECEMBER 14, 2008

THIRD SUNDAY OF ADVENT   SUGGESTED SERMON

The Eternal Son

Date preached:

By Dr. Robert M. Norris

Scripture: Hebrews 7:27—8:5, especially 7:28
For the law appoints as high priests men who have weakness, but the word of the oath, which came after the law, appoints the Son who has been perfected forever.

Introduction: At Christmastime, we focus on the miracle of the Incarnation: Jesus became flesh and dwelt among us! However, I'm afraid we often think of Him in the past tense: "Jesus *was* a man," or "Jesus *was* God's Son." The writer of Hebrews reminds us of the eternality of Jesus; the Christmas story was not over when Jesus ascended into heaven! Jesus is eternally the Son of God, which has many implications for us today.

1. **Jesus Is Sinless (v. 26).** "For such a High Priest was fitting for us, who is holy, harmless, undefiled, separate from sinners, and has become higher than the heavens." No other High Priest could claim perfection, for the High Priest offered sacrifices for themselves (v. 27), but Jesus needed no sacrifice.

2. **Jesus Offered a Perfect Sacrifice (v. 27).** "Who does not need daily, as those high priests, to offer up sacrifices, first for His own sins and then for the people's, for this He did once for all when He offered up Himself." Because Jesus needed no sacrifice, He was able to offer Himself *as* the sacrifice to end all sacrifices!

3. **Jesus' Sacrifice Was Once-for-All (v. 27b).** ". . . This He did once for all when He offered up Himself." All of God's work in history pointed to the sacrifice of Christ. Since His death and resurrection, everything looks back to the sacrifice of Christ for its foundation. Christ is the center of the history of grace. There is no grace without Him. Grace was planned from all eternity with Jesus Christ at the center and His death as the foundation.

4. **Jesus Has Been Appointed as a Perfect Son (v. 28).** The oath he's referring to is, "The LORD has sworn and will not relent, 'You are a

priest forever according to the order of Melchizedek'" (Ps. 110:4). So the final High Priest is the Messiah, the Son of God, in the order of Melchizedek, not Levi or Aaron, and is installed by an oath, not by the Law, which is passing away.

5. **Jesus' Ministry Is Forever (v. 28b).** ". . . The Son who has been perfected forever." Think about how uncertain our lives are. But Jesus never dies; He never has to be replaced by a new priest. He serves now and forever as our High Priest if we believe!

6. **Jesus Is Seated at the Right Hand of God (8:1).** ". . . We have such a High Priest, who is seated at the right hand of the throne of the Majesty in the heavens . . ." No Old Testament priest could ever say this. Jesus deals directly with God the Father. He has a place of honor beside God. He is loved and respected infinitely by God.

7. **Jesus Is Ministering in Heaven (8:2).** "A Minister of the sanctuary and of the true tabernacle which the Lord erected, and not man." This is what cast on Mount Sinai a shadow that Moses copied. We are shown that the one final and ultimate reality is God and His Son interacting in love and holiness for our eternal salvation.

Applications: These words, which were intended to bring some direct implications to the life of the first-century church, also bring to each one of us challenges to our own lives.

1. **Jesus Has Changed the Way We Look at the Future.** Humans have been made for hope. Death always appears as an enemy. The prospect of life that ends is alien to us because we were designed for eternity. Hope is, therefore, a part of our makeup. But the Christian alone has reason to believe in a blissful future. The reason is Jesus Christ.

2. **Jesus Has Changed the Way We Worship.** The shadow gave way to the reality! Jesus is the great High Priest, fulfilling the tabernacle, temple, priesthood, sacrifices, dietary laws, and seasonal acts of atonement and reconciliation. The worship life of God's people has now been refocused onto Jesus Himself!

3. **Jesus Has Changed the Way We Witness.** The message of the Scripture is designed to be proclaimed to the world. It is meant to be taken to every people, tribe, nation, and culture. That's why we as a church are committed to taking the gospel to every nation.

STATS, STORIES, AND MORE

More from Dr. Norris

At our home, we have on our downstairs walls silhouette drawings of each of our children. They are like shadows of our children; and as much fun as they are, and as much as they capture the reality of the outline of our children, they are only pictures of the reality they represent. So it is with the rituals and institutions of Israel. They were only shadows, and the author of Hebrews wants his hearers to understand that the shadows only point to a reality.

A History of Hope

These first Christians were in danger of losing sight of their hope, because their attention, like ours became fixed upon the temporal. When this happens we lose the strength, peace, and confidence that flow from the authentic Christian hope. Julian the Apostate, the nephew of Constantine, had been raised with both pagan and Christian teachers, but had chosen paganism for his faith. When he became emperor, he set out to win the empire back to paganism, and he sought to undo what his uncle had done in making Christianity the religion of the empire. But Julian was a thoughtful man, who asked himself why Christianity succeeded in winning the minds and hearts of people. He concluded that the reason Christians had, in a mere 300 years, succeeded in triumphing to become the religion of the empire that had persecuted them, was threefold:

1. The courage of the Christians in the face of persecution
2. The generosity of the Christians to the poor
3. The treatment of Christians for their dead.

The reason they were willing to face death rather than disown the Lord is that they were absolutely sure that because of Jesus Christ, death was for them nothing more than "one, short, dark passage to eternal light." Anyone can face death who knows that but moments later he will be in paradise. The reason they treated the poor so generously was that, because of their certainty of the amazing wonder of the world to come, they didn't have to hoard their property in this world and were free to be generous with it. The reason they treated their dead so lovingly and buried them in ways that so powerfully suggested their expectation that they would see their loved ones again, was precisely because of this strong Christian hope. In their burial customs, the Christians beautifully embodied a confidence in a happy future that the pagans did not have. Their hope directly affected the way in which they lived.

APPROPRIATE HYMNS AND SONGS

"Away in a Manger," James Murray & John Thomas McFarland, Public Domain.

"Infant Holy, Infant Lowly," Anonymous—Polish Caro, Public Domain.

"Joy to the World," Isaac Watts & George Frederic Handel, Public Domain.

"Thou Didst Leave Thy Throne," Emily Elliott & Timothy Matthews, Public Domain.

FOR THE BULLETIN

December 14, 872, marks the death of the Italian pope, Adrian II, the last married pope, who died at about age 80. ● On December 14, 1417, Sir John Oldcastle, one of John Wycliffe's strongest supporters and a Lollard leader, was captured, suspended over a slow fire by chains, and roasted to death for his faith in Christ. ● December 14, 1836, is the birthday of hymn writer Frances Ridley Havergal, born in the rectory at Astley, Worcestershire, England. Her father, Rev. William Havergal, was an Anglican clergyman who devoted himself to improving the church music in England, and who himself wrote over 100 hymns. Frances struggled throughout her twenties and thirties, pulled in one direction by the acclaim of great London crowds who loved her singing, and in another direction by the Holy Spirit. Then one day at age 36 she read a booklet entitled "All For Jesus," which stressed the importance of making Christ King of every corner and cubicle of one's life. Frances made a fresh, complete consecration to God. Today she is best known as the author of such hymns as "Like a River Glorious," "Take My Life and Let It Be," and "Another Year is Dawning." ● On December 14, 1853, through the efforts of zealous Wesleyans, the Illinois Institute opened its doors for the first time. Seven years later, amid financial struggles, the trustees requested help from the wealthier Congregationalists. Jonathan Blanchard, Presbyterian pastor and academic, was appointed president. He approached Warren Wheaton for a large donation of property and offered to name the school Wheaton College. "That will at least save your heirs the expense of a good monument," Blanchard said. Wheaton College has been training students ever since "For Christ and His Kingdom."

WORSHIP HELPS

Call to Worship

I waited patiently for the LORD; and He inclined to me, and heard my cry. He also brought me up out of a horrible pit, out of the miry clay, and set my feet upon a rock, and established my steps. He has put a new song in my mouth—praise to our God; many will see it and fear, and will trust in the LORD (Ps. 40:1–3).

Advent Scripture Reading

And behold, there was a man in Jerusalem whose name was Simeon, and this man was just and devout, waiting for the Consolation of Israel, and the Holy Spirit was upon him. And it had been revealed to him by the Holy Spirit that he would not see death before he had seen the Lord's Christ. So he came by the Spirit into the temple. And when the parents brought in the Child Jesus, to do for Him according to the custom of the law, he took Him up in his arms and blessed God and said: "Lord, now You are letting Your servant depart in peace, according to Your word; for my eyes have seen Your salvation which You have prepared before the face of all peoples, a light to bring revelation to the Gentiles, and the glory of Your people Israel." And Joseph and His mother marveled at those things which were spoken of Him. Then Simeon blessed them, and said to Mary His mother, "Behold, this Child is destined for the fall and rising of many in Israel, and for a sign which will be spoken against (yes, a sword will pierce through your own soul also), that the thoughts of many hearts may be revealed" (Luke 2:25–35).

Benediction

Serve the LORD with fear, and rejoice with trembling. Kiss the Son, lest He be angry, and you perish in the way, when His wrath is kindled but a little. Blessed are all those who put their trust in Him (Ps. 2:11–12).

Additional Sermons and Lesson Ideas

The Consolation of Israel
Date preached:
By Joshua D. Rowe

SCRIPTURE: Luke 2:25–35

INTRODUCTION: Have you ever hoped for something so intensely that it deeply affects you? You can hardly think of anything else, and nothing can console you except the fulfillment of your hope! That's the way Simeon hoped for Jesus Christ, the Consolation of Israel. We can learn a lot from this often-overlooked portion of the Christmas narrative.

1. God Keeps His Promises (vv. 25–29). The Holy Spirit revealed that Simeon, before he died, would see the Christ (v. 26). Joseph and Mary brought Jesus to him in the temple (v. 27). Simeon acknowledged that God was true to His word (v. 29).
2. Jesus Is Salvation (v. 30). When Simeon took Christ into his arms, he said, ". . . my eyes have seen Your salvation." Our salvation is not simply *because* of Jesus, our salvation *is* Jesus!
3. Salvation Is Offered to All (vv. 31–32). Simeon points out that Jesus was ". . . prepared before the face of all people . . ." (v. 31). In other words, salvation was no longer an invisible hope; it was now a Person! Simeon continues to describe Christ as, "A light to bring revelation to the Gentiles, and the glory of Your people Israel."

CONCLUSION: Won't you put your trust in Christ today as your consolation, as your salvation?

The Disciple's Diet
Date preached:
By Dr. Melvin Worthington

SCRIPTURE: Various

INTRODUCTION: God demands that we search, study, show, and share the Scriptures. In light of the nature of the Bible, Christians would do well to become students of this blessed book.

1. The Sharpness of the Scripture (Heb. 4:12). The Scripture discerns, divides, discloses, and directs.
2. The Standard of the Scripture (Ps. 119:9, 25, 28, 41, 58, 65, 91, 107, 116, 154, 169; Rom. 2). The Scripture defines the source, scope, and subjects of redemption, retribution, and remuneration.
3. The Search of the Scripture (Acts 17:10–15).
4. The Study of the Scripture (2 Tim. 2:15; Heb. 5).
5. The Showing of the Scripture (Phil. 1:27; 1 Thess. 1).
6. The Sharing of the Scripture (Matt. 28; Acts 1:8; 2 Cor. 5).

CONCLUSION: The disclosed, desired, and daily diet of the Christian is the sincere Word of God (1 Pet. 2:2). Christians should read, reflect, record, receive, respond, remember, retain, review, and reproduce the Word of God in their lives.

DECEMBER 21, 2008

A Stocking Full of Love

Date preached:

Scripture: 1 John 3—4, especially 3:1
Behold what manner of love the Father has bestowed on us that we should be called
children of God!

Introduction: Many of our Christmas traditions are rooted in church history, and if we know their origins we'll appreciate them more. The hanging of stockings by the fireplace is just about the first and oldest of our traditions. For most of human history, most people didn't have extensive wardrobes. Socks in particular had to be washed out at night and hung by the fire to dry for the next day. Centuries ago, a teenager named Nicholas from the city of Patara on the Mediterranean coast in ancient Turkey entered the ministry. He became a popular and beloved bishop in the city of Myra. In one of his ministry trips, Pastor Nicholas was in a particular city. While there he heard of a widower trying to raise three daughters. They were on the verge of starvation, and this man was unable to provide a dowry for his girls. As a result they were unable to get married. Even worse, they were in danger of being sold into slavery. Burdened for this family, Nicholas went to the home by night. The eldest daughter's stockings were hanging by the fireplace, and Nicholas reached through the window and tossed a coin into the stocking. He reportedly later did the same for the other girls. Thus it became a tradition on St. Nicholas' Day for children to hang their stockings by the fireplace where, during the night, a treat would be place in them. The Christmas stocking is appropriate to Christmas because it symbolizes the truth of the gospel. Like that poor family, we're grief-stricken, and impoverished in heart, enslaved by sin, and unable to save ourselves. But on Christmas Day, God put something into our stockings, so to speak. What He put there was better than gold—the feet of His own dear Son, feet that were to be nail-pierced for our sin. *How great is the love the Father has lavished on us, that we should be called children of God! And that is what we are!* (1 John 3:1 NIV).

1. **Look at God's Love (1 John 3:1)!** The first word of John 3:1 is a Greek term meaning, *Look at this, become aware of this, consider this.* The

older translations use the word *behold*, but that's not a term we use anymore. The real emphasis is—*hey, look at this, pay attention!* The Lord wants us to stop what we're doing and look at something He wants to show us. He wants us to pay attention. He wants us to see what kind of love the Father has given to us, that we should be called the children of God.

2. **When You Look at God's Love You Look at Jesus (1 John 3:16).** There are two "John 3:16s" in the Bible. In 1 John 3:16, we read: "By this we know love, because He laid down His life for us." In other words, if you could only draw one picture for the world to depict the concept of love, it wouldn't be a wedding ring, a sensual embrace, a romantic candle, or a sacrificial act of kindness. It would be the Cross of the Lord Jesus Christ.

3. **When You Look at Jesus You Lose Your Fears (1 John 4:7–19).** We can rely on His love at the crucial junctions of life. We can rely on His love when our strength fails, when our friends die, when our hearts break, when our minds reel, when our hopes are dashed, when our health is gone. We can rely on His love, and His love is embodied in Jesus Christ. So this verse says, in effect, whatever you're facing right now, rely on Jesus! We don't need to be afraid of anything in this life, because we can rest in the fact that come-what-may, God loves us and His perfect love casts out fear.

Conclusion: Perhaps today you feel lonely and you're fighting off the Christmas blues. Well, God loves you, and you can rely on His love. His love casts out fear. Behold what manner of love the Father has bestowed on us that we should be called the children of God. And that is what we are. Because the heavenly Father put the feet of Jesus Christ into your Christmas stocking 2,000 years ago in Bethlehem, you have a stocking full of love.

> *He left His Father's throne above so free, so infinite His grace—*
> *Emptied Himself of all but love, and bled for Adam's helpless race:*
> *'Tis mercy all, immense and free, for O my God, it found out me!*

STATS, STORIES, AND MORE

In a letter to an advice columnist in a Scottish newspaper, a reader wrote this story: "My boyfriend put heavy pressure on me to have an abortion. He said it wasn't the right time for us to have a baby. I agreed, but we split up soon afterwards. I thought I was over both him and the abortion and then I saw him pushing a pram (baby stroller). It turns out he had been seeing someone else while he was with me, who must have become pregnant around the same time as I did. I hate him and I hate myself for having the abortion. If I'd kept the baby I would have someone to love me."[1] She regrets having her abortion, but why? Because if she had kept the baby at least she might have one person in this world who loved her. Do you ever feel like that? All over the world, people are lonely. Several years ago when I was visiting my mother, an elderly widow living alone in her house in the mountains, I noticed that an old cat had showed up on the back doorstep. It was a wild cat, and to my surprise she was putting food out for it. Now, my mother was never much for having a pet. But I noticed that when she sat down on the back porch, the old cat came up and rubbed against her leg and she reached down and petted it. She looked up at me and simply said, "Every living thing in this world needs to be loved."

I've never forgotten that. We need all kinds of love connections in our lives. Babies need love. Children need love. Teenagers need love. Adults need love. The elderly need love. And even those creatures down at the animal shelter need someone to love them.

Now You Know the Rest of the Story

> *T'was the night before Christmas, when all through the house*
> *Not a creature was stirring—not even a mouse;*
> *The stockings were hung by the chimney with care,*
> *In hopes that St. Nicholas soon would be there.*

APPROPRIATE HYMNS AND SONGS

"O Little Town of Bethlehem," Phillips Brooks & Lewis Redner, Public Domain.

"O Holy Night," John Dwight & Adolphe Adam, Public Domain.

"Good Christian Men Rejoice," Latin Carol, 14th Century, Public Domain.

"Angels We Have Heard on High," French Carol, Public Domain.

---

[1] The Daily Record of Scotland, December 19, 2006.

FOR THE BULLETIN

December 21st marks the traditional death of the apostle Thomas in India. He was reportedly killed "in the 30th year of the promulgation of the gospel," by Brahmins who were seeking to end his evangelistic activities. Learning he was in a cave, they went to the mountainside, saw him through the narrow opening, on his knees with his eyes closed, in a rapture so profound he appeared to be dead. They thrust a lance through the opening, wounding him mortally. ● Thomas Becket, Archbishop of Canterbury, was born on this day in 1118. ● Hernando Cortes and the conquistadors slaughtered and enslaved thousands of the Aztecs and Incas. On December 21, 1511, at the risk of his own life, Pastor Antonio des Montesinos stood before his church in Hispaniola and thundered against the conquistadors: *I have climbed to this pulpit to let you know of your sins, for I am the voice of Christ crying in the desert of this island, and you must not listen to me indifferently. You are in mortal sin; you not only are in it, but live in it and die in it because of the cruelty and tyranny you bring to bear on these innocent people.* ● On December 21, 1620, the 103 Pilgrims aboard the Mayflower landed at Plymouth Rock. ● December 21, 1795, is the birthday of Robert Moffatt, Scottish pioneer missionary and Bible translator to South Africa. ● Pastor and hymnist, John Newton, died on December 21, 1807. One of his famous hymns had this stanza: *But to those who have confessèd, / Loved and served the Lord below, / He will say, "Come near, ye blessèd, / See the kingdom I bestow.*

PRAYER FOR THE PASTOR'S CLOSET

Bind me to Thyself as Thou bindest the planets to the sun, that it may become the very law of my nature to be lead by Thee. May I be content to know that goodness and mercy shall follow me without waiting to see them in advance of me. Amen. —GEORGE MATHESON

WORSHIP HELPS

Call to Worship

That which was from the beginning, which we have heard, which we have seen with our eyes, which we have looked at and our hands have touched—this we proclaim concerning the Word of life. The life appeared (1 John 1:1–2a NIV)!

Advent Scripture Reading

And Mary said: "My soul magnifies the Lord, and my spirit has rejoiced in God my Savior. For He has regarded the lowly state of His maidservant; for behold, henceforth all generations will call me blessed. For He who is mighty has done great things for me, and holy is His name. And His mercy is on those who fear Him from generation to generation. He has shown strength with His arm; He has scattered the proud in the imagination of their hearts. He has put down the mighty from their thrones, and exalted the lowly. He has filled the hungry with good things, and the rich He has sent away empty. He has helped His servant Israel, in remembrance of His mercy, as He spoke to our fathers, to Abraham and to his seed forever" (Luke 1:46–55).

Kid's Talk

The highlight of any Christmas Sunday or Christmas Eve service is reading the Christmas story to the children. We always put a large chair, like one a grandfather would sit in, on the stage. Beside it we'll put a fireplace or a Christmas tree. I have the children gather at my feet and, while "Silent Night" is playing softly in the background, I'll read from Luke 2 in the old King James Version. For some reason, I always have to fight back a few tears; and miracle of miracles, the children are always hushed and attentive.

Additional Sermons and Lesson Ideas

The Life Appeared!

Date preached:

SCRIPTURE: 1 John 1:1–4 (NIV)

INTRODUCTION: Here in the prologue of 1 John we have—not the history of Christmas—but the history of the Christ of Christmas. John gives it to us in four stages, and each stage is seen readily in the first phrase of each of these four verses.

1. The Beginning of Christ (v. 1): *That which was from the beginning.* . . . Three books of the Bible begin in the same way: Genesis, John, and 1 John all begin with "the beginning." Christ preexisted prior to His birth.
2. The Appearance of Christ (v. 2): *The life appeared.* . . . That's described in Matthew 2 and Luke 2.
3. The Preaching of Christ (v. 3): *We proclaim to you.* . . . This isn't a reality to be kept quiet. We shout it from the mountaintop.
4. The Joy of Christ (v. 4): *We write this to make our joy complete.* As we receive this message, we discover joy unspeakable and full of glory— joy to the world!

CONCLUSION: During this Christmas season, I hope you'll dedicate yourself fully to the Lord Jesus Christ, God in flesh, Christ by highest heaven adored, Christ the everlasting Lord. That which was from the beginning. . . . This life appeared. . . . We proclaim to you. . . . That your joy may be complete!

One Starry Night

Date preached:

SCRIPTURE: Luke 1:26–38

INTRODUCTION: A child opened a big box under the tree to find a giant doll that, when upright, towered over her. She promptly discarded the doll but had a ball playing in the box. We do the same at Christmas, discarding the Baby but having a great time with the wrappings. Gabriel's announcement reminds us of four things that demand our attention.

1. His Name (v. 31). *Jesus* is the Greek form of the Hebrew *Joshua— Salvation of Yahweh.* Woven into the syllables of His name, we see the suffering He would endure, the salvation He would bestow, and the splendor He would display.
2. His Nature—In Gabriel's announcement, four different "sonships" are ascribed. He is: (1) *Son of Mary* (v. 31); (2) *Son of the Highest* (v. 32); (3) *Son of David* (v. 32); and (4) *Son of God* (v. 35).
3. His Nobility (vv. 32–33). His is a *powerful* kingdom, a *permanent* kingdom, a *providential* kingdom, and a *political* kingdom, for one

day the earth will be full of the knowledge of the Lord (Hab. 2:14). It's also a *personal* kingdom, as He becomes King of our hearts.

4. His Nativity (vv. 34–35). Jesus was born of divine conception, of a virgin who had never known a man.

CONCLUSION: Mary's response to this message was: "Behold the maid-servant of the Lord! Let it be to me according to your word." When we come face-to-face with God's wondrous plan for us, there's no better response.

CLASSICS FOR THE PASTOR'S LIBRARY

A Serious Call to a Devout and Holy Life
By William Law

William Law was born to a village grocer in 1686, which meant he came of age just in time to become embroiled in the Hanoverian crisis that rocked England and the Anglican Church. Law's high church principles kept him from accepting George I as England's rightful king; and as a result, he was barred from the church pulpit and the university classroom. He became the private tutor to Edward Gibbon, father of the famous historian of the same name, and served as a spiritual advisor to the whole Gibbon clan. In later years, he retired to the house he had inherited from his father and maintained an intense personal ministry, writing a number of controversial books and promoting the practice of personal holiness.

Despite being unable to minister in the Anglican pulpit, Law was a devoted high churchman who anguished over the state of spirituality in England. During those days, Sunday worship was a popular formality in the lives of most people. There was little authentic Christianity being lived-out, and hypocrisy was in vogue. It was a day of public worship without personal piety.

Church-goers, said Law, are strict about showing up on Sunday, "but when the service of the Church is over, they are but like those who seldom or never come there. In their way of life, their manner of spending time and money, in their cares and fears, in their pleasures and indulgences, in their labor and diversions, they are like the rest of the world."

That's why Law wrote *A Serious Call to a Devout and Holy Life*. It was an appeal for Anglicans to practice throughout the week what they prayed and preached in the cathedrals and churches on Sunday, and it found a mark in many people. It was published in 1728, and among its readers were those who would become leaders of the great Evangelical Revival that swept England a decade later.

Law's writings inflamed the Wesley brothers, as well as young George Whitefield, who later wrote, "Before I went to the University I met with Mr. Law's *Serious Call*, but had not money to purchase it. Soon after my coming up to Oxford, seeing a small edition of it in a friend's hand I soon purchased it. God worked powerfully upon my soul, as He has since upon many others."

None less than Dr. Samuel Johnson gave this testimony, "I became a sort of lax talker against religion . . . and this lasted until I went to Oxford, where . . . I took up Law's *Serious Call*, expecting to find it a dull book (as such books generally are), and perhaps to laugh at it. But I found Law quite an overmatch for me; and this was the first occasion of my thinking in earnest of religion."

Interestingly, Law himself was never an evangelical and wanted little to do with the revival he helped kindle. As one historian put it, "Law was never in full sympathy with the Evangelical movement; he set the ball a-rolling but he did not follow its course."

A Serious Call combines medieval mysticism with High Church tradition, and it encourages intense personal devotion to Christ within the context of an organized system of personal disciplines. Using a parade of fictional characters, Law illustrates his theme that devotion to Christ must extend to all the sectors of daily life impacting how we spend our money, plan our day, treat our neighbors, and view our world. True holiness leads to true happiness, and every day should be organized around set hours of personal prayer. Not just the clergyman, but the tradesman, gentleman,

Continued on the next page

CLASSICS FOR THE PASTOR'S LIBRARY—*Continued*

and everyone else should practice a personal piety that pervades every part of life and is driven by a passionate desire to please God. The average church-goer should be as devout and devotional as the holiest bishop, for holiness should extend to all people and to all of life.

A Serious Call is available all over the Internet, and bound volumes can be easily located at used book Web sites. It's not the easiest of reading, and I bogged down here and there, primarily because I wanted to mull over what I was reading, and this kind of *lectio divina* takes time.

But who's in a hurry? Throw William Law in your briefcase and read one of his chapters from time to time as you feel led. It's especially rich when you're on a personal prayer or study retreat. Let its message slowly settle into your soul. After all, our times are not so different from those of William Law, and if ever a generation needed a serious call to a devout and holy life, it's now.

DECEMBER 28, 2008

SUGGESTED SERMON

You Tell Them!

Date preached:

By Dr. Larry Osborne

Scripture: Various, especially Acts 1:8
But you shall receive power when the Holy Spirit has come upon you; and you shall be witnesses to Me in Jerusalem, and in all Judea and Samaria, and to the end of the earth.

Introduction: Does Easter matter in December? So what if the tomb is empty? We ve just celebrated Jesus' birth, but what does it matter that He died and rose again? Great stories in the Old Testament and even in the New Testament tell of many who were risen from the dead, but they all died again. The big deal about Easter is not just that Jesus rose from the dead, but that He is still alive and well today and involved in our lives in a very active way.

1. **A Quick Look Back: It's a Good Thing Jesus Is Gone.**

   A. **He Went from *with* Us to *in* Us (John 14:16–20).** When Jesus spoke of His death and resurrection to the disciples, He said it's good that He would leave, so that the Spirit would live within us.

   B. **The Same Spirit and Power Jesus Had (Matt. 3:13—4:24).** When Jesus was baptized, the Holy Spirit descended upon Him. Just after that, He began His ministry! That Spirit is the same one that empowers us for ministry.

2. **A Closer Look at the Holy Spirit.** If we have the same Spirit as Jesus, why can't we do miracles left and right? We're given power to carry out God's assignment, not our wish list. Jesus only did as the Father commanded Him to (John 14:10, 31). In the same way, we were made for a specific purpose, to do various types of ministry by the power of the same Spirit (Eph. 2:10).

3. **A Look at Inside-Out Living.** When we speak of giving our lives to Christ, we speak of giving Him the steering wheel of our lives,

allowing the Holy Spirit to change us from the inside-out. But what does this mean practically in our lives?

A. **Inner Promptings (John 14:26).** When you become a follower of Christ, you will begin to receive inner promptings, a sense from the inside-out that "I ought to . . ." or "I ought not . . ." This doesn't mean we completely live by our feelings; we should always check the Scriptures to see if what we're being prompted to do is advocated by the Word of God. But, as we grow in Christ, we learn to understand and obey the prompting of the Holy Spirit.

B. **Spiritual Enlightenment (1 Cor. 2:10–16).** We understand the spiritual things of God because the Spirit is in us: ". . . we have the mind of Christ" (v. 16). We can understand things that once seemed foolish to us, but now we suddenly understand!

C. **Changed Desires (Phil. 2:13).** Many of you may think that whatever you want is the exact opposite of what God wants. But, if you are walking in obedience to the Lord, He will give you desires and fulfill them! Serving others, telling others about Christ, resisting temptation, praying, reading the Word: these things aren't done against our will or out of obligation. When we walk with the Lord, it's a joy to do His will.

D. **Spiritual Power (Acts 1:8).** Whatever God wants you to do, He will give you power to accomplish it. God gives us just what we need just when we need it.

4. **A Look at Our Responsibility: Witnessing 101:**

A. **If We Won't, No One Else Will (Acts 1:8).** It's been left up to us to tell the world about Jesus. If your coworker is facing a life crisis, who else will invite them to church or give them their testimony of how Jesus rescued them? It's up to us!

B. **Warning: Never Try This on Your Own (Matt. 17:14–21)!** If you go rant and rave to someone about God in your own power and for your own reasons, it's not going to work.

C. **Follow the Jesus Pattern:**
   (1) Look for open doors (John 4:4–26).
   (2) Earn the right to be heard (Matt. 7:29).
   (3) Speak the truth in love, not anger—or don't speak at all (2 Tim. 2:24–26).

Conclusion: It's a good thing Jesus left. It really is, because we have the Holy Spirit. He told *us* to tell them; it's *our* job! But we'll only do it right when we do it His way, empowered by His Holy Spirit; then, incredible things will happen.

STATS, STORIES, AND MORE

I Believe in the Holy Ghost
In her book, *A Little Pot of Oil,* Jill Briscoe describes being six years old during the Second World War, with bombs a daily part of her life in Liverpool, England. The Liverpool docks were pounded night after night, and she seldom slept in her little pink bedroom, but in a bomb shelter her father had dug out at the end of the garden. Huddled there, she would try to remember the prayers they had said in school that day. She was especially intrigued by the Apostles' Creed, which she now knew by heart. But one night the bombs were falling with such ferocity that she couldn't remember all the words. Suddenly her mind focused on the words: *I believe in the Holy Ghost.* The words frightened her a bit. Was there a Holy Ghost hovering nearby? She later wrote, "It took me nine more years to find out the truth: that the Holy Ghost was the Comforter, the 'one called alongside to help,' the Advocate, who was actually aware of my plight and was praying for me. That He was someone who could hold me together inside and hush my fears to sleep—God Himself, able to fill the empty places in my life, to fill me up when I was running on empty."[1]

APPROPRIATE HYMNS AND SONGS

"Go Tell It on the Mountain," John Work II, Public Domain.

"Shout to the Lord," Darlene Zscech, 1993 Hillsong Australia.

"Blessed Be the Name," Charles Wesley & Ralph Hudson, Public Domain.

"Majesty," Jack Hayford, 1981 Rocksmith Music c/o Trust Music Management.

---

[1] Jill Briscoe, *A Little Pot of Oil* (Sisters, Oregon: Multnomah Publishers, 2003), pp. 13–16.

FOR THE BULLETIN

On this day nearly a thousand years ago, December 28, 1065, Westminster Abbey opened and was dedicated in London, built by Edward the Confessor, the last of the old Anglo-Saxon kings, as a memorial to St. Peter. Unfortunately, Edward was unable to attend the dedication, being ill a few miles away. He died shortly afterward, and his remains are interred behind Westminster's High Altar. ● John Wycliffe, the "Morning Star of the Reformation," suffered a debilitating stroke while presiding over the Lord's Supper of Sunday, December 28, 1384. He was carried to his bed, where he passed away on December 31. Forty-one years later, still hated by his enemies, his bones were exhumed, burned, and thrown into the river. ● December 28, 1798, marks the birthday of Charles Hodge, one of America's greatest theologians, who studied the old and familiar Scriptures with fresh excitement. Three thousand pastors prepared for ministry in his theology classes at Princeton, and multitudes have benefited from his three-volume *Systematic Theology*. ● On December 28, 1993, South Africa's white parliament, sitting for the last time, buried apartheid, voting 237 to 45 to adopt an interim constitution leading to majority rule after the staging of the country's first all-race election.

Quote for the Pastor's Wall

ORDINARY PEOPLE—*Abraham Lincoln observed, "God must love ordinary people, because He made so many of them!"*

WORSHIP HELPS

Call to Worship
Blessed be the Lord, who daily loads us with benefits, the God of our salvation! Our God is the God of salvation; and to GOD the Lord belong escapes from death (Ps. 68:19–20).

Pastoral Prayer
Father, help us to be men and women who grow in our understanding of what it means to simply yield to that inside-out work You're doing in our lives. Help us to take that to the workplace, our neighborhoods, our friends, and loved ones who don't yet know You, and to respond to them as You would and as You do, in love. In Jesus' name we pray, Amen.

Suggested Scriptures

- Matthew 4:23—5:1; 12:24–37; 28:18–20
- Luke 3:21–23
- John 12:49–50; 16:7–13
- Acts 16:7
- Galatians 2:20
- Philippians 2:13
- 2 Timothy 2:24–26

Benediction
Salvation belongs to the LORD. Your blessing is upon Your people (Ps. 3:8). And the Lord will deliver me from every evil work and preserve me for His heavenly kingdom. To Him be glory forever and ever. Amen (2 Tim. 4:18)!

Additional Sermons and Lesson Ideas

Safe on the Rock
By Dr. Robert M. Norris

Date preached:

SCRIPTURE: Hebrews 6:19–20

INTRODUCTION: To weak and weary Christian people who were struggling with doubt and uncertainty, the author of the Hebrew letter pens these words to bring certainty to the uncertain, encouragement to the dispirited, and hope to the hopeless.

1. The Gospel Guarantees Us to Heaven (vv. 19–20). Jesus is described as "an anchor of the soul" in verse 19, who has entered into heaven as our High Priest. If your trust is in Christ, your future is anchored to Him.
2. The Gospel Encourages Us to Live with Heaven in Sight (v. 19). The idea that Jesus has guaranteed heaven to those who trust and follow Him is described as our "hope." We must always live with this truth in mind, even if unseen for now (cf. Heb. 11:1).
3. The Gospel Reminds Us of Our Hope of Heaven (vv. 19–20). The hope described in verse 19 is secured because of verse 20, the person of Christ has become our Mediator and High Priest!

CONCLUSION: Secure your eternal destination as you fix your eyes upon Christ, and set your heart upon Him and His promises and rest in the provision that He has made for His own.

Making Resolutions Realities
By Dr. Timothy K. Beougher

Date preached:

SCRIPTURE: Philippians 3:12–14

INTRODUCTION: This week millions of people across our nation will make resolutions; most resolutions are abandoned within two weeks. How can we make our resolutions our realities? Philippians 3:12–14 gives insight about reaching goals.

1. Fully Confess Your Shortcomings (v. 12a)—Paul confessed he had not yet "arrived." He still needed to grow. In what areas do you most need improvement?
2. Find Your Destiny (vv. 12, 14)—Paul pressed on to lay hold of that for which Christ laid hold of him. Do you have a driving agenda in life, given to you by Christ?

3. Forget the Past (v. 13)—When Paul said he was forgetting what lay behind him, he was referring to past accomplishments. Don't rest on your past deeds or be hindered by failures. Put it all behind you and under the blood of Christ.

4. Focus Your Aim (v. 13)—"One thing I do." What does God want you to do in the coming year?

5. Forcibly Pursue Your Goal (v. 14)—Paul's imagery of "pressing on" is of a runner straining for the tape (see Heb. 12:1–2).

CONCLUSION: Prayerfully set goals for the New Year, write them down, share them with someone, and devote the next 365 days to fulfilling them for the glory of God.

ORDINATION SERMON

Pastoral Preaching

By Dr. Melvin Worthington

Date preached:

Scripture: Various, especially 2 Timothy 4:2
Preach the word! Be ready in season and out of season. Convince, rebuke, exhort, with all longsuffering and teaching.

Introduction: God exercises a special care for the church by appointing pastors and teachers who watch over it as shepherds. Ministers are not appointed to do the work of the members, but to prepare members for their own work, that the whole church may be built up as the body of Christ. Perhaps the most pressing need in the church today is a renewed emphasis on clear, correct, concise, compassionate, and comprehensive preaching of the Word. A good pastoral preaching program embraces the following three things.

1. **The Pastor (Eph. 4:11–12; 1 Tim. 3; 1 Pet. 5:1–4). It is impossible to ignore the place of the pastor in a sound, scriptural preaching program. The man cannot be separated from the ministry.**

   A. **Consider His Character.** The pastor is characterized in the Scriptures as a chosen, called, commissioned, compelled, and consecrated man.

   B. **Consider His Credentials (1 Tim. 3).** His marriage, mate, money, motivation, and maturity must be considered if he is to serve effectively.

   C. **Consider His Charge.** The pastor is charged with the responsibility of leading and loving his congregation. He does this by what he teaches, by how he lives, and by investing himself in others.

   D. **Consider His Choices.** The pastor must recognize his gifts and be realistic in his goals, but at the same time rely on God's grace and retain God's guidelines. He must have time for meditation, those hours set aside for study, supplication, and solitude. Preparation time for the head and heart does not conflict with serving and sharing. He must have time for his marriage. The pastor who neglects his family and reserves no time for it invites disaster.

2. **The Preaching (2 Tim. 4:1–4).**

   A. **Consider the Aim of Preaching.** Effective preaching always aims the arrow of truth for a specific purpose. Preaching includes the ingredients of invitation, instruction, inspiration, indoctrination, initiation, and implantation. While not every sermon will include all the ingredients, over the long haul, pastoral preaching brings each area into focus.

   B. **Consider the Authority for Preaching.** Paul's final word to Timothy was "Preach the word!"

   C. **Consider the Accomplishment of Preaching.** Preaching of the Bible had a profound impact on the world as seen in Acts and the Epistles.

   D. **Consider the Absence of Preaching.** The decadent periods in history have been those times when preaching went into eclipse. Renewed preaching heralds the dawn of a reformation or a revival for the churches.

3. **The Plan (2 Tim. 4:1–4).**

   A. **The Preaching Plan Must Be Biblical.** The pastor cannot afford to get sidetracked in his preaching and spin his wheels on counterfeit contemporary controversies. While informing one's congregation about issues may have a place, it cannot substitute for preaching the Bible precept by precept and chapter by chapter. Preaching personal philosophical positions is a subtle temptation every pastor faces.

   B. **The Preaching Plan Must Be Balanced.** The effective program includes textual, topical, Bible characters, and themes as well as a solid expository base.

   C. **The Preaching Plan May Be Blended.** This means the program must include doctrine, the explanation of parables, the examination of miracles, and the weaving of variety and freshness into the delivery until the young and old alike know that the Bible is a practical Book for today's culture.

Conclusion: The pastor's preaching program is the key to a successful and satisfying ministry. The frustration, fears, and fights in many churches can be traced to an apathetic pulpit. Pastors, you must not neglect your preaching. Burn your appointment calendar if you must, but be ready on Sunday to preach the kind of sermon you will wish you had, if you meet God on Monday!

WEDDING SERMON
Wedding: A Celebration of Love

Family, friends, and brothers and sisters in Christ, we are gathered here today to celebrate the union of _____ (groom) and _____ (bride). Only a handful of events can inspire, encourage, and bring joy to our hearts like a wedding. We are not here today merely to see beautiful candles and clothing, to fellowship with friends and family, to give presents, and to take pictures. We're here to witness a solemn occasion before God Himself as these two people make a biblical covenant that must endure for the rest of their earthly lives.

Marriage is a union ordained by God and spoken of in the highest regard by Jesus Christ and His apostles. Scripture speaks of marriage as the picture and the very symbol of Christ's love for His people. Greater love no man has ever had than Him who laid down His own life for His people. Not only this, but He has given us His Scriptures as the authoritative Word to govern every aspect of our lives, including marriage. The Bible teaches that love is the bonding agent of friendship and marriage. We read in 1 Corinthians 13 (NIV):

> Love is patient, love is kind. It does not envy, it does not boast, it is not proud. It is not rude, it is not self-seeking, it is not easily angered, it keeps no record of wrongs. Love does not delight in evil but rejoices with the truth. It always protects, always trusts, always hopes, always perseveres. Love never fails.

_____ (bride), when _____, for the hundredth time, leaves his dirty clothes in the floor, remember that *love is patient.* _____ (groom), when _____ backs the car into a telephone pole, remember that *love is kind.* If you see others struggling in their relationships, while yours continues to blossom, offer your support and not your judgment: for *love does not envy, it does not boast, and it is not proud.* Speak to one another, always considering the other above yourself, for *love is not rude, and is not self-seeking.* When arguments arise, treat each conflict not as an argument to be won or lost, but as a new and distinct challenge to face together. When resolved, forget about them, for *love is not easily angered, it keeps no record of wrongs.*

Keep yourselves pure for each other and always be open and honest. Remember that when you say "I do" to one another, you are saying "I don't" to every other man and woman in the world. For *love does not delight in evil but rejoices with the truth. It always protects, always trusts, always hopes.*

And above all, remember that the Lord Himself has brought you together, and it is His purpose to sustain your relationship. He is both the author and sustainer of love. Love the Lord with all of your heart, mind, soul, and strength, and each other as yourselves, for Jesus Christ Himself gave us this as the greatest commandment applying to every area of life and marriage; strive for this goal every moment of every day and you can be assured that *love always perseveres; love never fails.*

Lord, may the commitment made here today encourage us; may it act as a testimony to challenge us; may it bring joy to our hearts and glory to Your name in which we pray, Amen.

_____, will you have this woman as your wedded wife, to live together after God's ordinance in the holy state of matrimony? Will you love her, comfort her, honor and keep her in sickness and in health; and, forsaking all others, keep only unto her so long as you both shall live?

The groom answers: I will.

_____, will you have this man as your wedded husband, to live together after God's ordinance in the holy state of matrimony? Will you love him, comfort him, honor and keep him in sickness and in health; and, forsaking all others, keep only unto him so long as you both shall live?

The bride answers: I will.

WEDDING SERMON

Wedding: A Celebration of the Gospel

Dear friends, we have gathered here today to unite in marriage
_____ and _____, and to shower
them with our love and to surround them with our prayers. Marriage
is history's most original relationship, for it was at the dawn of time
in the Garden of Eden that the Creator-God brought together the man
Adam and the woman Eve in a bond of mutual love and united them
in holy marriage with these immortal words: "Therefore a man shall
leave his father and mother and be joined to his wife, and they shall
become one flesh."

From that point and throughout the Bible, marriage is described as a
sacred intention for human society whereby lives are joined, loneliness
is dispelled, children are produced, families are raised, trials are met,
the gospel is advanced from generation to generation, and God is
glorified. Even the very Son of God Himself, our Lord Jesus, was born
into a human family, was obedient to Joseph and Mary, and, upon
entering His ministry, performed His first wonder at a wedding that
was an occasion of joy just as this one is, now, two thousand years
later.

The writer of the book of Hebrews said, "Let marriage be held in honor
by all and the marriage bed undefiled." The apostle Paul in the fifth
chapter of Ephesians compared the relationship between husband and
wife to the bond existing between Christ and His church, for he said:
"Husbands, love your wives, just as Christ also loved the church and
gave Himself for her."

"This is a great mystery," wrote the apostle, "but I speak concerning
Christ and the church. Nevertheless let each one of you in particular
so love his own wife as himself, and let the wife see that she respects
her husband."

Our commitment to each other is a reflection of our dedication and
devotion to Christ, who pronounced His vows for us on Calvary's Cross.

On the Cross, He demonstrated His love for us. On the Cross, He thought of us and gave Himself for our well-being. His processional wasn't down a rose-petaled aisle like this one, but down the Via Delarosa. His wedding music was a death march. His altar was the blood stained timber of Calvary. His wedding ring was the crown of thorns atop His brow. But truer vows have never been spoken, and richer love has never been seen.

The Bible teaches that God has loved us from the foundation of the world. Yet by our very nature, we have all been unfaithful to Him and unfit to live under the same roof, as it were, with Him; we have fallen short of His glory. Nevertheless, in His infinite love, God devised a way for us to be united with Him, by sending His only begotten Son to this planet like a Bridegroom in search of a bride. and when the kindness and the love of God our Savior appeared, not by works of righteousness which we have done, but according to His mercy He saved us, through the washing of regeneration and the renewing of the Holy Spirit.

The Bible says: "He died for all, that those who live should live no longer for themselves, but for Him who died for them and rose again. . . . . Therefore, if anyone is in Christ, he is a new creation; old things have passed away; behold, all things have become new . . . (for) God was in Christ reconciling the world to Himself, not imputing their trespasses to them . . . For He made Him who knew no sin to be sin for us, that we might become the righteousness of God in Him."

If Jesus Christ so gave Himself at the altar of Calvary for us, we should give ourselves as living sacrifices for Him; and we should give ourselves in love for one another.

At this marriage altar today, we give this man and this woman into a relationship that reflects and relates to the supernatural love of our all-sufficient Savior. Without a spiritual foundation, there can be no enduring bonds, for happy homes and holy ones are built only on the cornerstone of Christ Himself. All other ground is sinking sand.

So I want to implore you, _____ and _____ and I implore all who are here today gathered, to make and keep

Jesus Christ as your own Savior and Lord. Honor Him as King and Commander. Obey Him as Lord and Leader. Trust Him as your Strength and your Song.

_____ (groom), if you are ready to take _____ as your wife, will you please repeat after me these words: Today with love and loyal commitment, I take you, _____, as my wife, leaving all others, to have and to hold from this day onward, for better or for worse, in sickness and in health, in poverty and in wealth, with the love, joy, and peace as God helps me, that I may be your faithful husband henceforth, until death shall part us.

_____ (bride), if you are ready to take _____ as your husband, will you please repeat after me these words: Today with love and loyal commitment, I take you, _____, as my husband, leaving all others, to have and to hold from this day onward, for better or for worse, in sickness and in health, in poverty and in wealth, with the love, joy, and peace as God helps me, that I may be your faithful wife henceforth, until death shall part us.

WEDDING SERMON

Wedding: A Celebration of Friendship

Dear friends, we have gathered here as witnesses and well-wishers to unite _____ (groom's name) and _____ (bride's name) in the holiness of sacred marriage.

Those who enter such a hallowed relationship are not just partners in the bonds of matrimony; they are two people in the process of becoming one flesh, dearest friends, lifelong confidantes, alter egos, loving yoke-fellows, best buddies, fellow students in the school of life, and fellow servants in the work of God. They are two planets orbiting the same star, two ropes forming one cable, two halves becoming one whole.

This kind of partnership isn't grown in a day or a night; it's a life-long endeavor, for as someone said, "It takes a long time to grow an old friend." And friendship is the essential word. I know that many people prefer the word "love," as Elizabeth Barrett Browning said when she wrote her famous poem: "How do I love thee? Let me count the ways. / I love thee to the depth and breadth and height / My soul can reach . . ."

But love is simply friendship set afire; and friendship is the fuel of love and the flowing fountainhead of a long and happy marriage. A good friendship is like a prize-winning cake, made of quality ingredients dispensed in the right measurements. The recipe is found in the cookbook of God's Word, where we read, for example, in Romans 12 (NIV): "Love must be sincere. Hate what is evil; cling to what is good. Be devoted to one another in brotherly love. Honor one another above yourselves. Never be lacking in zeal, but keep your spiritual fervor, serving the Lord. Be joyful in hope, patient in affliction, faithful in prayer . . . Practice hospitality . . . Live in harmony with one another. Do not be proud . . . Do not be conceited . . . Be careful to do what is right in the eyes of everybody. . . ."

This is intentional love, for we can't rely merely on romantic feelings and physical attraction through the years and fears and tears of life. The feelings of romantic love are important, of course, and we must tend to them, stoking them as we would a fire in the hearth; but feelings, by their very nature, are fluctuating emotions. The attitudes of zeal and fervor and hope and faithfulness and hospitality and harmony are not.

Happiness is a feeling, but joy is a disposition. Excitement is an emotion, but zeal is an attitude. Cheerfulness and joy are attitudes that mark a happy home, and they are regrettably rare in our relationships; for many marriages are ruined by partners who let themselves become irritable, bad-tempered, demanding, and disagreeable. Proverbs 17:22 (Good News Translation) says, "Being cheerful keeps you healthy. It is slow death to be gloomy all the time."

An easy smile isn't always easy, but it's always needed, and a joyful heart is essential to a happy home. Cheerfulness is sunshine streaming through the windows of life; but anger and dissension are icy storms that paralyze the lifelines of a relationship. God's recipe for a happy home uses simple, wholesome ingredients, like a cup of cheerfulness, a pound of patience, a gallon of grace, and a spoonful of sugar. If you combine these ingredients and bake at 350 for a lifetime, your home will be filled with the aroma of friendship, lifelong, loving, and loyal. And so today, _____ and _____, I implore you: Don't just love one another as the world defines love, but work heartily each and every day to become and to always be one another's closest friend.

If here and now you are ready to pledge yourselves to one another in such a way, will you please join hands for the saying of your vows.

_____ (groom), do you take this woman as your wedded wife, to live together after God's ordinance in the holy state of Matrimony, to love her, comfort her, honor, and keep her in sickness and in health; and, forsaking all others, keep yourself only unto her, so long as you both shall live? *The Man shall answer*, I Do.

_____ (bride), do you take this man as your wedded husband, to live together after God's ordinance in the holy state of matrimony, to love him, comfort him, honor, and keep him in sickness and in health; and, forsaking all others, keep yourself only unto him, so long as you both shall live? *The Woman shall answer*, I Do.

Then you are each given to the other in the holy bonds of marriage as husband and wife both now and until death shall you part.

FUNERAL SERMON

Suitable for the Death of a Believer
The Death of a Saint

By Rev. Todd M. Kinde

Scripture: Genesis 23:1–20, especially verses 2 and 19
And Abraham came to mourn for Sarah and to weep for her . . . . And after this, Abraham buried Sarah his wife in the cave of the field of Machpelah, before Mamre (that is, Hebron) in the land of Canaan.

Introduction: We find in Genesis chapter 23 the death of a saintly woman and the response of a saintly husband to her death. We will learn, then, how we as followers of Christ are to respond to death when we walk through the valley of its shadow.

1. **We Grieve at the Time of Death (21:1–2).** There is something sudden and final about the way this chapter begins. Yet, there is something of fulfillment and completion about it as well. Sarah's life was certainly one of struggle—being given to two other men while married to Abraham, tension with Hagar, the Egyptian maidservant, battles with infertility, moving around the country and living in a tent. Yet, her life was also one of blessing—seeing her husband grow stronger in faith, giving birth to Isaac which brought her laughs of joy, living beside the oases and the groves of trees, experiencing the faithfulness of God's Word, living in anticipation of the land belonging to her son's sons. After all is said and done, Sarah had a good life. She ended it with joy and satisfaction in the Lord her God. But her life has ended, and for Abraham this brings a deep sense of loss. Abraham mourns and weeps for her (v. 2).

   Death is a time of loss and grief. We as Christians should be the first to acknowledge this truth. Death is a result of our fall into sin (Gen. 2:17; Rom. 3:23). We are created as human beings with bodies. It is not the way it is supposed to be when our spirit is removed from our body and we cease to live on this earth. It is a horrible thing that we experience physical death, lose our bodies, and lose physical contact with our loved ones.

   Abraham weeps at this loss. So, too, does our Lord. The Bible says that at the funeral of Lazarus, "Jesus wept" (John 11:35). Jesus enters into our pain, into our loss, into our grief. "For we do not have a High Priest who cannot sympathize with our weaknesses . . ." (Heb. 4:15).

2. **We Resolve to Live Intentionally Reliant on God When Confronted with Death (21:3–16).** Abraham needs a burial place for his bride. He owns no property. He is a stranger in the land. Yet, the Hittites appear to have great respect for Abraham calling him a "mighty prince" or a "Prince of God." Although the Hittites offer him a gift of land, He will accept no gift from the world. The Hittites by speaking well of Abraham and by offering him a borrowed place to bury his wife are attempting to keep Abraham landless. Though they respect him, at least in words of honor, they are threatened by his presence and seek to deter him from owning land and of losing their own hold on the land.

   Abraham will not receive something for nothing from the pagan culture. He pays full price for the chosen place, the cave of Machpelah and the adjacent grove of trees. No human being can say they had a part in making Abraham the great man that he had become. All that Abraham has is a gift not from men but from God.

3. **We Live with Bold Faith in Christ When Confronted with Death (21:17–20).** The land transfer is finalized. We also see the final act of Sarah's burial in the cave. The text is clear to highlight the fact that Abraham now owns a piece of the land (vv. 18, 20). The importance of this detail is that it shows us faith, faith that God will fulfill His Word and promise to Abraham by giving the land. He buries Sarah in this first installment of land in anticipation of inheriting the entire land.

   In chapter 22 when Abraham offered up Isaac we learned that Abraham believed God could raise the dead (cf. Heb. 11:17–19). Abraham purchases a burial plot in the Promised Land for his now dearly departed wife in anticipation that God will raise her and give her the promise fulfilled.

   This burial site would become the burial place of Abraham himself and in future years also of Isaac, Rebekah, Leah, and Jacob. We read in Hebrews 11:13 that "These all died in faith, not having received the promises, but having seen them afar off were assured of them. . . ." The spiritual heritage of one generation was passed on to the next. An intergenerational legacy that anticipates the fulfillment of God's promises. So we do mourn, but we do not mourn as those who have no hope (1 Thess. 4:13–18; 1 Cor. 15:51–58).

Conclusion: We commemorate those who have died in the Lord and are with Him waiting for the resurrection of their bodies. We honor them and we honor the Lord by pressing on in the faith of Christ. We are confronted with the truth that we will all face death because of sin. Those who die outside of Christ will be lost in grief and torment for an eternity under God's wrath. But we are comforted by the truth that Christ has overcome sin and death and that those in Him will be in the blessed presence of God who made us and rules over us (Rev. 14:12–13).

FUNERAL SERMON

Suitable for the Funeral of an Unbeliever
He Knows Our Griefs

Today we have gathered in memory of _____

Personal Comments

Scripture: 2 Chronicles 6:29–30

Introduction: This wonderful passage is part of the prayer Solomon offered at the dedication of the temple in the Old Testament. "Whatever prayer, whatever supplication is made by anyone, or by all Your people Israel, when each one knows his own burden and his own grief, and spreads out his hands to this temple: then hear from heaven Your dwelling place, and forgive, and give to everyone according to all his ways, whose hearts You know, for You alone know the hearts of the sons of men." This Scripture passage tells us several things about our God.

1. **God Knows Our Grief.** This passage tells us that we can come to God with whatever prayer, whatever supplication we may need to make out of our own burden and out of our own grief. When you read the Bible, you find so many people whose hearts were grief-stricken as ours are today. There's a story about King David when his child was at death's door, how he wept and fasted and fell on his face and thought he himself would die from his anxious grief. Later when his oldest son was killed, the great king was so grief-stricken his wails were heard all across Jerusalem. In the New Testament, we have a story of Jesus visiting the gravesite of his friend who had died. The mourners were still there, four days after the funeral. The family members were struggling with their questions, and Jesus Himself wept by the tomb of His friend. Grief is a natural part of life and it's an appropriate response to loss. It is normal and healthy to grieve, though it hurts so much to do so. There are many aspects to grief. Sometimes we feel overwhelming sadness. Other times we feel anger. We have moments of depression and regret. There's often a numbness that comes. All these are normal, but painful; and the Bible assures us that God knows every pang of the heart and He cares for us in our

grief. He feels our sorrow. He is touched by our anguish. An ancient English Psalter has a beautiful stanza about this: "Jehovah hear thee in thy grief, / Our fathers' God defend thee still, / Send from His holy place relief, / And strengthen thee from Zion's hill.

2. **God Hears Our Prayer.** This passage also tells us God hears our prayers: *Whenever prayer, whenever supplication is made by anyone . . . then hear from heaven.* . . . It's wonderful to have friends who comfort us, but none can comfort like our Lord. Remember the old hymn that says: "What a Friend we have in Jesus, all our sins and griefs to bear! / What a privilege to carry everything to God in prayer! / O what peace we often forfeit, O what needless pain we bear, / All because we do not carry everything to God in prayer." During times of anguish and sorrow in my own life, I've often gone to the Bible and found verses of cheer, then gone to my journal and written out prayers as best I could, claiming those verses and asking God to relieve my distress and give me peace. Prayer is like going to the Lord for His comforting hugs and embrace. It's turning to a power greater than our own, and tapping into a presence that soothes and calms our troubled spirits.

3. **God Forgives Our Sin.** This verse also tells us that God forgives our sin. Verse 30 says: ". . . then hear from heaven Your dwelling place, and forgive." The Bible teaches that God is a God of mercy, quick to forgive. It's in His very nature to forgive sin. It comes to Him naturally. None of us knows the heart of another person, and I cannot tell you whether any particular individual is in heaven or hell. God alone knows, but we do know one thing—God is a God of infinite mercy; and I find great comfort in that. When I don't know where else to go or what else to think, I just fall into the arms of God's mercy and rest myself there.

Conclusion: When we ponder God's mercy, of course, it always takes us back to the old rugged cross of Jesus Christ. God spells mercy with the letters J-E-S-U-S. The Bible teaches that all of us have fallen short of God's glory, and that the wages of sin is death. But God demonstrates His love for us in this, that while we were yet sinners, Christ died for us. And if we confess with our mouth Jesus as Lord and believe in our hearts that God has raised Him from the dead, we shall be saved, for everyone who calls on the name of the Lord shall be saved (Rom. 3:23; 5:8; 6:23; 10:9–10, 13). We cannot be responsible for anyone else's soul, and so we leave our loved ones in God's hands. But we are responsible for our own souls, and at this very moment of sadness, I would encourage you to turn to Christ and find in Him a God who knows our griefs, hears our prayers, forgives our sins, and heals our hearts.

FUNERAL SERMON
Suitable for a Suicide Victim
By Pastor Al Detter

Introduction: I believe God has a word for us today in this very difficult hour. There are no easy or pat answers. But God's Word is sure and alive and relevant. David said in Psalm 119:28, "My soul weeps because of grief. Strengthen me according to Your word." In verse 93, he said, "I will never forget Your precepts, for by them You have revived me." And in verse 143, "Trouble and anguish have come upon me, yet Your commandments are my delight" (NASB). The Bible is God speaking to us and in times of tragedy, its power is incredible. The Word of God is an anchor in times of stormy weather. Today, I want to offer five anchors to steady our lives in the storm of life that has burst upon us.

1. **The Anchor of Sympathy.** I want you to know that Jesus knows all about this. He feels what you feel. He weeps. His heart is touched with your grief. Hebrews 4:15 says of Jesus that He is a High Priest who sympathizes with us. And because of His sympathy, we're told in the next verse to draw near to Him with confidence, that we may receive mercy and grace to help in our time of need.

2. **The Anchor of Explanation.**

   A. **Cancer of the Soul.** What happened to our friend causes a lot of questions. One big question is "Why?" I really can't answer that question to anyone's satisfaction, but some understanding would help us here. Our friend had some kind of terminal cancer of the soul. It's like physical cancer. Cancer in the body continues to grow until it chokes the life out of you. And all the while, family, friends, doctors, nurses, and hospitals are all involved. The same is true about terminal cancer of the soul. It continues to gnaw away. Friends, family, therapists, small groups, and medicines may be used, but sometimes it doesn't heal. And the person does something. When that happens, I believe there's some moment of insanity. He loses his ability to think like we do. The disease has crippled him. And when he ends his life, he really doesn't know what he's doing. In some ways, it's like those who crucified Jesus. They thought they knew what they were doing. But Jesus said, "Father, forgive them, for they do not know what they are doing." Our friend wasn't able to reason like you and I can.

B. **Attack of the Enemy.** There's another piece to this. The Bible tells us that we each have a spiritual enemy. His name is Satan. He is real. The Bible says that he's the father of lies. He and his evil hosts are master deceivers. And Jesus tells us his agenda. He wants to destroy as many as he can. So he tells us lies. When we're wounded and weak, we begin to believe them. What happened to our friend is not the way to solve problems. But the cancer finally overtook him. It helps to have some understanding of what happened. That's an important anchor.

3. **The Anchor of Affirmation.** We all did the best we could. We all loved our friend. His family did everything they could think of to help him. Everyone went the extra mile. And now we are tempted in our emotional trauma to ask where we've failed and what else we could have done? The truth is, everyone did the best they could and more. Guilt is a device in the hands of Satan and we rebuke his lies. When the waves of doubt and guilt assail, grab hold of this anchor. Remember how you cared. Remember how you loved. Remember how you tried. It will help heal our broken hearts. This anchor really helps.

4. **The Anchor of Destination.** At times like this, people begin to wonder where our friend is. Did he go to heaven? We can be comforted that suicide is not the unpardonable sin. When you truly have forgiveness, pardon, and everlasting life, you go to heaven when you die. Romans 8:35–39 is clear. Nothing is able to separate the believer from Christ, including death. Jesus is clear in John 10:28 that those with eternal life can never be snatched from the Father's hand. The real question before us is not our friend's eternal destination; it's ours. There are two great certainties in everyone's life. We're going to die *and* we'll stand before God someday (Heb. 9:27). No exceptions. With these two absolutes, it's amazing how few people prepare to meet God. Yet each of us is only one heartbeat away from death. If we choose to follow Jesus Christ as Lord and trust Him to forgive our sins as we turn from them, we will ultimately

have eternal life in Christ; that's the biggest anchor we could ever have.

5. **The Anchor of Celebration.** Family and friends, listen to me. We can't let the events of this week and the struggles of recent years overshadow our friend's life. In Psalm 139, we learn that God determines how many days we live and when. So God planned that in all of history, our friend and we would live at the same time and that our lives would intersect. I thank God for that. Our friend's life has made a difference for good in our lives and we need to celebrate that. We need to let the phenomenal friend we knew cast the biggest shadow over our lives!

Conclusion: To our friend's family: we'd be kidding ourselves not to think some hard days will be ahead. Time and friends will help heal the sorrow. We'll never heal completely. But these anchors will help. So let's draw strength from God and from each other. Let's remember the good times we used to have with our friend. Let's celebrate that we're all better people because we knew him. Let's believe that God will do what He said He will do. When life goes bad, He promises to work things together for good for those who love God (Rom. 8:28). I'm here to tell you, some good days are ahead!

Special Services Registry

The forms on the following pages are designed to be duplicated and used repeatedly as needed. Most copy machines will allow you to enlarge them to fill a full page if desired.

Sermons Preached

Date	Text	Title/Subject

Sermons Preached

Date	Text	Title/Subject

Marriages Log

Date	Bride	Groom

Funerals Log

Date	Name of Deceased	Scripture Used

Baptisms/Confirmations

Date	Name	Notes

Baby Dedication Registration

Infant's Name: _____

Significance of Given Names: _____

Date of Birth: _____

_____

Siblings: _____

_____

_____

Maternal Grandparents: _____

Paternal Grandparents: _____

Life Verse: _____

Date of Dedication: _____

Wedding Registration

Date of Wedding: _____

Location of Wedding: _____

Bride: _____

     Religious Affiliation: _____

     Bride's Parents: _____

Groom: _____

     Religious Affiliation: _____

     Groom's Parents: _____

Ceremony to Be Planned by Minister: _____ By Couple: _____

Other Minister(s) Assisting: _____

Maid/Matron of Honor: _____

Best Man: _____

Wedding Planner: _____

Date of Rehearsal: _____

Reception Open to All Wedding Guests: _____ By Invitation Only: _____

Location of Reception: _____

Wedding Photos to Be Taken: _____ During Ceremony

                              _____ After Ceremony

Other: _____

Date of Counseling: _____

Date of Registration: _____

Funeral Registration

Name of Deceased: _____

Age: _____

Religious Affiliation: _____

Survivors: _____

    Spouse: _____

    Parents: _____

    Children: _____

    Siblings: _____

    Grandchildren: _____

Date of Death: _____

Time and Place of Visitation: _____

Date of Funeral or Memorial Service: _____

Funeral Home Responsible: _____

Location of Funeral or Memorial Service: _____

Scripture Used: _____ Hymns Used: _____

Eulogy by: _____

Other Minister(s) Assisting: _____

Pallbearers: _____

_____

Date of Interment: _____ Place of Interment: _____

Graveside Service: _____ No _____

Subject Index

Scripture Index

END USER LICENSE AGREEMENT

...MENT. BY CLICKING ON THE "I ACCEPT THE TERMS OF THE LICENSE AGREEMENT" BUTTON AND CLICKING THE
...ND BY AND ARE BECOMING A PARTY TO THIS AGREEMENT. THIS PRODUCT REQUIRES USER REGISTRATION AND
...ION IS NOT CONFIRMED. IF YOU DO NOT AGREE TO ALL OF THE TERMS OF THIS AGREEMENT, CLICK THE "CANCEL"
...RODUCT TO THE PLACE OF PURCHASE FOR A FULL REFUND.

...and may contain electronic text, graphics, audio, or other resources ("Content") and related explanatory written materials
...upgrades, modified versions, updates, additions and copies of the Software. "You" means the person or company who is being
...documentation. "We" and "us" means Libronix Corporation and its parent company, Logos Research Systems, Inc.

...nse to use one copy of the Software and "unlocked" Content on any single computer, provided the Software and Content are in use
... Software is "in use" on a computer when it is loaded into temporary memory (RAM) or installed into the permanent memory of a
...CD-ROM or other storage device.

...manently installed on the hard disk or other storage device of a computer (other than a network server) and one person uses that computer
...that person may also use the Software and Content on a portable or home computer.

...ent that is NOT licensed to you. This Content is "locked" in electronic form and is included for your convenience should you desire to "unlock"
...it. Content that you "unlock" is covered by this agreement.

...ll right, title and interest in the Software and Documentation. Ownership of the Content remains with Copyright holders.

COPIES

...y of the Software solely for backup or archival purposes, or
...oftware to a single hard disk, provided you keep the original solely for backup or archival purposes.

AY NOT DO
...Content, and Documentation are protected by United States copyright laws and international treaties. You must treat the Software, Content, and Documentation
... copyrighted material—for example a book. You may not:
...he Documentation,
...the Software or Content except to make archival or backup copies as provided above,
...dify or adapt the Software or merge it into another program,
...verse engineer, disassemble, decompile or make any attempt to discover the source code of the Software,
...place the Software or Content onto a server so that it is accessible via a public network such as the Internet,
...sublicense, rent, lease or lend any portion of the Software, Content, or Documentation, or
...reverse engineer, disassemble, decompile or make any attempt to "unlock" or circumvent the digital copyright protection of the Content.

TRANSFERS
You may transfer all your rights to use the Software, Content, and Documentation to another person or legal entity provided you transfer this Agreement, the Software, Content, and Documentation, including all copies, update and prior versions to such person or entity and that you retain no copies, including copies stored on computer.

LIMITED WARRANTY
We warrant that for a period of 90 days after delivery of this copy of the Software to you:
—if provided, the physical media on which this copy of the Software is distributed will be free from defects in materials and workmanship under normal use, and
—the Software will perform in substantial accordance with the Documentation.
To the extent permitted by applicable law, THE FOREGOING LIMITED WARRANTY IS IN LIEU OF ALL OTHER WARRANTIES OR CONDITIONS, EXPRESS OR IMPLIED, AND WE DISCLAIM ANY AND ALL IMPLIED WARRANTIES OR CONDITIONS, INCLUDING ANY IMPLIED WARRANTY OF TITLE, NONINFRINGEMENT, MERCHANTABILITY OR FITNESS FOR A PARTICULAR PURPOSE, regardless of whether we know or had reason to know of your particular needs. No employee, agent, dealer or distributor of ours is authorized to modify this limited warranty, nor to make any additional warranties.

SOME STATES DO NOT ALLOW THE EXCLUSION OF IMPLIED WARRANTIES, SO THE ABOVE EXCLUSION MAY NOT APPLY TO YOU. THIS WARRANTY GIVES YOU SPECIFIC LEGAL RIGHTS, AND YOU MAY ALSO HAVE OTHER RIGHTS WHICH VARY FROM STATE TO STATE.

LIMITED REMEDY
Our entire liability and your exclusive remedy shall be:
—the replacement of any diskette(s) or other media not meeting our Limited Warranty which is returned to us or to an authorized Dealer or Distributor with a copy of your receipt, or
—If we or an authorized Dealer or Distributor are unable to deliver a replacement diskette(s) or other media that is free of defects in materials or workmanship, you may terminate this Agreement by returning the Software and Documentation and your money will be refunded.
IN NO EVENT WILL WE BE LIABLE TO YOU FOR ANY DAMAGES, INCLUDING ANY LOST PROFITS, LOST SAVINGS, OR OTHER INCIDENTAL OR CONSEQUENTIAL DAMAGES ARISING FROM THE USE OF THE INABILITY TO USE THE SOFTWARE (EVEN IF WE OR AN AUTHORIZED DEALER OR DISTRIBUTOR HAS BEEN ADVISED OF THE POSSIBILITY OF THESE DAMAGES), OR FOR ANY CLAIM BY ANY OTHER PARTY.

SOME STATES DO NOT ALLOW THE LIMITATION OR EXCLUSION OF LIABILITY FOR INCIDENTAL OR CONSEQUENTIAL DAMAGES, SO THE ABOVE LIMITATION MAY NOT APPLY TO YOU.

TERM AND TERMINATION
This license agreement takes effect upon your use of the software and remains effective until terminated. You may terminate it at any time by destroying all copies of the Software and Documentation in your possession. It will also automatically terminate if you fail to comply with any term or condition of this license agreement. You agree on termination of this license to either return to us or destroy all copies of the Software and Documentation in your possession.

CONFIDENTIALITY
The Software contains trade secrets and proprietary know-how that belong to us and it is being made available to you in strict confidence. ANY USE OR DISCLOSURE OF THE SOFTWARE, OR OF ITS ALGORITHMS, PROTOCOLS OR INTERFACES, OTHER THAN IN STRICT ACCORDANCE WITH THIS LICENSE AGREEMENT, MAY BE ACTIONABLE AS A VIOLATION OF OUR TRADE SECRET RIGHTS.

GENERAL PROVISIONS
1. This written license agreement is the exclusive agreement between you and us concerning the Software, Content, and Documentation and supersedes any and all prior oral or written agreements, negotiations or other dealings between us concerning the Software.
2. This license agreement may be modified only by a writing signed by you and us.
3. In the event of litigation between you and us concerning the Software or Documentation, the prevailing party in the litigation will be entitled to recover attorney fees and expenses from the other party.
4. You agree to register this product with Libronix Corporation within 30 days. (Registration may be accomplished via the Internet or by mail. Registration helps protect the owners and publishers of copyrighted Content and encourages more publishers to release their Content electronically.) You may register anonymously but we may not provide certain types of support or opportunities to participate in certain online features if you choose to do so. After 30 days the software may cease to function until it receives confirmation of registration.
5. You represent that if you choose to provide name, address, credit card, or any other information that it will be your true information. You may choose or be assigned a user name, confirmation code, and/or password in connection with your use of the Software. You agree to keep your confirmation code and password confidential. We disclaim responsibility for unauthorized use of your credit card or password.
6. Registration with Libronix Corporation implies registration with the Content owners whose Content you have licensed for use with the Software. We may share your registration information with the owners of Content you have licensed. We will honor your indication that you do not want registration information shared with any other third party. (You may indicate this during registration if you choose to provide name, address, etc.)
7. You agree that the Software may detect the presence of a connection to the Internet and communicate with servers controlled by Libronix in order to submit anonymous statistical information on use of the Software and Content and to detect and download updates to the Software and Content and new Software and Content for which you may have chosen to purchase licenses. You agree that new and updated Software and Content downloaded by the Software from the Internet are covered by this license.
8. This license agreement is governed by the laws of the State of Washington, USA.
9. You agree that the Software will not be shipped, transferred or exported into any country or used in any manner prohibited by the United States Export Administration Act or any other export laws, restrictions or regulations.
10. The controlling language of this agreement is English. Any translation of this agreement that you may have received is provided only for your convenience.